The Augustan Court

R. O. Bucholz

The Augustan Court

Queen Anne and the Decline of Court Culture

Stanford University Press, Stanford, California 1993

Stanford University Press
Stanford, California

Printed in the United States of America

CIP data appear at the end of the book

Published with the assistance of
Loyola University of Chicago

To My Beloved Laurie

Wer ein holdes Weib errungen,
stimm' in unser'n Jubel ein.
Nie wird es zu hoch besungen,
Retterin des Gatten sein.

—*Fidelio*, Act II

Acknowledgments

Like the archetypal courtier, I have contracted many debts in the writing of this book. Unlike that sometimes ungrateful figure, I take much pleasure in this opportunity to acknowledge them. My oldest intellectual obligation was incurred while I was an undergraduate at Cornell. There, I had the good fortune to cross paths with five men who not only fired my interest in the early modern period, but taught me nearly everything I know about how to write its history: Colin Brooks, Frederick Marcham, Michael MacDonald, and, especially, Daniel Baugh and Clive Holmes. As a graduate student at Oxford I was equally fortunate in my choice of mentors. I owe a profound debt to the late G. V. Bennett, who suggested the subject, saw the potential for something more than a narrowly political study, and oversaw the work in its initial stages. Subsequently, I came under the tutelage of P. G. M. Dickson. Demanding yet patient, critical yet encouraging, attentive yet neither overbearing nor fussy, Professor Dickson is the very model of an Oxford supervisor. Whatever intellectual rigor or stylistic felicity the following may contain owes a great deal to his direction.

I have been equally fortunate in, and, I fear, importunate toward, those who have helped, by their criticism, to turn the resulting doctoral thesis into a book. I would like to thank all who read and commented upon the manuscript, in whole or in part, at various stages in its development. They include Colin Brooks, Jo Hays, David Hood, Christopher Johns, Gary de Krey, Paul Langford, David Lemmings, John Phillips, William Speck, William Weber, and Patrick Woodland. Technical advice and assistance were rendered by David Cressy, Sharon Olson, Alan Turner, and Patricia Warren. The figures were realized by John New and George Owendijk. Computing facilities were provided by Professor Hood and by the Biology Department of Loyola University of Chicago.

There would have been little to compute or comment upon if the owners and keepers of numerous collections, both public and private, had been less generous in allowing me to examine and quote from them. I would like to thank His Royal Highness the Prince of Wales and the trustees of the Chevening Estate for allowing me to consult the Stanhope of Chevening MSS, His Grace the Duke of Devonshire for permission to examine the Chatsworth MSS, the Marquess of Lothian for making available the Melbourne Hall MSS, Lord Bathurst for providing access to the Bathurst Loan, Lord Dartmouth for permission to examine the Dartmouth MSS, Lord Egremont for allowing me to consult the Petworth House Archives, and Mr. Charles Lloyd-Baker for making available the Sharp MSS. Crown copyright material in the Public Record Office is reproduced with the kind permission of the controller of Her Majesty's Stationery Office. I am likewise grateful to the board of the British Library, Bodley's librarian, the curator of manuscripts of the Huntington Library, the Royal College of Surgeons, and the keepers of the archives at the record offices of Derbyshire, Gloucestershire, Kent, Greater London, Staffordshire, West Sussex, and Worcestershire for allowing me to consult and quote from manuscripts in their care. I owe a particular debt to Drs. Eveline Cruickshanks and David Hayton of the History of Parliament Trust for allowing me to consult copies of division lists, members' biographies, and other material in their possession. (They are equally deserving of thanks for the numerous lunches and teas and the general encouragement that they have provided to me and other poor and gloomy graduate students over the years.) Indeed, I would like to thank the staffs of each of these institutions; that of the Newberry Library, Chicago; and the libraries at New College, Oxford; Cornell; California State University, Long Beach; and Loyola of Chicago for putting up with my insistent and sometimes unreasonable demands. I owe a particular debt to the staffs of the interlibrary loan departments of the last two institutions, who did much by their industry and ingenuity to lessen the apparent disadvantage of living and working an ocean and a continent away from my sources.

What remained of that disadvantage was virtually nullified by the generosity of those institutions that provided financial support for travel to collections. My oldest and greatest material debt is owed to the trustees of the Keasbey Memorial Foundation, who funded my first two years in Oxford in a style to which it was all too easy to become accustomed. Subsequently, I received additional funding from the Bryce and Reed Fund at Oxford, from the British Council, and from Loyola University. I am especially grateful to Loyola for a generous subvention that facilitated the publication of this work. I must also thank the history departments of Cal State Long Beach, Cornell, and Loyola, first for having the goodness to employ me, but also for providing successive intellectual homes, which have been at once warm and stimulating. I can truly say that my fellow historians have done far more to sustain me with their patience, encouragement, and collegiality than they will ever know.

Finally, I wish to thank my family, in particular my mother, Lillian Bucholz, for providing unstinting emotional and material support. I owe a recently contracted debt to my daughter, Katie, who has shown far greater patience to her distracted father than he has had any right to expect from a newborn. But my greatest obligation is that, no doubt to be forever outstanding, which I owe to the dedicatee of this work. Unlike some indifferent royal patron, she has labored mightily, as editor, typist, private secretary, analyst, sounding board, and cheerleader, to make this work both possible and presentable. Over the twelve years it has taken her to do this, she has assumed within our household not only most of the duties for which Queen Anne could call upon a staff of nearly 1,000, but also a number of positions unknown to the Augustan Court, such as "mistress processor of the words" and "lady keeper of the floppy discs." Unlike many of the Queen's servants, she has done so without grumbling or expectation of gain. Rather, she has performed these tasks with a selflessness and a grace that lend true meaning to the phrase "better half." If all of this suggests that I have pursued an absolutist policy in our house, I can only affirm what I have known from the beginning: that I have not had these things as of right, but at the pleasure of my sovereign lady.

R.O.B.

Rogers Park
16 October 1991

Contents

Tables and Figures

Tables

Figures

Note: The values given in the tables and figures are based upon a thorough revision and recounting of those that appeared in R. O. Bucholz, "The Court in the Reign of Queen Anne" (D.Phil. thesis, Oxford University, 1987). The major discrepancies are explained by the addition of two societies, the chaplains in ordinary and the yeomen of the guard, whose omission from the thesis no longer seems warranted.

Abbreviations

Add. MSS	Additional Manuscripts, British Library, London
A.O.	Archives Office
App.	Appendix
B.I.H.R.	*Bulletin of the Institute of Historical Research*
B.L.	British Library, London
Bodl.	Bodleian Library, Oxford
Cal. Ref. Mus.	*A Calendar of References to Music in Newspapers Published in London and the Provinces (1660–1719)*, ed. M. Tilmouth, Royal Musicological Association Research Chronicle, nos. 1–2 (1961–62)
Camd. Soc.	Camden Society
Commons Journals	*Journals of the House of Commons* XIII–XVII [1702–14]
C.S.P.D.	*Calendar of State Papers, Domestic Series* [1660–1704] (1860–1947+)
C.T.B.	*Calendar of Treasury Books*, vols. I–XXXI [1660–1718], ed. W. A. Shaw (1904–62)
C.T.B. & P.	*Calendar of Treasury Books and Papers, 1727–45*, ed. W. A. Shaw (1897–1903)
C.T.P.	*Calendar of Treasury Papers, 1557–1738*, ed. J. Redington (1868–89)
D.N.B.	*The Dictionary of National Biography*, ed. L. Stephen and S. Lee (1908–9)
E	Exchequer Papers, Public Record Office, Chancery Lane, London
E.	Easter
Eg. MSS	Egerton Manuscripts, British Library, London

E.H.R.	*English Historical Review*
G.L.R.O.	Greater London Record Office, London
Harl. MSS	Harleian Manuscripts, British Library, London
Harl. Soc.	Harleian Society
Hayton and Jones	*A Register of Parliamentary Lists 1660–1761*, ed. D. Hayton and C. Jones (Leicester, 1979)
H.J.	*Historical Journal*
H.L.Q.	*Huntington Library Quarterly*
H.M.C.	Historical Manuscripts Commission
LC	Lord Chamberlain's Papers, Public Record Office, Chancery Lane, London
London Stage	*The London Stage 1660–1800*, vols. I–II, ed. E. L. Avery, W. Van Lennep, et al. (Carbondale, Ill., 1960)
Lords Journals	*Journals of the House of Lords* XVII–XIX [1702–14]
LS	Lord Steward's Papers, Public Record Office, Chancery Lane, London
Ms.	Michaelmas
n.d.	not dated
n.s.	new series
Parl. Hist.	*The Parliamentary History of England*, vol. VI [1702–14], ed. W. Cobbett (1810)
P.R.O.	Public Record Office, Chancery Lane, London
R.O.	Record Office
S.P. Dom.	State Papers, Domestic Series, Public Record Office, Chancery Lane, London
T.R.H.S.	*Transactions of the Royal Historical Society*

The Augustan Court

CHAPTER I

Introduction and Background

The inhabitants of early modern Europe were in no doubt as to the significance of courts. The crowds who flocked to the prince's household in search of employment, influence, prestige, or entertainment; the multitudes who cheered its alfresco processions and festivals; and the wider public that devoured the numerous private letters, "secret" memoirs, ballads, broadsides, and prints relating its splendors and intrigues all appear to have shared a single conviction: that the court was the very center of earthly power, the arbitrator of good taste and the fount of worldly success. It is true that there were, and had always been, alternative routes to power, wealth, status, and pleasure. But it is equally true that during the period between the Renaissance and the French Revolution, the princely courts of western Europe came to dominate access to these goals as never before or since. When Norbert Elias characterized the subject of his pathbreaking work as *Die höfische Gesellschaft*—the court society—he was describing accurately not only the society of the prince's household, but, to some extent, that of early modern Europe as a whole.[1]

It is thus somewhat surprising that, until the initial publication of Elias's work in 1969, professional academics had, for the most part, ignored the early modern court as a subject in its own right. Certainly popular historians and, presumably, their publics have never lost interest in the lives and loves, scandals and intrigues of monarchs and their great courtiers. But, as this characterization suggests, this work is often excessively narrow, focusing on a small clique at the top of the court hierarchy. It is also, more often than not, prurient in its interests, credulous in its use of primary sources, and cavalier in its overall scholarship.[2] As a result, its subject has been made to seem trivial in comparison to the more pressing concerns of professional historians.

Their concerns have, naturally, derived from the ideological assumptions, expectations, biases, and debates prevailing when the historians in question have written. Those writing in the nineteenth and early twentieth centuries, an age of European dominance and emerging liberal democracy, were generally far more interested in the growth of empire and the development and inevitable triumph of representative institutions over absolutism and its attendant superstitions.[3] Historians writing in the mid to late twentieth century, increasingly aware of race, class, and gender biases, increasingly suspicious of Eurocentric and elite perspectives, have sought to recover the experiences and worldviews of heretofore neglected groups. To each of these "schools," whether Whig, Marxist, or revisionist, the court has seemed elitist, reactionary, and wasteful.[4]

There are as many practical reasons for the relative neglect of court history as there are ideological or political. There is, first, the problem of definition. In contemporary usage, the word "court" denoted at once a physical place, a group of people, a form of behavior, and a set of attitudes. Moreover, none of these meanings is entirely clear-cut in its own right. In its geographic sense, the court was located wherever the ruler happened to be. Since most early modern rulers were at least somewhat peripatetic, the court was a movable feast that might be sampled at any given time at any one of a number of royal palaces and hunting lodges, or, when on progress, virtually anywhere in the realm. The history of the court is therefore not the history of Whitehall or Versailles, though it must include an awareness of the history, expenses, and physical arrangements of all royal or princely residences.

Demographically speaking, the court in its narrowest and most manageable sense might be said to comprise the ruler's personal retinue. But this definition, too, is imprecise. A distinction must be drawn between those members of the court who served him in some permanent, formal domestic capacity (court officers and servants) and those who merely attended his person and court out of habit, with no formal domestic duties there (courtiers or habitués). Moreover, because the process by which the functions and offices of government went "out of court" was by no means complete during the early modern period, contemporaries (in England, at least) tended to apply the term to any person or group employed by or associated with the Crown. In this larger sense "the court" sometimes expanded to include the current ministry; the body of its supporters in parliament; the whole of the paid administration, whether at the center or in the localities; or even the totality of all those in the country at large who supported the monarch and his or her aims.[5] Modern historians, to whom the process of government's "going out of court" is more apparent, have less excuse for using the term ambiguously. The present study is primarily concerned with the court in its narrower sense of household servants, courtiers, and the environment they inhabited.[6] However, it should be obvious that their service and that environment cannot be understood without reference to the court in its wider senses.

When used in these wider senses, the noun "court" begins to shade off into something of an adjective. Thus, historians have sometimes written, not always convincingly, of a "Court" party in parliament.[7] Contemporaries occasionally spoke of "court ways," or referred to someone's behavior as being very "court" or "like a courtier's." Such references, almost always pejorative, suggest that in the contemporary mind the court instilled a way of life, a set of assumptions, and a code of behavior. Indeed, the word was until recently commonly used as a verb—as in "to court"—which was itself loaded with similar connotations. While analyses of the "Court" party in parliament or the contemporary debate about the role of the courtier are beyond the scope of this study, it is hoped that the following will provide something of a corrective to old stereotypes by elucidating how court servants and courtiers actually behaved, in parliament and out.

The historian who chooses to examine the court in its geographic and demographic senses must also realize—as contemporaries certainly did—that the court was a microcosm of the wider world, to which it was often held up as an example. First, the court was unusual among early modern institutions in containing men and women from nearly every contemporary social group: royalty, nobility, gentry, clergy of all ranks, professionals of all kinds, middling and menial servants, laborers, and even impoverished pensioners.[8] Any historian who seeks to understand the court as a totality, and, in particular, the patronage links between court elites and their social inferiors, must be prepared to examine every member of this hierarchy, from lords chamberlain and steward down to the lowliest laundress or soil carrier.

Moreover, courts were unusual in having administrative, financial, political, social, and cultural aspects, none of which can be examined properly in isolation from the others. Appreciation of this integral character is crucial not only for historians of the court but for other specialists as well. For example, while historians of literature and art have always been aware of the role of courts as patrons and subjects for writers and artists, they have only recently understood the degree to which the nature and amount of such patronage were directly related to financial, political, and social realities at court.[9] Similarly, the possibilities for political influence by courtiers were dependent not only upon the personality of the ruler, but also upon administrative, social, and even architectural realities. Finally, and perhaps most importantly, the court's ability to attract the attention and hold the loyalty of the aristocracy was, to a varying extent in each case, dependent upon its size, structure, financial health, political arrangements, and cultural pretensions. Clearly, any serious attempt to examine the early modern court must do so holistically.

A second and equally daunting practical reason for the neglect of court history is the problem of evidence. Unlike a legislative body or a trading company, the court was not, by and large, an institution of record. While all courts generated vast amounts of paper in the form of ordinances, accounts, minutes, and proceedings, as well as private correspondence, diaries, journals, and manuscript poems and plays, the majority of the political and social business transacted there was done ephemerally, often secretly, by word of mouth, by gesture, or even by facial expression. As a result, the careful historian must, like the assiduous courtier, be sensitive to information that is often conveyed subtly, incidentally, inadvertently, even unconsciously by his subjects. He must, like the courtier, see and hear everything, yet take nothing for granted. If, for example, he would know where the prince's favor lay, he must go beyond the mere opinions of courtiers by measuring them against the hard evidence of results. If he would know how the inhabitants of the court deported themselves, he must look beyond books of rules and ordinances to as many examples of the actual behavior of courtiers as he can find, for the ultimate authority in a court was not legislation or rubric, but precedence, usage, routine, and the whim of its master. Finally, where he lacks written evidence altogether, the modern historian of the court must turn to other forms of information and to the methodologies used to "read" them. In short, he must be willing to enter into the territory of the art historian, the anthropologist, and the sociologist if he is to have any hope of charting the sometimes cryptic activity of the courtier.

Perhaps it is not surprising that the requirements of precise yet flexible definition, holistic scope, and methodological diversity called for above have rarely been met by the latest generation of court historians. The modern reassessment of the court's role in early modern continental history began for most scholars in 1969 with the first publication of Norbert Elias's *Die höfische Gesellschaft*. Elias is a sociologist whose attempt to use Louis XIV's Versailles as a model for all court societies now seems naive: if any early modern European court was unique in its size, structure, and political, social, and cultural arrangements, it was Versailles under the Sun King. Elias's failure to recognize this is easily explained by his less than solidly empirical treatment of both Versailles and, especially, the other courts that are supposed to have been so much like it. Nevertheless, his work is pathbreaking in a number of ways. First, he reminds us that courts were important to contemporaries and, thus, eminently worthy of study by anyone concerned with accurate knowledge of the past.[10] Second, he argues for the need to see courts as whole societies, encompassing everyone from the king down to the lowest menial, all interacting with each other to some degree.[11] Finally, while recognizing the importance of written evidence, he argues for the analysis of such seemingly superficial features of court life as daily etiquette and palace architecture as being equally indicative of the social and political realities at court.[12]

In fact, Elias's work has had some influence upon German scholars since 1933, when it first appeared as a *Habilitationsschrift* at the University of Frankfurt. But it has had far less impact elsewhere, perhaps because of delays in providing English, French, and Italian translations.[13] For English readers the first serious attempt to pursue many of these themes came in 1977 with the publication of *The Courts of Europe: Politics, Patronage and Royalty 1400–1800*, edited by A. G. Dickens. This work, comprising article-length studies of twelve early modern courts by as many authors, is necessarily uneven. A number of the articles follow the timeworn procedure of simply relating the rise and fall of successive favorites, factions, or artistic styles without placing them within the wider court society noted previously. But the best pieces—those by Knecht on Francis I, Evans on the Austrian Habsburgs, Elliott on Philip IV, and Hatton on Louis XIV—examine their subjects in the holistic fashion advocated above, defining those subjects for future scholarship in the process.[14]

Unfortunately, while there has been a great deal of subsequent scholarship on the early modern court, little of it has lived up to these models. Rather, it has generally been narrow in scope, content to borrow its themes from the history of politics, literature, or art in the most stereotypical way. For example, despite a veritable explosion of new work on the princely courts of Renaissance Italy, much of it published by the Centro Studi Europa della Corte, most of our knowledge about these institutions is still confined to their role as artistic and literary patrons.[15] Indeed, the great question for historians of the Italian courts is as old as Burckhardt: were courts good for Renaissance art, literature, and scholarship, and if so, why did the Renaissance end?[16] By contrast, there is next to no work on the administration and finances of these institutions, with the significant exception of the papal court.[17]

Surprisingly, much the same can be said of the court of France. There exists a fine general survey by J.-F. Solnon.[18] But apart from the scholarship of R. J. Knecht on Francis I,[19] work on individual courts has been as narrow in focus and, sometimes, clichéd in subject matter as that on the courts to the south. Historians of the French court have followed the French monarchy and its contemporary observers in concentrating upon the outward projection of royal power through public ceremony, art, and architecture.[20] Some of the work on ceremony, in particular, is highly sophisticated in its exploration of the political and social significance of royal word and gesture. But, as if dazzled by the Sun King or overawed by the sheer scale of Versailles, French historians have been almost entirely silent about the size and structure of the household, its finances, recruitment, work, emoluments, or tenure of office at the middling and lower ranks.[21] The King's immediate circle, the great officers and nobles, and the court's role in the domestication of the latter have all received a great deal of attention.[22] But even at this level, the mechanics of court politics, the extent of influence by favorites and mistresses, and the methods and membership of the great patronage networks have yet to receive close scrutiny. For too long, historians of the French court have contented themselves with extensive and, often, uncritical quotation of the memoirs of Saint-Simon or the letters of Liselotte, Duchess of Orléans.

Like their counterparts beyond the Pyrenees, historians of the Spanish court have tended to concentrate upon those of its aspects that most interested contemporaries. To foreign observers, the most remarkable thing about the Spanish Habsburg court was its extreme formality. Consequently, there exist several printed primary and secondary works on Spanish court ceremony and etiquette.[23] His Catholic Majesty's own subjects paid equal attention to the contemporary debate over the role of the *valido*, or favorite-minister. This subject, too, has received attention in recent years.[24] There is a first-class article on the finances of the court in the seventeenth century[25] and some fine work on the art, architecture, and gardens of that institution under both the Habsburgs and the Bourbons.[26] In 1980 Jonathan Brown and J. H. Elliott combined these themes with an analysis of the diplomatic situation of the Habsburg monarchy to produce *A Palace for a King: The Buen Retiro and the Court of Philip IV*. Though concerned with the construction and subsequent history of a single palace, this beautifully illustrated work provides a model for the integration of the administrative, political, social, and cultural aspects of courts.[27]

But it is, above all, historians of the various German courts who have pursued this holistic approach most consistently and successfully. Historians of the imperial and lesser German courts write from within what is probably the longest and most distinguished tradition of continental court historiography.[28] That tradition has always emphasized the relationship of the imperial, royal, or electoral household to the development of the state. Specifically, German historians, like their French counterparts, have tended to see the court as an important weapon in the arsenal of absolutism, its purpose to attract and hold the attention and loyalty of the *Hof-Adel*, or court nobility. As in French historiography, this has led to much fine work on court art, festival, and culture.[29] But, of equal importance, it has also led to a number of works on the structural and financial bases of these households and the prosopography of their inhabitants,[30] work that is lacking for the French court. This difference is partly explained by the depth and rigor of the German tradition, by the influence of Elias's work, and by the relatively small scale of so many German courts—perfect doctoral thesis subjects—in comparison to the immense scale of Versailles. For whatever reason, this "school" has made the greatest contribution to our knowledge of the structure and workings of the early modern continental court.

Like their German counterparts, historians of the early modern English court have dwelt upon the relationship of the court to the development of a centralized, bureaucratic state. The modern study of the Tudor court began in the early 1950s with the writings of G. R. Elton and W. C. Richardson.[31] Both authors were less interested in the court per se than in the answer to a very old question: when did the business of government finally and irrevocably move out of court, thus becoming more rational, national, and modern? Elton, in particular, argued that the household reforms fostered by Thomas Cromwell at the end of the 1530s were the crucial step in the process, which was, in turn, part of a veritable revolution in the interlocking relationship of state, church, and people. As is well known, Elton's assertion of a "Tudor revolution in government" set off one of the great historiographical debates of the twentieth century.[32] What is perhaps less obvious is that Elton's work led a new generation of historians, many of them Elton's pupils, to reassess the Tudor court.

Out of this new generation, the most prominent, sophisticated, and suggestive work has been produced by David Starkey. First in a remarkable doctoral dissertation, then in a series of important articles, Starkey has reasserted the "household" character of politics and government under the first two Tudors. More specifically, he has related the administrative and structural development of the household (especially the privy chamber) to high politics, crown finance, the architecture of royal palaces, the vagaries of royal personality, and contemporary beliefs about the sacred character of monarchy.[33] Some of Starkey's work has appeared in an important recent collection that he edited entitled *The English Court: From the Wars of the Roses to the Civil War*. The articles contained therein, along with those published elsewhere by Simon Adams and Dale Hoak, provide the best introduction to the structural and political development of the Tudor royal household.[34] To this should be added the work of Sydney Anglo and Roy

Strong on Tudor pageantry and cultural patronage.[35] Finally, much of the best recent work on this subject has been synthesized by David Loades in *The Tudor Court*. With chapters on administration, structure and finance; politics and religion; social life and culture; and imagery and pageantry, this work is a valiant attempt to integrate all aspects of court life. Unfortunately, its vast time scale (1460–1603) and modest length (192 pages, plus appendices, notes, etc.) sometimes force the author to resort to narrative where analysis is called for. Moreover, its division by topic instead of reign sometimes obscures the degree to which the court's face changed with that of the monarch.[36] Still, this study's holistic scope complements the depth of the article literature; taken together, they offer a fairly complete picture of the nature and development of the Tudor royal household.

Like their Tudor counterparts, historians of the early Stuart court have been preoccupied with the relationship of the royal household to the state—or, more precisely, to the state's collapse at midcentury. For years, Whig historians have sought a partial explanation for the Crown's increasing political and financial difficulties in the early Stuart court's reputed corruption, extravagance, frivolity, and general moral laxity.[37] There was, too, its later association with Arminianism and, in the popular mind especially, Catholicism, which contributed to its increasing isolation from the mainstream of upper-class and popular opinion during the reign of Charles I. The court is thus seen, according to this view, as contributing to the general unpopularity of the crown and the rise of a "Country" or "Puritan" opposition in parliament. That institution threatened to seize the initiative from the King and court in the 1620s and, after the hiatus of the Personal Rule, finally did so in the early 1640s.[38]

In the last two decades, historians of literature, art, and pageantry have used an interdisciplinary approach to argue that the cultural manifestations, at least, of early Stuart extravagance were anything but frivolous. Rather, they have demonstrated, and delineated in some detail, an attempt by the first two Stuart kings to project an image of divinity, unity, and order in the buildings, the paintings, and, especially, the masques that they commissioned.[39] However, while this work is fully conversant with the political, theological, and aesthetic milieu of the early Stuart court, it has tended to ignore the wider audience beyond the precincts of Whitehall. In *Court Culture and the Origins of a Royalist Tradition in Early Stuart England*, R. Malcolm Smuts has argued that for all the iconographic ingenuity and dramatic splendor of early Stuart court pageantry and art, its message was largely lost upon the great mass of the people, who rarely saw their monarch and his retinue in person, out of doors, as they had seen Queen Elizabeth and her court. Rather, under Charles I an ever higher proportion of the political nation found itself out of contact and sympathy with the artistic amusements of an increasingly narrow and isolated court. Smuts's work, while giving due weight to the quality and complexity of Jacobean and Caroline court culture, nevertheless appears, in the end, to provide evidence for the old Whig point of view.[40]

Still, most of the best recent work on the early Stuart court has come in the wake of the debate, begun in the 1970s, over revision of the Whig view on the causes of the English Civil War.[41] Whether produced by avowed revisionists or not, most of this new work stresses the court's continuing role as the principal point of contact between center and locality; the permanent primary venue for the transaction of political business; the fount of honor, office, and sometimes wealth; and, up to the death of Buckingham (1628), the tolerant home of a wide variety of views among the nobility and gentry. Neil Cuddy, Roger Lockyer, Kevin Sharpe, and, in particular, Linda Peck have provided sophisticated portrayals of individuals and groups of courtiers and the patronage networks that surrounded them.[42] Caroline Hibbard has analyzed the political and diplomatic significance of Henrietta Maria's court and the Catholic faction at Whitehall.[43] Finally, all historians of the early Stuart court owe a significant debt to a somewhat older work, Gerald Aylmer's *The King's Servants: The Civil Service of Charles I 1625–1642*. Though dealing with the central government as a whole, this contains the most authoritative treatment of the administration, structure, finances, conditions of service, and personnel of the Caroline royal household. Indeed, Aylmer's pioneering use of prosopographical analysis has provided a model and a challenge too rarely accepted by historians of the English court.[44]

Taken together, all of this work has served to demonstrate repeatedly the importance of the court for the history of English government, politics, finance, society, and culture during the Tudor and early Stuart periods. Whatever the ultimate significance of the "Tudor revolution" or revisionist interpretations of the relationship between King and parliament, it is abundantly clear that the royal household was an important and often powerful institution at the very center of the English polity right up to the moment of its dissolution in the 1640s (and at the center of the later historiographical debate about its nature and development). Thus it is altogether remarkable that, apart from a handful of scholarly articles and the sometimes acute generalizations to be found in biographies and political histories,[45] there is next to no significant work on the courts of the later Stuart period. Rather, historians of the late seventeenth and early eighteenth centuries have, perhaps understandably, chosen to concentrate on those developments that had the most positive and lasting influence upon the next hundred years: the Glorious Revolution and the ensuing wars with France; the resulting expansion and elaboration of the central administration; the commercial and financial revolutions; the rise of the professions; the birth of two great political parties; the growth of London and its distinctive "town" culture; and the related beginnings of widespread public patronage of the arts. In comparison, the later Stuart court has come to seem frivolous, reactionary, and, ultimately, irrelevant to these dramatic and seemingly modern developments.

And yet, if Tudor and early Stuart historians are correct about the court's leading role in so many areas of national life before the Civil War, then the loss of that leadership under the later Stuarts is of obvious relevance to every one of the above developments. The present study of Anne's court, therefore, is intended to fill a gap in our understanding not only of the later Stuart court, but of the constitutional, political, financial, social, and cultural history of Augustan England. It seeks to explain why an institution that had once dominated national life in each of these areas had, indeed, declined into a state of near irrelevancy to them by 1714. More specifically, it seeks to determine why members of the ruling elite were initially drawn to the court (either as employees or habitués); and why the court (and therefore the monarchy) failed to retain their interest and loyalty. In addition, it seeks to explain how Anne's court sought to portray itself and its mistress to the population at large, whether that portrayal was accepted, and how possible acceptance might have affected the balance of political, social, and cultural power in Augustan England. In order to answer these questions, it is necessary to examine every aspect of court life: its administration and finances; its personnel and distribution of patronage; the work and emoluments associated with household office; the politics and political influence of household officers; and the ceremonial, artistic, and social role of the court.

Finally, the decline of the court as a serious factor in the social and political life of the nation can only be understood in the context of the whole later Stuart period. It is therefore necessary, before turning to Anne's reign, to review the history of the court during the reigns of Charles II, James II, and William III.[46]

Charles II

Even for those of Anne's courtiers who were too young to have had direct personal experience of her uncle's court, its reputation and influence must have been considerable. Its memory was kept alive by an endless stream of popular anecdotes, anti-court propaganda, and Grub Street memoirs, culminating in those of Count Grammont, first translated into English in 1714.[47] That memory has been perpetuated into our own day by the diaries of John Evelyn and Samuel Pepys, numerous collections of correspondence, and, less reliably, a host of popular biographies of rakes and mistresses.[48] Taken singly or together this material tends to paint the court of Charles II as the very epitome of Stuart exuberance, extravagance, and corruption, a hotbed of political and amorous intrigue; in short, the last truly gay and splendid court in English history. Allowing for its obvious hyperbole, there is much more than a grain of truth in this picture, particularly for the beginning of the reign and in light of what was to follow. If Anne's courtiers and servants were to find her house wanting, it was because they had known, thought they had known, or had heard about something very different.

The court of Charles II was a potential source of profit, power, and prestige, though in differing degrees, to all who inhabited it. As the court was restored in 1660, its large size—nearly 1,100 places, over half of which were suitable for those of gentle or noble birth—provided wide opportunities for employment. These were made wider still by the existence of ancillary courts for Henrietta Maria, the Queen Mother (with around 140 places); the Duke and Duchess of York (around 300 places); and, from 1662, Catherine of Braganza, the Queen Consort (around 120 places); not to mention literally hundreds of supernumerary, extraordinary, or reversionary positions.[49]

As this last suggests, the "old administrative system," described by G. E. Aylmer,[50] and the standards it fostered were restored along with the monarchy in 1660. Though outright sinecures and life tenures were in the minority, they were not uncommon. For the rest of the King's servants, work was rarely strenuous and job security was excellent. When Sir Stephen Fox was removed from his clerkship at the greencloth for having voted for Danby's impeachment in December 1678, he protested, brazenly but accurately, "Upon strict and very deliberate inquiry it may be asserted that no precedent can be found for it."[51]

In the end Fox was restored to his place, though not before raising the possibility of selling it.[52] Sale of office was a common and quite acceptable surrogate pension plan for those departing from royal service, as well as a legitimate and valuable source of supplementary income for department heads, who generally acted as brokers in the transactions of subordinates.[53] Because most household offices had their ancient, often pitifully small and erratically paid salaries restored or raised only slightly in 1660, most of their holders still found it necessary to supplement their established income by taking fees and other nonmonetary perquisites. This practice was, naturally, open to abuse: the Venetian resident complained, "At the Court here no progress can be made and nothing obtained without presents or without money."[54] Ironically, the one significant administrative reform of the court at the Restoration, Charles II's surrender of his rights of purveyance, actually increased the opportunities for abuse, since it was usually a department's accounting officer who became its purveyor.[55] As a result, certain well-placed middling officials like Fox could make quite substantial fortunes out of household service.[56]

It was not necessary to be in active service to make one's way at court, financially or otherwise. Charles II was not, as his father had been, a very formal man. Both the Earl of Halifax and Sir Charles Cotterell, his master of the ceremonies, were driven to despair over their master's failure to observe the dignity befitting the royal state.[57]

Though the King liked his solitude more than is often supposed,[58] his tendency toward accessibility, informality, and conviviality—at least in comparison to his father and brother—brought him into regular contact with a wide range of his subjects, from government ministers and lords of the bedchamber to merchants and monied men, artists and scientists, peeresses and prostitutes, middling and menial servants.[59]

Many of these individuals found the King as generous as he was open. Charles II maintained an established pensions list that had grown to £180,000 per annum by the time of his death.[60] To this should be added the many grants of royal lands or leases at preferred rates he made throughout the reign; numerous pensions paid directly out of the revenue; individual payments out of the secret service and privy purse (neither of which had to be publicly accounted for); and, finally, the hundreds of sinecures, many of them in the customs service or on revenue commissions, which courtiers and favorites could fill. In short, the restored court was, as fully as its predecessors had been, "a market place for the disposal of an ever-increasing volume of cash, pensions, jobs, monopolies, and favours of all kinds."[61]

The most spectacular example of royal largesse in action, and one that conveniently illustrates each of these methods of payment, is provided by the notorious career of Barbara Villiers, the "little lecherous girl" who rose from the King's bed to become Duchess of Cleveland; a lady of the Queen's bedchamber; and mistress of Nonsuch Palace, Bushey Park, and a host of smaller properties. The wages of sin also included £10,000 out of the customs, £10,000 out of the beer and ale excise, £5,000 out of the post office, £1,000 out of First Fruits and Tenths, and individual payments of up to £30,000 to supply her gambling debts and other contingencies. Finally, the Duchess was granted the reversion, and so the disposition and sale, of all places in the customs and green wax.[62] Few dug so deeply into the King's pockets as Cleveland or her great rival, Portsmouth, but even a cursory examination of the *Calendars of Treasury Books* demonstrates that relatively minor courtiers and servants, like the Chiffinchs, the Killigrews, Edward Progers, or Henry Savile, could do very well for themselves, if on a smaller scale, out of their attendance at court.[63]

Political as well as financial capital could be amassed at the Restoration court. Those who shared the King's bed, his bottle, or his purse were generally assumed by contemporaries to possess his ear as well.

The significance of bedchamber influence and court intrigue upon royal policy deserves more detailed and hardheaded study than it has yet received. However, there is evidence that mistresses like Cleveland and Portsmouth and middling servants like Chiffinch and Progers played a part in influencing appointments, as well as in such dramatic events as the fall of Clarendon and the Popish Plot, albeit more often as go-betweens and couriers than as actual initiators and shapers of policy.[64] Whatever their real influence, the relatively free access to the royal ear enjoyed by mistresses and middling courtiers and the regulation of that access by very minor court officers lent even the latter a prominence and a prestige they would not otherwise have had. Thus, "great men" like the Duke of Lauderdale were anxious to stay on the good side of the "little people," as the following letter from his agent at court attests: "The greatest part of the King's servants are truely very kind & respectfull at all times in your concernes, especially Mr Windam & Mr Griffin, Grooms of the Bedchamber, Mr Progers, Mr Rogers, the Gentlemen Ushers, & Mr Cheffins is very civill & kind at all times."[65]

A more important consequence of Charles II's informality and liberality, in that its appeal went far beyond a small circle of professional courtiers and household servants, was his court's openness, hospitality, and obsession with diversion. During the first half of the reign especially, when Catholics were still welcome at court, almost anyone of gentle birth and appearance could turn up, as Pepys did one September day in 1662, and practically rub elbows with the King and Queen, the Duke and Duchess of York, the future Duke of Monmouth or Lady Castlemaine (the future Duchess of Cleveland). The diarist remarks: "They being all together, was such a sight as I could never almost have happened to see with so much ease and leisure."[66]

The court offered far more to men and women of Pepys's class during the heady years immediately following the Restoration than a glimpse of the royal family. Many would have had lodgings there: Whitehall alone had almost 1,400 rooms.[67] Others might have turned up for a free meal at one of 21 great tables that served a total of about 450 dishes at a cost to the crown of over £60,000 per annum.[68] Finally, there was the "Merry Monarch's" patronage of art and pleasure to take advantage of. In the winter of 1662–63 the French ambassador described the social and cultural routine of Charles's court as follows: "There is a ball and a comedy every other day; the rest of the days are spent at play, either at the Queen's or at the Lady Castlemaine's, where the company does not fail to be treated to a good supper."[69] Those of a more reflective disposition could, as John Evelyn sometimes did, admire the King's collection of Dutch and Italian masters as well as new commissions by Lely, Kneller, Streeter, and Verrio; attend the choral services of the King's chapel to hear the work of the young Blow, Humfrey, and Purcell; or stroll through the gardens and parks of the King's palaces at Greenwich, Hampton Court, or St. James's as laid out or improved by Le Nôtre or Rose upon Charles's instructions.[70]

The elevation of St. James's park and mall and Newmarket into places of fashionable resort have been attributed to the influence of Charles II and his court.[71] The Restoration court has also been credited with introducing or popularizing French taste in music, dancing, gardens, furniture, costume, and table manners;[72] Dutch taste in architecture, painting, silverwork, and embroidery;[73] the orchestral accompaniment of choral anthems;[74] the comedy of intrigue and the rhymed heroic drama;[75] the man's vested suit;[76] periwigs for both men and women;[77] the guitar;[78] champagne;[79] tea;[80] and, perhaps most fortunately, ice cream.[81] To this should be added the court's interest in the early careers of Blow, Grinling Gibbons, Humfrey, Kneller, Purcell, and Riley, as well as its employment of many of the most famous "wits" of the time in the chamber and bedchamber, including Buckingham, Dorset, Mulgrave, Rochester, Bulkeley, Guy, Killigrew, and Savile.[82] Admittedly, some of these attributions of stylistic innovation and influence are based on tenuous evidence or mere "tradition," and many aspiring artists (Dryden and Butler, for example) found the King and his court far more interested intellectually than financially in their careers.[83] Nevertheless, there seems to have been a clear assumption on the part of contemporaries that cultural innovation and patronage depended on the court.

It is this reputation, rather than the supposed creation of a Stuart "court art," that was Charles II's real cultural achievement. Despite the undoubted propaganda value of Dryden's heroic plays and Verrio's ceiling painting, the King's financial resources and attention span were both too limited for any truly comprehensive Royalist program such as Louis XIV was fostering across the Channel. Rather, by distributing his artistic patronage widely yet discriminately, by remaining open to new talent and stylistic innovation, Charles II restored the court's traditional leadership as an artistic patron and a clearinghouse for new styles after the nearly fatal Interregnum hiatus. This, in turn, made the court attractive not only to those with political and financial ambitions, but to anyone interested in what was new, what was fashionable, or what was fun. Thus, in the spring of 1663, while Sir Richard Fanshaw was away on a diplomatic mission, Sir Ralph Freeman let the latter's lodgings at Whitehall "to accommodate his daughter, who desired to see the Court entertainments, as balls and plays, which have been frequent this last winter."[84] Balls, plays, art work, gardens, gambling, free meals, and intrigues of all kinds provided sufficient excuse for Restoration society to go to court, or at least to keep itself apprised of the court's activities when forced to remain in the country.[85] Conversely, one of the King's frequent progresses to Newmarket or Winchester would, according to the French ambassador, leave "one of the greatest towns in the world . . . turned into a solitude."[86] The court thus provided access to the great, place, profit, art, diversion—and, possibly, as a subtle by-product, attachment to the principle of monarchy.

However, not everyone appreciated the dizzy pace of Restoration court life. Administrators and courtiers complained frequently of the difficulties of carrying on business while on progress.[87] Poor, lethargic Prince George of Denmark simply found the court's routine exhausting: "We talk here of going to tea, of going to Winchester, and everything else except sitting still all summer which was the height of my ambition. God send me a quiet life somewhere for I shall not be long able to bear this perpetual motion."[88] More severe critics, both contemporary and modern, have found the social whirl of the Restoration court not merely tiring but empty, amoral, and coarse. Anthony à Wood, remembering a royal progress to Oxford during the plague year of 1665, puts the opposition case with graphic eloquence: "Though they were neat and gay in their apparell, yet they were very nasty and beastly, leaving at their departure their excrements in every corner, in chimneys, studies, colehouses, cellars. Rude, rough, whoremongers; vaine, empty, carelesse."[89]

There was indeed a great deal of carelessness, coarseness, and crassness, not to mention cruelty and violence, at the court of Charles II,[90] a corollary of the openness and moral laxity that otherwise made it such an exciting and attractive place. Francis North, Lord Guilford, was advised upon his first coming to court to "keep a whore," for "he

TABLE 1.1

Annual Average Expenditure of the Household, 1660–1685

Department	Lord Treasurer Southampton			Treasury Commission and Lord Treasurer Clifford		Lord Treasurer Danby			Treasury Commission
	Ms. 1660– Ms. 1663 (£)	Ms. 1663– Ms. 1664[a] (£)	Ms. 1664– Ms. 1667 (£)	Ms. 1667– Ms. 1669[a] (£)	Ms. 1669– Ms. 1673 (£)	Ms. 1673– E. 1676 (£)	E. 1676– E. 1677[a] (£)	E. 1677– E. 1679 (£)	E. 1679– E. 1685[a] (£)
Household	130,081	62,785	100,310	61,816	112,117	132,390	88,938	151,894	53,677
Chamber	19,667	25,181	17,327	14,287	33,779	37,861	34,867	37,947	16,855
Stables	3,789	2,718	2,649	2,600	8,781	11,838	12,200	12,393	5,684
Works	11,333	12,354	9,798	10,384	14,726	14,680	12,248	13,487	15,169
Great ward.	17,060	42,552	35,511	21,575	21,020	20,945	20,982	24,629	9,467
Robes	2,352	15,838	3,800	3,250	4,938	7,616	2,450	4,625	3,300
Salaries (estimate)	25,000	—	25,000	12,500	25,000	25,000	—	25,000	20,833
Gent. pens.	4,000	—	6,120	—	4,266	7,049	5,862	5,740	4,165
Jeweler and goldsmith	16,036	10,000	17,305	1,365	30,861	14,296	12,014	13,839	3,004
Privy purse	14,177	20,986	17,761	16,082	40,892	41,464	38,794	30,111	23,171
Works—Windsor	—	—	—	—	—	—	6,314	1,189	200
Tents and toils	2,091	1,100	1,307	600	1,169	1,951	2,000	1,182	—
Total	245,586	193,514	236,888	144,459	297,549	315,090	236,669	322,036	155,525

SOURCES: Figures derived from tables of exchequer issues in Chandaman, *English Public Revenue*, App. 3, pp. 350–51, 354–55, 358–59, 362–63. These figures are probably slight underestimates since they do not take into account issues out of the revenue that did not go through the exchequer. The figure for salaries paid at the exchequer is an estimate based upon the civil establishments. No such payments appear to have been made during the years of retrenchment. The above figures are not strictly comparable to those in Table 1.2, which are based on departmental declared accounts.

[a]Period of retrenchment.

was ill looked upon [at court] for want of doing so." But his brother, the Reverend John North, clerk of the closet to Charles II, claimed that "for the number of persons that resided in the court, a place reputed a centre of all vice and irreligion, he thought there were as many truly pious and strictly religious, as could be found in any other resort whatsoever."[91] Indeed, one need only remember the presence of men like Burnet, Compton, and Evelyn or women such as Margaret Blagge, Anne Killigrew, or Anne Kingsmill, afterwards Countess of Winchilsea, at the Restoration court to realize that its essential characteristic was not so much licentiousness as diversity: it managed to attract both the best and the worst of contemporary society.

Yet even at the height of its glory and fame under Charles II, the royal household began to exhibit tendencies, and to be affected by financial, political, and social realities, that would progressively undermine its attractiveness in subsequent reigns. The openness, diversity, and cosmopolitanism of the court were steadily eroded from the late 1660s on as security tightened and increasing numbers of Catholics were banished from Whitehall.[92] The Exclusion Crisis and its aftermath completed this process, and also served to alienate or proscribe courtiers on the opposite side of the religious and political divide. Even the substantial group of moderate Anglican courtiers that remained began to suffer a thinning of ranks during the second half of the reign. Toward the end of the 1670s in particular, the small circle of court "wits" that had so dominated the artistic and social life of the capital began to die, drift away, or become submerged in the political struggle then gripping the nation.[93] Finally, the quality of court life began to be affected by the King's chronic financial difficulties.

From the first, Charles II was living well beyond his means. Indeed, Professor Chandaman has argued that his household expenses and largesse to courtiers made a major contribution to the chronic insolvency of the Crown, which occurred despite a total revenue (ordinary and extraordinary) that should have been adequate from the 1670s onward.[94] Table 1.1 indicates that Charles's household expenditure sometimes exceeded £300,000, a figure matched by only one of his successors listed in Table 1.2. Consequently, household expenditure was one of the chief targets of the treasury's periodic attempts at retrenchment between 1660 and 1685 (see Table 1.1). As early as 1663, Lord Treasurer

TABLE 1.2
Annual Average Expenditure of the Household, 1685–1727

Department	James II (£)	William III (£)	Anne (£)	George I (£)
Household	76,784	99,145	89,828	87,252
Chamber	30,662	38,351	28,941	39,996
Stables	10,367	17,734	7,948	10,908
Works and gardens	22,730	47,963	37,390	33,966
Great wardrobe	19,552	30,857	19,940	23,112
Robes	2,757	4,946	3,676	3,564
Salaries	13,798	21,469	20,221	29,040
Gent. pens.	7,889	5,338	6,238	5,760
Jeweler and goldsmith	13,243	12,679	12,743	8,532
Privy purse	28,427	37,787	27,490	30,324
Works-Windsor	2,674	847	5,060	—
Total	228,883	317,116	259,475	272,454

SOURCES: *Columns 1–3*: Figures derived from the departmental declared accounts and statements of exchequer issues printed in the introductions to *C.T.B.*, vols. VIII–XXVIII, supplemented by Chandaman, *English Public Revenue* (Table of Exchequer Issues, Michaelmas 1684–Michaelmas 1688), p. 363; E 403 2203–14 (Exchequer Issues on Debentures, 1690–1716) and records of issues in *C.T.B.*, vols. VIII–XXVIII, for salaries paid at the exchequer; LS 4/14 and LS 4/18 (Pedes Parcellarum) for missing household accounts; and *Wren Society*, Vols. IV, VII, for works and gardens accounts. In each case I have followed J. M. Beattie's procedure of dividing the total expenditure for each reign by the number of months accounted for and multiplying by twelve.
Column 4: J. M. Beattie, *English Court*, p. 112.

Southampton persuaded the King to eliminate most of the tables of hospitality, some 200 diets. This measure alone resulted in savings of almost £30,000—albeit over the loud protests of courtiers deprived of free meals.[95]

The "rougher hands" of the treasury commission of 1667 went further. The commissioners confronted the old administrative system head-on and, in the process, initiated the long struggle to impose treasury control on the court's ancient independent jurisdictions. They began by asserting the treasury's right to call for and examine departmental accounts, to modify establishments, and even to direct how individual household paymasters should dispose of their funds.[96] This aroused considerable departmental resistance at first,[97] but after the treasury's primacy was confirmed by the order in council of 31 January 1668, the commissioners went on to pursue the goals of tenure and salary reform; speedy declaration of accounts at the exchequer, in English; and the submission of weekly certificates of receipts and remains by all spending departments.[98] Most of these reforms, like the spending goals they were designed to facilitate, petered out within a year of their enactment (see Table 1.1), but they proved to be important as precedents. All were revived for good, with the King's full backing and without recourse to the privy council, by the treasury commission of 1679.[99] As a result, the annual expenditure of the royal household averaged only £155,525 during the last five years of the reign, making those years the most economical of any under the later Stuarts (see Tables 1.1 and 1.2).

These economies did not affect the King's courtiers and servants equally. For the former, court life undoubtedly grew marginally less inviting as the reign wore on, at least in comparison to the profligate years immediately following the Restoration. The elimination of tables in 1663; the abolition of Valentine's Day gifts in 1668[100] and New Year's gifts in 1681;[101] the discontinuance of the elaborate three-day garter ceremony after 1674;[102] the reduction of the instrumental forces in the chapel and the retrenchment of the King's French and Italian Musicks in the late 1670s and early 1680s[103] all compromised the material, cultural, and social opportunities of the court in the eyes of habitués and casual visitors. But it must be stressed that these opportunities remained considerable, especially in comparison to what they would be in subsequent reigns. For those with the freedom to come and go, the court's luster was tarnished slightly; it was not eclipsed.

The various retrenchments and reforms of Charles II's reign had a far greater impact upon his sworn servants and tradesmen. Some had their places eliminated or their emoluments reduced. The retrenchments of 1663, 1668, 1676, and 1679 all involved year-long suspensions of virtually all salaries and pensions, many of which (at the lower echelons of household service especially) were already in arrears.[104] Finally, when salaries were paid, the Crown's financial situation often forced the treasury to distribute them in the form of orders or tallies in anticipation of future revenue. Since that revenue was invariably subject to long delays, individual servants often had to put their tallies onto a buyer's market, selling at a discount for far below what was actually owed them.[105] Even at the highest level, the Duke of Ormonde felt himself compelled to sell "his uncertain pension of a thousand pounds a year as Gentleman of the Bedchamber" in 1673. At a lower level, a musician named John Banister supplemented his court income by founding the first series of public concerts in London in 1672.[106]

Nonetheless, for as long as Charles II sat on the throne, individuals like Ormonde and Banister remained the exception. In general, Restoration courtiers and servants continued to attend, artists and tradesmen to entertain and supply the court, the first group in perpetual hope of political, financial, and social gain, the other three in fear of losing old arrears. For his part, the "Merry Monarch" seems to have been perfectly willing to run up large debts in order to maintain his own standard of living, his generosity to particular favorites, and his court's magnificent facade in general. In this he was largely successful. Money was always found for the King's personal entertainment, for mistresses and favored courtiers and servants.[107] It was in 1683, in the midst of the most stringent retrenchment of the reign, that he undertook construction of his English Versailles at Winchester.[108] Just one week before the King's death, John Evelyn could still marvel at the opulent tableau:

> The unexpressable luxury, & prophanesse, gaming, & all dissolution, and as it were total forgetfullnesse of God (it being Sunday Evening) which this day sennight, I was witnesse of; the King, sitting & toying with his Concubines Portsmouth, Cleaveland, & Mazarine: &c: A french boy singing love songs, in that glorious Gallery, whilst about 20 of the greate Courtiers & other dissolute persons were at Basset round a large table, a bank of at least 2000 in Gold before them, upon which two Gent: that were with me made reflexions with astonishment, it being a sceane of uttmost vanity; and surely as they thought would never have an End: six days after was all in the dust.[109]

The price for Charles's "unexpressable luxury" in the face of his straitened finances was largely paid by his inferior household servants, to whom he owed over £135,000 at the time of his death.[110] From this point on, however, the court's increasing inability to reward its friends and pay its servants would begin to lead men and women of every rank to look elsewhere for their entertainment.

James II

Despite the first signs of decline under Charles II, historians have generally traced the beginnings of the court's long slide into staid respectability to the accession of his brother, James. According to the great antiquarian Samuel Pegge, "All state sunk, from that time, like a Meteor, to rise no more"; even that monarch's most recent and sympathetic biographer appears to share this view.[111] Certainly the new King possessed none of his brother's prodigality. As Duke of York, James had had a well-deserved reputation for frugal and able management of his own household.[112] As King, he was to pursue the only original and long-term plan of the later Stuart period for solving the court's chronic financial and administrative problems. As indicated in Figure 1.1, he began by reducing the size of the royal household by over one third, some 470 places. He also eliminated the remaining life tenures, restrained fee taking, demanded more work from his remaining servants, and—armed with a revenue that was to yield an average of £1,600,000 per annum—raised salaries in compensation.[113] In his days as lord high admiral, James had justified this practice by arguing that it would teach his servants to "value their employments, and not subject them to a necessity of base compliances with others to the King's prejudice, by which to get one shilling to himself he must lose ten to the King."[114] Table 1.2 indicates that James's philosophy was highly successful. The new household was, at just under £229,000 per annum, the cheapest of all the later Stuart courts, omitting that of Charles's last, anomalous years. It was also the only solvent one: the servants of James II never complained about arrears, and, despite the chaos of 1688, he does not appear to have left any debts to speak of.

On the other hand, these reforms did much to reduce further the employment and financial opportunities of the court, particularly for those of middling rank. Over 200 of the eliminated places had been suitable for gentlemen. Moreover, James's native sobriety impelled him to restore much of his father's emphasis on ceremony and etiquette,[115] to abandon his brother's men of wit and pleasure,[116] and to attempt to reform the moral standards of his house: "Our master has already declared that no man shall ever be admitted into Court, that either fights a duel, is drunk or keeps a woman openly."[117] The new King attempted to set a good example by banishing from court his erstwhile (and pregnant) mistress, Catherine Sedley, in January 1686, though not before creating her Countess of Dorchester.[118] In effect, James was ridding the court not only of a particular group of people,

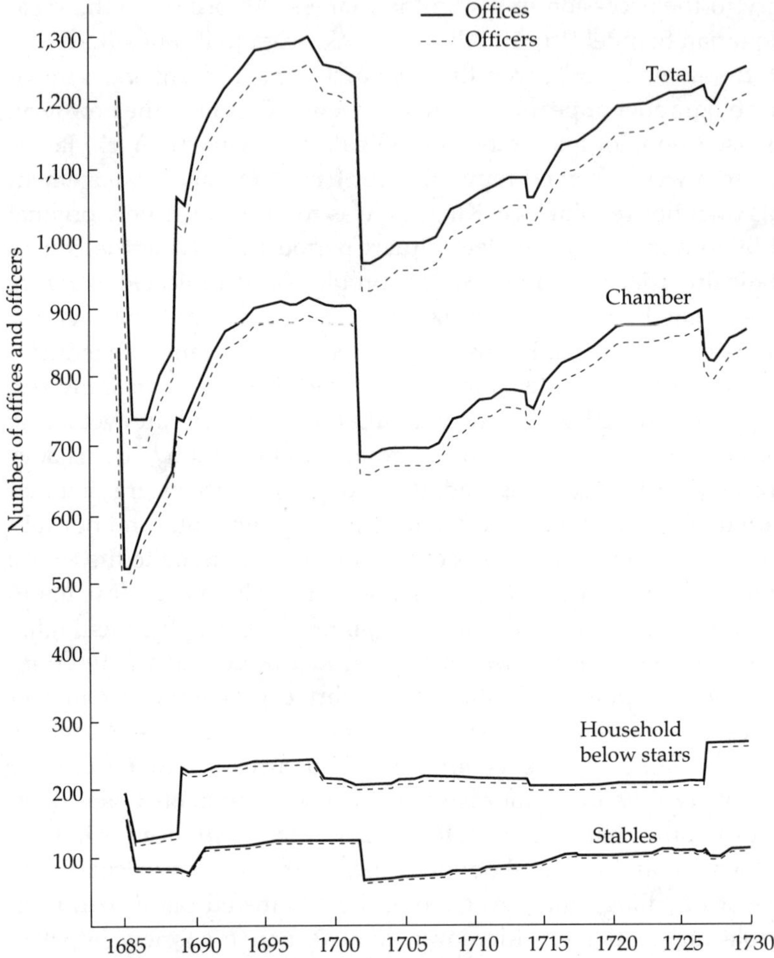

Fig. 1.1. Household offices divided into departments, 31 Dec. 1684–31 Dec. 1730. Data from LC 3/3–13, 29–33, 53, 56–57, 61–64, 73; LC 9/342; LS 13/7–14, 18–23, 37–68, 255–63; E. Chamberlayne and (from 1704) J. Chamberlayne, *Anglia Notitia*; J. Chamberlayne, *Magnae Britanniae Notitia*; G. Miege, *New State of England*; idem, *Present State of Great Britain*.

but of the openness, the informality, and the moral laxity that had made it a diverse and interesting place under his brother.

But in other ways the new court did its best to attract the more respectable side of later Stuart society. There were frequent balls and plays during the early years of the reign.[119] The King's Roman Catholic chapel, complete with a Gregorian choir and an occasional castrato soloist, attracted the curious: when Evelyn attended a service there in 1687 he found "much crowding, little devotion."[120] More devout Protestants could still accompany Princess Anne to the Anglican chapel to hear the anthems of Blow and Purcell, survivals from the religious and aesthetic diversity that had characterized Charles's court.[121]

The Catholic chapel was part of £35,000 worth of renovations undertaken by the new regime at Whitehall. Designed by Wren, decorated by Gibbons and Verrio, filled with new commissions by Gennari, Kneller, Riley, and Wissing as well as the last complete set of new tapestry hangings ever ordered by an English monarch, the additions to Whitehall realized a vision of the main royal residence that Charles II had contemplated but never had the means to carry out.[122] As this implies, James II was surprisingly good to the arts. It is a remarkable fact that he and his court attended a higher proportion of the plays given in London during his reign than any other later Stuart monarch, including his theater-loving brother.[123] Indeed, in July 1688, with his world beginning to crumble, it was reported, "Last Saturday his Majesty was pleased to order an entertainment to be given to the officers of the army at the camp."[124]

If James's court failed to attract the persons and loyalty of the English ruling class, it was not for want of trying, on an aesthetic plane at least. But no amount of cultural refinement or court entertainment could overcome the King's unpopular politics. They eventually drove away all good, and many not so good, Protestants, just as his native sobriety drove away the men and women of pleasure, and his thrift the sinecurists and hangers-on. In each case, James's overriding consistency of mind in the areas of religion, decorum, and administration banished or alienated from court groups and individuals who might have provided differing views. Indeed, he managed to estrange even those, often of impeccable Royalist pedigree, from whom no disagreement was to be expected and for whom the royal house (in every sense of the term) had been both a natural habitat and an object of unquestioning loyalty. Sir William Trumbull was shocked, upon going to court late in the reign, to find James "in his nightgown at the fireside with a company of Irish and unknown faces."[125] The court of James II was less costly and more efficient than its predecessor. As a partial consequence, it failed, unlike the earlier court, to provide the King with information and diversity of opinion, a point of contact with his most important subjects, and a home and source of inspiration for his supporters.

William and Mary

If the royal state began to sink under Charles II and James II, it was to decline even more rapidly under William and Mary. Surprisingly, the reason for this had less to do with the financial difficulties of the new regime than with its need to establish its own legitimacy and to distance itself from its predecessor. It is certainly true that the financial settlement finally voted by parliament in March 1690 was, as Clayton Roberts has shown, temporary, inadequate, and encumbered. Though William and Mary collected the hereditary excise without recourse to parliamentary sanction, and were granted the temporary excise for life, the customs was only voted for a term of four years, renewed in 1694 for five. Altogether these duties yielded an average of only £942,179 per annum between 1692 and 1694, some £500,000 to £600,000 short of what the Crown's annual ordinary expenditure is estimated to have been during that period. Worse, this revenue was encumbered with charges amounting to some £200,000 per annum needed to service the growing war debt.[126]

But financial uncertainty had done little to restrain Stuart extravagance in the past, and it did not do so now, owing to the new regime's pressing need to maintain the royal state and, with it, an appearance of legitimacy. Even before ascending the throne the new monarchs apparently promised to restore the establishment of the household to its pre-1685 levels.[127] A glance at Figure 1.1 reveals that they more than fulfilled that promise: at the time of Mary's death in 1694 the court approached 1,300 places (not counting her own personal servants), making it almost twice as large as the court of James II.

This increase in the size of the royal household (and payroll) was matched by an equally spectacular increase in the most conspicuous form of royal consumption, new building. In this case, the demands of the royal state were made more urgent by William's poor health, which necessitated residence away from Whitehall, which was damp and sooty.[128] As early as April 1689, without so much as a makeshift financial settlement of their own, William and Mary began to knock down portions of Tudor Hampton Court. They purchased Kensington House from the Earl of Nottingham for 18,000 guineas in June and began to alter it in July. Within two years they had spent over £100,000 on the two structures. By the spring of 1696, almost two years before the settlement of a permanent and unencumbered civil-list revenue, the building of Wren, the carving of Gibbons, the ironwork of Tijou, and so on had cost the crown over £131,000 at Hampton Court, £92,000 at Kensington, and an additional £83,000 for work on the gardens of those palaces.[129] The dual monarchs' vast household establishment and grandiose building projects (which more than doubled the annual expenditure of the royal works) cost, on average, £317,116 per annum (Table 1.2), a figure only exceeded by Charles II at his most extravagant.

The sudden expansion in the household's payroll and physical establishment in 1689 did not, by and large, benefit James II's old servants, about half of whom lost their places at the beginning of the new reign. Some had fled with their master to France.[130] A very few others were proscribed because of their Catholicism.[131] But the vast majority were simply purged—almost the only instance between 1660 and 1730 in which that word is appropriate—for their association with the old regime, sometimes after charges of disloyalty to the new one.[132] These changes were to have far-reaching consequences. First, with James's servants went the last of those families who had served the Stuarts through the darkest of times, and who formed a natural court community: Apsleys, Bathursts, Granvilles, Oglethorpes, Wyvills, and Yarboroughs.[133] Contrary to contemporary propaganda, they were not replaced by hordes of rapacious Dutchmen. For the most part, the King's Dutch friends were confined to a very few, though strategic, positions: Overkerk was named master of the horse; Zuylesteyn, master of the robes; Portland, groom of the stole and keeper of the privy purse, with his secretary Henning as deputy keeper; Abraham Rottermondt, royal apothecary; and, finally, Randolph du Kien, keeper of the closet.[134] The last four appointments were particularly significant, for they placed the regulation of access to the King, much of the responsibility for his health, and his most personal source of funds firmly in the hands of Dutchmen, arrangements that were strengthened by new bedchamber ordinances in 1689. This, combined with the new King's native reclusiveness, severely diminished the opportunities for bedchamber politicking and petitioning, at least on the part of Englishmen, which had been such a marked feature of court life under Charles II.[135]

The bulk of new household appointments in 1689 went to Englishmen who had supported William both politically and financially. Among the former were four signers of the famous invitation that led to the Revolution. Compton was restored to the deanery of the chapel of which James had deprived him; Devonshire was made lord steward, and Sidney and Lumley became gentlemen of the bedchamber. Churchill, Drumlanrig, Mordaunt, Ormonde, and the young Thomas Wharton were rewarded for their parts in the Revolution with places in the bedchamber or at the greencloth. At the middling and lower echelons the new court was filled with individuals whose pedigrees were not only Whig, as with the numerous Russells,[136] but occasionally downright Republican. Among the new appointments were a Bryan Fairfax, a Henry Ireton, and a Henry Cromwell, each a direct descendant of Civil War protagonists. Later in the reign young Philip Meadows, son of Cromwell's knight marshal, was allowed to purchase his father's old place back. Even their majesties' seamstress and starcher, one Edith College, was the daughter of Stephen College, the "Protestant joiner" executed for treason in 1681.[137]

While 1689 made the Tories into an opposition party, it transformed the Whigs into the party of the court, but with a crucial difference. In replacing the old Tory court community with one made up of individuals of Whig or Republican background, the new monarchs brought to Whitehall men and women who knew nothing of courts, who had lived in the political wilderness for decades if not their entire lives, and for whom "the Court" in its widest sense had always been the enemy. Such a "Court party" could never look upon the royal household as its physical or spiritual home any more than it could venerate divine-right monarchy. This attitude, as well as the preferment of pure party politicians like Wharton, goes far toward explaining why, in future years, the court (in every sense of the term) would figure less as an object of loyalty to be fought for than as a glittering prize to be fought over.[138]

If the preferment of William's political allies brought sweeping social and ideological changes to the court, that of his financial backers was equally significant. Most were made accounting officers and purveyors, often replacing men of 10, 20, and even 30 years' experience.[139] According to Sir Stephen Fox, this had disastrous results for the King's business.[140] Fox was hardly disinterested, having himself been driven from the greencloth almost immediately after the Revolution, but there is considerable evidence for a decline in the administrative standards of the government in general, and the household in particular, once "Whig disaplin" (as he termed it) took over.[141] Preoccupied with his crusade against Louis XIV, the otherwise conscientious William tolerated the revival of supernumerary appointments, sale of office, and life tenures within his own house.[142] Moreover, at least one of his "Revolution Officers" (as they were dubbed by one displaced Tory)[143] turned out to be unusually corrupt even by contemporary standards. In 1691 the new treasurer of the chamber, Sir Rowland Gwynne, was found to have embezzled between £3,000 and £4,000 out of his department. The money was never recovered from Gwynne and had to be supplied out of the pocket of his successor, Lord Edward Russell, so that the resultant arrears could be paid.[144] While old Royalists like Fox and Sir Benjamin Bathurst were not above picking the King's pocket, they seem to have known how to do it without stopping the King's business altogether.

It was inevitable, given the pedestrian standards of William's household administration, the size and expense of his establishment, and the inadequacy of his financial settlement, that he would soon be unable to pay his servants. As early as June 1691, with the revenue anticipated to 1695 because of the war, the board of greencloth reported the servants below stairs to be over £42,700 (about six months' pay) in arrears and the purveyors threatening to cut off supplies.[145] By February 1695 the servants below stairs were sixteen months in arrears and in "a Starving & Wretched Condition." The purveyors had cut off some provisions, forcing the chamber servants to supply their table out of their own pockets.[146] As the war dragged on and the Crown's financial situation worsened still further with the recoinage, the treasury increasingly resorted, as it had under Charles II, to tallies of anticipation and fictitious loan. This did more for the appearance of the Crown's books than for the financial well-being of its servants.[147] Finally, in the winter of 1696–97, with arrears to some individuals running at over two years,[148] Lord Steward Devonshire and Comptroller Wharton made this desperate suggestion to the cofferer of the household, Francis, Earl of Bradford: "yor Lopp ought (as being Cofferer) forthwith to advance One Thousand Pounds, as yor Predecess^rs^ have alwaies done upon like emergencies."[149]

Bradford's reply—if he made one—to this ludicrous (and in fact unprecedented) suggestion is not known, but there is no evidence that he ever made such a loan. Fortunately, the household's debts eased after 1697. First, with the coming of peace, parliament finally granted the King a civil-list revenue of £700,000 per annum, which was, for the moment at least, permanent, adequate, and unencumbered.[150] The peace also allowed William to begin to deliberate over the minutest details of his household establishments.[151] Unfortunately, the new establishments only managed to cut expenditure by about £15,000 and reduce the size of the household payroll by about 50 places. Moreover, they received the royal signature too late (October 1701 for the household below stairs, December 1701 for the chamber) to have had much effect before the reign's end.[152] Even the timely provision of an adequate civil-list revenue did little to reduce the debts and arrears that had accrued during the war years. William III died owing his household servants and purveyors £307,283 19*s*. 6¾*d*., a full year's expenditure and well over twice the debt left by his most profligate predecessor, Charles II.[153]

Still, that King had shown how an insolvent court, unable to pay or show extraordinary favor to its middling and menial servants, could nevertheless remain entertaining and attractive to the highest levels of aristocratic and gentle society. Unhappily, William's poor health, shyness, and general antipathy to the English nobility precluded such inclinations on his part. On the rare occasions when he met the latter socially, it was generally as a dinner guest, not a host.[154] Fortunately for the popularity of the new regime, William was content to delegate the monarch's social responsibilities to Mary,[155] who had been brought up at the Restoration court and seems to have been well-equipped to maintain its cultural and social traditions. It was Mary who, during William's absences on campaign, supervised the new building at Hampton Court and Kensington, demonstrating her keen interest, considerable technical knowledge, and good taste to Sir Christopher Wren's satisfaction.[156] She brought the same qualities to her patronage of the theater, the royal gardeners, and the musicians of the chapel royal. Her relationship with Henry Purcell, who composed six birthday odes for her, was especially noteworthy.[157] Finally, she popularized the art of embroidery, the collecting of delftware, and the ownership of pug dogs among women of the upper classes.[158] This, along with her husband's enthusiasm for painting, gardening, and the work of Huguenot, Dutch, and English fine craftsmen such as Marot, Tijou, and Tompion suggests that, in the realm of the fine arts at least, the court remained as significant under William and Mary as it had been under their predecessors.[159]

Mary's outgoing personality, in marked contrast to William's sober disposition, seems to have fit her to maintain the court's social role as well. She was, perhaps, the last of the Stuarts to possess some measure of her uncle's vivacity, gregariousness, and, at times, downright silliness. For example, after her arrival from the Netherlands in 1689 she was widely reported to have come to Whitehall "as to a Wedding, riant & jolly." The next morning she went about "in her undresse" testing the beds and opening the closets of her new home.[160] According to John Evelyn, she was quick to reestablish the old Stuart court routine: Mary, "within a night or two, sate downe to play at Basset, as the Q. her predecessor us'd to do: smiled upon & talked to every body; so as no manner of change seem'd in Court, since his Majesties last going away." Evelyn adds, "This carriage was censured by many."[161] Bishop Burnet, a dutiful Whig and a champion of Mary, insisted that her behavior was calculated by William as part of the new regime's refusal to apologize for overturning the old.[162] Certainly, her willingness and ability to continue the old Stuart court traditions of drawing rooms, balls, plays at court, and the like was invaluable to a regime anxious to maintain a facade of "business as usual" and to a king with more pressing concerns than the entertainment of the English nobility.[163]

But there were limits to William's willingness to perpetuate, let alone identify himself with, the culture of the Stuart court. Mary discovered those limits upon his return from the Irish campaign in the summer of 1690. During his absence, she had led a full and not always discreet social life. This had included a much-noticed visit to the playhouse to see a performance of Dryden's *The Spanish Friar*, the plot of which concerns a usurpation, whose beneficiary is a queen.[164] Worse, the hapless Queen "gave as much ocation for discours" a few days later with a shopping excursion to the establishments of a number of London tradeswomen of apparently dubious reputation. Her day culminated in a visit to "one Mrs. Waiss, a Famous woman for telling fortunes," who, unknown to Mary, had been predicting the imminent return of King James.[165]

William was not pleased with his consort's behavior and, upon his return from campaigning, made his displeasure known both privately and publicly, "saying to the Qu: that he heard she dined at a Bawdy hous & desired the Next time she wentt he might goe too." In fact, "slumming" had been a popular and perfectly acceptable activity at the old Restoration court, a fact that Mary alluded to when she replied that "she had done nothing but what the late Qu: had done." William's response—"he asked if she meant to make her her example"—implied a rejection not only of Mary of Modena's behavior but of everything the restored Stuarts and their courts had stood for.

As reported by the anonymous author of the above newsletter, the effect of this exchange upon the Queen was immediate and dramatic: "But it was borne wth all the submission of a good wife who leaves off all to the direction of the K & diverts her selfe wth walking six & seven Mile a day & looking after her buildings Making of Fringes, & such like Inocent things."[166] Suddenly, Mary's interest in Wren's alterations to Hampton Court and Kensington, her concern for the musical standards of the chapel royal, her collection of delftware, and her embroidery all take on a new light. Along with the King's interest in painting, gardening, and craftsmanship, they appear to represent a conscious rejection of the most public and least respectable aspects of Stuart court life, and an equally conscious attempt, more drastic than James II's, to create an alternative that would be culturally satisfying and legitimizing, but above all private and free from scandal. At the end of the reign John Tutchin, author of the *Observator*, caught its style perfectly when he wrote, "King William never incouraged the Devil's-Shop, the Play-House, so much as once during his Reign with his Presence."[167]

Having abolished the openness and banished the personnel of the old Stuart court, the dual monarchs set about purging it of much of its gaiety as well. Under William and Mary household officers were not only forbidden to engage in "swearing and cursing, prophaning the Lord's day, drunkenness, and such immoralities"—all perfectly acceptable among Charles II's boon companions—but were for the first time required to attend daily morning chapel services and to keep a monthly fast day.[168] Mary's fun-loving spirit did occasionally peek through, as when she managed to sneak a visit to the *Folly*, London's floating bawdyhouse cum music hall in the Thames.[169] But after her death, in December 1694, she was more often remembered for having "brought religion and virtue in fashion at Court, as well as over the whole nation."[170]

In the wake of his consort's death, William and the court retreated even further from public view or notoriety.[171] When in England, the King preferred to live at Hampton Court or Kensington rather than the more centrally located, but unsalubrious, Whitehall. Drawing rooms seem to have been infrequent, and when they were held the King was "observed to not talk much to ladys."[172] Balls and plays were held only upon royal birthdays, if at all. In 1696 Princess Anne, acting as royal hostess, opted for a ball, having "heard the king dos not care for plays."[173] He does not appear to have cared much for dancing either, for he was reported to have been "extremely out of humour" on the night in question.[174] It is therefore hardly surprising that William did not lament the destruction of Whitehall by fire in January 1698.[175] Not only was its location bad for his precarious respiration, but it was the only one of his English residences with a theater large enough to accommodate such onerous entertainments, or lodgings plentiful enough to house a significant proportion of the entertainees.

If William failed to bring his subjects to court, he likewise failed to bring the court to his subjects. The first years of the reign had seen a number of public appearances by both William and Mary, in keeping with the need to establish the legitimacy and popularity of the new regime.[176] But after 1689 public appearances by the King were rare, whether owing to shyness, poor health, or a legitimate fear of assassination.[177] For whatever reason, William was persuaded to undertake only one major progress, during the electoral summer following his triumph at Namur in 1695. This was, for the most part, quite successful, the people demonstrating plenty of enthusiasm for the Protestant champion and he, in turn, rising to the occasion with grace.[178] But at times the King's reserve, fatigue, security concerns, or just poor planning appear to have defeated the object of the enterprise. For example, according to Edward Harley, "It is said in Warwickshire and many other places the King greatly disappointed the country, not coming the roads where they waited to see him."[179] At Oxford, admittedly the most Jacobitical city in England, the King refused a dinner, it was said out of fear of being poisoned.[180]

There is evidence that in the few years remaining to him after the war, William III made some attempt to revive the ceremonial, political, and social sides of court life, as he had, briefly and belatedly, its administrative and financial standards. Upon his return from the continent in 1697, a triumphal procession through London was staged, and he allowed himself to be fêted at the Middle Temple.[181] During the parliamentary session of 1699–1700, drawing rooms were held more frequently, and in the following session, the King fêted the whole of his loyal House of Commons after the anti-French resolution of 18 February 1701.[182] After the destruction of Whitehall, work at Hampton Court, which had been suspended on Mary's death, was resumed. Indeed, a few days before the King's own demise, orders were given to fit up a theater there.[183] But as with William's belated attempts at good husbandry, these efforts were far too little, too late, to be more than isolated glimmers of a once-brilliant past. Whereas the royal household had been, under Charles II, the very center of an open, attractive, and vibrant court culture—political, social, and aesthetic—it had become, by the death of William III, "the residence of secluded Royalty, pointed out from afar, difficult of access save on formal occasions of proverbial dullness."[184]

Contrary to much received opinion about the "fat, dull and persevering lady"[185] who succeeded William on the throne, this was no more the sort of household envisaged by Queen Anne (herself a child of the Restoration court) than was the role of "Doge of Venice" that it implied. Just as she confronted the central problem of postrevolutionary monarchy—how to maintain freedom of action in the face of parliamentary domination of her finances and party domination of parliament—so she confronted the related problem of how to maintain an attractive and impressive court life within the financial and political constraints imposed upon the later Stuarts. It is well known that Anne, like her father, presided over a household that was relatively efficient, inexpensive, and free from scandal. It is less well known that she also made some attempt to provide a court life that was, in her terms, entertaining, inspiring, and popular, as her uncle's had been.

The following chapters chronicle this attempt and its ultimate failure. That failure has often been attributed to defects of Anne's personality. It is certainly true that her court was, like those of her predecessors, in part a reflection of the personality of the monarch. But of at least equal importance in explaining that failure is the legacy of the previous 40 years. That legacy included an antiquated and inflexible administrative system, an inadequate revenue, and an accumulation of debt going back to Charles II. The Queen's task was rendered more difficult by the virtual extinction of the old guard of household administrators and the lack of adequate facilities after the destruction of Whitehall. Gone, too, were many of the old court families that had looked to the royal household for leadership, livelihood, or hospitality. In their place had arisen two parties bent upon reducing court posts to little more than the spoils of victory. Finally, there was the apparent loss of the habit, once so common among the English ruling class, of simply "going to court." Just as the power and authority of the monarch were being challenged in the constitution so was the preeminence of the court in government and society as a whole. The English royal household was being replaced as an employer by a burgeoning governmental bureaucracy and the rising professions; as a source of easy profit by the joint-stock companies and government funds; as a political center by parliament and its attendant parties' various watering holes; as an entertainer and artistic patron by the public theater and concert hall; and as a provider of conversation and companionship by the coffeehouse and club. The court as it existed under Queen Anne, like personal monarchy itself, was to see the inevitable culmination of these trends tending toward its decline, even as it made one last, desperate attempt to resist them.

CHAPTER II

Administration and Finance

In the early editions of *Anglia Notitia*, Edward Chamberlayne eulogizes the administrative and financial structure of the later Stuart court in the measured and self-satisfied tones usually reserved by contemporaries for the "Ancient Constitution" itself:

> The Form of Government is, by the Wisdom of many Ages, so contrived and regulated, that it seems to such as seriously consider it, almost impossible to mend it, if the prescribed Rules of Government be duly and impartially executed. The Account (which is of many Natures, and is therefore very difficult, must pass through many hands, and is therefore very exact) is so wisely contrived and methodized, that without the Combination of every one of these following Officers, viz. The Cofferer, a Clerk of the Green-cloth, a Clerk Comptroller, a Clerk of the Kitchen, of the Spicery or Avery, or a particular Clerk, together with the Conjunction of a Purveyor and Waiter in the Office, it is impossible to defraud the King of a Loaf of Bread, or a Pint of Wine, a Quart of Beer, or Joynt of Meat, or Money, or any thing else.[1]

Here, as elsewhere, Chamberlayne's work gives every evidence of having been informed not only by data provided by the Restoration court, but by its characteristic attitudes as well. Old Stuart servants like Sir Charles Lodowick Cotterell and Sir Stephen Fox shared his faith in the ancient forms, precedents, and "Rules of Government" as embodied not only in books of ordinances but especially in long-standing tradition and usage.[2] According to Fox, the "Whig disaplin" of William's reign failed precisely because it abandoned "ye Rules of the House."[3]

Certainly the first impression conveyed by the official household records as preserved in the LC and LS series in the Public Record Office, apart from their sheer bulk, is of a vast and complex but efficient institution coping smoothly with an equally vast and varied amount of business. Long series of establishments, contracts, estimates, warrants, tradesmen's bills, receipts, and accounts document each one of the steps extolled by Chamberlayne, which were necessary in order to equip royal palaces and yachts; arrange coronations, progresses, and funerals; or appoint, pay, house, feed, and clothe royal servants.[4] These records do provide glimpses of occasional disruptions of routine: messengers of the chamber caught smuggling goods from Europe; complaints about the portions and quality of the food served at the royal tables; servants failing to attend or perform their duties.[5] But in each case the lord chamberlain or board of greencloth appears to have acted quickly and decisively, correcting abuses, drawing up new rules and ordinances, and suspending, though rarely removing, the offending parties. Finally, the Queen's business would seem to have been paid for with equal dispatch and completeness, for the accounts declared by household paymasters at the exchequer rarely show a deficit.[6]

Early modern historians have long been aware of the dangers of taking contemporary administrative and financial records at face value. To address only the last example, departmental declared accounts only registered the year's business, not its debt; that is, bills and wages paid, not those contracted for and earned. The following pages will attempt to penetrate the positive exterior of the household's accounts to determine its actual financial health. First, however, the administrative framework that was supposed, among other things, to manage those finances must be examined.

Administration

The author of *Anglia Notitia* was at least half right when he described the form of government of the royal household as a product of "the Wisdom of many Ages."[7] The structure of the household, as restored in 1660 and largely inherited by Queen Anne in 1702, was a Tudor and early Stuart modification of a medieval prototype. The end result of this long period of gestation, and the most basic problem for those whose job it was to manage the court, was its lack of a central coordinating authority. Rather, each of the household's various departments, subdepartments, and societies[8] had its own peculiar, time-honored but by no means necessarily well-defined relationship to the whole. For administrative purposes at least, these various entities may be roughly

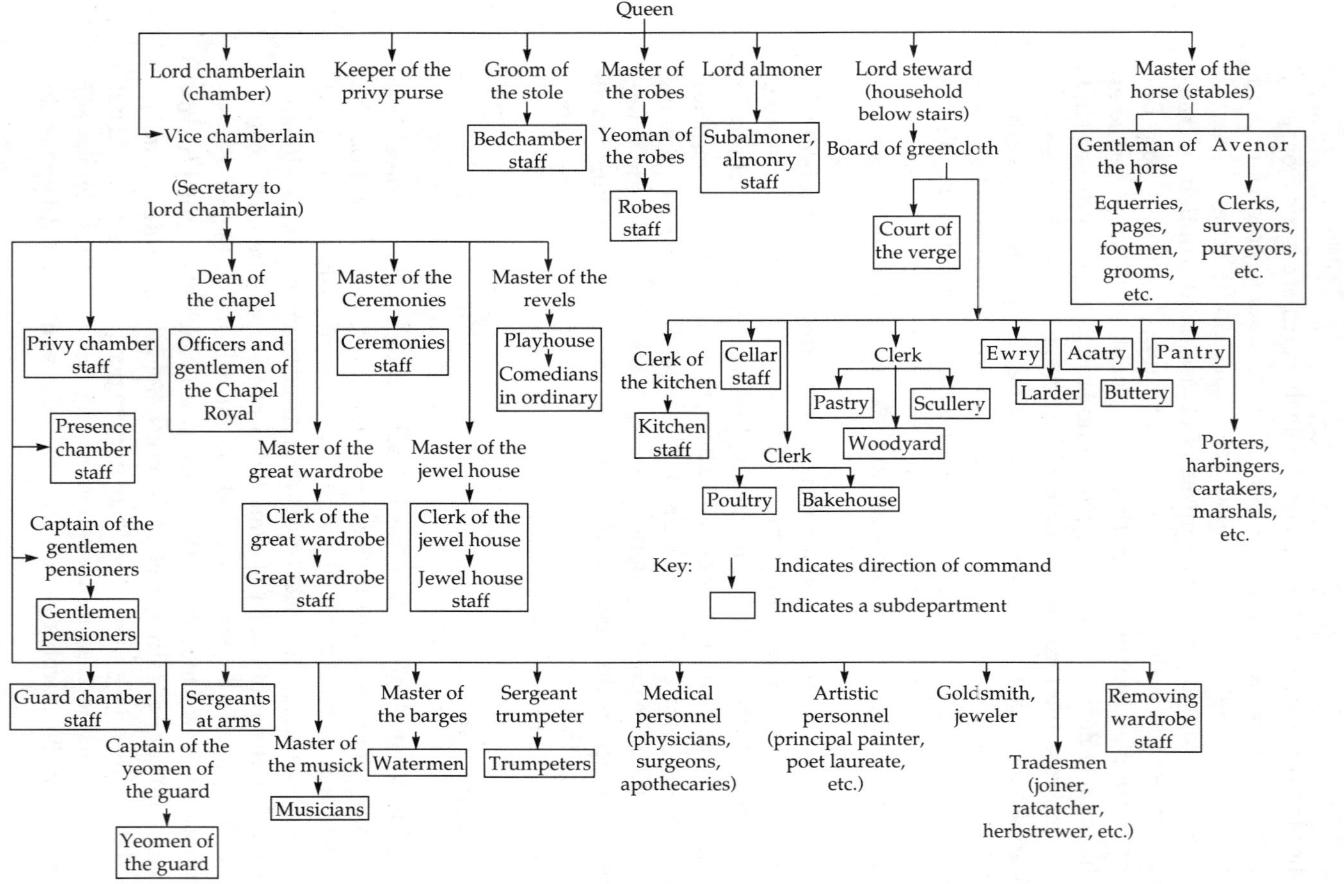

Fig. 2.1. Departmental organization of the household. Data from sources cited in Chapter 2, n. 4.

divided into three main departments (or collections of subdepartments): the chamber, which was concerned with the ceremonial and aesthetic life of the monarch; the household below stairs, concerned with her culinary and domestic needs; and the stables, which provided her transportation.

Of these, the chamber was by far both the largest (Figure 1.1) and the most loosely organized (Figure 2.1). At its head was the lord chamberlain (or, in his absence, the vice chamberlain), who received his orders directly from the Queen. These were communicated verbally through the gentleman usher, daily waiter in attendance to the bewildering array of gentlemen, gentlemen ushers, grooms, and pages who served in the public rooms; through their respective masters to the officers of the ceremonies, revels, the Queen's musick and her watermen; through their respective captains to the gentlemen pensioners and yeomen of the guard; and through its dean to the gentlemen and children of the chapel royal. Financially independent subdepartments providing matériel, such as the great wardrobe, works, or jewel house, received their orders via lord chamberlain's warrant to their respective masters.[9]

Toward the end of the seventeenth century, and during the 1680s in particular, the lord chamberlain's authority began to be questioned by the heads of a number of these subdepartments, most of whom were his social and political equals. However, in every case but one the vigorous and politically significant lords chamberlain of that decade, Arlington and Mulgrave, were successful in asserting their primacy.[10] The exception was the royal bedchamber and closet, whose precincts and personnel, after a running battle throughout the early 1680s, finally came under the jurisdiction of the groom of the stole.[11] This arrangement was to be strengthened by the new bedchamber ordinances of 1689 (which remained in effect under Anne) as well as by the naming of two such powerful personalities as the Earl of Portland and the Duchess of Marlborough to the groomship almost in succession. Otherwise, the lord chamberlain's administrative authority went virtually unchallenged during Anne's reign, despite the relatively uninspiring quality of her first two holders of that office (the Earls of Jersey and Kent) and the frequent absences of the third (the Duke of Shrewsbury).[12]

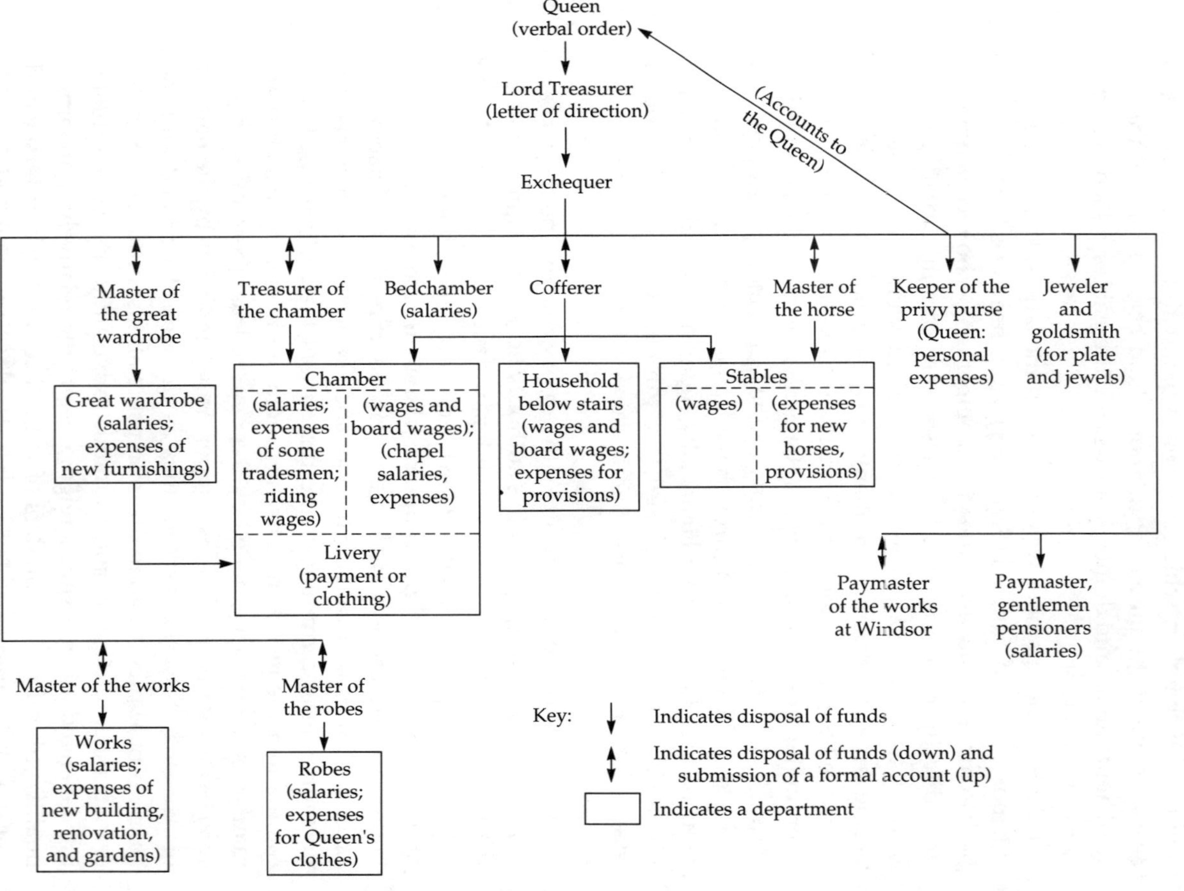

Fig. 2.2. Financial arrangements of the household. Data from sources cited in Chapter 2, n. 4.

Unfortunately, the lord chamberlain was not his department's chief financial officer. Anciently, that function had been fulfilled by the treasurer of the chamber. After the household reforms of the 1530s, however, the chamber's treasurer actually paid and accounted for only a portion of the wages and bills of the servants in the lord chamberlain's jurisdiction, most notably the servants in the public rooms, some of the artisans, and the yeomen of the guard (Figure 2.2). Other subdepartments and societies, such as the ceremonies, the revels, and the gentlemen pensioners, had their bills paid and accounted for with the treasurer, but received their salaries directly at the exchequer. The great wardrobe, robes, and works—subdepartments of great antiquity and historical independence—though administratively subordinate to the lord chamberlain, were financially completely autonomous, receiving their money on imprest and accounting for it at the exchequer directly. This put the lord chamberlain in the position of having to order matériel—anything from new curtains to major renovations of palaces—without knowing or being held responsible for the cost. In addition, many chamber servants, including the lord chamberlain himself, received livery or payments in kind out of the great wardrobe. Finally, they received the bulk of their wages and boardwages, as did the servants of the stables, on the establishment of the household below stairs (Figure 2.2).[13]

Both the stables and the household below stairs were smaller and more tightly and intelligibly organized than the chamber. The stables, with its assortment of equerries, pages of honor, footmen, grooms, purveyors, and stable keepers, received the Queen's orders, often at a moment's notice, from her master of the horse. He also received the department's imprests and accounted for its extraordinary expenditure (horses, equipage, provisions, etc.) at the exchequer; however, the department's wages were paid, as noted in the previous paragraph, by the cofferer of the household at the board of greencloth. This body, headed by the lord steward (the ultimate administrative authority below stairs), consisted of the treasurer, comptroller, and master of the household (mostly sinecures), the cofferer (the department's financial and accounting officer), and the four clerks and clerks comptroller of the greencloth (who performed most of the board's real administrative work). It coordinated the work of the various catering offices below stairs (see Figure 2.1), disciplined recalcitrant officials, and acted as a court of law for "the Verge," that area within twelve miles of the royal household, excluding the city of London and other liberties. The board's intrusion into the affairs of the chamber and stables also derived from the reforms of the 1530s. Cromwell seems to have realized that, in the absence of a single overarching authority for the household as a whole, the board of greencloth was the one body of sufficient weight and collective experience to have any possibility of coordinating this vast aggregate of departments, subdepartments, and societies.

But Cromwell's household reforms went no further, and subsequent efforts to rationalize this haphazard structure, such as that of the 1630s, proved abortive.[14] When, in the late seventeenth century, the need for reform once again became paramount, the initiative had passed out of the hands of individual department heads and even the privy council into those of the treasury.[15] As noted in the previous chapter, by the time of William III's household reforms at the end of the century, the treasury's right to impose its will upon the household's spending departments was no longer at issue. But the treasury's apparent success in this area is at least partially explained by its limited objectives and its halfhearted manner of pursuing them. The most lasting of its so-called reforms merely involved the grafting of some form of treasury authority, often an officer or a procedure, onto the existing structure, not its radical renovation. Thus, the treasury asserted its right to determine the establishments of household departments such as the chamber and household below stairs, but made no real attempt to rationalize them by causing their administrative and financial business to be transacted in the same place. Nor did it make any effort to "establish" those departments or offices such as the great wardrobe, robes, jeweler, and goldsmith, which had never known a budget and where most of the expenditure was in the form of tradesmen's bills—much easier to inflate than a payroll.

Similarly, while the treasury asserted its right to direct how the departments of the royal household spent their money (in particular, demanding estimates for proposed work in the great wardrobe), it found no effective way to determine whether the amounts it authorized were justified. This should have been of great concern, for the practice of naming household administrators as purveyors and suppliers to their own departments encouraged overspending, especially when poundage taken in the former capacity was directly dependent upon the amount of goods or business provided in the latter. Since the treasury obviously could not rely upon the officers of the household to police themselves, its usual procedure was to erect an outside comptroller subject to its own authority, as it did in the chamber after the scandal of the early 1690s and as it was to do after a similarly disturbing inquiry into the great wardrobe in 1728.[16] But such measures were only as good as the men named to carry them out. In 1712 the comptroller of the accounts of the treasurer of the chamber was himself found to have taken illegal fees from those he was supposed to regulate.[17] The comptroller of the great wardrobe was to prove, at best, ineffective in stopping the rising tide of that department's expenditure into the 1740s.[18] In the end, the imposition of treasury control, the initiation of new ordinances and procedures, and the erection of separate comptrollers answerable to it, far from rendering the royal household more time- or cost-effective, merely created one more office, one more step, one more vague level of jurisdiction in a structure already overburdened with all three. It is thus no accident that the period when the treasury's hegemony was being asserted also saw the marked increase in jurisdictional and procedural disputes noted above.

The resultant administrative chaos, so well camouflaged in official records, emerges quite clearly from the private correspondence, memoirs, and diaries left by household administrators, in particular the notebooks of Sir Clement Cotterell.[19] Cotterell was master of the ceremonies from 1710 until his death in 1758 and had served under his father as assistant before succeeding him in the mastership. His office was responsible not only for the ceremony and protocol surrounding ambassadorial entrances and audiences, but also for the domestic arrangements of foreign dignitaries. As a result, he was familiar with most aspects of the household's administrative system. Despite continued attempts to improve coordination under Queen Anne, Cotterell's notebooks, from the time of his initial appointment, are full of examples of various offices "blundering one among another."[20] On the occasion of a visit in 1722 by an envoy from Tunis, he writes as follows:

The steps taken towards him [the envoy] are thus. My Lord Chamberlain by his Letter to the Lords Commissioners of the Treasury signifies the Kings plea-

> sure that so much should be paid to me to deliver to Juluff Chagia lately arrived from Tunis upon this by their Lordships orders Mr Lowndes Secretary to the Treasury writes a letter to the Auditor of the Exchequer to issue the Money to the Cofferer of the Household, this is done, but still it seems I cannot recive [*sic*] the necessary imprest from the Green Cloath, till my Lord Chamberlain signifies the King's pleasure in this affair to my Lord Steward & the rest of the board, by another Letter which I hope will be done. I am particular in the necessary forms because I see all officers forget these things from time to time, & so cause much trouble and attendance before they can fall into the right way.[21]

Clearly, the involvement of the treasury in this transaction, far from lending direction or efficiency, merely gave Cotterell yet more "trouble and attendance." Other accounts from Anne's reign suggest that his experience was by no means unique; indeed, even the Queen and the Duke of Marlborough occasionally found it difficult to get what they wanted out of the royal household.[22]

Such a tortured and tangled system could only be worked by a cadre of old hands of the sort Cotterell eventually became: able but none too scrupulous, at home with "the necessary forms" but not above bypassing them when expedient. In this regard the Queen was lucky, for, despite the purges of the previous reign, she inherited a number of administrators of long and continuous experience or pedigree, like the Cotterells in the ceremonies or the Killigrews in the revels.[23] She was also able to bring back a number of old Stuart servants who had lost their posts under William and Mary, such as Sir Stephen Fox, who became a commissioner of horse and one of the compilers of her first establishment,[24] and Thomas Atterbury, her clerk of the cheque to the messengers, "which place he enjoyed before the revolution."[25] Anne's household administration also benefited from the experience (if not necessarily the integrity) of a number of those who had served her as Princess: her old comptroller, Sir Benjamin Bathurst, and her master of the horse, Viscount Fitzharding, became cofferer and treasurer of the chamber, respectively, in the new household. Her groom of the stole (and principal favorite), the Countess of Marlborough, not only retained that post under the new Queen, but assumed those of mistress of the robes and keeper of the privy purse as well.

Finally, a number of Anne's household administrators proved themselves for the first time after her accession, most surprisingly so in the case of her much maligned master of the horse, the Duke of Somerset: his correspondence and accounts reveal him to have been a conscientious manager of her stables.[26] More importantly, Thomas Coke, who came to London at the end of William's reign as a young and pleasure-loving M.P. from Derbyshire, is revealed in his private papers to have been an able, assiduous, and highly versatile vice chamberlain, a post that he held from 1706 until his death in 1727.[27] Along with Sir John Stanley and John Evans, respectively secretary (1697–1719) and clerk (?1708–27) to the lord chamberlain, Coke took care of a vast amount of chamber business, sometimes by warrant or letter, more often by personal visit. This team gives every evidence of having worked smoothly, with only occasional reference to the lord chamberlain, to plan the monarch's schedule, arrange entertainments and processions, furnish the royal palaces, determine disputes among royal servants, and regulate London's theatrical companies.[28] Since none of Anne's lords chamberlain were active administrators, as Arlington and Mulgrave had been, the vice chamberlain's attendance upon the monarch was especially important to her. Indeed, Coke refused to leave the court even to campaign for his reelection to parliament during the summer of 1710.[29] It is thus little wonder that the Queen allowed him £1,000 per annum out of the privy purse "in consideration of his constant waiting and attendance on her person and the extraordinary expense occasioned to him thereby."[30]

Subsequent chapters will explore more fully the quality of Anne's household administrators and the environment they provided for her and her guests. For the moment, it is sufficient to point out that men such as Coke and Cotterell did much by their vigor and flexibility to mitigate the worst effects of an antiquated administrative framework, accomplishing the Queen's business often as much in spite of "the prescribed Rules of Government" as because of them. Moreover, they would appear to have done so with a minimum of the sort of large-scale corruption common in earlier reigns. Nevertheless, neither their relative efficiency and rectitude on the one hand, nor the inefficiency and petty corruption they resisted on the other, ultimately had much effect on the most fundamental problem facing the royal household at the turn of the eighteenth century: shortage of money.

Finance

In *The English Court in the Reign of George I*, Professor Beattie has demonstrated that the court's financial problems at the beginning of the eighteenth century were essentially those of the civil list writ small.[31] As noted in Chapter 1, it was not until 1698 that parliament recognized the monarch's changing constitutional position, absolved him from having to pay for the nation's military and naval forces, and granted him a separate and permanent civil-list revenue. This was to be raised out of the customs, the hereditary and temporary excise, the post office, and what remained of the King's other hereditary revenues, all of which, it was hoped, would yield a total of £700,000 per annum.[32] It should be understood at the outset that this figure was based upon no very reliable estimate of what William's civil expenses actually were, nor was it guaranteed by parliament should the assigned revenues fail to meet it. In fact, the legislators who drew up the first civil-list settlement were so confident of its adequacy that they made provision to claim any surplus over the above figure for their own purposes.[33] It was on this basis that in 1701 parliament appropriated £3,700 per week (£192,400 per annum) out of the excise "for the Publick Use and Service."[34]

If the first civil-list act reflected the monarch's gradual retreat from the business of government, it also reflected the fact that this retreat was by no means complete by the end of the seventeenth century. The civil-list revenue was granted to William III in order to pay not only for the service of the royal household and state, but also for the expenses of the civil government, still the King's government. These included the salaries of the judges and the officers of the central administration, the expenses of the diplomatic service, pensions, bounties, and secret service.[35] In theory, the royal household was budgeted to receive just under 40 percent of the civil-list revenue.[36] In practice, and particularly during periods of shortage, it often received a far smaller proportion—a sacrifice to the need to keep other, more essential, government services running.

Immediately upon Anne's accession in 1702 the Commons began to consider a provision for her civil establishment.[37] As in 1697–98, no estimate of the new Queen's potential expenses was called for, nor was one provided by the treasury. What the latter did provide was a statement drawn up by Secretary Lowndes of William's civil-list revenues. Unluckily for Anne, this showed a yield of £709,423 4*s*. 5½*d*. for his last full year on the throne (25 Dec. 1700 to 25 Dec. 1701), even after deducting the £3,700 per week appropriated for the service of the public.[38] Armed with this comforting bit of information, the House proceeded to grant the new Queen virtually the same settlement, with the same encumbrances, as her predecessor had enjoyed, passing the bill on 26 March 1702. The bill passed the Lords on the following day and was ready for the royal signature on the 30th.[39]

From the first, the honorable members seem to have been convinced that they had acted not only quickly but generously in light of the unprecedented burden of the war and the memory of previous Stuart extravagance and corruption. The latter, in particular, would appear to have given some members pause, for, as Gilbert Burnet hinted, "many seemed to apprehend, that so great a revenue might be applied to uses not so profitable to the public, in a reign that was like to be frugal, and probably would not be subject to great accidents."[40] This attitude, owing more to Country tradition than a realistic assessment of the Crown's legitimate needs, persisted among the gentlemen of the House of Commons to the end of the reign, effectively forestalling any further attempt to augment the Queen's civil-list settlement.[41]

Nevertheless, it was immediately apparent to Anne and her closest advisers that between the war and the "great accidents" it was to wreak upon the economy, the revenue settlement of 1702 was neither so certain nor so generous as its authors imagined.[42] She told them as much in her speech of acceptance, predicting, "It is probable the Revenue may fall very Short of what it has formerly produced."[43] Table 2.1, column 1, fully bears her out: not once in Anne's reign did her civil revenues yield the expected £700,000. Rather, after the deduction of the £3,700 earmarked for public uses, they averaged only £597,842 per annum during the period of Godolphin's tenure at the treasury. Nor was the whole of even this lesser figure necessarily at the Queen's disposal. At her acceptance of the civil-list settlement she promised to donate a further £100,000 for the first year's service of the war.[44] In fact, over the next eight and a half years (the period up to Godolphin's fall) she contributed an average of £41,177 per annum "for the service of the pub-

TABLE 2.1
Annual Yield of the Civil-List Revenue Compared to Issues to the Civil Departments, 8 March 1702 to Michaelmas 1714

Year	Revenue (£)	Issues (£)	Difference[a] (£)
8 Mar. 1702–Ms. 1702	250,691	115,537	+135,154
Ms. 1702–Ms. 1703	601,084	547,192	+53,892
Ms. 1703–Ms. 1704	676,826	629,147	+47,679
Ms. 1704–Ms. 1705	595,999	757,118	−161,119
Ms. 1705–Ms. 1706	562,867	656,136	−93,269
Ms. 1706–Ms. 1707	637,001	731,252	−94,251
Ms. 1707–Ms. 1708	609,244	793,013	−183,769
Ms. 1708–Ms. 1709	579,326	711,908	−132,582
Ms. 1709–Ms. 1710	568,627	814,078	−245,451
Ms. 1710–Ms. 1711	513,615	637,918	−124,303
Ms. 1711–Ms. 1712	565,405	675,166	−109,761
Ms. 1712–Ms. 1713	587,022	585,185	+1,837
Ms. 1713–Ms. 1714	562,650	1,104,024	−541,374
Total	7,310,357	8,757,674	−1,447,317

SOURCE: Statements of revenue and expenditure printed in the introductions to *C.T.B.*, vols. XVII–XXVIII.
[a]See Chapter 2, n. 78.

lic."[45] Further, in 1704 she donated the income from First Fruits and Tenths, worth about £13,000 per annum, to the poor Anglican clergy ("Queen Anne's Bounty").[46] As a result, during the period up to the change of ministry in 1710 the Queen had at her disposal, on average, a mere £543,665 per annum with which to pay the expenses of her household and the civil government of the nation, which were supposed, according to the civil establishments, to cost £666,765 per annum.[47] With little hope of any further help from parliament, she would have "to be frugal" indeed.

Fortunately, if Anne inherited the problems of William's household structure and civil-list settlement, she also inherited and profited by some of his attempted solutions to those problems. Despite the claims of both Sir Stephen Fox and the Duchess of Marlborough,[48] her original establishments for both the chamber and the household below stairs were quite clearly more stringent versions of those drawn up at the end of the previous reign.[49] Their most important innovation was the elimination of over 250 places, mostly in the chamber. While some of these were purely honorary positions (for example the 86 gentlemen of the privy chamber stricken from the establishment), enough salaries were eliminated to bring the established expense of these two departments down about £10,000 from 1689. All told, Anne's court was smaller and less costly than that of any other later Stuart except her father (see Table 1.2). It promised to be still smaller and less costly in future, for the new establishments earmarked over 40 additional paying positions for elimination upon the deaths of their current holders.[50]

The new court recalled the spirit of James II, too, in its greater dedication to administrative reform and financial rectitude. One of the Queen's first instructions to her new board of greencloth was the warrant of 29 June 1702, later embodied in a general order in council for the whole administration, prohibiting sale of office.[51] This was followed on 29 January 1703 by a warrant designed "to reduce Our Present Officers Allowances to a certainty" by eliminating the greencloth's ancient rights of "Wast [*sic*], Command and Remaines" whereby officers of the board could claim leftover provisions. In compensation they were granted a stipend of 24*s*. per diem, or £438 per annum.[52] This policy was later extended to the surveyor of the royal pictures, the watch and clock maker, and the writer and embellisher, all of whom were granted fixed salaries ranging from £60 to £200 per annum in lieu of individual bills for work performed.[53] It is a measure of the inadequacy of Anne's financial settlement that, unlike her father, she did not have the resources to extend this policy further. This illustrates the fundamental paradox of early modern administration: in order to be cheaper and more efficient, it would have had to be better funded.

Since this was not the case, the treasury was left to pursue less radical measures, such as the traditional call for the completion and declaration of outstanding accounts and the return of outstanding plate.[54] In addition, the treasury demanded that in future all warrants for such plate should be accompanied by an estimate of cost, like warrants of the great wardrobe.[55] At the departmental level, the new establishment empowered the greencloth to choose among competing provisioners: "The Several Purveyors, Tradesmen, and Others that make Provision for Our House or Stables shall be soe Admitted, that Our Officers of the Greencloth be left free to contract with those that will Serve best, and at most reasonable Rates."[56] In practice, this meant that the board no longer swore purveyors and tradesmen into ordinary service for the duration of the reign. Rather, the Queen contracted with them a year at a time, an arrangement that the Duchess of Marlborough also pursued, successfully, in the robes.[57] Taken together, these provisions, like the new establishments, amounted to a less drastic attack upon the fundamental administrative and financial problems of the court than that launched by Anne's father. But in light of his eventual fate they perhaps represented a more prudent and potentially effective compromise between reform and frugality on the one hand, and the need to maintain the dignity (and patronage opportunities) of the royal state on the other.

In later years, the Duchess of Marlborough took credit for many of these reforms. According to one preliminary draft of her *Conduct*, "All that the Queen did when she came first to the crown to prevent selling in the greencloth, & other offices was at my solicitation."[58] Elsewhere, Sarah claims to have saved the Crown a total of £100,000 by her vigilance and reforms in the robes; though in the printed version she toned this down to a mere £90,000.[59] Like Sarah's claims of political significance and importance as a patron, these assertions must not be dismissed out of hand. She does appear to have eliminated the sale of purveyorships and the taking of poundage in the robes.[60] She did declare her accounts promptly and they demonstrate substantial savings over the robes expenses of Anne's predecessor, if not quite as substantial as she later claimed.[61] Most importantly, the Duchess of Marlborough was to prove invaluable to the Queen in fielding (and usually discouraging) a wide variety of petitions for places, pensions, and individual bequests. This saved her mistress much time, trouble, and money, as well as the resentment that comes from having to say "no," which Sarah, of course, took upon herself.[62]

But there is no evidence in the extensive correspondence between the Queen, Godolphin, and the Churchills for the Duchess's supposed influence on the Crown's general policy of attack on corruption, fee taking, and administrative venality. Nor do Sarah's assertions sit well with her periodic borrowings and pilferings out of the privy purse, which Anne was apparently blackmailed into allowing. These amounted, by the time of the Duchess's removal, to £32,800.[63] In fact, there was a general resolve toward good husbandry within Anne's immediate circle, and there are more likely candidates than Sarah for the role of its guiding spirit. For example, Lord Treasurer Godolphin had begun his career as a page of honor and was, later, master of the robes at the court of Charles II. This, along with his experience at numerous treasury boards, would have made him familiar with the problems of household administration and finance from every angle and could only have convinced him of the need for retrenchment and reform. Indeed, Godolphin's presence at the treasury at the end of William's reign and the beginning of Anne's suggests that he may have had the greatest influence upon the reformed establishments of those years. Moreover, it can be proved from the Queen's correspondence that it was he and not Sarah who guided her in the elimination of fee taking at the greencloth in 1703.[64]

Nor should it be forgotten that Queen Anne was the daughter of James II and had been raised at the court of that efficient and frugal monarch. As Princess, she frequently involved herself in the business of her own household, examining accounts, making specific orders for provisions, noting when servants were lax in their attendance or tradesmen's work was poor.[65] Indeed, while looking over some bills in the spring of 1697 ("& amongst other faults I found, I thought ye expences of oyle & vinegar weare very extravagant") Anne herself discovered, through the interrogation of several inferior officers, that her comptroller, Sir Benjamin Bathurst, was selling places in her household.[66] It is probably the shock of this revelation, and not Sarah's urgings, that explains the attack on venality at the beginning of her reign. Princess Anne's reaction to Bathurst's mismanagement, as conveyed to the Countess of Marlborough, both demonstrates her own resolve and gives a good idea of what she expected of her servants: "I think it is very hard that I who love to live well, should pay more & yet bee worse served than any body upon earth & therefore I will try if I can to put things in a better method, tho it will bee impossible for me to have everything don to my mind unless I could meet with a Mrs. Freeman [the Countess of Marlborough] in every post of my family."[67]

Despite this last bit of flattery and the eventual preferment of Mrs. Freeman to three of the most prestigious posts in the new household, as Queen, Anne was to rely at least as much on her lord treasurer and her own innate vigilance to have things "don" to her mind. As is well known, she attended more cabinet meetings than any other monarch in British history. During the early years of her reign she also attended the treasury board on several occasions.[68] As a result, she was closely involved, along with Godolphin and Fox, in drawing up her first establishment, "in wch Her Maj^{tie} was very circumspect and knowing" according to the latter.[69] After Godolphin was named sole lord treasurer, he continued to attend her on a near daily basis with treasury business, as did his successor, Oxford, in later years.[70] Between their visits, the constant access of department heads such as the lord steward and master of the horse, and Sarah's correspondence, Queen Anne continued to be involved with the minutest details of her household's administration right up to the end of her reign.[71]

A partial record of that involvement, in the form of Anne's answers to petitions submitted to her treasury board, has been preserved in the minutes of that body. Their examination amply confirms Dr. Shaw's assessment that they are "terse and brief but . . . distinguished by strong common sense."[72] They also reveal a certain amount of characteristic Stuart imperiousness and cunning, particularly when dealing with the debts of her predecessor. Queen Anne did not repudiate the debts of William III, but she was highly selective about those she paid.[73] For instance, in 1702, when William's former master of the horse, Overkerk, petitioned to be reimbursed for expenses he had incurred in that post, he was told that though he would be paid for horses presented to the King of the Romans, the Queen would "not pay for such equipage as was bought and never used."[74] Similarly, in 1703, when Sir Godfrey Kneller petitioned to be paid for £570 worth of paintings of the royal family, he was informed, "Her Majesty does not care for the picture of [i.e., costing] £350"—an equestrian portrait of William—"the others are to be paid for."[75] To Thomas Tompion, petitioning for over £500 worth of clocks and watches, the Queen's disingenuous reply, as recorded in the minutes, was: "Her Majesty has no occasion for his clocks and watches."[76] Clearly, Anne's dislike of "Mr. Caliban" and all those associated with him dovetailed nicely with the new regime's emphasis on frugality. In fairness, it should be pointed out that she was the most generous of the later Stuarts to those truly in need, whatever their personal and political associations. At the same time, she was equally careful not to overpay her servants or enlarge her establishments without due cause.[77]

This emphasis on good husbandry, combined with the relatively economical starting point provided by Anne's original establishments, resulted in an average annual household expenditure of just under £259,500, significantly less than that of either her predecessor or her successor (Table 1.2). This in turn, combined with Godolphin's able management of available funds, explains why, despite inadequate revenue yields, the early years of Anne's reign were not marred by the chronic financial difficulties experienced by her uncle and brother-in-law from the inception of their reigns. But as the total civil expenditure increased and the civil revenue continued to decline still further, the household portion of that expenditure began to be squeezed (Table 2.1).[78] As early as April 1704 the great wardrobe had to be denied requested funds by the treasury. A similar request in April 1706 received a similar reply: "There is no money at present. As soon as there is his Lordship will direct for that Office."[79]

Tradesmen's bills for furniture delivered or for servants' liveries such as those that constituted the bulk of great wardrobe expenditure were one thing; arrears owed to the purveyors who supplied the daily provisions needed to feed, heat, and light the court were quite another. By December 1706 this service, too, was apparently beginning to suffer, for in that month the clerks of the greencloth wrote at length to the cofferer of the household, Francis Godolphin, of "the pressing necessityes of y[e] Family."[80] Table 2.2 indicates that issues to the household below stairs had fallen during the previous exchequer year (Michaelmas 1705 to Michaelmas 1706) by something like 25 percent, from an average of £79,500 per annum for the previous three years to just over £60,000 for this one. The board's transparent attempt to gain the attention of Godolphin *père* through the influence of Godolphin *fils* seems to have worked, for issues to the household below stairs rose to nearly £80,000 again the following year. This temporary increase was accomplished by the diversion to the household paymasters of proceeds from loans on the security of the sale of the Queen's tin. Still, this did nothing to remedy the effects of the previous shortage. In August 1707 the board reported the household servants and purveyors nearly three quarters in arrears,[81] and this just prior to the department's leanest year of the reign (Table 2.2). Despite two relatively good years before Godolphin's fall (Table 2.2), and his continued diversion of the proceeds from the tin sales into the civil-list account,[82] in May 1710 the board of

TABLE 2.2

Issues to the Queen's Household out of Her Own Civil List, 1702–1714

Department	to Ms. 1702 (£)	1702–3 (£)	1703–4 (£)	1704–5 (£)	1705–6 (£)	1706–7 (£)	1707–8 (£)	1708–9 (£)	1709–10 (£)	1710–11 (£)	1711–12 (£)	1712–13 (£)	1713–14 (£)
Household	15,000	75,612	82,181	80,735	61,038	79,842	54,007	96,880	80,136	54,760	107,081	60,919	144,537
Chamber	—	30,310	26,120	28,969	23,317	27,786	21,465	37,586	26,385	22,791	20,799	19,259	64,354
Stables	—	13,750	—	9,000	5,000	13,000	—	2,000	12,000	1,500	9,000	16,000	12,500
Works	4,911	26,820	29,025	28,473	26,568	25,590	50,585	24,869	58,336	16,352	25,879	4,893	74,474
Works-Windsor	1,300	5,375	2,948	3,240	6,770	3,554	9,481	2,907	7,602	1,630	2,032	—	10,887
Great ward.	14,008	15,576	15,430	20,000	15,000	17,394	19,606	27,156	9,400	14,238	2,500	20,712	47,936
Robes	—	5,000	5,000	5,000	—	—	7,000	3,000	3,000	4,000	4,000	4,000	5,105
Salaries paid at exchequer	10,427	23,058	16,022	22,077	18,742	18,258	19,010	18,942	13,974	20,806	20,060	18,669	13,012
Gent. pens.	3,000	9,000	6,000	6,000	4,500	4,500	6,000	6,000	3,000	7,500	3,750	4,530	11,072
Jeweler	10,000	24,050	6,937	4,446	7,600	6,648	9,286	11,319	6,934	14,559	11,698	18,097	16,505
Privy purse	6,900	26,600	17,700	22,800	26,000	25,500	27,000	26,500	22,575	27,500	29,500	27,500	26,811
Gardens	1,036	—	—	—	—	—	—	—	—	—	—	—	—
Total	66,582	255,151	207,363	230,740	194,535	222,072	223,440	257,159	243,342	185,636	236,299	194,579	427,193
Above as a % of total issues to civil departments (Table 2.1)	57.6	46.6	33.0	30.5	29.6	30.4	28.2	36.1	29.9	29.1	35.0	33.3	38.7

SOURCES: As for Table 2.1; also E 403/2203–14 (Exchequer Issues on Debentures, 1690–1716).

greencloth reported the servants below stairs to be a full year in arrears, the purveyors fourteen months in arrears and "reduced to a most deplorable Condition, having exhausted all their Stock, and strained their utmost Creditt for Her Ma^{ts} Service, insomuch that diverse declare themselves intirely disabled to Serve ye next Month of June 1710."[83]

By that date the crisis had extended itself to the other household departments, though, as in previous reigns, it was those who served at the lower echelons of the court hierarchy who suffered most from the Crown's financial difficulties. Thus, Anne was unable to pay for much of the work supplied by artisans and small tradesmen at Hampton Court.[84] Lord Almoner Sharp found money so difficult to come by that he occasionally had to supply the Queen's charity out of his own pocket.[85] As early as June 1707 the messengers of the chamber were owed a year and a quarter's payments on bills.[86] However, chamber servants with greater social pretensions, such as the physician Sir David Hamilton, appear to have been paid quite regularly up to the time of Godolphin's fall in the late summer of 1710.[87] Indeed, the *Treasury Books* indicate that those great and middling officers who received their salaries directly at the exchequer, such as the vice chamberlain, the ladies and women of the bedchamber, and the maids of honor, were all paid fairly promptly, often within days of the end of the quarter.[88]

For those less fortunate, it was perhaps inevitable and certainly understandable that many abandoned (if they had ever embraced) the high administrative standards set by their superiors at the beginning of the reign. These servants began to exploit other nonestablished forms of income, often at the Queen's expense. For example, despite her desire to reduce all emoluments "to a certainty," rights of poundage, waste, command, and remains still survived among most of the clerks and subclerks below stairs. By mid-reign complaints about the quality of the food served at the royal tables led to the discovery of widespread abuses of those rights in the scaldinghouse and larder. The officers of these subdepartments appear to have taken in provisions far in excess of what was actually needed for the Queen's service, thereby increasing their income from poundage. They would then use a number of ingenious rationalizations to declare the choicest part of these provisions "waste," and thus claim it for their own use, leaving the rest to be served to the Queen and her guests.[89] Even more shocking was the discovery in 1712 that William Vanbrugh, the comptroller of the accounts of the treasurer of the chamber, had been taking unauthorized fees from those whose salaries he regulated. Vanbrugh defended himself in terms that must have sounded depressingly familiar to his superiors at the treasury: "The value and support of his employ was sunk so low that it would not support him or the credit of the office, and he must depend on the goodwill he sometimes had to 'cheque.'"[90]

In lieu of the funds necessary to raise salaries and so justify the elimination of such practices, the authorities concerned could do little more than suspend the offending parties, enjoin them to greater rectitude upon their restoration, issue new and probably equally circumventable ordinances for the department concerned, and hope for the best. The Queen's other reforms also seem to have foundered upon the rock of her inadequate revenue. The campaign to recover old plate failed because most of its holders turned out to be owed more in arrears of salary than the plate itself was worth; thus it was cheaper for the treasury to simply let them keep it in partial compensation.[91] As for the greencloth's newly acquired power to vary those who purveyed to the household below stairs, the department's contract books continued to list the same names year after year. Perhaps the board was satisfied with their service; more likely it could not find anyone else willing to do business with it.[92] Finally, despite its proscription at the beginning of the reign, sale of office continued on a modest scale at Anne's court, often with the Queen's permission, as a compensation for service ill-rewarded up to that point.[93] In every one of the above cases a reform was abandoned or vitiated and a destructive fee, perquisite, or privilege condoned because the Crown did not have enough money to pay its servants.

Even the Queen's resolve seems to have faded by mid-reign. Sometimes it fell victim to her sense of charity, as when she refused Godolphin's suggestion to retrench the pensionary watermen.[94] It was probably her love of pomp and ceremony that caused her to continue to fill nearly all of those offices marked in 1702 for termination at the demise of their current holders.[95] Finally, in demanding more work from fewer servants, Anne, like her father previously, put herself in the position of having to increase their emoluments in order to pay them for it, as noted above in the case of Vice Chamberlain Coke. In particular, by insisting that on her frequent excursions to Kensington and Windsor she be accompanied by the full royal retinue—including the gentlemen and children of her chapel royal, the officers of her removing wardrobe and jewel house, the gentlemen pensioners, ushers, and necessary women—she was compelled between 1705 and 1712 to restore each of these societies to riding wages at the levels they had enjoyed under the similarly peripatetic Charles II.[96] These increases illustrate not only the Queen's weakening resolve, but also the near impossibility under the old administrative system of taking any perquisite or privilege away once it had been granted.

But it was not burgeoning expenditure, corruption, or inefficiency, such as had plagued the household administration of Charles II, that threatened to bring the royal service to a halt in 1710. The primary cause was the Queen's increasingly inadequate revenue. By Michaelmas 1710, just after Godolphin's fall, the civil-list revenue had fallen short of the intended £700,000 per annum by a total (over eight and a half years) of £868,335.[97] Thanks to Godolphin's various stratagems, noted previously, the total debt on the civil-list account was only £511,762, significantly less than a year's average civil expenditure. However, this figure included a debt of £81,394 in the household below stairs, £38,165 in the chamber, £27,534 in the great wardrobe, and £45,000 in the works, roughly equal to an average year's expenditure in those departments.[98] While the household departments were intended to receive £258,000 per annum, or about 39 percent of a total civil budget of £666,765,[99] Table 2.2 shows that after exchequer year 1702–3 they did not again receive that proportion of the civil revenue under Lord Treasurer Godolphin. In short, bad as things were for the servants of the civil government by the time of his dismissal, they were worse for those who served in the Queen's "family."

This crisis, part of a general breakdown in government finances at Godolphin's fall,[100] was inherited by the new treasury commission of August 1710. Their new blood, and the exhilaration of having finally freed herself from Whig bondage, seem to have revived Anne's old zeal for reform. She began to attend the treasury board once again, and at their first meeting together, on 16 August, she enjoined them "to be good husbands for the public in the first place and for her Civil List in the second place and that they do endeavour to get her out of debt (especially to her poor servants) as fast as possibly they can."[101] On 28 August the board, in the tradition of all such bodies since 1667, instructed all civil departments to submit weekly certificates of receipts, payments, and remains, "expressing particularly the persons to whom the payments [were] made."[102] Two days later, the Queen declared that no salaries or pensions should be augmented.[103] This was followed on 1 September by the obligatory call for outstanding accounts. Possibly owing to the long delays (or noncooperation) anticipated in fulfilling that request, on 14 September came the unprecedented demand that each household department submit an estimate of its median expenditure for the previous seven years and for the exchequer year about to begin.[104] As Professor Beattie has pointed out, this was an isolated incident in Anne's reign. Nevertheless, it represents the treasury's first attempt to base its plans vis-à-vis the household upon a realistic appraisal of what expenditure had actually been in the past and was likely to be in the future. As such, the directive of 14 September was to be an important precedent, which would be revived for good in 1718, in the treasury's long struggle for control of the spending departments.[105] At the least, it demonstrates both the seriousness with which the commission of 1710 viewed the situation and the depth of their resolve to deal with it effectively.

Contrary to much received opinion,[106] the commission's resolve was shared and its efforts were extended by the Earl of Oxford after his appointment as lord treasurer in June 1711. Almost immediately upon taking office he launched an inquiry into the administrative and financial practices of the great wardrobe.[107] In September, the privy council issued another order forbidding sale of office.[108] In February 1712 the treasurer called for detailed statements of departmental debt and, recognizing where funds were most needed, directed that a weekly payment of £2,000 to the household below stairs should take precedence over all other issues to the civil departments.[109] But the great wardrobe inquiry came to nothing because of the treasury's characteristic reluctance to do more than merely reiterate existing ordinances, when what was required was the thorough overhaul of the department's antiquated billing and accounting procedures.[110] There is evidence that Anne continued to tolerate sale of office.[111] Far more importantly, the treasury's attempted marshaling of available funds failed for the simple reason that there were so few funds available to marshal.

According to Table 2.1, the civil-list yield for the new ministry's first full year in office (Michaelmas 1710 to Michaelmas 1711) was only £513,615, the lowest of the entire reign. Despite almost £130,000 of additional moneys derived from the continuing sale of the Queen's tin,[112] her household received only £185,636 that year, barely 70 percent of its annual established expenditure (Table 2.2). As before, the Queen's servants and purveyors below stairs suffered most of all, receiving only £54,760, or about 64 percent of their established salaries and expenses. It is therefore little wonder that in the middle of the exchequer year the board of greencloth once again felt the "indispensible Necessity" of reminding the treasury of "the difficultyes that at this time attend Her Ma^ts^ Houshold Service & Servants, by reason there is due to them an entire Yeare ye last of March past." Once again the purveyors, most of whom "suffer extreamly by ye Arreares of ye late King," are said to have exhausted both their stores and their credit, while the Queen's inferior servants "are reduced to the utmost necessityes."[113] As in previous reigns, the treasury's attempts to rectify the situation often only served to aggravate it. When payments were made, they frequently came in the form of exchequer bills, tin tallies, or, once, in tallies of fictitious loan, rarely in amounts proportional to the relatively small sums owed their recipients and always subject to considerable discounts.[114] Things improved slightly during exchequer year 1711–12, when the royal household received £236,299 as a result of Oxford's emergency measures, noted above. But in the following year issues to the household departments once again fell to £194,579, the third-lowest total of the reign (Table 2.2).

Quite understandably, the Queen's servants, unaware of the subtleties of her revenue situation, could think of no one else to blame but the Queen's ministers. Their resentment was ably expressed by one Richard Watts, a gardener at Windsor, who is reported to have complained, "Damn ye present Ministry, they pay no body, But the late Ministry were honest Men, and paid every Body."[115] Though other statements by Watts indicate that he was no friend to the new ministry, the Tories, or even "ye Family of the Stewards" in general, his sentiments seem to have been shared by royal servants of all political persuasions.[116] Naturally, the Whigs in particular charged that since the civil-list revenue was manifestly adequate, the only explanation for the civil-list debt was Oxford's diversion of that revenue for purposes of political corruption.[117] To Oxford's detractors, the Queen was quick to point out that he had inherited both the revenue and the debt situation from his predecessor, but in private her correspondence to him hints at great anxiety about what was to become of her "family."[118]

Oxford's immediate response to this situation was to propose the civil-list lottery of 1713. This enabling act, 12 Anne c. 11, gave the Queen permission to mortgage £35,000 per annum out of her civil-list revenues to pay the interest on an immediate loan of £500,000, which was to be used to pay five quarters' arrears to every servant. Oxford has been much criticized for this measure.[119] It was certainly of doubtful constitutional propriety, an affront to the Queen's hereditary rights, and ultimately destructive of the Crown's long-term financial position, given the need to continue paying interest for the next 32 years. But it is difficult to imagine precisely what else the lord treasurer could have done in the context of the current financial and political situation. Any quick attempt to cut civil expenditure still further via even a temporary retrenchment would only have hurt those already suffering without addressing the crushing problem of past debt. An increase in the Queen's civil-list provision was out of the question, given the widespread conviction that it was already more than adequate and the Oxford ministry's precarious situation in parliament. In fact, during the debates on the lottery the honorable members of both parties spent more time trying to affix blame for the debt upon each other's period in office than in attempting to ascertain the Crown's legitimate needs.[120] In these circumstances, it is a tribute to Oxford's parliamentary skill that he was able to push even this stopgap measure through.

Both Oxford and the Queen were fully aware that the lottery was only a temporary measure. With the end of the war they, like William III earlier, began to seek a more permanent solution to the problems of the civil list. As the treasurer's credit with parliament waned, and with it any possibility of an increase in the Queen's civil-list revenue, the only possible alternative was a reduction in her civil expenditure. In February 1714 the treasury drew up proposals for yet one more retrenchment of the civil establishment.[121] Unlike previous retrenchments, however, this reduction was to be chiefly in extraordinary expenditure for goods and services, rather than in places or salaries, a tacit admission that these had already been cut about as far as was consistent with the splendor of the royal state or the financial and physical health of the royal servants. Thus, while the household below stairs was to undergo "a reasonable retrenchment" of, presumably, redundant offices and fees, most of its projected reduction in expenditure of about £10,000 was to come "by buying provisions, etc., with ready money out of a weekly sum to be constantly issued for that purpose." Likewise, £5,000 was to be saved in the great wardrobe "by paying with ready money," as well as by the elimination of some of the salaries and liveries anciently paid there that now "appeared needless." Some £3,000 was to be trimmed in the chamber "out of Stationers' and Messengers' Bills, etc.," while £5,000 was supposed to be made up in the jewel house by pursuing the recall of old plate more vigorously. The Queen herself was to sacrifice some of her traveling to and building at Windsor, to judge from the £4,000 each to be saved in the stables and the works there. However, the two heads of expenditure most personal to the monarch, her privy purse and robes, were to remain at £30,000 and £3,000 respectively, "being for the Queen's own use." Likewise, the total of the salaries paid at the exchequer to the vice chamberlain, ladies and women of the bedchamber, maids of honor, and so forth was to remain at £20,000, a tribute to the political and social clout of these officers. Thus, the Queen's servants, especially those at the top, were to suffer relatively little for a reduction in the household's established expenditure of from £258,000 to £212,000 per annum.[122] This latter figure would have formed roughly the same proportion as before of a total civil establishment of £542,270 3*s.* 2*d.*

It is a sad comment on the state of the civil-list revenue that the framers of the new civil establishment found it necessary to pitch its total expense some £150,000 below the advertised yield of £700,000 per annum. Even so, this new establishment, for all its originality of means and moderation of ends, would probably have proved unworkable if instituted. Perhaps the Queen's interest in Windsor could have been subdued. Nor was the assumption that the end of the war would bring a decline in both messengers' and stationers' bills unwarranted. But the new arrangements for paying purveyors and tradesmen in the household below stairs and great wardrobe would have required a far more steady and secure source of "ready cash" than could ever be expected from the civil-list revenue in its current, unaugmented state. Likewise, the projected return of old plate by displaced officers could only occur if they had been paid up to the time of their dismissal, an equally unprecedented and unlikely event for the same reason. Nor was any retrenchment of inferior officers likely to appear "reasonable" to Queen Anne, given her awareness of, and concern over, their past difficulties.

Finally, and above all, it is to be wondered how far such measures could have been carried forward in the early eighteenth century without serious damage to the service of the royal household or the dignity of the royal state, which, as we shall see, were already somewhat compromised under Anne. Though corruption and waste did exist at her court, they did so to a far lesser degree than in previous reigns. Even at its most extravagant, her household was significantly less expensive than those of her uncle, her brother-in-law, or the distant cousin who succeeded her. Only her father's court was cheaper, and, as already noted, the political and constitutional realities of later Stuart England had exacted a price for such economies. Not until a rather different set of political and constitutional realities began to evolve in the 1780s could further reductions in the size and expense of the royal household, accompanied by the administrative overhaul long needed, be seriously contemplated.

For whatever reason, on 21 June 1714, only a few weeks before the Queen's death, Lord Steward Poulett reported to the board of greencloth that she, having reviewed all of the additional warrants for places, pensions, and salaries granted since 1702, "was graciously pleased to approve & direct ye continuance of each of them" almost without exception. She was also pleased to continue to her servants all of their customary rights, fees, and privileges and to enjoin her lord steward to protect them in the enjoyment of the same: in short, as the old regime gave way to the new, the old administrative system was to remain unchanged. Queen Anne ended this final message to her servants with a curious postscript, part reassurance, part apology, part admission of defeat: "Y^{e} late inquiryes into y^{e} Severall parts of y^{e} Expense were only intended to find out such reasonable abatem$^{ts.}$ as might make y^{e} future paym$^{ts.}$ both to y^{e} Servants and Purveyors more punctuall & certain, and thereby render Her Ma$^{ts.}$ Service more easy."[123]

The Queen's abandonment of these enquiries put the matter firmly back into the hands of Lord Treasurer Oxford. In the short term, his lottery had been remarkably successful. It had raised the hoped-for £500,000 very quickly, and both its internal accounts and those of the civil departments indicate that that sum was religiously applied to the purpose for which it had been voted (see Tables 2.1 and 2.2).[124] However, in the long term it created even more debt (over £600,000) while doing nothing to change the conditions that had led to its enactment.[125] The temporary nature of the measure soon made itself apparent. By January 1714 Oxford was once again forced to issue tallies of fictitious loan, amounting to £60,000, to the household paymasters.[126] In March it was reported with approbation by the government that the treasurer had paid the tradesmen "to Midsummer last, one third part in tin tallies without interest, but will be paid in about two years, and the other two thirds in ready money."[127]

It is therefore not surprising that Queen Anne died owing her household servants £153,020 14*s.* 3¼*d.*, over half a year's expenditure.[128] No doubt this figure would have been greater still had the reign lasted even a year longer. There is no reason to believe, given the Queen's refusal to give herself over to a single party, the continuance of divisive party issues such as the succession, and the widespread conviction that her revenues were already quite adequate, that any future lord treasurer would have been any more successful than Godolphin or Oxford at solving the problems of the civil list. It was not until 1727, with a Hanoverian firmly established on the throne of a single party state and Sir Robert Walpole at the head of that party in the House of Commons, that parliament could be persuaded to make a permanent augmentation of the civil-list revenue to, in effect, £900,000 per annum.[129] Unfortunately, it made no provision to pay the arrears of Anne's servants, many of which were still outstanding.[130] In the following chapters it will be shown that the Queen's inability to pay her own servants had sweeping consequences, not only for the political, social, and cultural life of her court, but for the nation as a whole.

CHAPTER III

Patronage

T. F. Tout, the great historian of early English government, once wrote: "To understand that machine properly one has to learn something about the men engaged in working that machine."[1] This was as true under Queen Anne as it was under any of her medieval predecessors, for in the absence of anything like a modern civil service, the quality of her administration was a direct reflection of that of her administrators. Having surveyed the machinery of Anne's household administration and finances, we must now meet the men and women who worked and profited from, changed and were changed by it. The present chapter and the two that follow will be concerned with the Queen's servants, their recruitment, work, rewards, and condition at retirement. Underlying these basic concerns will be two more subtle but important questions: why did men and women want to serve at court; and what does this desire and its manner of fulfillment tell us about the court's role in Augustan politics and society as a whole?[2]

The demand for places in the Queen's household was always great. Sarah, Duchess of Marlborough, writes of "the great solicitations" at Anne's accession, and her correspondence alone contains more than enough petitions, recommendations, and refusals to confirm this.[3] In April 1704, when it became known that Lord Chamberlain Jersey would be removed, the Duke of Newcastle, the Earl of Bridgewater, and the ultimately successful Earl of Kent were among those who expressed interest in the place. News of Cofferer Bathurst's death within the same month unleashed a similar set of petitions, causing Lord Treasurer Godolphin to complain to the Duchess: "What would you doe if you had all the trouble I have undergon this week, and have still to undergoe with 55 [Newcastle], and 19 [Buckingham] and a hundred more? Among others, Sir Stephen Fox has taken it into his head to persecute mee about the Cofferer's place."[4] Four years later a contemporary noted, "So many think themselves fit for Chamberlain that the fear of disobliging a multitude still keeps in Lord Kennt."[5] Both the Queen and her lord treasurer referred in similar terms to "a thousand pretenders" or "a thousand solicitations" even for a dresser's place.[6]

In the wake of Godolphin's own fall in 1710 "the rout" for place was so great that, as Lady Pye noted to Abigail Harley, it was "impossible to satisfy all."[7] To take just one example, after the Duke of Somerset's removal as master of the horse in January 1712, the Dukes of Argyll, Beaufort, Ormonde, and Shrewsbury, the Earls of Strafford and Dartmouth, and Lord Masham were each rumored at one point or another to be either actively soliciting or under consideration for the vacancy. Perhaps owing to the Queen's "fear of disobliging a multitude" (a verdict endorsed by the French ambassador), all were ultimately unsuccessful, the place remaining in commission until Anne's death, in 1714.[8] No doubt the rout would have been greater still had the arch-Tory Viscount Bolingbroke received the treasurer's staff at the end of the reign. While nearly all of the examples for which we have evidence concern high-ranking "prestige" posts, there seems to have been no shortage of men and women anxious to take up even the most menial positions at the court of Queen Anne.

That both the demand for office and the extent of its fulfillment were dependent upon the actions not only of the Queen and her department heads, but of her ministers as well, illustrates the fundamentally ambiguous nature of patronage within the royal household and the central administration as a whole. In theory, the structure of household patronage was quite clear (Figure 3.1). The monarch appointed all the great household officers, such as the lord and vice chamberlains; the lord steward, and the officers of the greencloth; the groom of the stole and ladies of the bedchamber; the masters of the horse, robes, jewel house, great wardrobe, and buckhounds; the captains of the gentlemen pensioners and yeomen of the guard; the lord almoner and dean of the chapel royal. In addition, the Queen had the disposal of the most prestigious and lucrative middling posts, including the women and maids of honor in the bedchamber; the equerries and pages of honor in the stables; and the clerks, gentlemen, and sergeants of the various catering subdepartments below stairs, though here royal initiative

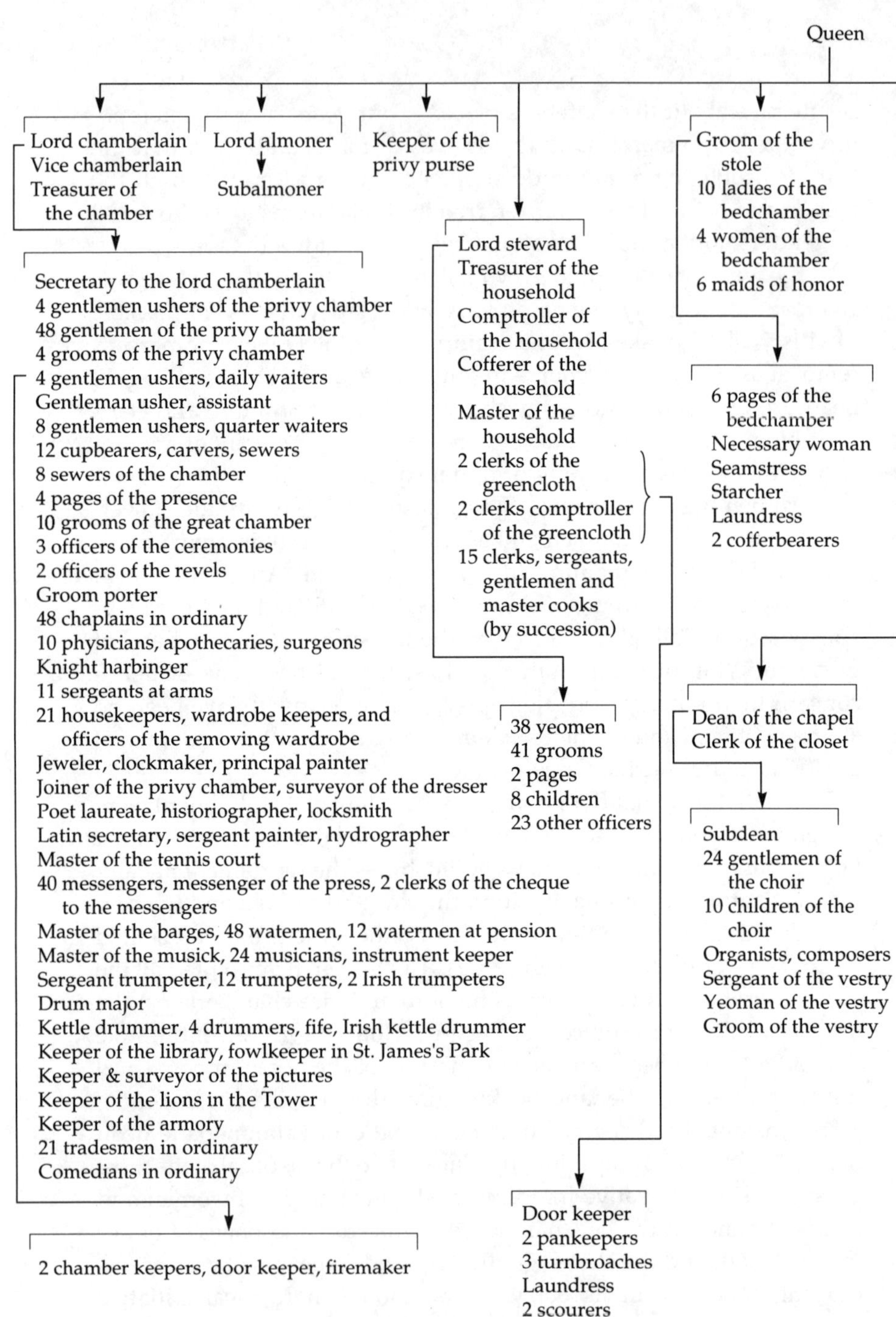

Fig. 3.1. Household patronage. Data from sources cited in Figure 1.1.

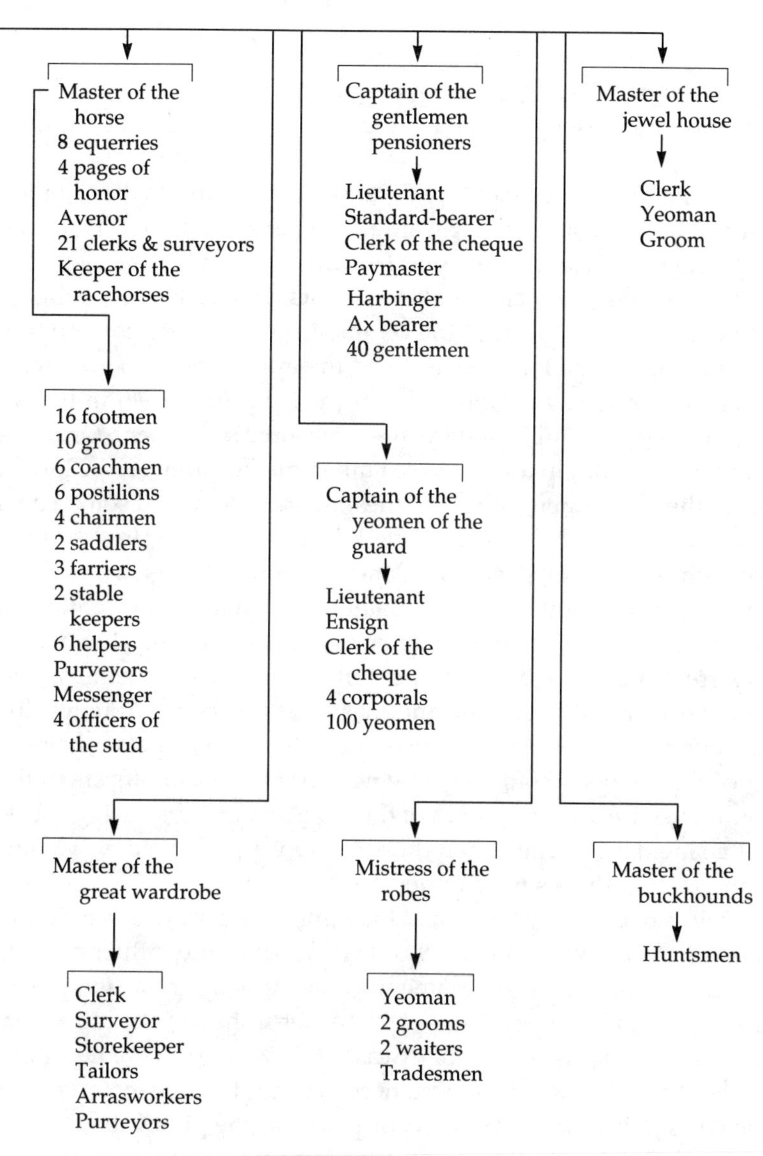

Key:
↓ Appoints the following officers

should have been circumscribed by a strict order of succession that was supposed to fill those offices from below.[9] Altogether, the Crown had about 90 of the most desirable posts in the royal household in its own gift.

The remaining household patronage was meant to be divided among those great officers who were also department heads. Thus, the lord chamberlain had in his disposal a patronage field of over 400 middling and menial chamber attendants, artists, and tradesmen, ranging in status from the masters of the ceremonies and revels down to the royal watermen. The lord steward had the appointment of about 110 yeomen, grooms, pages, and children (really apprentices) in the catering subdepartments, though the household's "Ancient Order of Succession" should, in theory, have limited his freedom. At the lowest levels of the department, turnbroaches, doorkeepers, and soil carriers were appointed by the individual clerks and clerks comptroller of the greencloth in turn. The captain of the yeomen of the guard had the appointment of 107 officers and yeomen; the captain of the gentlemen pensioners, 46 officers and gentlemen of the band. Finally, the master of the great wardrobe appointed about 60 tailors, arrasmakers, and tradesmen to his department; the master of the horse, roughly the same number of footmen, grooms, and other stables personnel; the dean of the chapel, about 40 gentlemen, children, and officers of the choir and vestry; and the groom of the stole and mistress of the robes, about 20 menial servants when those two posts were held by a single person, as they always were under Anne (Figure 3.1).[10]

However, to determine who had the right to dispose of a place is not necessarily to know who had all or even most of the influence in its disposal. Historians of government and patronage have long been aware of the advantages to the place seeker in having an influential patron to back up his suit; in many cases this was a positive necessity. The extent to which a patron was necessary under Queen Anne is of particular significance, especially for places in the gift of the Crown, for it is only in recent years that the traditional Whig picture of Anne as a well-intentioned but weak, dull, and easily led monarch has begun to be seriously questioned. That picture was first and most vividly drawn by Sarah, Duchess of Marlborough, who wrote of the appointments made by Anne and her husband, George, in the period prior to

1702, "They wou'd take no body into their service but upon my recommendation."[11]

Though prudence later impelled Sarah to delete this from the final version of her *Conduct*, numerous letters from Anne's days as Princess appear to confirm it. For example, when, in the mid-1690s, Sarah recommended an impecunious cousin named Abigail Hill for Anne's service, the Princess replied:

As to what you say about Mrs Hill you may asure your self she shall have ye place you desire for her when ever Bust dyes, I have thought myself engaged to you these many yeares for Mrs Chudsleigh but have no other promis upon my hands nor never will engage my self in nothinge without knowing first whether any thing y^t^ lyes in my power can be ye least servisable to deare Mrs Freeman who need never use any arguments for any thinge she has a mind to but y^t^ tis her desire for her commands weighs more with me then all ye world besides.[12]

As Sarah often noted, her correspondence with Anne from before her accession is full of such assurances, and they continued to be expressed, albeit with decreasing ardor and frequency, throughout the early years of the new reign.[13] As Queen, Mrs. Morley would appear to have been as good as her word, for there is a great deal of evidence of her "deare Mrs. Freeman's" influence upon a wide range of household appointments. Admittedly, much of this evidence is open to question, coming as it does from the Duchess's own, by no means impartial, writings. However, most of her claims are substantiated by letters of thanks or other forms of acknowledgment from those she is supposed to have helped. Even these are not entirely above suspicion, given the typical courtier's propensity to bow and scrape, equally and indiscriminately, before any benefactor, whether potential or actual.[14] Still, the sheer number of such acknowledgments, the Queen's frequent professions, and the Duchess's role as a clearinghouse for petitions, which gave her, in effect, a right of first refusal, all suggest real power over the disposal of household office.

Nevertheless, it should not be assumed that this power was given by the Queen without reason, against her best interests, or irrevocably. Early in the reign, the disadvantages of being thought the tool of a favorite, later highly resented by Anne, seem to have been outweighed for her by the screen that the Duchess provided from the "thousand solicitations" noted above. Not only did Sarah weed out or discourage obviously unsuitable candidates for household office, but her involvement gave the Queen time to consult with Lord Treasurer Godolphin, the Duke of Marlborough, and, of course, the Duchess herself about more serious prospects.[15] Moreover, though Sarah made clear to each petitioner that any final decision was ultimately the Queen's, her role as the chief conduit of both petition and response brought her most of the resentment felt by disappointed applicants, thus sparing Anne.[16] Finally, if Queen Anne seems to have followed the advice of her three best friends—the Churchills and Sidney, Lord Godolphin—almost invariably during the early days of her reign, it should be remembered that their interests, experience, and (in the case of the lord treasurer and captain general, at least) political philosophy, like their ideas on administration and finance, would have given her little cause to do otherwise: apart from Sarah's Whiggery, they were virtually identical to her own. This unity of purpose and sentiment, albeit short-lived, makes any attempt to separate the influence of Sarah and the Churchill circle from the new Queen's own wishes and interests at the beginning of the reign more than a little artificial.

The unity of experience and purpose shared by the new Queen and the Churchills (including Godolphin) is evident in their choice of whom to retain and whom to discard from among William's old household servants in 1702. Altogether, Queen Anne retained 695, or 57 percent, of her predecessor's household servants. These formed an even higher proportion, about 73 percent, of the new, much smaller court.[17] Gone, of course, were nearly all of the Dutchmen who had served in William's bedchamber, robes, and stables. No doubt many wished to return to their homeland after their master's death, and others would have had to be replaced by women in any case. But Anne's experience as Princess at the hands of William's Dutch guards during her quarrel with Mary had not disposed her to be merciful to the remainder.[18] Indeed, one of her first (and most uncharacteristic) acts as Queen was to purge the stables of all of William's old grooms, most of whom were Dutchmen.[19] Later, she apparently instructed her board of greencloth not to prefer any foreigner without her permission, though in practice she was not nearly so strict once the reign was well under way.[20]

The other group purged from the court in 1702 were those officers of extreme Whig or Republican ancestry who had been preferred in 1689. Here, too, Anne's experience during the previous reign was important. She avenged Lord Wharton's attempt to dissuade William from granting her a separate revenue as Princess by forcing him to surrender his comptroller's staff, in her presence, to the High Tory Sir Edward Seymour.[21] In most cases, however, it was probably her dislike of extreme Whiggery in general, as well as her sense of administrative propriety, that caused her to replace a number of "Revolution officers" with the old Tory-Royalist administrators whom they had replaced in 1689, such as Sir Stephen Fox and Thomas Atterbury. She likewise found room at her court for representatives of some of the old Tory-Royalist families who had been ousted at the Revolution, such as the Bathursts, the Grahmes, the Granvilles, the Oglethorpes, and the Yarboroughs.[22] Finally, and somewhat less typically, she restored to her chapel royal one Stephen Crispian, who had been removed from the choir in 1697 for refusing to sign the Association.[23] It is thus perhaps little wonder that the Duchess of Marlborough was later to charge that, at her accession, Anne threw "herself and her affairs almost entirely into the hands of the Tories."[24]

However, since over half of William's servants were retained, the new court must have included many nominal Whigs. Indeed, in keeping with the duumvirs' desire to base their support upon the moderate men of both parties,[25] the Queen retained a number of moderate Whigs who had particularly distinguished themselves during the previous reign by their treatment of either her or her friends, the Churchills. For example, the Duke of Devonshire and his son, the Marquess of Hartington, were most likely retained as lord steward and captain of the yeomen of the guard, respectively, on the twin strengths of the Duke's role in Princess Anne's escape from her father in 1688 and his subsequent loyalty to Marlborough upon the latter's committal to the Tower in 1692.[26] Another of the "Revolution officers," the Earl of Bradford, had been a Royalist during the Civil War; had served in Charles II's household but lost his places in 1687 for opposing James II's religious policies; and had also remained loyal to Marlborough in 1692. Such a record of behavior was perfectly calculated to win the new Queen's approbation: it goes far toward explaining his retention as treasurer of the household and that of his son-in-law, Sir William Forrester, as a clerk of the greencloth.[27] Forrester was also, along with Vice Chamberlain Peregrine Bertie and Master of the Household Sir Thomas Felton, an anti-Junto Whig. Bertie and Felton were more closely associated with Robert Spencer, Earl of Sunderland, an old Churchill ally toward whom Anne had at last begun to warm by 1702.[28] Finally, the new Queen retained a number of middling servants whose sympathies were demonstrably Whig, such as John Bigg, William Churchill, Sir Stephen Evance, Sir Edward Lawrence, Sir Philip Meadows, Thomas Orme, Anthony Rowe, and James Tyrrel.[29] Clearly, far from placing her household affairs "almost entirely into the hands of the Tories" at the beginning of her reign, the new Queen was striving for the same sort of balance within her "family" that her ministers were seeking in the government at large.

At or below the middling levels of household service, few of William's old servants could have had much opportunity to ingratiate themselves with the new Queen or her ministers. Here, the Countess of Marlborough, with her extensive knowledge of the court and its inhabitants, was crucial in vouching for those whose only prior distinction was the rather dubious one of having served "Mr. Caliban." Thus, she successfuly championed the cause of Sir Edward Lawrence, a gentleman usher who had bought his place in 1700 for £800 and who, "by his Majesty's death, and his Servants not being pay'd, . . . had lost both his money and his Salary too."[30] Sarah was also instrumental in continuing a number of relatives of the Countess of Scarborough, a close personal friend and a lady of the new Queen's bedchamber.[31] What is most significant about these examples is that neither Lord Chamberlain Jersey's rights of patronage within his own department nor Lady Scarborough's access to the Queen as a bedchamber attendant were thought to be enough, on their own, to guarantee the continuation of these servants in their posts. This is particularly remarkable in Lawrence's case since it was presumably Jersey who had supervised and profited by his original purchase. The perception that the Countess of Marlborough was the chief and surest avenue of access to the Queen, even where others had the right of appointment, seems to have been widespread, if Sarah herself may be believed: "The storys of this kind are endless."[32]

Turning to those who were preferred into the royal household for the first time in 1702, much the same pattern emerges of the Queen's rewarding of individuals who had demonstrated their faithfulness in the previous reign, and relying upon the Countess of Marlborough's opinions for those of whom she had no experience. The previous chapter noted Anne's preferment of old personal servants such as Sir Benjamin Bathurst; John, Lord Fitzharding; and the Countess herself into high-ranking administrative posts in the household below stairs, the chamber, and the bedchamber and robes, respectively. To this may be added the preferment of Ladies Beverwort and Frescheville, Agneta Cooper, Beata Danvers, and Abigail Hill into the same bedchamber posts they had held under the Princess. Charles Scarborough and Edward Griffith were promoted to clerkships at the greencloth from their old positions as a groom of the bedchamber and secretary, respectively, to Prince George. Griffith, in particular, had distinguished himself by risking arrest on the Prince's behalf in 1688 and he was one of Sarah's numerous in-laws (through her late sister Barbara) to boot.[33] Altogether, the new Queen preferred about 33 of her old servants into the main court, plus 10 from the household of Prince George, 14 from that of the late Duke of Gloucester, and, rather more surprisingly, another 5 who had served her late sister, Queen Mary. Anne's dedication to those who had faithfully attended her or her family is further illustrated by her ready compliance with Sarah's request to award a pension of £200 out of the privy purse to Abigail Hill's sister Alice, she "haveing served my poor dear child & being ye only one y^t^ is not provided for."[34]

Finally, it should be noted that the new Queen's favor was reserved as much for old friends as it was for old servants. It was on this basis that she named the Duke of Somerset master of the horse and his Duchess, as well as the Countess of Scarborough, a lady of her bedchamber. Though none of these had served Anne previously, each had remained loyal during her quarrel with Mary. The Somersets had offered her the use of Syon House when she had nowhere else to go,[35] and Lady Scarborough had continued to pay her respects to both the Princess and the Countess of Marlborough throughout the debacle, despite her position as a lady of Mary's bedchamber and the latter's express orders forbidding her to do so.[36]

Even after the preferment of so many old friends and retainers, there still remained almost 200 places to fill in the new household. It was here, in helping Mrs. Morley to decide among individuals she hardly knew, that Mrs. Freeman really came into her own, offering her advice freely and apparently quite successfully. For example, she later recalled having "prepared a list of ye Ladies of ye best quality ye nerest ye Queen [in] age & most Suted to her temper to be Ladies of ye Bedchamber."[37] Among those named on the list were two of Sarah's daughters, Henrietta Godolphin and Anne Spencer. She also took credit for the preferment of the Duchesses of Ormonde and Somerset, Ladies Burlington, Hyde, and Scarborough, and for Lady Frescheville's initial introduction into Anne's service many years before;[38] letters of thanks exist, however, only for Ladies Hyde and Scarborough.[39] Sarah's opinions were also sought, and proved equally decisive, in filling middling bedchamber posts in the Queen's gift, such as those of the women and maids of honor. They continued to be important up to 1709.[40]

It was not at all unusual for a department head such as the Countess (from late 1702, the Duchess) of Marlborough to advise the Queen on appointments within her own area of responsibility. More striking is Mrs. Freeman's influence on appointments in departments other than her own. Prior to 1702 she nearly infringed upon Bathurst's rights of patronage as treasurer of the Princess's household on more than one occasion.[41] Her decisive involvement in chamber patronage at the Queen's accession has already been noted. Likewise, in the stables, Sarah successfully recommended Richard Arundell, William Bretton, and Thomas Meredith to lucrative posts. As in the chamber, the influence of the department head, though a favorite this time, was still not thought sufficient to sway the Queen by itself; Sarah later recalled, "The Duke of Somerset did not think his Right in that Place what he cou'd intirely depend upon, and desired me that I would joine with him."[42] As late as April 1709 Peter Wentworth reported that a rumor of an impending vacancy among the equerries had inspired "five or six to ask't of the Duke of S[omerset] & the Dutchess of M[arlborough]," though, ominously for Sarah, it was his direct application to the Queen that eventually prevailed.[43]

Still, prior to her fall, the Duchess was acknowledged by the Earl of Kent, John Charlton, and—probably less sincerely—the wife of Thomas Mansell for their respective appointments as lord chamberlain, master of the jewel house, and comptroller of the household, all in 1704.[44] In the following year she was thanked by her daughter on behalf of her husband, the Earl of Bridgewater, for his appointment as master of the horse to Prince George, and in 1708 by the wife of another relation, Edmund Dunch, for his preferment as master of the household.[45] Finally, it was Sarah who procured for Lord Monthermer, her son-in-law and the Duke of Montagu's son, a reversion, rare in Anne's reign, to his father's mastership of the great wardrobe, to which he succeeded in 1709.[46] Indeed, as will become clear in subsequent chapters, the Duchess did her level best to fill the court with her own relations, dependents, and personal servants. Even if we insist on seeing a method to Mrs. Morley's apparent meekness, it is clear that, for the first half of the reign at least, the traditional picture of Mrs. Freeman's influence over household appointments is generally correct.

Nevertheless, it must not be forgotten, as the general public and, later, Mrs. Freeman herself forgot, that even at its height, that influence had its limits. Indeed, the widespread and ultimately exaggerated public perception of Sarah's absolute power over household appointments often brought her as much resentment and embarrassment as it did gratitude and prestige. Such was the case when her importunate in-law, the Duke of Montagu, insisted that his son, Monthermer, be made captain of the yeomen of the guard while waiting to succeed to the mastership of the great wardrobe. The Duchess knew that Anne would find such a request unreasonable and so quashed it, albeit with some difficulty.[47] On another occasion, family loyalty did force her to support a petition for further employment from her brother-in-law, Griffith, which she later agreed the Queen was right to refuse.[48] Finally, suppliance could very quickly turn to bitterness among those who did not appear to benefit from Mrs. Freeman's power. Thus, in 1705, when Bridgewater was about to replace the mentally ill Earl of Sandwich as master of the Prince's horse, Godolphin warned Sarah, unless Lady Sandwich "bee in some measure satisfyed, whenever it is known Lord Bridgwater succeeds, she will impute it to you."[49] It is thus little wonder that Sarah later recalled in her *Conduct*, "I was fearful about everything the Princess did, while she was thought to be advised by me."[50]

More damaging than any public misconceptions about her influence was the exaggerated notion that the Duchess herself eventually came to have about it. The glibness with which she writes of procuring this or that place for a petitioner, the great number of acknowledgments she received from those who were successful, and the frequent, and frequently cloying but not always sincere, professions of submission she received from her "faithful Morley" should not blind us to the fact that Anne was Queen, and had always been perfectly capable of denying the Churchills and even her "dear Mrs. Freeman."[51] Both Lord Treasurer Godolphin and the Duke of Marlborough spoke with respect of Anne's ultimate right of acquiescence or denial in matters of household patronage. For example, when Lord Steward Devonshire died in August 1707, Godolphin wrote to the Duke, "The Queen seems resolved that his son [Hartington] shall succeed to his employment," adding, "I hope she will lett my Lord Manchester return to his [former] place, of Captain of the Yeomen of the Guard," which would become vacant upon Hartington's succession.[52] In fact, she did not prefer Manchester but instead another Whig, Viscount Townshend, who was, admittedly, equally agreeable to the ministry. On another occasion, the Duke of Marlborough, having been exposed for promising a household place that he could not deliver, vowed to Sarah: "I promis you eareafter [*sic*] I wil never have any ingagements that may be in the least uneasy to the Queen."[53] The difficulties that the duumvirs later experienced in attempting to persuade Anne to prefer Junto Whigs into any part of her civil government strongly suggest that she would never have tolerated appointments to her own "family" against her will or what she perceived to be her best interest. It is significant that her household suffered no political removals from April 1704 to April 1710. The preferment of moderate Whigs and even some Harleyites into those places that did fall vacant because of death or surrender suggests a continued dedication on Anne's part to the cause of moderation, or at least a give-and-take relationship with decided limits upon her willingness to do the former.[54] Her ability and increasing willingness to do the latter became strikingly evident in April 1710, when she named the Duke of Shrewsbury lord chamberlain without so much as consulting with her lord treasurer or captain general.

Only the Duchess of Marlborough seems to have seriously questioned the Queen's ability, and even her right, to make up her own mind. Her attitude, as well as Anne's increasing independence of thought and deed, is evidenced by a series of incidents that occurred in 1709, when Mrs. Freeman's credit had already reached low ebb and Mrs. Morley was anxious to reassert her independence. In February of that year the Queen increased the emoluments of her starcher, Elizabeth Abrahall, by granting her a daily bottle of wine on the household establishment. Though Abrahall was a member of the bedchamber staff and so technically under Sarah's immediate jurisdiction, Anne neither consulted nor informed her groom of the stole about the change. Worse, though Abrahall had begun her career in the Churchill household, Sarah suspected her of being in league with Mrs. Masham, whom she naturally assumed to be behind the affair.[55]

Nevertheless, for the moment, the Duchess held her fire to await the outcome of another matter. The Queen had been speaking for some time about preferring a new bedchamber woman to take over from the aging Beata Danvers. Sarah "got the Duke of Marlborough & my Ld Godolphin to press the queen mightily to take in Mrs. Vain [i.e., Fane]," née Stanhope, a former maid of honor whose politics were congenial to the Churchills.[56] However, at the end of July the Queen informed her groom of the stole that she had instead preferred Beata's daughter, Isabella Danvers, at her mother's request. Once again, Sarah saw the hand of her rival, Masham, in the affair.[57] She opened with a short letter on 29 July decrying the influence of "one who is thought soe unfitt for it by all people that are reasonable & good."[58] Perhaps because this cut a bit too close to her own situation, the Duchess shifted tactics in her next attack, on 6 August, by lecturing the Queen on the rights of her household officers: "That your majesty may not think me so much in the wrong when I say I am not used as others are of my rank I beg leave to explain that matter to you, when a place is vacant under any of your other offices, tho your ma^ty^ does not allow them immediately to fill it, yet some regard is had to them & their recommendation." After giving a number of examples, Mrs. Freeman opened a new front, that of Mrs. Abrahall's portentous bottle of wine, contending: "The other instance I have complained of is still more perticular, for I defy any body to shew that att any time, or in any reign that an inconsiderable under officer had ever any sort of addition to their place with out acquainting the principal."[59]

Here, full blown, is all the presumption of a favorite, or rather the desperation of one who knows her days of favor to be numbered. Although, or perhaps because, the Duchess is here questioning the Queen's rights of patronage for places in the Crown's gift, as well as her right to reward her servants as she saw fit, Anne did not at first respond. She only did so after two more salvos from Sarah (the second dated 26 October), which were intended to forestall the preferment of Abrahall into the seamstress's place, rumored to be coming available owing to the illness of its incumbent, Mrs. Rhansford. In the second of these volleys the groom of the stole reminded her mistress, "That place is in the disposal of my office as much as a footman is in the Duke of Somersetts."[60] This time the Queen could not forbear, and responded on the next day: "When ever he recommends any body to me he never says it is his right but submitts to my determination, & has don soe upon occasions in wch you have recommended people to me in posts under him." Anne's pointed reference to Sarah's interference in other people's fields of patronage was followed by a categorical denial of Masham's or anyone else's influence upon the above transactions. The once-compliant Mrs. Morley, referring to the prospect of Rhansford's death, concluded by informing Mrs. Freeman:

> I shall then hearken to no body's recommendation but my own . . . y^{t} being a post y^{t} next to my bedchamber women is ye nearest to my person of any of my Servants, & I beleeve no body, nay even you your Self if you would judg impartialy, could think it unreasonable y^{t} I should take one in a place soe neare my person y^{t} weare agreeable to me; I know this place is reckoned under your office, but there is no office whatsoever y^{t} has y^{t} intire disposal of any thing under them, but I may putt in any one I please when I have a mind to it.[61]

Clearly, even if we allow the young Princess more of a mind of her own than is readily apparent, the mature Queen had come a long way. The above amounts to an assertion by the once-faithful and submissive Morley of her absolute right to fill not only places in her own gift but any place within her "family" as she saw fit, a claim that even the most ambitious of her Stuart predecessors had been dissuaded from making. In fact, the letter of the law, as contained in the latest chamber establishments and bedchamber ordinances, was on the side of the Duchess of Marlborough, stating quite clearly: "All the Inferior Servants of the Bedchamber are in ye disposal of ye Groome of ye Stool."[62] Legal precedent, too, would appear to have supported Sarah's case, for when, on three separate occasions, Charles II had attempted to assert a right to appoint to offices in the gift of the lord chamberlain, the master of the jewel house, and the board of greencloth, respectively, he was defeated, either in privy council or the courts, or by personal persuasion.

But it is also true that in at least two of the above instances the appointing officer, having defended his general right, deferred to the King's wishes in filling the particular office over which they had clashed, as a matter of diplomacy, not precedent.[63] In the same reign Lord Steward Ormonde did so on a number of occasions without a struggle.[64] We have already noted several instances in Anne's reign when department heads, such as Lord Chamberlain Jersey and Master of the Horse Somerset, either consulted with the Queen or sought Sarah's influence with her before filling places in their own gift. On at least two occasions Anne preferred inferior servants below stairs without consulting her lord steward.[65] Once, in August 1705, she went so far as to forbid the board of greencloth to swear in Devonshire's nominee for the place of yeoman of the kitchen in order to prefer someone else.[66] The Hanoverians seem to have been capable of similar behavior, and department heads soon learned the wisdom of at least making a show of submitting their choices for royal approval.[67] Obviously, whatever an officer's theoretical rights, it was good and prudent policy to secure the monarch's approval, tacit or otherwise, in making any appointment, no matter how small. Though supported by laws and ordinances, Sarah's claim that she was in the right failed according to the highest authority at court, that of usage. She seems to have admitted as much in a final, taunting letter to Anne on 29 October: "So far Mrs Masham is in the right for tis generally true, there being noe law against it, but then it is as true that you use that officer [the Duchess of Marlborough] ill & unkindly."[68]

The greatest significance of the events of 1709 lies not in the light they shed on the Crown's rights of patronage, nor in indicating how far Sarah's credit with Anne had fallen by that date. Rather it lies in their demonstration of how independent the Queen had become in such matters. Sarah, who simply could not conceive of Anne as having a mind of her own, attributed her increasingly contrary behavior to the influence of Mrs. Masham.[69] The latter's influence on politics and appointments in general will be examined in Chapter 6. It is sufficient here to note that unlike her great Whig rival, Abigail left very little evidence of her involvement in household patronage.[70] Such involvement would not have been consistent with the Queen's reputed aversion to making "a great lady" of her, nor with her increasing fear of being spied upon. Anne had had some experience with spies in her "family" during her falling out with Mary, and again during her quarrel with Sarah.[71] Later, she was to fear that Abigail and her sister Alice were watching her.[72] Given her recent experiences with the Duchess of Marlborough, it hardly seems likely that the Queen would have allowed Mrs. Masham to preside over the appointment of a new nest of potential informers. The Duke of Shrewsbury was closer to the truth when he informed one disappointed applicant, "Those are matters she is grown very nice in, and not willing to admit any who are not perfectly well known to her."[73] Clearly, Anne had learned the lesson of not placing, or being seen to place, all her trust in the advice of a single favorite.

Nor was the Tory ministry that came to power in 1710 altogether successful in its attempt to dominate household patronage and turn it to political advantage, for, as Jonathan Swift lamented to Stella, "They have cautioned the queen so much against being governed, that she observes it too much."[74] It is true that she gradually allowed the Oxford ministry to use most of the great household offices for ministerial patronage. But this, for the most part, involved the removal of Whigs whom she had preferred at the behest of her previous ministry into places that, though prestigious and lucrative, involved very little attendance upon her person, such as the offices of the upper greencloth and the masterships of the buckhounds and jewel house.[75] Those offices that did involve close personal attendance or were held by old friends were not allowed to become party fodder. For example, though prevailed upon to dismiss Somerset as master of the horse, Anne only did so, despite his half-hearted loyalty to her new ministry, after he had offended her personally by lying about his vote in the Hamilton affair.[76] Moreover, as seen above, she chose to leave his post vacant rather than replace her old friend with one of the Tory competitors for the office, which had traditionally been held by a favorite. Anne also refused to remove the Duchess of Somerset, despite even greater pressure from the ministry and the Tory party in general for her to do so.[77] It is equally significant that neither the Duchess of Devonshire nor the Countess of

Scarborough ever seems to have been in danger of losing their bedchamber posts, despite the Whig-opposition politics of their respective husbands.[78] This refusal to politicize the bedchamber by exploiting spousal connections undoubtedly weakened the political significance of court office. But, for Anne, the issue was more fundamental and no different from the one she had argued with Sarah, one that ultimately struck at her notion of the prerogative. As she reportedly informed her new ministers, "if it were so, that she could not have what Servants she liked, she did not find how her Condition was mended."[79]

Anne's growing insistence on this point is most dramatically illustrated by the case of her old friend and treasurer of the chamber, Viscount Fitzharding. When he died in December 1712, Lord Berkeley of Stratton noted that his two posts (he had also been a teller of the exchequer) would be "very welcome to the ministry who have long had an eye upon them, but the Queen had the goodness to keep him in for his life."[80] There followed a delay of about eight months before she chose as his successor in the treasurership John West, Lord Delawarr, an old servant of the Prince's with vaguely Tory principles. This may not have been entirely to the liking of Lord Treasurer Oxford, who had a multitude of more prominent Tories to satisfy. A number of those near the treasurer apparently attempted to get Delawarr to refuse the post. This convinced him that the appointment "was purely the pleasure of the Queen without any of the advise of the ministry."[81] Possibly because of a desire to slip a more suitable candidate by the Queen, more likely because of his diminishing capacity by the late summer of 1713, Oxford sent a blank warrant for her to sign. Anne's response, dated 21 August 1713, was indignant and revealing:

> I was very much surprised to find by your letter that, though I had told you the last time you weare hear I entended to give the Treasurer of the Chamber to Lord De Laware, you will bring me a warrant in blank. I desire you would not have soe ill an oppinion of me as to think when I have determined anything in my mind I will alter it. I have told Lord De Laware I will give him this office and he has kissed my hand upon it. Therfore when you com hither bring the warrant with his name.[82]

Whatever the cause of Oxford's slip, the former Mrs. Morley here demonstrates all the stubbornness and consciousness of her own regality that one expects of a Stuart. She was clearly much changed from the meek-sounding woman whose highest ambition in life was to serve her beloved Freeman. While it is difficult to determine the degree of control exercised by Queen Anne over household patronage at the beginning of the reign owing to the general congruence of her interests and sentiments with those of the Churchills, it is clear that well before its end she had become a force to be reckoned with, increasingly willing to override the advice of ministers and favorites, to defend her own rights of patronage, and even to invade those of her great officers to ensure a "family" that was both congenial and trustworthy.

Fortunately, Queen Anne was so good a mistress, and her relationship with most of her great officers was so harmonious, that she did not feel the need to do this very often. For the most part, and especially in filling places involving little attendance upon her, she allowed her great officers the free exercise of their rights of appointment in patronage fields, which, for the lord chamberlain or lord steward, could be very large indeed. What little evidence we have as to how inferior posts were filled suggests a pattern not unlike that already described for places in the Queen's gift. First, as at the Queen's accession in 1702, the vast majority of incumbents were left in place at the appointment of a new department head, and few were subject to removal for political reasons subsequently. Nor does there seem to have been any attempt on the part of the great department heads to build up a clique or "interest" of important fellow countrymen to lend prestige at home and at court, as was so common a century earlier. With the security of tenure noted above, there were too few vacancies caused by death or surrender, except perhaps in the largest departments, to allow for clientage on a grand scale. Moreover, department heads occasionally found their freedom of action compromised by the interference of a more powerful patron, such as the Duchess of Marlborough, as noted previously.[83] Finally, the lack of a clear ladder of promotion in most departments militated against lasting patron-client relationships—as Sarah frequently and ruefully noted in marginal comments on letters and petitions from those who later proved disloyal.[84]

The only exception to this was the practice, adopted by most department heads, of finding room for up to half a dozen personal servants in subordinate positions, often of considerable responsibility.[85] Thus, the litigious Duke of Montagu preferred his highly competent solicitor, Edmund Dummer, to the clerkship of the great wardrobe. Similarly, the Duchess of Marlborough took Rachel Thomas—"a woman," wrote Sarah, "of whose honesty I had great experience"—out of the Churchill household and made her a "yeowoman" and chief accountant of the robes.[86] There were advantages for the selecting officer in preferring his own servants into the Queen's household besides his prior knowledge of their suitability and trustworthiness. Their supplementary court income allowed him to pay less out of his own pocket, while their long-term presence in London attending to the Queen's business left them equally well placed to attend to that of their noble master as well.[87] On the other hand, there could be disadvantages for middling and menial servants in being too closely associated with a great patron: at Sarah's fall in January 1711 her successor as groom of the stole and mistress of the robes, the Duchess of Somerset, broke tradition and replaced some of the old Churchill retainers in those departments with her own people from Petworth.[88] Nevertheless, the vast majority of those preferred from noble into royal service were able to effect a permanent transition: even Rachel Thomas was considered so honest by the new mistress of the robes that she was retained as "yeowoman," despite her connection to the old.

Unfortunately, not all Queen Anne's great household officers left administrative or estate correspondence from which to identify personal servants. Even if they had, it is highly unlikely that any but the very smallest departments could have been filled by the personal servants of a single nobleman. This is obviously the case with the 400 places in the gift of the lord chamberlain. Clearly, like Anne herself, her department heads would have had to rely upon the advice and testimony of another, say a private secretary or clerk, in attempting to fill places in their gift. While this process was undoubtedly more often informal and verbal than otherwise, a rare opportunity to watch it at work is provided by the correspondence of the Duke of Shrewsbury with his secretary, Sir John Stanley, during the former's first, brief tenure as lord chamberlain to William III, from the autumn of 1699 to the spring of 1700.[89] Because of Shrewsbury's poor health and political cautiousness, he was, by and large, an absentee lord chamberlain. As a result, he relied heavily upon Stanley and his twice-weekly letters from court to report vacancies; to ascertain the lord chamberlain's title to fill them;

to be aware of the individual reputations and quality of competing candidates; and to give a considered personal opinion of each one's suitability for the post in question. The final decision was Shrewsbury's.

While the process by which household office was filled is fairly clear, the specific criteria applied in doing so are much less apparent. The Shrewsbury-Stanley correspondence is almost unique in its concern with household patronage. Unfortunately, because it covers so short a period, and one prior to Anne's reign, it is of only limited use. None of the great household officers left anything like the equivalent of Harley's collection of treasury and revenue papers, which contains large numbers of petitions and recommendations, often annotated by their recipients. There are, in short, no explicit statements, either of general principles or of specific reasons why one candidate for household office was chosen over another. In the absence of such evidence, examination of the Queen's servants themselves, as individuals and en masse, is necessary. This will also throw light on the equally important question of why men and women sought court office in the first place.

CHAPTER IV

Personnel

Previous chapters have portrayed the court as a classic premodern institution. Its structure had been dictated by history; its formal procedures by custom; its day-to-day operation by the predilections and competence of individual officers; and its officers by the personal decisions of the Queen and other great patrons. Consistent with this picture, there were no formal, standardized requirements, no specific professional credentials that automatically qualified one for employment at the court of Queen Anne. The university background enjoyed by 187 of her servants was a prerequisite only for the 82 men who served her in the capacity of chaplain (Table 4.1). An additional 46 servants in a wide variety of mostly middling posts had attended an Inn of Court (Table 4.2). In brief, for most of the Queen's servants, including her clerical staff, higher education was more a mark of social distinction than professional competence.[1] Such hallmarks of the modern civil service as formal interviews and entrance examinations, already in place in some of the revenue departments, were unknown in the royal household.[2]

Nor would they have been everywhere appropriate to an institution of its unique character and purpose. At its most basic level, the court existed to provide for the domestic needs of the monarch: her food, lodging, transportation, safety, health, and entertainment. As we shall see, such positions were, by and large, filled by men and women who possessed some experience or professional reputation in these areas. But an equal number of those employed by the court were there to enhance the royal state, fill out the Queen's entourage, and, generally, to provide a good show. Their presence reminds us that, whatever its immediate aims, the ultimate purpose of a court was far less tangible, less rational or "modern" than that of any other government department: to promote veneration of a divinely appointed hereditary monarch and

TABLE 4.1
University Education of Anne's Household Officers

	Rank of officer			
	High	Middle	Low	Total
Total number of officers who attended a university	20	154	13	187
Above as a % of total number of household officers[a]	36.4	28.3	1.4	12.3
Total number of officers who took an undergraduate (B.A. or M.A.) degree				
Earned	10	112	11	133
Honorary	1	1	2	4
Total number of officers who took a graduate degree				
Earned	3	67	1	71
Honorary	12	26	2	40
Breakdown by Institution				
Oxford				
Attended	12	81	6	99
Undergraduate degree				
Earned	6	51	4	61
Honorary	1	1	1	3
Graduate degree				
Earned	3	40	0	43
Honorary	9	13	2	24
Cambridge				
Attended	8	59	1	68
Undergraduate degree				
Earned	3	41	7	51
Honorary	0	0	2	2
Graduate degree				
Earned	1	22	1	24
Honorary	5	13	1	19
Other universities				
Attended	0	10	0	10
Undergraduate degree				
Earned	0	4	0	4
Honorary	0	0	0	0
Graduate degree				
Earned	0	4	0	4
Honorary	0	0	0	0

SOURCES: See Appendix B.

[a]I.e., 55 high officers, 544 middling officers, 926 low officers = 1,525 total officers.

TABLE 4.2
Legal Education of Anne's Household Officers

	Rank of officer			
	High	Middle	Low	Total
Total number of officers who attended an Inn of Court	4	42	0	46
Above as a % of total number of household officers[a]	7.3	7.7	0	3.0
Total number of officers who were called to the bar	0	9	0	9
Breakdown by Institution				
Middle Temple				
Attended	1	12	0	13
Called to the bar	0	5	0	5
Inner Temple				
Attended	3	16	0	19
Called to the bar	0	0	0	0
Lincoln's Inn				
Attended	1	12	0	13
Called to the bar	0	3	0	3
Gray's Inn				
Attended	0	6	0	6
Called to the bar	0	1	0	1

SOURCES: See Appendix B and information provided by David Lemmings.
[a]I.e., 55 high officers, 544 middling officers, 926 low officers = 1,525 total officers.

to perpetuate the social system over which she presided. The question of which candidates for household office could best further these aims went far beyond the issue of simple professional competence. Its answer required a definition of "merit" that balanced the personal, political, social, and economic circumstances of Queen, patron, and client in ways that seem irrational and unfair to modern observers.

In fact, that balance was constantly debated in its own day, and varied from office to office and individual to individual. It is therefore hardly surprising that no general statements of criteria for selection to household office have come down to us. But there does exist an even better source of evidence: the officers themselves. In the absence of formal guidelines for the filling of household positions, the following chapter seeks to discover the informal, unarticulated criteria used by patrons and selecting officers through the examination of those whom they patronized or selected. Specifically, it uses the techniques of prosopographical analysis to construct a collective biography of all 1,525 men, women, and children who served in the royal household between 1702 and 1714.[3] This "group portrait" should provide some idea of what the Queen and her administrators looked for in those whom they selected to serve her. Indeed, it will demonstrate that those selections were far more rational—given contemporary expectations of what a court should be—than is often assumed to be the case. This examination will also give some indication of why those preferred into household office had sought it in the first place. This question will be taken up in greater detail in the next chapter.

Professional Standards and Reputation

As indicated above, most service and artistic positions at court necessitated some degree of professional competence. Below stairs, the "Ancient Order of Succession" was intended to ensure that those who drew up the Queen's accounts, cooked her meals, or provisioned her house received sufficient training by ascending the rungs of two separate ladders of promotion, one for clerical staff, the other for culinary and victualing officers.[4] As we shall see, promotion along the first ladder was increasingly uncertain owing to the interference of great patrons and the preferment of well-bred outsiders.[5] But under Anne it was still possible to rise from the very lowest rungs of the second ladder to the ranks of sergeant, gentleman, or master cook in the appropriate catering subdepartment.[6] Likewise, a number of the gentlemen of the Queen's chapel royal had been trained there as boys.[7] In keeping with her elevated administrative standards, Queen Anne granted few reversions, which involved a promise to succeed to an office, but no training.[8] However, she did allow extraordinary or supernumerary service at full, half, or no pay until an ordinary (i.e., permanent and established) position became vacant.[9]

This begs the question of precisely how extraordinary, supernumerary, and inferior officers were selected in the first place. Most inferior kitchen servants seem to have been the offspring of senior kitchen personnel.[10] But the children of the chapel were, presumably, initially selected upon the basis of some previously demonstrated aptitude for singing. In fact, the vast majority of the court's service personnel re-

TABLE 4.3
Outside Occupations of Anne's Household Officers

	Rank of officer			
	High	Middle	Low	Total
Total number of officers for whom an outside occupation is known	54	336	339	729
Above as a % of total number of household officers[a]	98.2	61.8	36.6	47.8
Breakdown by Occupation				
Arts and scholarship	4	46	122	172
Government and local office	32	68	19	119
Inn or tavern keeping	0	0	1	1
Landowning	32	97	10	139
Landowning (family)	14	23	0	37
Law	0	7	0	7
Medicine	0	20	2	22
Mercantile and finance	2	27	28	57
Military				
Army	10	60	23	93
Navy	1	4	0	5
Religious	3	70	13	86
Service	2	19	23	44
Sports and gardening	0	1	4	5
Trades and crafts	0	3	29	32
Transport	0	2	86	88

SOURCES: See Appendix B.
[a]I.e., 55 high officers, 544 middling officers, 926 low officers = 1,525 total officers.

ceived their training and established their professional credentials long before their initial household appointments. We have already noted that a number of menial servants had proved themselves in the households of noble department heads before coming to court. Others, notably those with medical, artistic, trade, or transport backgrounds (Table 4.3, sub "Breakdown by Occupation"), had established their professional reputations among their peers and the general public at large. Presumably, this reputation was the main consideration in their individual appointments.

Perhaps the most impressive of those officers who had proved their mettle in the wider world were the Queen's chaplains and medical personnel. The former were drawn from among the most promising preachers, scholars, and controversialists in England.[11] Twenty-one of these individuals went on to deaneries, twenty to bishoprics. While much of this advancement was undoubtedly due to political factors, prosopographical analysis of the chaplains in ordinary nevertheless conveys the overall impression that they were drawn from the cream of the Anglican religious establishment. Likewise, the Queen's physicians included two presidents and four censors of the Royal College of Physicians.[12] Most of her medical personnel could point to long lists of significant medical publications and noble patients.[13] It was probably David Hamilton's success in treating feminine disorders that recommended him to the barren Queen.[14] John Arbuthnot is supposed to have proved himself by his life-saving emergency treatment of Prince George when the latter fell ill at Epsom early in the reign.[15] Drs. Thomas Lawrence and Sir Thomas Millington and the apothecary Daniel Malthus had each built up a considerable clientele among the various branches of the Churchill family circle.[16] On the other hand, Dr. John Radcliffe, who had treated Anne as Princess and was perhaps the most eminent medical man of his day, never received preferment from her as Queen, almost certainly because he refused to take her obstetrical problems seriously.[17] Dr. Samuel Garth, another prominent physician, was also conspicuously absent from the royal sickbed, no doubt because of his reputed atheism and demonstrative Whiggery.[18] Clearly, professional competence, no matter how important for the Queen's medical personnel, could not entirely make up for personal or political incompatibility.

While personality and politics could also have a negative effect upon preferment to prestigious "cultural" posts—as with Jonathan Swift's abortive attempt to become historiographer royal[19]—most were filled on the basis of merit. Anne's two historiographers, Thomas Rymer and Thomas Madox; her principal painter, Sir Godfrey Kneller; her library keeper, Dr. Richard Bentley; and even her much abused poet laureate, Nahum Tate, all made significant contributions to the scholarly and artistic life of the nation both before and during their preferment at court. Much the same was true of her musicians and, especially, the gentlemen of her chapel royal. The latter were selected from among the best vocalists in England and together formed its premier choral establishment, a worthy vehicle for the compositions of members such as John

Blow and William Croft, or outsiders like George Frideric Handel.[20] Finally, a good scholarly or artistic reputation earned outside the court might lead to preferment into a purely honorary or ceremonial post. This was true of Kneller, who was also a gentleman of the privy chamber; the antiquary John Chamberlayne, also of the privy chamber; the historian James Tyrrel, who was made a cupbearer; the poet William Walsh, gentleman of the horse; a number of the medical personnel; and three of the seven members of the legal profession with places at court (Table 4.3, sub "Breakdown by Occupation").[21]

At the lower levels of household service, stables posts, in particular, demanded expert equestrian knowledge. In correspondence with the Earl of Oxford dated November 1711, the Queen's studmaster, Thomas Pulleine, displays an extensive knowledge of breeds and training methods.[22] Andrew Snape, junior, her sergeant and marshal farrier, whose family had served in the royal stables since the Tudor period, made use of a similar expertise in his fine folio of 1683, *The Anatomy of an Horse*.[23] Evidence from the stables of Charles II and the estate correspondence of Anne's master of the horse, the Duke of Somerset, indicates that such knowledge was expected of the lowliest groom or postilion, and that it was important in determining appointments.[24]

At the very highest levels, however, technical expertise was only one of many considerations that might affect appointments. For example, when, in 1697, the Duke of Shrewsbury recommended Sir Charles Shuckburgh to succeed to the mastership of the buckhounds, he began by stressing the candidate's excellence in this field: "Shuckburough [*sic*] . . . is the only man in his Majesty's dominions that I believe has a pack of hounds that are truly bred of the old fleet northern kind, and understands the best how to make them hunt and run." But what probably weighed more heavily in Shuckburgh's eventual preferment was the information that he was "extreme zealous in the interest of the Government" and had "a great power among the loyal Church party" of Warwickshire.[25] In 1712 a shrewder, more experienced Shrewsbury once again recommended for a vacancy at the head of the buckhounds. This time he wrote on behalf of his kinsman, the Earl of Cardigan. Cardigan, though an avid sportsman, was put forward for Lord Treasurer Oxford's consideration on this sole basis: "You may depend upon his being gratefully your servant."[26] That Shrewsbury's candidate was appointed without any discussion of his technical qualifications suggests that, at this level, political considerations were far more important.

Politics

The majority of those appointed to great and middling household office under Queen Anne were selected not for their abilities, knowledge, or experience, but for their "interest," whether political, economic, or social. Anne herself would have denied this: one of her arguments against preferring Mrs. Fane at her ministry's behest was that "she would not have any marayd person for the intrest."[27] But, as noted in Chapter 3, political behavior and reputation had had a great deal to do with whom she had chosen to retain from William's household; at the highest levels, it was to continue to have a major influence upon whom she preferred into her own. For example, despite the Duchess of Marlborough's claim to have sought out ladies "of ye best quality ye nerest ye Queen [in] age & most Suted to her temper" to serve in the bedchamber, it can hardly have been a coincidence that this resulted in a remarkably even balance between women whose husbands or fathers were Tories (Ladies Abingdon, Frescheville, Hyde, and Ormonde); and those married to or descended from Whigs (Ladies Beverwort, Hartington, Scarborough, and Somerset). In theory, this left Sarah, her two daughters, and the Countess of Burlington holding the balance, if in practice tipping it increasingly toward the Whigs.[28]

Where it is possible to determine the politics of those appointed over the next twelve years, they correspond, more often than not, to those of the ascendant party at the time of appointment. Thus, Sir Nathaniel Napier, a High Tory M.P. with Jacobite tendencies, was made a gentleman of the privy chamber in February 1704, two months before the leaders of his party fell from their powerful positions within the Marlborough-Godolphin ministry. After the fall of the High Tories in April, the politics of new appointees, where known, tends to be moderately Whig in color. This was true of John Charlton, William Feilding, William Lowther, and Thomas Meredith, appointed master of the jewel house, lieutenant of the yeomen of the guard, a gentleman of the privy chamber, and an equerry, respectively, in 1704; Philip Cavendish and Philip Sherrard as sergeant porter and a gentleman of the privy chamber, respectively, in 1705; Viscount Townshend as captain of the yeomen of the guard in 1707; the Earl of Cholmondeley, Edmund Dunch, and Henry Ashurst as treasurer and master of the household and a gentleman of the privy chamber, respectively, in 1708; Sir John Holland as comptroller of the household in 1709; and Horatio Walpole, Thomas Windham, and Wyriott Owen as corporals to the yeomen of the guard and a gentleman of the privy chamber, respectively, in the early months of 1710. Two of the above individuals were peers, eight were (or were about to be) members of the lower house (see Appendix C). Five in particular were members of the Walpole-Townshend Norfolk connection, which was increasingly important to the parliamentary health of the Marlborough-Godolphin administration.[29]

After the fall of that administration in the summer of 1710, there were few vacancies at the middling levels of household service for Tories to fill. The exceptions led to the preferment of Carew Mildmay in December 1710, Richard Lockwood in May 1711, and Sir John Statham in May 1714 as gentlemen of the privy chamber; and Sir John Walter in February 1711 as a clerk of the greencloth. But at the highest levels, Queen Anne tolerated what amounted to a gradual purge of Whig officeholders, including some of those preferred at the instigation of her previous ministry, and their replacement by Tories of varying persuasion. Thus, Lord Steward Devonshire was replaced in October 1710 by the Duke of Buckingham; Comptroller Holland, Cofferer Godolphin, Captain of the Yeomen Townshend, Master of the Jewel House Charlton, and Master of the Buckhounds Chetwynd in the spring of 1711 by Sir Thomas Mansell, Samuel Masham, Henry Paget, Heneage Finch, and Sir William Wyndham, respectively; Captain of the Gentlemen Pensioners St. Albans in January 1712 by the Duke of Beaufort; Master of the Household Dunch that summer by Sir William Pole; and Treasurer of the Household Cholmondeley in the summer of 1713 by George, Lord Lansdowne. All of the new appointees sat in parliament (see Appendix C) and most were personal associates of either Oxford or Bolingbroke. Clearly, the previous administration had taught the Queen to regard these posts as majority fodder.[30]

Nevertheless, the significance of politics as a factor in deciding household appointments should not be overestimated. While of undoubted importance in filling most great and some middling positions, these form only a small proportion of the total number of household appointments made between 1702 and 1714. Moreover, none of the appointments noted above involved close daily attendance upon the monarch. This is in marked contrast to posts in the bedchamber, where personal and social considerations also mattered and from which there were no purely political removals.[31] In short, Queen Anne attempted to keep purely political appointees to a minimum and at a distance. This helps to explain her refusal to fill the mastership of the horse, a great office that did involve close daily attendance, after Somerset's fall in January 1712. It is significant, too, that most of those named prior to 1710 had to wait for a vacancy to open up through death or surrender.

Indeed, the lack of a strong political profile could sometimes be an asset in the hunt for great household office. This was Arthur Maynwaring's explanation for why the much abused Earl of Kent (nicknamed "Bugg" because of an odor problem) was preferred to the lord chamberlainship in April 1704: "As the Politicks then stood when neither Side was to be much oblig'd or displeas'd it seem'd to me as if Bugg had been fortunately made by providence to supply a vacancy that was to be fill'd up with something very insignificant."[32] Six years later, when the Queen replaced Kent with the Duke of Shrewsbury, it was the Duke's rather ambiguous politics that enabled her to claim that the move did not presage a ministerial revolution. Indeed, at those moments when the Crown was anxious to assert its independence of party, it was possible to win preferment at court even if one's politics were ostensibly out of favor. Thus, the nominal Tory Thomas Coke was named vice chamberlain in December 1706 and the Whig Crewe Offley became a gentleman of the privy chamber in July 1714.[33] In conclusion, while politics might have aided or hindered court preferment, they can be shown to have been a simple, decisive factor in only a few cases, mostly at the top. As a result, the royal household, despite its great size, was of limited usefulness to the current ministry in obliging those with political ambitions.

"A Good Estate"

No political affiliation is known for the vast majority of the 1,525 men, women, and children who saw service at the court of Queen Anne, nor is it likely that party politics had a significant influence upon their initial appointment. For those at the lowest levels, this goes without saying. For most of those in the middle, and even a few at the top, a more general, socioeconomic rather than strictly political, notion of "interest" would have recommended their appointment. For these officers "a good estate" was often a useful, if not sufficient, condition for preferment. In a minority of cases that estate was of a nonlanded kind. This applies to the 27 middling merchant/financiers and the majority of the professional men with ceremonial posts at court (Table 4.3, sub "Breakdown by Occupation"). Among these were George Morley, M.P., of Lincoln's Inn and the Inner Temple, a master in Chancery and commissioner of prizes who served Anne as a sewer, then a carver; Sir Jonathan Andrews, an East India Company merchant and eventual director of the company, assistant of the Royal Africa Company and a member of the London Lieutenancy, sworn a gentleman of the Queen's privy chamber; and Sir Steven Evance, M.P., who had lent vast sums of money to William's government, was a proprietor of the Sword Blade Company, and had interests in prospecting and fishing in addition to being the Queen's jeweler.[34] Despite Evance's eventual suicide, these were very solid citizens indeed. It was presumably hoped that, as with the artists and scholars appointed to ceremonial posts, their presence at court would lend it prestige as well as gain their general support for the Queen's interests in parliament, the City, and the country at large, irrespective of the complexion of her current ministry. At a somewhat lower level, much the same was probably true of the preferment of John Stone, "certified to be a substantial, well affected apothecary at Kensington," as a groom of the great chamber; or the appointments of the 28 smaller tradesmen, who appear to have had some influence in City politics.[35]

But the oldest and most common meaning of "a good Estate," as well as the clearest indication of "interest" to contemporary eyes, was an estate composed of land. Thus, Sarah later justified her recommendation of the Duke of Somerset to be master of the horse, despite his being "very unreasonable and troublesome," on these grounds: "I thought him honest and in the Queen's interest because of his great state." The latter included his own Seymour lands in Sussex and Wiltshire and his wife's vast Percy inheritance in the north.[36] Likewise, defenders of Kent's appointment to the lord chamberlainship could point to his extensive holdings.[37] For those at the top, landownership had a direct political significance: ten of the Queen's great officers, including Somerset, had a parliamentary interest that spanned at least one county.[38]

While political influence was obviously useful, the primary significance of a landed estate was that it conferred status and respectability upon its holder. Altogether, at least 139 of Anne's 1,525 household servants can be shown to have owned land (Table 4.3, sub "Breakdown by Occupation").[39] This figure is almost certainly an underestimate: as indicated in Table 4.4b, a place of residence has been found for only 331, or about 55 percent, of the 599 great and middling officers (adding "High" and "Middle" columns together). The smaller percentage of lower servants for whom we possess such information is less worrying, since most would have had to live in or near the metropolis owing to the relative constancy of their attendance and the smallness of their emoluments. Even without them, it is significant that 32 of 50 great officers (64 percent) and 97 of the 281 middling officers (34 percent) for whom a place of residence is known had landed estates (Table 4.3, sub "Breakdown by Occupation," compared to Table 4.4b). Moreover, these figures do not include the 37 individuals, mostly women in high or middling bedchamber positions, whose fathers or husbands owned land (Table 4.3, sub "Breakdown by Occupation"). In short, the court was staffed at the senior level by representatives of the class thought to comprise the natural inheritors of political, social, and economic power in the localities.

However, examination of the regional distribution of officeholders does not suggest a comprehensive attempt to spread patronage or interest evenly or proportionally throughout the country (Table 4.4b). Rather, those counties with the highest proportion of court officers were not necessarily those with the greatest gentry, or even Royalist gentry, populations. In Chapter 3 the failure of Anne's great department heads to fill the court with clients from powerful local families was noted. Instead, the fact that those outlying counties with the greatest representation at court were so well represented can usually be explained by the presence there of several members of one, two, or at most three families. Often, these had a long-standing tradition of court service, but only a moderate significance in local or national politics.[40]

Most seem to have been at least as interested in forging marital connections with other court families as with the politically significant gentry of their respective local communities. This was true of the Daltons, Wyvills, and Yarboroughs of Yorkshire, the Dacres of Hertfordshire, the Dummers of Hampshire, the Eccles of Surrey, and the Napiers of Dorset.[41] In short, the Queen's desire to be served only by those she knew or who had served the Stuarts in previous reigns and her anxiety to keep her court private and free from politics all tended to confine its appeal to a relatively narrow clique of court families, landed, but not always wealthy or politically active. The resulting concentration of royal favor served to isolate the court from the broad political and social clientele that Charles II's household had appealed to so successfully, and that now regarded parliament and the ministers who controlled it as the focus of their interests.

The relatively high proportion of household officers residing in the Home Counties is explained less by family connections than by these areas' increasing convenience as suburbs of the metropolis. As for London and its environs, at least 63 of the Queen's servants can be shown to have possessed Middlesex residences in addition to their country homes (Table 4.4b). For those with no land in the country, especially lower officers, London and Middlesex easily outstrip all other places of domicile, with 249 permanent residents (Table 4.4b, sub "Middlesex," subtracting the 63 individuals possessing a second, non-Middlesex residence). This figure would obviously be greater were the domiciles of more of Anne's menial servants traceable. As a result, a comparison of Tables 4.4a and 4.4b only begins to suggest the degree to which London and the Home Counties drew those who were born or raised elsewhere. Specifically, of a total of 300 officers whose place of birth or father's place of residence was outside London, 60 moved to the metropolis, 28 bought town houses in the city, and a further 18 moved to one of the Home Counties.

Table 4.4a indicates that most of those born away from London came from the North and the West, but a small yet significant number (77) hailed from beyond England's borders. Some of those from the continent were survivors from the great cosmopolitan courts of Anne's uncle and father, such as the painter Kneller and the musician Jacob Kremberg. But most of the Europeans at court were Protestant refu-

TABLE 4.4

Geographical Distribution of Anne's Household Officers

	A. Place of Birth or Father's Residence				B. Place of Residence While in Service			
	Rank of officer				Rank of officer			
	High	Middle	Low	Total	High	Middle	Low	Total
Total no. of officers for whom locality is known	47	239	92	378	50	281	168	499
Above as a % of total no. of household officers[a]	85.5	43.9	9.9	24.8	90.9	51.7	18.1	32.7
	Breakdown by Locality				*Breakdown by Locality*			
Bedfordshire	1	4	0	5	1	2(1)	1	4(1)
Berkshire	3(2)[b]	5	4	12(2)	3(1)	5(2)	4(1)	12(4)
Buckinghamshire	1(1)	6(1)	0	7(2)	0	7(3)	2	9(3)
Cambridgeshire	0	4	0	4	0	8(1)	0	8(1)
Cheshire	2(1)	5	1	8(1)	1(1)	3	1(1)	5(2)
Cornwall	2	3(1)	0	5(1)	3	3(1)	0	6(1)
Cumberland	0	1	0	1	0	1	0	1
Derbyshire	3(1)	6	2	11(1)	5(3)	4	0	9(3)
Devonshire	2	2	0	4	2(1)	1	0	3(1)
Dorset	0	5	1	6	0	5(1)	0	5(1)
Durham Co.	0	0	0	0	0	0	0	0
Essex	1	5	0	6	2(1)	11(6)	1	14(7)
Gloucestershire	2	2	2	6	3(2)	4(2)	2(1)	9(5)
Herefordshire	0	4	0	4	0	4(1)	0	4(1)
Hertfordshire	3	7(2)	2	12(2)	2(2)	10(2)	1	13(4)
Huntingdonshire	0	3	0	3	0	1	0	1
Kent	0	5	1	6	1(1)	10(3)	1(1)	12(5)
Lancashire	0	4	1	5	0	0	0	0
Leicestershire	0	2(2)	1	3(2)	0	2	0	2
Lincolnshire	0	4	0	4	2(1)	4(2)	1(1)	7(4)

Middlesex	6(3)	50(12)	23	79(15)	22(15)	146(38)	144(10)	312(63)
Monmouthshire	0	0	0	0	0	0	0	0
Norfolk	2	8(1)	2(1)	12(2)	2	5(1)	1	8(1)
Northamptonshire	3(1)	9	3	15(1)	3(2)	4(1)	0	7(3)
Northumberland	0	1	0	1	0	0	0	0
Nottinghamshire	0	2(1)	1	3(1)	0	3	0	3
Oxfordshire	1	5(1)	1	7(1)	4(3)	12(1)	0	16(4)
Rutlandshire	1	2(1)	0	3(1)	0	1	0	1
Shropshire	1	7(2)	1	9(2)	2(2)	2(1)	1(1)	5(4)
Somersetshire	2	6(1)	1	9(1)	2(1)	3	0	5(1)
Southamptonshire	1	6(1)	0	7(1)	0	8(3)	0	8(3)
Staffordshire	4	2	1	7	2	3	0	5
Suffolk	2	2	1(1)	5(1)	1	5(2)	0	6(2)
Surrey	2	5(1)	0	7(1)	1	14(4)	13(5)	28(9)
Sussex	0	2	2	4	1(1)	3(1)	1	5(2)
Warwickshire	1	5	1	7	0	2	1(1)	3(1)
Westmoreland	0	1	0	1	0	0	0	0
Wiltshire	1	7(1)	0	8(1)	2(1)	2	1	5(1)
Worcestershire	0	3	0	3	1	2(2)	1	4(2)
Yorkshire	2	21	1	24	1(1)	15(2)	2	18(3)
Channel Islands	0	2	0	2	0	1	0	1
Ireland	1(1)	7	4	12(1)	0	3	0	3
Scotland	0	3	1	4	0	2(1)	0	2(1)
Wales	1	2	0	3	1(1)	1	0	2(1)
American Colonies	0	2(1)	0	2(1)	0	0	0	0
France	0	9(1)	21(1)	30(2)	0	0	0	0
German States	0	7	11	18	0	0	0	0
Netherlands	1	1	3	5	0	0	0	0
Italy	0	0	1(1)	1(1)	0	0	0	0
Total localities	52	254	94	400	70	322	179	571

SOURCES: See Appendix B.

[a]I.e., 55 high officers, 544 middling officers, 926 low officers = 1,525 total officers.

[b]Numbers in ( ) refer to officers whose fathers claimed more than one place of residence (Table 4.4a) or to officers who possessed more than one residence themselves (Table 4.4b).

gees, usually Frenchmen who had come over with or been appointed by William III, such as the tailcartaker Jacob d'Abbadie; the clerk to the treasurer of the chamber, Moses Girardeau; and the trumpeter John St. Amand. In cases such as these, the Queen's aversion to foreigners in general and to clients of "Mr. Caliban" in particular appears to have been overcome by her sympathy for those who had fled popish tyranny.

Seven of the Queen's twelve servants from Ireland had been appointed under William III, and two had served under him on campaign there, but in all other respects (apart from that of having sought their fortune at the English court) this diverse group is hard to classify.[42] It is more significant that, apart from Anne's two doctors, Arbuthnot and Hamilton, her court included few if any Scots. The political implications of this were not lost upon Lord Treasurer Godolphin, who wrote to Lord Seafield in the summer of 1705: "As to the argument of English influence, how can the Queen but bee influenced by her English servants when she has no Scots servants near her person, at least during a sessions [*sic*] of Parliament, which is the time when the greatest affairs of that kingdom are transacted."[43] The Union occurred too late in the reign (1707) to upset the stability of court families and personnel noted in this chapter. The absence of Scots from the court previously reflects not only the absentee quality of the Queen's government in Scotland, but also the cool, indeed tense, state of Anglo-Scottish relations that she inherited from William. The result was obviously as damaging to local interests as it was to the Queen's.

"A Good Family"

Although a good estate, preferably landed, was a valuable asset to anyone seeking great or middling office, it was not essential, especially for the latter. When Lady Scarborough recommended her cousin Richard Dalton to the Queen's favor, she stressed a much more important, if obviously related, qualification, in labeling him "a Gentleman of a good family and in low Circumstances."[44] Whatever one's current financial situation, "a good family," that is, noble or gentry status, was considered an absolute necessity in filling most great and middling positions, respectively. Indeed, nothing less than an earldom would do for the four greatest household posts, those of lord chamberlain, lord steward, master of the horse, and groom of the stole. Defenders of Kent's appointment to the first of these posts could point not only to his estates but to his being "the first earl of England."[45] By the same token, when England's senior Protestant duke, Somerset, was about to lose his mastership of the horse in December 1711, the Countess of Strafford objected to one of his potential successors as follows: "I should think L^{d}: Dartmouth not won of consideration enough for A place of that profitt."[46] The remainder of the great household offices were always held by a peer except for those of vice chamberlain and the masterships of the jewel house and buckhounds.

At the middle rank of household service, gentry status was an almost universal prerequisite, whether in filling a clerkship of the greencloth (worth over £1,000 per annum) or a gentleman usher's place, "the Lowest office for a Gentleman" according to one holder[47] (worth from £80 to £200 per annum). Indeed, despite a wide variety in the emoluments and prestige of the offices they held, Queen Anne's middling servants exhibited a remarkable degree of social homogeneity. For example, a comparison of the six men who served her as clerks of the greencloth with the five who were her gentlemen ushers, daily waiters, reveals that what separated the personnel of these two societies was not the greater social status, wealth, or political significance of the former, but that of their relatives and friends. Only three of her clerks of the greencloth, Col. Charles Godfrey, Sir William Forrester, and Sir John Walter, possessed landed estates at the time of their initial court appointments.[48] Far more important to Godfrey's preferment was his marriage to Arabella Churchill, the Duke of Marlborough's sister. Likewise, Forrester owed his position to his uncle, Treasurer of the Household Bradford. Among the nonlanded men, Charles Scarborough was the son of Sir Charles Scarborough, physician in ordinary to Charles II; the younger Charles was himself a former servant of Prince George's. Edward Griffith had also both served the Prince and married into the Churchill family circle. Finally, Anthony Rowe was one of the "Revolution officers," having received his place as a reward for his financial services to William in 1688. Three of the six were also members of parliament (see Appendix C), but in at least two cases, those of Forrester and Godfrey, this, too, had more to do with family connection than individual merit.

In contrast to this, the five gentlemen ushers, daily waiters, lack only one thing: prominent social and political connections. Admittedly, one of them has remained a virtual unknown to modern scholarship. Sir William Oldes, a former servant to Queen Mary, knighted upon his promotion to Black Rod in 1710, is otherwise untraceable.[49] The group included, too, one striking example of social mobility. Sir David Mitchell had begun life as a cabin boy in a merchant vessel but had risen first to a command in the Royal Navy and then to a comfortable retirement by the time of his initial court appointment in 1689. A knighthood followed in 1698, and he purchased the lease of an estate at Popes, Hertfordshire, in 1700.[50] The other three, Francis Ashton, Jeremiah Chaplaine, and William Saunderson, all possessed landed estates at the time of their initial appointments.[51] Moreover, Chaplaine, Mitchell, and Saunderson all attained to solid gentry marriages, though, significantly, nothing like the triumphs of Godfrey and Griffith.[52] In fact, only Chaplaine could boast a prominent relative, his cousin Lady Scarborough. In short, both groups were cut from the same socioeconomic cloth. The difference in their respective fortunes at court was determined by the presence at or absence from court of socially and politically prominent relatives. A similar socioeconomic homogeneity can be observed among the largest society of middling officers at court, the gentlemen of the privy chamber.[53]

Gentry background was beginning to be required even below stairs. It is true that household clerks like Alexander Gretton, Henry Lowman, John Price, or John Shaw had risen from humble backgrounds, through the ranks, over long careers, to an artificial gentility. This was consistent with the "Ancient Order of Succession" that was supposed to govern preferment in the catering subdepartments. In every case, their connections, where traceable at all, were to other menial servants below stairs rather than to established gentry families.[54] However, at the accession of George I in 1714, Henry Lowman "esq." discovered the significance of his origins, the limits of his prospects, and the real value of his courtesy status. Of German birth, he was a clerk of the kitchen by 1691, and a favorite of William, Anne, and George. This seemed to make him a likely candidate to succeed to a clerkship of the greencloth, theoretically the next stage in the "Ancient Order." But by 1714 the greencloth was, as indicated above, the province of men with better connections and pedigrees than Lowman's. He was repeatedly passed over by the first two Hanoverians, it was said because of "objections as to his Genteelity," and died, still a clerk of the kitchen, in 1749.[55]

Indeed, from at least the reign of Charles I onwards, political and, especially, social considerations made it increasingly difficult for servants below stairs to rise to the masterships, clerkships, and even yeomen's positions that had once been their right.[56] This explains the presence of men like James Clerke, "of London, Gent" among Anne's clerks of the kitchen. Granted arms in December 1688, Clerke had been constable of Dublin Castle and steward to the first Duke of Ormonde as lord lieutenant of Ireland. It was almost certainly the latter's patronage as lord steward that brought Clerke to the household in 1673 at the relatively advanced rank of supernumerary sergeant of the chandry.[57] The increasing preferment of men like Clerke into ever more subordinate positions below stairs was closing off one of the few social ladders open to menial officers at the court of Queen Anne, in a period usually said to be one of upward mobility.

The one remaining department where social homogeneity was not strictly maintained and where a real rise in social status was still possible was, surprisingly, the royal bedchamber. It is true that the groom of the stole and ten ladies of the bedchamber were among the best-born women in England, while the six maids of honor were drawn from prominent gentry families. But the social pretensions of the real working core of the department, the four women of the bedchamber and its various seamstresses, starchers, and so on, were more variable. These positions often paid quite handsomely, up to £500 per annum in the case of the women of the bedchamber. But they also involved their holders in strenuous and menial work.[58] As a result, they tended to attract women of gentry or near-gentry background whose families had fallen on hard times. The resultant social ambiguity confused even Sarah; she recalled years later:

> I had some scruple in speaking for [Abigail Hill] because her misfortunes had obliged her to serve, & upon that I ask'd adviss, to which my friends said I need not make any difficulty in that for if she had not been a Gentle woman

that there was non in the Princess's family at that time that were Gentle women, except Mrs. Danvers, who had in some measure lost the advantage of her birth, by having marryed a trades man.[59]

From her position in the bedchamber, Abigail Hill was able to resuscitate her family's fortunes through royal favor; though Anne insisted that she continue to perform the relatively menial duties of a dresser, even after her husband's elevation to the peerage in 1712.[60] The Danvers, too, retrieved their gentle status somewhat through the marriage of their daughter, Isabella, also a dresser, to an Irish bishop, John Harstongue.[61] The Queen's seamstress, Anne Rhansford, was succeeded in that post by a daughter who married a son of John Moore, Bishop of Ely.[62] Several of Anne's maids of honor, the products of solid gentry families, were able to marry into the peerage.[63] Finally, it is worth remembering that the Duchess of Marlborough herself began her court career as Sarah Jennings, maid of honor to the Duchess of York, from which position she, too, engineered an advantageous marriage. Clearly, a post in the Queen's bedchamber was a potential ladder upon which an ambitious young woman could rise in status by gaining access either to the monarch's person and favor or, more commonly, to those well-born and eligible young men who still frequented the court. For the rest of the Queen's servants, household office was more a recognition of and a reward for one's place in society, not a means to improve it.

Court Families

It should be apparent from the discussion so far that a family background of household service was likely to lead to court office. In the following section, it will be argued that such "court" connections were shared by nearly half of Anne's servants. However, connection took numerous forms, and its elucidation requires careful genealogical analysis. Direct succession from parent to child was not common: only 41 of Anne's servants succeeded a parent, and the same number were themselves succeeded by a child (Table 4.5). There were no officially inheritable offices at court, though succession from father to son was tacitly observed immediately before, during, and after Anne's reign in the masterships of the ceremonies and barges and in the knight mar-

TABLE 4.5
Succession of Anne's Household Officers from and by Relatives

	Rank of officer			
	High	Middle	Low	Total
A. Succession from a Relative				
Officers who succeeded a parent	3	15	23	41
Above as a % of total number of household officers[a]	5.5	2.8	2.5	2.7
Officers who succeeded another relative	–	13	25	38
Above as a % of total number of household officers[a]	–	2.4	2.7	2.5
B. Succession by a Relative				
Officers who were succeeded by a child	2	16	23	41
Above as a % of total number of household officers[a]	3.6	2.9	2.5	2.7
Officers who were succeeded by another relative	–	16	32	48
Above as a % of total number of household officers[a]	–	2.9	3.5	3.1

SOURCES: See Appendix B.
[a]I.e., 55 high officers, 544 middling officers, 926 low officers = 1,525 total officers.

shal's, library keeper's, and sergeant trumpeter's places.[64] The Queen also allowed the Marquesses of Hartington and Monthermer to succeed to their fathers' places as lord steward and master of the great wardrobe in 1707 and 1709, respectively. However, she categorically refused to allow the daughters of the Duchess of Marlborough to do the same at the latter's fall in January 1711.[65] Occasionally, fathers were able to surrender their places to sons or even to sons-in-law while still living. Thus, Charles Nicholas Eyre, cupbearer, gave way to his son, Charles Chester; and Samuel Brown, yeoman of the pastry, to his daughter's husband, Thomas Salter, in the latter case for an annuity of £10 for the rest of Brown's life.[66] Since the Queen herself was rarely able to provide similar annuities for retiring servants or their surviving dependents, every effort was made to find room for the offspring of those who had died young. For example, when Samuel Chambers died in 1706, his son, Robert, was immediately preferred into his place as a child of the scullery. Robert must have been well under age at the time,

TABLE 4.6
Anne's Household Officers with Relatives at Court, 1660–1760

	Rank of officer	Officers w/ proved relatives	Officers w/ probable relatives	Total	Total as a % of total number of officers[a]
	High	45	3	48	87.3
	Middle	150	79	229	42.1
	Low	132	237	369	39.8
	Total	327	319	646	42.4
Breakdown by Periods Before, During, and After Anne's Reign					
1660–1702	High	38	4	42	76.4
	Middle	111	61	172	31.6
	Low	78	165	243	26.2
	Total	227	230	457	30.0
1702–1714	High	29	0	29	52.7
	Middle	104	26	130	23.9
	Low	96	143	239	25.8
	Total	229	169	398	26.1
1714–1760	High	37	0	37	67.3
	Middle	82	47	129	23.7
	Low	77	148	225	24.3
	Total	196	195	391	25.6

SOURCES: See Appendix B.
[a]I.e., 55 high officers, 544 middling officers, 926 low officers = 1,525 total officers.

for in 1710 the board of greencloth found him still "to Young to undertake the Labour & performe the Duty of his said Place." This caused them to name John Griffin, a pankeeper in the scullery, Chambers's deputy, reserving a salary for the latter until he was old enough to do the work himself.[67] Finally, the Queen's master cooks apparently had the right to start their sons upon the ladder of kitchen preferment as children of that department: at least three of them did so.[68]

While such well-documented examples of succession within a single family are rare, as are those of active solicitation by a family member like Lady Scarborough's in 1702, Table 4.6 suggests that they form the tip of a much larger iceberg of family relationship. The number of Anne's servants who can be shown through genealogical and other sources to have had a family member at court sometime during the century 1660–1760 is calculated in Table 4.6, column 1 ("Officers w/proved relatives").[69] Unavoidably, these figures omit large numbers of servants for whom no family is traceable, but who, in many cases, shared the same surname. Where they held similar posts, or, in the case of particularly common surnames, actually succeeded each other, they are included in Table 4.6, column 2, as officers with "probable" relatives at court. Given the stringency of this rule and other deficiencies in the data, the totals given in columns 3 and 4 ("Total" and "Total as a % of total number of officers") are more likely to understate the degree of family connection than overstate it.

According to the composite figures contained in Table 4.6, columns 3 and 4, over two fifths (42.4 percent) of the Queen's servants could point to a blood relative who was at court between the years 1660 and 1760. The lower portion of Table 4.6 breaks this information down by periods before, during, and after Anne's reign. Just over a quarter (26.1 percent) could point to a relative at her own court (Table 4.6, sub "1702–1714"), and, perhaps more significant for those seeking employment, a somewhat higher proportion (30.0 percent) could trace kin to the courts of her predecessors (Table 4.6, sub "1660–1702"). These proportions are significantly greater for those at the highest levels, a not unexpected reminder of the exclusivity and continuing sociopolitical importance of the group from which they were drawn. But the high proportion of officers of all ranks with kin at previous and subsequent courts (Table 4.6, sub "1660–1702" and "1714–1760") suggests continuity at all levels. This is perhaps most tangibly expressed in Figure 4.1, where the "Total" column for the whole period 1660–1760 is less than half again as high as the columns for the three constituent periods, indicating substantial overlap among the three subpopulations.

Figure 4.2 breaks this evidence of family continuity down into reigns. As might be expected, 232, or just over 15 percent, of the Queen's servants could trace family back to the Tory court of her uncle and roughly the same proportion could do so to the court of her father. More surprisingly, an even higher number, 366, or exactly 24 percent, could do so to the relatively Whig court of her brother-in-law, William III. This column, nearly twice as high as that for relatives at the courts of either Charles II or James II, along with the high number of officers with kin at the courts of George I and George II, suggests that Anne's court was not dominated by Tories, Royalists, and Jacobites. Clearly, despite the proscription of extreme Whigs at the Queen's accession and

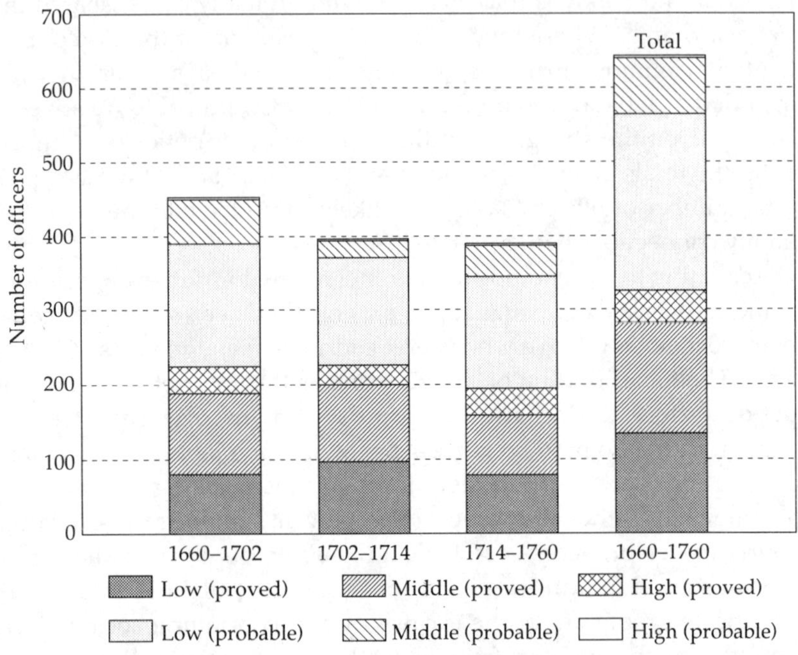

Fig. 4.1. Household officers with proved and probable relatives at court (added together), 1660–1760. Data from sources cited in Appendix B.

of a number of Tory families at her death,[70] most court families weathered those two great and potentially disastrous watersheds intact.

If officers known to have had family members at court between 1660 and 1760 are divided into types of relationship (Table 4.7, sub "1660–1760"), virtually every one can be shown to have had a parent, a child, a sibling, or a spouse there. That 118 of the Queen's servants had a father in court service, 17 a mother, 101 a son, and 12 a daughter suggests that if direct succession from parent to child was rare, many children nevertheless chose to follow in their parents' footsteps in the general choice of a court career. Moreover, Table 4.7, sub "1702–1714," indicates that *simultaneous* service by parents and children, such as that provided by the Duchess of Marlborough and her daughters or the Queen's three master cooks and their sons, was not unusual. In addition, servants with siblings (35 with brothers, 6 with sisters), spouses (16 husbands, 16 wives), and in-laws at court (30 brothers-in-law alone)

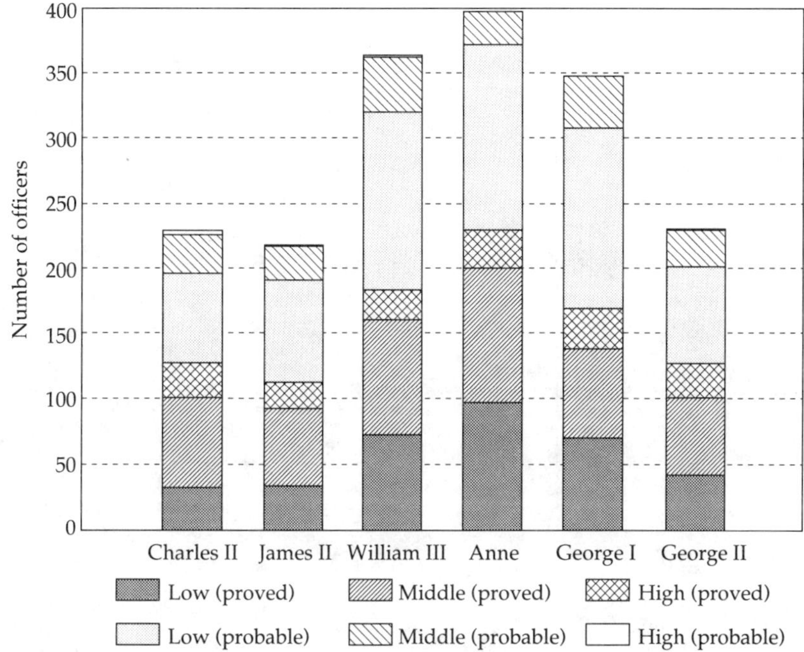

Fig. 4.2. Household officers with proved and probable relatives at court (added together), divided into the reigns during which those relatives served. Data from sources cited in Appendix B.

between 1702 and 1714 were numerous (Table 4.7, sub "1702–1714," rows 7–8, 12–14). Admittedly, Anne's reign was something of a special case, for her sex dictated that most of her personal attendants would be women, thus making sisters, wives, and female in-laws potential colleagues. Three of the Queen's great officers—Lord Steward Devonshire and Cofferers Godolphin and Masham—had wives in the bedchamber. Two other male servants, Vice Chamberlain Coke and the standard-bearer to the gentlemen pensioners, Charles Fane, married maids of honor.[71] One post, the keepership of Kensington Palace, was shared between a married couple, Henry and Mary Lowman. Another post, the keepership of Westminster Palace, was actually passed down via marriage through the female line from John Wynyard, whose family had held it since at least the reign of James I, to his daughter Anne; then, at her death, to her husband John Incledon; at his death, to their

TABLE 4.7

Types of Family Relationship Claimed by Anne's Household Officers with Relatives Serving at Court

Type of relationship	Relative served in period 1660–1760				Relative served in period 1702–1714			
	Rank of officer				Rank of officer			
	High	Middle	Low	Total	High	Middle	Low	Total
Great-grandparent	0	3	0	3	0	1	0	1
Great-grandchild	1	1	0	2	0	1	0	1
Grandparent	4	13	1	18	0	1	1	2
Grandchild	5	3	4	12	0	1	1	2
Father/mother	13/3	59/11	46/3	118/17	2/2	18/2	30/1	50/5
Son/daughter	17/3	35/8	49/1	101/12	5/1	14/4	27/1	46/6
Brother/sister	8/4	32/7	16/2	56/13	2/3	21/3	12/0	35/6
Husband/wife	9/11	9/11	7/8	25/30	4/6	6/6	6/4	16/16
Uncle/aunt	9/0	29/4	2/0	40/4	1/0	6/2	1/0	8/2
Nephew/niece	3/2	17/8	5/0	25/10	2/2	5/5	2/0	9/7
Cousin	10	25	1	36	10	18	0	28
Fr/mr-in-law	21/5	19/3	9/1	49/9	5/2	9/1	8/0	22/3
Son/dr-in-law	10/3	10/0	8/0	28/3	4/0	4/0	6/0	14/0
Bro/sis-in-law	14/7	28/11	8/0	50/18	9/4	14/6	7/1	30/11

SOURCES: See Appendix B.

daughter Jane Grace; and finally, at her death, to her husband, Nathaniel Blackerby.[72]

The most remarkable example of family connection in general and marital connection in particular at the court of Queen Anne was the vast clan headed by Sarah Churchill, Duchess of Marlborough. Sarah herself rose from a relatively subordinate position (maid of honor to Anne's stepmother, Mary, Duchess of York) to engross the three most prestigious and lucrative court positions open to a woman: groom of the stole, mistress of the robes, and keeper of the privy purse. Her husband, John, himself the son of a clerk of the greencloth, rose from the equally humble post of page of honor to serve first James II and then William III as a lord of the bedchamber. Two of their daughters, Ladies Godolphin and Sunderland, were ladies of Anne's bedchamber. The former was married to one of the Queen's cofferers, later groom of the stole to George I; the latter's husband also served Anne's successor as groom of the stole. Both Lords Godolphin and Sunderland were themselves the sons of former court officers who had gone on to bigger things.[73] A third Churchill daughter, the Countess of Bridgewater, was married to Prince George's master of the horse and a future lord of the bedchamber to George I. The fourth daughter, the Duchess of Montagu, was married to Anne's second master of the great wardrobe, himself the son of the first. Through John's sister, Arabella, the Churchills were in-laws to Charles Godfrey, successively master of the jewel house and a clerk of the greencloth to Queen Anne. Two of his daughters had served as maids of honor to Anne as Princess. One married Edmund Dunch, her master of the household; the other married Hugh Boscawen, comptroller of the household to George I. Sarah procured a second clerkship at the greencloth for another brother-in-law, Edward Griffith. A third clerkship went to John Charlton, steward to her son-in-law Sunderland. She may have been instrumental in getting her uncle, Martin Lister, named a physician in ordinary. Finally, as she would long ruefully remember, it was the Duchess of Marlborough who first introduced her impecunious cousins, the Hills, into royal service, with eventual dire consequences. It is little wonder that contemporaries remarked upon the Duke's "great appetite for offices for his relations."[74] The Marlboroughs' efforts on behalf of those outside their immediate family circle must also be recalled.[75]

The Churchill connection was paramount, but a number of other families maintained a significant presence at court over an equally long period of time. These included the Granvilles[76] and Villiers,[77] most numerous at the Tory-Royalist courts of Anne's father and uncle; and the Cavendishes[78] and Russells,[79] especially common at the Whig-Republican courts of her brother-in-law and, to a lesser extent, of her two Hanoverian successors. Some families were particularly associated with certain departments, such as the Blands, Dummers, Elringtons, and the Montagus at the great wardrobe;[80] the Centlivres, Chambers, Murrays, Parsons, Prices, Salters, and Webbs below stairs;[81] or the ten Killigrews (four under Anne) and nine Russells (again four during Anne's reign) who inhabited the chamber.[82] The society most dominated by kinship was undoubtedly that of the Queen's watermen. Under Anne there were 21 families with two watermen each, including the Endfields and Hills with three apiece and the Warners with five. Between 1660 and 1760 there were four Hills, seven Masons, and seven Warners. These three families supplied all seven masters of the barges from 1614 to 1736.[83]

Family connection was obviously an important factor for entry into court service, as it was for entry to parliament and many government offices. It was no accident that contemporaries sometimes referred to the staff of the royal household as the Queen's "family." Anne herself acknowledged the importance of kinship when, in 1703, she assured Sarah that though the Earl of Bridgewater (Sarah's son-in-law) was "no Solomon," she would nevertheless prefer him to the head of the Prince's stables: "Y^t^ wch weighs most with me is ye neare relation he has to my dear dear Mrs Freeman."[84] Given the importance of tradition in the life of a court and the absence of formal training and admissions requirements, it made some sense to prefer those whose families had proved themselves by loyal and competent past service. Court families tended to raise their offspring with some knowledge of the protocol, usage, and taboos of the household departments they administered. Moreover, the practice of granting court office to the descendants of a previous officer relieved the Crown of the responsibility to provide pensions for retired servants or their dependents. Finally, the court's reliance upon family connection for its personnel was entirely appropriate to what was, after all, the personal household—the "family"—

of a hereditary monarch and the apex of a social system founded upon birth and marital alliances.

In conclusion, exclusivity, favoritism, and nepotism were entirely in keeping with contemporary expectations of a court. Indeed, when allowances are made for those expectations, the variety of criteria used to fill different offices, as noted above, make a great deal of sense. It must have seemed altogether appropriate that only those offices demanding technical expertise be filled by individuals with long experience and good professional reputations; that service posts be filled by those who knew how to serve; ceremonial posts by those who would do most credit to the ceremony; honorary posts by those who either deserved or would feel obliged by the honor; great offices with minimal duties by those with political ambitions or more "interest" than ability; posts near the Queen's person by those whom she liked; and places of all kinds and at all levels of her court "family" by the kin of those who had proved their loyalty to her real family over several generations. An emphasis upon family connection was particularly appropriate to an institution dominated by precedent and tradition, yet lacking a formal procedure for instilling them. Under Anne, these criteria resulted in a comfortable and relatively private environment for the Queen, a reasonably efficient administration for her house, and the best moral and social model for the nation in several reigns at a time when many thought standards in these areas to be slipping.

But there was another, still more important role for a court, more often articulated by historians than by contemporaries: that of attracting and obliging the political, financial, social, and cultural leaders of the nation. In this, Anne was only marginally successful. Room was found at court for some important political, business, and cultural figures, as has been seen. But often, these filled honorary or near sinecure positions. In subsequent chapters it will be shown that the Queen's failure to make more demands on their time and pay them more frequently and adequately caused them to center their efforts outside the court. The one significant exception, the Marlborough connection, undoubtedly involved a rising family, significant in many areas. But the unique favor shown them and their clients in the first half of the reign only served to highlight the Queen's apparent lack of generosity to rivals. In general, the favor shown to old families with long-standing court connections when filling the majority of household posts tended to bring the same families to court again and again, without regard for their current importance in the new world growing beyond St. James's. The result was a population of solid, respectable, and trustworthy courtiers that was (apart from the Churchills and a few other great officers) only intermittently and tenuously connected with the emerging political, professional, cultural, or social elites of the early eighteenth century.

CHAPTER V

Work, Emoluments, and Tenure

Having identified the Queen's household servants, this study must now determine the conditions of their service: its nature, difficulty, duration, and reward. At first glance, this information would appear to be readily available for any court of the period, for there exist numerous contemporary establishments, ordinances, accounts, and guidebooks that purport to describe in great detail precisely what each household officer did and how each was rewarded for doing it.[1] However, as has been noted in previous chapters, such "official" sources can rarely be taken at face value. Historians (and some contemporaries) have long suspected that most household posts were near-sinecures. Administrative historians in particular have also been aware that the established salaries of court officers were only the tip of an indeterminately sized emoluments iceberg that included nonestablished fees, perquisites, grants of money, land, and favor, and other, less tangible compensations. As with so much else at court, practice rather than prescription, usage rather than directive, custom rather than legislation is the thing.

The present chapter, therefore, goes beyond official sources in an attempt to determine where the balance lay between practice and prescription and between work and reward generally for the Queen's servants. It seeks to determine not only how hard they worked and how well they were paid, but what variables in this equation attracted them to and held them at court. We shall see that the terms of the equation varied considerably from rank to rank and office to office. In general, it will be argued that most household posts were not sinecures and that some at the middling and lower ranks involved a great deal of hard work. However, it will also be seen that deputization, duplication, and rotation allowed the Queen's household servants a certain amount of discretion in choosing how often or how hard to work.

In fact, this flexibility, along with other intangibles such as prestige and security of tenure, may have meant more to most household servants than the material rewards of their service. Below the level of the great officers, where those rewards were in decline but still impressive, the Crown's decaying financial position left salaries moderate and often poorly paid or unpaid. A number of attempts to calculate the value of nonestablished fees and perquisites suggest that, despite some spectacular exceptions, these were generally too modest to make much of a difference in the sometimes dire financial situations of most household servants. In short, the present chapter will argue that court office could not, by and large, make one rich or catapult one into a higher socioeconomic rank. This in turn suggests that the question "Why did men and women want to serve at the court of Queen Anne?" ought to be rephrased thus: "What sorts of men and women wanted, and were able, to serve there?" The answer to this question should illuminate some of the findings of the previous chapter.

Attendance and Work

Official documents convey an impression of the court as a vast and well-regulated machine every one of whose 1,000 or so places furthered the ceremonial or domestic life of the monarch. However, as noted in Chapter 2, the unofficial correspondence of courtiers and others sometimes suggests otherwise. Sir John Clerk of Penicuik, an occasional visitor to court in his capacity as a commissioner for the Union from the summer of 1706 to the spring of 1707, noted of the Queen that "no Court Attenders ever came near her," and of her summer residence at Kensington that it was "a perfect solitude": "I never saw any body attending there but some of her Guards in the outer Rooms, with one at most of the Gentlemen of her Bedchamber."[2]

Clerk's mistaken belief that Queen Anne had male bedchamber attendants reminds us that his was not the practiced eye of a courtier. Nevertheless, his general impression receives some confirmation from the testimony of others who knew the court well. For example, in the wake of Guiscard's attempt on Harley's life in the spring of 1711, Lord Chamberlain Shrewsbury, who had by his own admission "lived in four Courts," worried that the Queen might be subject to similar attempts "for want of attendance."[3] Since low attendance implies sinecurism, this sort of evidence has led historians to disregard the court as a working institution and to depict most offices at the Stuart court as sinecures or near-sinecures.[4]

The issue is in fact complex. It is true that there were a few outright sinecures at court. For example, the keepership of the royal palace at Whitehall continued to pay £550 per annum well past the middle of the eighteenth century despite the fact that the palace itself had burnt down at the beginning of 1698. For most of that time the post was held by Percy Kirke junior, who had succeeded his father as keeper in 1691, at the age of seven. The younger Kirke continued to enjoy the profits of the place, with no apparent inconvenience to an active military career, until his death in 1741.[5] Similarly, the naval officer Philip Cavendish, the diplomat Sir Philip Meadows, the historian James Tyrrel, and the poet William Walsh were all able to add between £33 6*s.* 8*d.* and £155 to their annual incomes for very little attendance or work as sergeant porter, knight marshal, a cupbearer, and gentleman of the horse, respectively. However, the equation between work and its rewards was rather more complicated for the rest of the Queen's servants.

The combination of little or no work and large profit was most closely associated in the contemporary mind with the 30 or so great offices in the household. Thus, when the Earl Poulett concluded his brief career as first lord of the treasury to become lord steward in June 1711, he observed to Sir William Trumbull: "I confess to you one has prepared me to have a most delicious taste of the ease and leisure of the other."[6] Certainly, none of the great household offices, apart from those in the bedchamber, sentenced their holders to frequent attendance or strenuous duties. But technically, the great department head was the ultimate authority, and so personally responsible for the continued functioning of his domain. He was the proper liaison between the Queen and the staff of secretaries and clerks who handled the day-to-day administration of his department. It was his right to approve or reject any departmental policy or appointment not within royal jurisdiction; his signature that had to be obtained on contracts and warrants for matériel; and his own personal estate and reputation that were at stake when departmental accounts came before the exchequer.[7] Finally, every great household officer was expected to turn out in full regalia and give his attendance upon the Queen on great state occasions, such as royal birthdays, funerals, or services of thanksgiving.[8]

Some department heads, such as Lord Chamberlain Kent or the two Montagus (*père et fils*) who served as masters of the great wardrobe, appear to have delegated their authority as much as possible, rarely appearing at court or in the administrative records of their respective departments.[9] It was not uncommon for the vice chamberlain or the lieutenant of the yeomen of the guard to officiate at an ambassadorial entrance or even a royal birthday for their respective superiors.[10] In the case of Lord Chamberlain Shrewsbury or Captain of the Yeomen Townshend, this was necessary because each held an important diplomatic post for a major portion of his period in household office.[11] Lord Steward Buckingham, Comptroller Mansell, and Master of the Buckhounds Wyndham used their offices as convenient and relatively flexible situations from which to pursue higher political ambitions. Finally, and perhaps most commonly, court office at this level could provide worthy but sufficiently undemanding employment for the lazy or incompetent scion of an important family, such as Kent, the Montagus, or Prince George's master of the horse, the Earl of Bridgewater. But other great officers, whether out of a sense of duty, self-importance, or a desire to make as much political capital as possible from their free access to the monarch, seem to have attended assiduously and taken a real interest in the affairs of their departments, most notably Vice Chamberlain Coke, Lord Almoner Sharp, and Master of the Horse Somerset.[12] In short, it was perfectly possible to treat great household office as a sinecure, but such office also afforded wide scope for activity and attendance on the part of those who wished to make use of it.

Anne's two successive grooms of the stole, the Duchesses of Marlborough and Somerset, used this freedom to stay away from the court for long periods of time. But their subordinates, the ten ladies of the bedchamber, formed the one set of great household officers whose personal attendance was regular and indispensable. They were supposed to attend the Queen on a rotating basis, one week at a time. Though allowances had to be made for the Duchess of Ormonde, who accompanied her husband as lord lieutenant of Ireland from mid-1703 to mid-1705, and for the frequent illnesses of the other ladies, one such officer was always in attendance, more during periods of political crisis.[13] Her duties were to assist the Queen at her dressing and meals; to introduce guests into her presence; and, in general, to provide her with aristocratic companionship.[14] In practice, this usually meant long hours standing, either about the chair of state at drawing rooms; in the House of Lords when the Queen sat in on debates; or at the backstairs upon less formal occasions. Only the Queen's passion for gambling provided an occasional opportunity to sit down to a game of bassett, ombre, or picquet.[15] Obviously, boredom and long periods away from one's family were, after the demands upon physical stamina, the greatest liabilities to the post of lady of the Queen's bedchamber. Though the Duchess of Marlborough asserted that Anne "treated her chief ladies and servants as if they had been her equals," it is little wonder that a woman of Mrs. Freeman's attainments found the post "a good deal of trouble & attendance."[16]

The 300 or so officers in the middling ranks of household service may be divided by function into three broad categories: administrators and clerical staff; gentlemen and women waiters in the public rooms, bedchamber, and stables; and artistic and professional personnel. Among the most prestigious and demanding middling places were those of the administrators who, in effect, deputized for the great department heads. These included the lord chamberlain's secretary, the four clerks of the greencloth, the deputy master and clerk of the great wardrobe, the avenor and clerk martial in the stables, and (in much smaller areas of responsibility) the subalmoner and subdean of the chapel. These officers, generally recruited from solid gentry families, were in almost daily contact with their superiors, informing and advising them about appointments, disputes, expenditure, and any other business requiring the authority of a great officer. Where the nominal department head was particularly inactive, middling secretaries and clerks exercised wide discretionary powers to screen petitions, distribute lodgings, discipline subordinates, and order matériel without reference to a higher authority.[17]

These officers must therefore be distinguished from the numerous lesser clerks and yeomen who churned out the endless stream of letters, warrants, ordinances, and accounts required to keep the household's administrative machinery in operation. The latter were rarely of gentry status, and often began their court careers as the personal servants of their respective superiors.[18] A third group, the various sergeants, gentlemen, and clerks nominally in charge of the catering subdepartments below stairs and also technically of middle rank, were meant to have risen either from the ranks of subordinates in the first two cases, or from inferior clerkships in the third. However, with the elimination of most of the great tables under Charles II and the consequent decline in the amount of work performed by their departments, many of these places became virtual sinecures. This allowed the Queen's administrators to eliminate two such posts and amalgamate another five into two on the establishment of 1702. It also increasingly allowed the Crown to fill the remainder with men of superior birth from outside the department, a trend that continued after Anne's death.[19]

The gentlemen waiters of the chamber and stables formed the largest single bloc of middling posts at court. Most had retained their time-honored, if somewhat undemanding, duties well into the eighteenth century. The major exception, the 48 gentlemen of the privy chamber, had lost nearly all of their duties and corresponding rewards by 1702.[20] There remained on the chamber staff around 220 gentlemen ushers, grooms, sewers, pages, gentlemen pensioners, and yeomen of the guard.[21] Their primary function was to open doors, light the way for visitors, and generally to provide the public rooms with a gentle or martial presence. This work probably involved more tedium than exertion. A typical day in the public rooms was supposed to begin between 8:00 and 9:00 in the morning and conclude at 9:00 in the evening (later on ceremonial occasions), with time off in the afternoon for a meal.[22] The intervening hours were most likely spent on foot, wearing stiff clothing in drafty or overheated rooms, amid company hardly likely to speak to a mere gentleman usher or groom.

Fortunately for those concerned, attendance was divided up by weeks, months, or quarters (depending upon the individual society), so that only a fraction of the chamber servants was in waiting at a given time and few were required to wait for more than a quarter out of every year. Thus, a visitor to St. James's when the court was in residence should have encountered 40 yeomen of the guard lining the great staircase and guard chamber, with a yeoman usher to open the door to the latter. At the opposite end of the guard chamber would have stood a gentleman usher, quarter waiter, to open the door and, if necessary, light the way into the presence chamber. This room was supposed to be lined by 2 sergeants at arms and between 12 and 40 gentlemen pensioners on Sundays and other special occasions. At all times, the far end of the presence would be inhabited by a groom whose duty was to open the door and light the way into the privy chamber. At the far end of the latter stood 2 gentlemen ushers of the privy chamber, who provided the same service into the drawing room.

Both the privy chamber and the "withdrawing room," as the drawing room was sometimes still called, were relatively recent additions to the architectural and social topography of the court.[23] As a consequence of this, the gentleman usher of the privy chamber was supreme in both. Otherwise, the work of the public rooms was coordinated from the presence by the gentleman usher, daily waiter, in attendance. This officer, subordinate only to the lord and vice chamberlains, undertook a wide range of duties, including the swearing-in of new chamber officials; the supervision of the various inferior grooms, pages, chamber keepers, and firemakers who delivered messages and kept the public rooms clean and warm; and the regulation of the social and sartorial standards of visitors to those rooms.[24] Visitors to the backstairs should have been greeted at the bottom by a page and at the top by a lady or a woman of the bedchamber.[25] Also in ostensible attendance at the backstairs was an equerry of the stables, ready to accompany the Queen's coach on horseback at a moment's notice if she chose to take the air.[26]

The historian Tindall maintained that Queen Anne "required a strict attendance from all persons in their respective stations."[27] *Pace* Clerk and Shrewsbury, whose views were noted earlier, most of the administrative and literary evidence left behind by court officers suggests that, below the level of the great officers, this was generally the case. Only once, in December 1704, was Anne's lord chamberlain forced to issue an order demanding the attendance of the chamber servants in their proper waitings.[28] Only once, in May 1708, was a chamber servant suspended for failing to attend; even this appears to have been a mistake, for the officer in question was soon after restored to his post with full pay.[29] These figures compare favorably with those for Anne's immediate predecessors and successor, whose administrators were, on the whole, less watchful than hers.[30] Another official index of attendance, the payment of riding wages by the treasurer of the chamber, indicates that even at her "out-of-town" residences of Hampton Court, Kensington, and Windsor, the Queen insisted upon a full complement of chamber servants.[31] Early in the reign, this even included one each of the cupbearers, carvers, and sewers, whose sole remaining function by the later Stuart period was to be present at court "that so strangers and men of quality . . . [would] not finde it empty."[32] Finally, the correspondence of middling chamber and stables personnel, most notably that of the equerry Peter Wentworth, makes clear that one's week, month, or quarter of waiting was to be taken quite seriously.[33]

However, while the Queen expected to be attended by the proper number of officers in all stations, she did not necessarily require that each of her officers attend equally. In the household below stairs, where the work was generally most strenuous and the pay too poor to permit retirement, she sometimes allowed servants who were too young, too old, or too ill to perform their duties to name a deputy from among their fellow officers.[34] In the chamber and stables, where middling servants frequently had other posts or interests outside the court, she often tolerated less formal arrangements. Thus, when the mother of Richard Arundell, a page of honor, requested that he be allowed to delay his period of attendance, the Queen wrote to Sarah, "It is certainly very reasonable she shou'd please her self, onely she must send to one of the other pages to wait for her son."[35]

Peter Wentworth sometimes waited for months at a time on behalf of fellow equerries serving in the military or diplomatic corps.[36] The extent to which such arrangements could become institutionalized is indicated by a list of the grooms of the great chamber and pages of the presence drawn up for a new lord chamberlain in 1685. It distinguishes between those who "have constantly wayted" (ten grooms and two pages) and those who "live in ye Country & Seldome wayte" (four grooms and two pages).[37] Recent work on the chapel royal under Queen Anne suggests that here, too, there was a small core of active waiters and others who, for reasons of age or distance, treated their posts as near sinecures.[38] Similar arrangements must have been made for those Churchill servants in the robes and bedchamber who accompanied the Duke of Marlborough on campaign, and for James Vernon junior and Horatio Walpole, whose diplomatic posts prevented attendance for years at a time as a groom of the bedchamber to Prince George and a corporal to the yeomen of the guard, respectively.[39] A post in the diplomatic service may help to explain the most remarkable example of Queen Anne's flexibility about attendance, that of Francis Coleman of her woodyard. Not only was Coleman nominally pursuing a degree at Cambridge during the period of his court employment, but the admissions register of Corpus Christi College lists him as "Groom of the Woodyard, and Resident at Vienna."[40]

The most important and hardworking of Anne's servants were the four women or dressers of the bedchamber. Though this was a middling post, the women chosen to fill it were often of inferior gentry status or lower, such as Abigail Masham. Unlike the aristocratic ladies of the bedchamber, the Queen's dressers were, in effect, personal maids, performing a wide variety of indispensable but menial tasks about her, known collectively as the "royal body service." An account of those tasks, the only such description by a contemporary household servant, survives in the words of Mrs. Masham, as conveyed through her friend Arbuthnot:

> The bedchamber-woman came in to waiting before the queen's prayers, which was before her majesty was dressed. The queen often shifted in a morning: if her majesty shifted at noon, the bedchamber-lady being by, the bedchamber-woman gave the shift to the lady without any ceremony, and the lady put it on. Sometimes, likewise, the bedchamber-woman gave the fan to the lady in the same manner; and this was all that the bedchamber-lady did about the queen at her dressing.
>
> When the queen washed her hands, the page of the back-stairs brought and set down upon a side-table the basin and ewer; then the bedchamber woman set it before the queen, and knelt on the other side of the table over-against the queen, the bedchamber-lady only looking on. The bedchamber-woman poured the water out of the ewer upon the queen's hands.
>
> The bedchamber-woman pulled on the queen's gloves, when she could not do it herself.
>
> The page of the back-stairs was called in to put on the queen's shoes.
>
> When the queen dined in public, the page reached the glass to the bechamber-woman, and she to the lady in waiting.
>
> The bedchamber-woman brought the chocolate, and gave it without kneeling.
>
> In general the bedchamber-woman had no dependence on the lady of the bedchamber."[41]

The involvement of the lady, woman, and page of the bedchamber in such routine tasks as putting on the Queen's gloves and shoes owed as much to Anne's poor health as to the proprieties of the body service. The duty of nursing her when she was ill fell largely upon the shoulders of her dressers. During the early years of the reign, the brunt was borne by Beata Danvers and Margery Fielding, who had served Anne since her infancy. But by mid-reign, they themselves had grown infirm, and the increasingly demanding task of looking after the Queen was assumed by Abigail Hill.[42] As Anne's most recent biographer, Edward Gregg, has pointed out, whatever Abigail's possible political significance, it was as a nurse that the Queen chiefly valued her. Anne rarely allowed her to go out of waiting, and frequently required her to stay up all night, or at least sleep in the next room. After her marriage to Samuel Masham in the summer of 1707, Abigail continued to wait as often as her own poor health and frequent pregnancies would allow.[43] When she herself was unable to do the duty, her sister Alice did so. Indeed, it was in order to lighten the load on the recently married Masham that the younger sister was preferred to a dresser's place in September 1707. Since the marriage was supposed to have been kept a secret from Abigail's former employer, the Duchess of Marlborough, Anne justified the appointment to her groom of the stole by arguing, rightly enough, that her faithful nurse was overworked in any case: "For tho Hill does not complain I see her soe very much fatigued every morning y^{t} she goes out of waiting."[44]

Anne's poor health also made great demands upon her medical staff. One and often more of her physicians attended daily even when she was in the best of health. When she was ill, the whole society, as well as her apothecary, Daniel Malthus, might be summoned to the royal sickbed at a moment's notice and for hours on end.[45] The Queen's infirmities, coupled with her straitened circumstances, ensured that other middling and lower specialty posts, such as those of the artists and musicians, required little attendance by mid-reign. One nearly contemporary guide book states frankly, "[The musicians] attend at all Balls, Bith [*sic*] Days etc., when they are commanded; but their Places are liable to little Trouble, and [are] no other than a sort of Sine Cure."[46] On the other hand, the Queen's piety and love of sacred music caused her to demand the regular attendance of her chapel-royal vocalists even at her "country" residences.[47] The former quality also seems to have ensured that each of the Queen's 48 chaplains in ordinary fulfilled his annual week of attendance.[48] Finally, the demands of the war and following peace ensured that by the end of the reign the messengers of the chamber—really diplomatic couriers with law-enforcement capabilities—had "been more employed within these three years than in thirty years before," according to Secretary Bolingbroke.[49]

Unlike the Queen's middling servants, who had largely lost their counterparts in the great aristocratic houses of England, the work of most of her 500 to 600 menial servants and tradesmen was virtually indistinguishable from that of equivalent positions serving the nobility or the general public. The function of the Queen's cooks, confectioners, and scullery personnel, her necessary women and laundresses, her footmen and grooms, purveyors and tradesmen was to keep the Queen's house clean, warm, furnished, and well lit, and its inhabitants clothed, fed, mobile, and entertained. This was the same work that many of them performed for additional income when out of waiting, either in private houses or for the public at large (see Table 4.3, sub "Breakdown by Occupation"). This plurality of employment was made possible, as at middling levels, by the duplication of office and the rotation of attendance in most subdepartments—features unique to court service—and probably by the widespread use of unofficial deputies against the Queen's wishes, especially below stairs.[50]

In summary, most great offices allowed their holders wide discretion in deciding how much to attend or involve themselves in the day-to-day administration of their respective departments. Such administration was generally the province of middling clerks and secretaries. Below the level of the great officers, there were few outright sinecures at court. However, duplication of office, rotation of attendance, and occasional unauthorized deputization within most subdepartments and societies lightened work and made prolonged absence by some holders possible. The work of these bodies was generally performed by a cadre of habitual waiters, like Abigail Masham and Peter Wentworth. As a result, though all officers did not wait equally, at least one officer of each type was in attendance at any given time.

In light of this attendance, it may be asked why observers as diverse as Clerk and Shrewsbury appear to have complained of its lack. The answer probably lies in the difference between what contemporaries called "close waiting," that is, the formal attendance and performance of duty by weeks, months, or quarters required of household officers as described above; and the less formal, more social sort of attendance at court that anyone of sufficient birth might give. The latter was the sort of waiting that Sir Benjamin Bathurst, treasurer to the Duke of York, described when, in 1683, he spent a day with the King at Winchester "walking up and down and giving [his] attendance at Court."[51] The first kind of attendance was, as we have seen, carefully observed under Queen Anne. But without the second, the flocking to court of great numbers of the nobility and gentry, her house would nevertheless have presented a barren appearance, especially to an observer who knew little of the court, such as Clerk, or who had known it in better days, such as Shrewsbury. In Chapter 1, it was noted that the informal attendance of the nobility and gentry had indeed declined toward the end of the seventeenth century. As will be noted in Chapter 7, it continued to do so for most of Anne's reign owing to the diminishing financial, political, social, and cultural opportunities of her court.

Emoluments: High Officers

As with work due, the rewards of office as calculated in official establishments and guide books can rarely be taken at face value.[52] These show a steady rise in the wages and boardwages of most offices between 1660 and 1702. Those at the highest level, in particular, increased in apparent value two- and three-fold, rising from a few hundred pounds to between £1,000 and £1,400 per annum for most department heads and lords of the bedchamber, £2,000 for the master of the great wardrobe, and £3,000 per annum for the groom of the stole.[53] However, most of these increases in established fees came in compensation for the loss of tables of hospitality, fees of poundage, and other perquisites that were, more often than not, of even greater value.[54] For example, in January 1680 Sir William Boreman, a clerk of the greencloth, calculated the past and present value of Lord Steward Ormonde's place, with a view to its possible sale. Boreman concluded that though it had paid only £100 in salary under the early Stuarts, Ormonde's post had actually been worth an additional £3,000 per annum in perquisites and fees, not counting proceeds from the sale of office in the lord steward's gift. But the retrenchment of tables in 1663 and subsequent economies had reduced this figure to "less than a quarter" of this amount by the time of Boreman's writing.[55] Contemporary estimates of the value of tables alone under Charles I suggest that he was exaggerating only slightly.[56] Similarly, a modern calculation of the value of poundage in the great wardrobe indicates that its elimination for a fixed salary in 1669 resulted in a net loss to the master of that department of £500 per annum.[57] It is probable that most of the great offices experienced a similar decline in value.

Even where the financial compensation offered by the Crown was not unreasonable,[58] the attempt to reduce the emoluments of the great officers to fixed monetary salaries left them almost entirely dependent upon the health and dispatch of the royal treasury, both of which left much to be desired under the later Stuarts. As early as 1673 the Duke of Ormonde was compelled to sell "his uncertain pension of a thousand pounds a year as Gentleman of the Bedchamber." As we have seen, less than a decade later the retrenchment of 1679 caused him to consider abandoning his other court post in the same way.[59] During the lean years of William's reign, the greedy and litigious Earl of Montagu obtained a renewal of his patent as master of the great wardrobe that allowed him to resume his fees of poundage in the event of nonpayment of his established salary.[60] Under the later Stuarts, the sale of inferior offices was a partial compensation for the great officers' loss of fees and perquisites and the uncertainty of their fixed salaries. But, as noted in Chapter 2, Queen Anne effectively closed off this avenue of reward, or at least made it much more difficult of access.[61]

Admittedly, Anne's financial situation, though serious, was never so desperate as that of Charles II or William III at their nadirs. Consequently, her ladies of the bedchamber were generally paid on time, and the rest of her great officers did not experience significant arrears until the later years of the reign.[62] But when arrears did begin to accumulate, the reforms of the later seventeenth century left most such officers exposed, without an alternative set of fees and perquisites to fall back on. Moreover, even when those salaries were promptly paid, they were finite, and so represented a limitation, unknown to previous generations, on the amount of wealth that great household office could generate.

Some idea of the extent of the loss may be gathered from the value of the two remaining great offices whose holders were still allowed to take fees of poundage on the business transacted in their departments: the cofferer of the household and the treasurer of the chamber. The cofferer took 6*d*. in the pound. The average annual expenditure of the household below stairs under Queen Anne was £89,828. Omitting the £6,860 paid annually in salaries to the officers of the greencloth and not subject to fees, this should have yielded to the cofferer about £2,074 per annum, over four times his established salary of £500 per annum.[63] The treasurer of the chamber took his fees on a scale that varied according to the size of the bill or salary being paid, and that averaged between 4 and 5 percent. At an average annual chamber expenditure of £28,941 under Queen Anne this should have yielded him between £1,100 and £1,500 per annum. This was between three and a half and five times his established salary of £314 1*s*. 4*d*.[64] Thus, each of these officers could expect to make at least twice as much as the majority of their colleagues on fixed household incomes. If we recall that the amount of business transacted in all household departments was considerably greater under Charles II and William III and again under George I,[65] it is clear that the elimination of nonestablished sources of income for the great offices seriously compromised their potential value.

The monetary fees that remained to them were of negligible value.[66] More considerable were a number of material perquisites paid only once. For example, the lords chamberlain and steward, the treasurer and comptroller of the household, and the master of the horse were, along with other cabinet-level officers and ambassadors, allowed 1,000 ounces of plate out of the jewel house, fashioned to its recipients' specifications. The plate itself was worth only £400, but its fashioning, upon which no limit was set, generally cost the Crown between £2,900 and £3,000.[67] Legally, this plate remained the property of the Crown and was supposed to be returned when the recipient left office. However, the treasury's poor record of payment of established salaries under the later Stuarts led most of the great officers to claim their plate as a permanent souvenir of their time in royal service. While there were periodic attempts to reclaim old plate, in most cases the officer in question either obtained a royal discharge or simply waited the treasury out.[68]

Additionally, some of the Queen's great officers were entitled to certain of her personal effects after her death. Her groom of the stole had a right to her old clothes and bedchamber furnishings, including the royal deathbed. In the wake of Anne's demise in 1714, the Duchess of Somerset received both furnishings and the sum of £3,000 for goods that the new King wished to retain.[69] The lord chamberlain was allowed used mourning cloth that had hung in the public rooms. This he generally distributed among the inferior servants of the chamber and bedchamber, as Lord Chamberlain Shrewsbury carefully put it, "as a gift from me to them & not of any right or fee belong$^{n.}$ to them."[70] Finally, the master of the horse was allowed his pick of any of the deceased monarch's horses, carriages, and equipage, though the Crown was saved this expense at Anne's death, the mastership having been in commission since 1712.[71]

By far the most substantial and sought-after nonmonetary perquisite attached to great household office was the accommodation granted to most such officers in at least one and usually more of the Queen's residences.[72] For example, the Duchess of Marlborough had lodgings at Hampton Court, Kensington, St. James's, and Windsor Castle in addition to the lodge in Windsor Great Park, which came with her rangership there. Each of Anne's four successive lords steward, none of whom was a particular favorite, nevertheless received lodgings in each of the above palaces except St. James's, where it would have been superfluous for most great officers. These lodgings generally consisted of elaborate suites of rooms fully worthy of their inhabitants' noble status and life-style. The groom of the stole's apartments at Kensington consisted of "10 rooms & Closetts"; those of the lord steward at Windsor, "3 Rooms one Closet and Stoole Room, w$^{th.}$ 2 little Rooms w$^{th.}$ out Chimneys."[73] Others had private kitchens and accommodation for servants. The convenience of such arrangements is obvious. A great officer would have had to spend several hundreds per annum to rent comparable accommodation in an equally fashionable location. It is therefore understandable that the distribution of lodgings in the royal palaces was a frequent source of dispute among the great household

TABLE 5.1
Grants and Favors to Anne's Household Officers

	Rank of officer			
	High	Middle	Low	Total
Total number of officers receiving grants	42	87	88	217
Above as a % of total number of household officers[a]	76.4	16.0	9.5	14.2
Breakdown by Type of Grant or Favor				
Pension upon retirement	2	11	29	42
Pension upon decease, to surviving family	1	7	38	46
Pension held concurrently with household post	11	20	2	33
Sinecure	20	16	5	41
Land (grant or lease)	6	11	0	17
Royal bounty	16	18	10	44
Christening plate	11	15	1	27
Furniture	0	5	0	5
Misc. gift	3	2	0	5
Misc. favor	2	7	4	13
Total number of grants and favors	72	112	89	273

SOURCES: See Appendix B, *C.T.B.*, vols. I–XXXI, passim, and LS 13/38–50.
[a]I.e., 55 high officers, 544 middling officers, 926 low officers = 1,525 total officers.

officers;[74] that the acquisition of the best ones appears to have been a sign of royal favor;[75] and that, once lodgings were acquired, lavish sums were spent by their occupants to make them even more habitable.[76]

If the size and quality of a great officer's accommodations were an index of royal favor, the accommodations themselves were a potential means of cultivating that favor through convenient access to the royal person. No doubt this happened. However, the grants or favors enjoyed by roughly 77 percent of the Queen's great household officers (Table 5.1) must not be taken as direct evidence of it. Most turn out to have been made by one of Anne's predecessors. For example, all but three of the awards of land or leases at preferred rates enjoyed by the Queen's great officers were made prior to 1702.[77] In fact, the lavish Crown grants of the 1660s and the sale of fee farm rents in the 1670s left the last Stuart with precious little land to give away. According to the Duchess of Marlborough, "At the Queen's accession to the government she used to lament to me that, the Crown being impoverished by former grants, she wanted the power her predecessors had enjoyed to reward faithful servants."[78] Moreover, the furor over William's Irish grants caused parliament to include clauses in the Act of Settlement of 1701 and the Civil List Act of 1702 limiting royal initiative on the alienation of Crown lands.[79] In the end, Anne's only large, outright gift of land to a courtier was that of Woodstock Manor to the Duke of Marlborough in 1706, hardly a direct result of the access or favor enjoyed by her groom of the stole.[80]

Most of the largest pensions enjoyed by Anne's great household officers had likewise been bestowed prior to 1702. Two had gone to natural sons of Charles II: £5,350 per annum out of the excise and post office to the Duke of Northumberland, Anne's keeper of Hampton Court Palace; and £2,800 out of various sources to the Duke of St. Albans, captain of the gentlemen pensioners. Her treasurer of the household, Lord Lansdowne, inherited £3,000 per annum out of the Duchy of Cornwall from his uncle, the Earl of Bath, Charles II's groom of the stole. Less spectacularly, the Queen's most senior bedchamber lady and the widow of an old Royalist, Anne, Lady Frescheville, had been awarded a pension of £500 per annum by Charles. Finally, Charles Godfrey, successively master of the Queen's jewel house and a clerk of the greencloth, received £1,000 per annum out of the secret service. This sum had originally been awarded to his wife, Arabella née Churchill, by James II, whose mistress she had been.[81]

In contrast, Queen Anne's own grants, apart from a pension of £2,000 per annum collected retroactively out of the privy purse by the Duchess of Marlborough, were relatively modest in scale. As Princess or Queen she awarded annual pensions of £600 (later raised to £1,000) to Lady Fitzharding as former governess to the Duke of Gloucester, and £400 to Edward Griffith, a clerk of the greencloth and faithful former servant of Prince George.[82] Bishops Compton and Sharp received individual payments of royal bounty money ranging up to £180, but this was almost certainly intended for distribution as charity.[83] Finally, eleven great officers took advantage of a custom whereby the Queen awarded plate worth between £25 and £100 (depending on the social rank of the recipients) to the parents of a child she had been asked to christen.[84] Though Sarah later claimed that Queen Anne had "no native generosity,"[85] the moderate size and number of these awards surely owed as much to the Crown's straitened financial circumstances as they did to the frugality of its wearer.

In summary, great household office was not a source of great fortune. However, it was still capable of providing a substantial, if not always dependable, supplementary income in return for a small investment of time and trouble. For example, the lord chamberlain could expect to make an average of £1,315 per annum in wages, boardwages, livery, and fees of honor. This was his reward for as little attendance as he cared to give; perhaps £150 per annum in fees; and the expense of entertaining, which all great officers were expected to incur.[86] This expense was greatly mitigated by the possession of palace lodgings, and was a regular part of aristocratic life in any case. It is true that arrears of salary of up to a year and a quarter were common toward the end of the reign, and that department heads occasionally found themselves having to dip into their own pockets to keep their offices running.[87] But the £3,400 worth of plate that most kept upon departing from royal service should have made up for any shortfall on the part of the Crown.

It should also be noted that a well-paying sinecure, pension, or occasional gift could double or treble the established income from great household office. Lady Fitzharding's pension, when combined with her husband's salaries and fees as treasurer of the chamber and a teller of the exchequer, yielded them anywhere from £2,500 to £3,300 per annum.[88] The comparable figure for the Duke of St. Albans was £3,800; that for the Duke and Duchess of Somerset almost £4,300.[89] The Duchess of Marlborough was the most prosperous of the Queen's servants, her places and pension yielding an average of at least £7,600 per annum before fees and taxes.[90] Admittedly, this was merely a drop in the very deep bucket of £60,000 per annum that the Marlboroughs, together, are supposed to have enjoyed from the Crown at the height of their power.[91] Further, with or without bonuses, the salaries quoted above are still fairly low in comparison to the £10,000 that Edward Chamberlayne thought to be the average annual income of a typical peer.[92] Nevertheless, it should not surprise us to find that even with its diminished luster, the unique combination of light work and emoluments of over £1,000 per annum rendered great household office attractive even to those who appear to have needed it least. Of the seven peers (excluding the Marlboroughs) generally acknowledged to be the wealthiest in England during the first quarter of the eighteenth century (Beaufort, Bedford, and Newcastle at over £30,000 per annum; Devonshire, Ormonde, Somerset, and Lord Brooke at over £20,000 per annum), four at one time or another either were at Anne's court themselves or had a spouse there (Beaufort, Devonshire, Ormonde, and Somerset), while a fifth (Newcastle) solicited to be there.[93]

Finally, it should be noted that for men such as this, a white or a gold staff might have a value beyond that of mere money.[94] The prestige of great household office alone may have been enough for nonentities from important families, such as Bridgewater or Kent. For those of greater ability or electoral significance, like the Dukes of Buckingham, Devonshire, Shrewsbury, and Somerset, the Earl of Jersey or Sir Edward Seymour, it could still provide sufficient portfolio for a seat in the cabinet.[95] Prior to Anne's reign, politicians in decline such as the Earls of Arlington and Sunderland found the household a convenient refuge from places of "business" and political exposure. Under Anne, the Dukes of Buckingham and Shrewsbury, Viscount Townshend, and Sir William Wyndham found their court posts equally convenient starting points from which to aspire to places of more serious business or political significance.[96] In each case, the unique, if diminished, attractions of great household office enabled the Queen to satisfy an important, useful, or ambitious—if not always able—member of the aristocracy without subjecting him to the responsibility, the drudgery, or the public scrutiny of a real "place of business."

Emoluments: Middling Officers

Unlike those of their superiors, the established emoluments of the Queen's middling servants varied greatly in size. At the top, vying with the great officers, the four clerks of the greencloth had in 1703 been given raises to £938 per annum in compensation for their loss of fees. But below the clerk of the great wardrobe, paid £300 per annum, and the clerks of the kitchen, paid £250 per annum, most household clerks received salaries of between £50 and £100. For inferior clerks, the hope of rising to a higher salary through the "Ancient Order of Succession" grew ever dimmer under the later Stuarts.[97] Among the gentlemen waiters in the chamber, bedchamber, and stables, those who served the monarch personally, generally members of the latter two departments, did best. Women of the bedchamber received £500 per annum; equerries and maids of honor, £300 per annum; and pages of honor, £156 per annum. Those who waited in the public rooms, at a distance, did less well. Their salaries ranged from £200 per annum for the gentlemen ushers of the privy chamber, down to a perfunctory £33 6*s*. 8*d*. for the cupbearers, carvers, and sewers, whose attendance was, admittedly, nominal by mid-reign. Those "specialists" who came into close and frequent contact with the Queen also tended to do well. For example, the annual salaries of her physicians ranged between £200 and £400. Others with more occasional duties, such as her Latin secretary, poet laureate, or historiographer, earned between £80 and £200 per annum. However, even more than for the great officers, the vagaries of the Queen's civil list could render such figures almost meaningless. Those few who received their salaries directly at the exchequer, such as her dressers and maids of honor, were generally paid on time. But the vast majority of middling servants who were paid by household paymasters appear to have found themselves in a predicament similar to that of the physician Sir David Hamilton, who reported his salary to have been half a year in arrears by mid-1710, three years in arrears by mid-1713.[98]

While the treasury's program of exchanging fees and perquisites for fixed salaries had not, apart from the clerks of the greencloth, penetrated to this level of officeholding, the nonestablished emoluments that remained to middling household officers were often only of moderate value or otherwise encumbered. For example, most clerks and subclerks in the chamber, great wardrobe, jewel house, and below stairs were allowed either a percentage in kind of the goods that passed through their hands or, far more commonly, poundage on the financial business transacted in their offices. The former was certainly open to abuse, especially when the departmental clerk was also its purveyor.[99] But the latter, when taken at the usual rate of one penny in the pound, tended, with a few spectacular exceptions, to add no more than £20 to £30 per annum to a clerk's established income.[100] Among gentlemen waiters, the four gentlemen ushers, daily waiters, were entitled to collect a fee from officers sworn by them into the chamber, which yielded an average of between £20 and £40 per annum apiece. However, that average obscures the fact that these figures fell off sharply after the initial spate of appointments at the beginning of the reign. Thus, the value of this perquisite declined just as arrears began to mount.[101] Most middling officers had the right to collect fees of honor at varying rates from newly created peers, bishops, baronets, and knights. These should have yielded averages ranging from £20 to £40 per annum, but there is evidence that these fees were becoming increasingly difficult to collect by the late seventeenth century.[102] A few middling servants were still entitled to livery money, again at amounts ranging from a few pounds up to £40 per annum.[103] Finally, all who traveled with the Queen received riding wages. These usually averaged out to about £10 per annum per officer, but indispensable personal servants such as the Queen's physicians, closet keeper, or officers of the robes could make up to £50 per annum in this way.[104] However, it should be remembered that both livery money and riding wages were in the nature of reimbursements for necessary expenses. Both were, moreover, ultimately as dependent upon the state of the royal treasury as wages and board-wages, and were therefore as subject to late payment or nonpayment.

Less tenuous were the provisions and shelter that the Crown still provided for many middling household servants. The Queen's chamber attendants (i.e., cupbearers, carvers, sewers, gentlemen, gentlemen ushers, and grooms of the privy chamber), her chaplains, clerks of the greencloth, maids of honor, and (on hunting days) equerries were all still allowed separate tables twice daily when in attendance.[105] In addition, most of those who lived within palace walls had a daily ration of bread, beer, coal, firewood, and candles.[106] Nearly all of the above-named officers had their own individual apartments, or at least rooms set aside for whoever of their society was in attendance.[107] Some of those who were not lodged at court received lodging money at around £100 per annum, which perhaps gives some idea of the amount to be saved in town rents by those who were provided with free court accommodations.[108] Since most officers at this level had to wait for only a quarter out of every year, some turned their accommodations into a source of outright profit by subletting, usually without permission. Other officers, or their dependents, clung to their court lodgings long after they had departed the Queen's service, again without permission.[109]

It was well that Anne's middling servants exploited the culinary and domestic arrangements of their places, for three other traditional avenues to personal enrichment once open to such officers and still available to their superiors—promotion, pluralism, and the cultivation of royal favor—were being closed off under the last of the Stuarts. It is true that the chaplains' lack of a salary was "abundantly made up to them, by being constantly in the [Queen's] Eye, for spiritual Preferment."[110] But for all other societies of middling household office, promotion to a place of business was virtually unheard of. Promotion within the household was almost as rare. Previous retrenchments, the wholesale removals of 1689, the telescoping of five clerkships into two in 1702, and the increasing preferment of men from outside the department throughout the period left the "Ancient Order of Succession" to clerkships below stairs a tangled wreck. Most other household departments were either too small or too fragmented to have a fully developed structure of promotion for middling officers. As a result, only 52, or 9.6 percent, of Anne's middling officers ever achieved advancement from their initial household posts. On the other hand, because of the relatively undemanding nature of court service, over twice that number—117, or 21.5 percent—of the Queen's middling servants were able to supplement their incomes by means of second posts either within the household or, with equal frequency, in the national administration.[111] Such posts generally were complimentary in function, were adjacent to each other on a ladder of promotion, or involved at least one sinecure such as the keepership of a royal palace, or, outside the household, a seat on a revenue commission. Thus, the Queen's service suffered relatively little for a substantial increase in these servants' income.[112]

In previous reigns, one of the chief attractions of middling court office, for both its holders and their families, had been its ability to bring men and women of very ordinary gentry background into close and frequent contact with the monarch, which in turn provided them with the opportunity to curry royal favor and solicit royal largesse.[113] However, toward the end of the seventeenth century the increasing prominence of the royal bedchamber and closet over the public rooms in the social and domestic life of the monarch tended to limit contact with middling chamber servants.[114] Queen Anne's sex, poor health, and native reclusiveness accelerated this trend, ensuring that she had very little contact with any of her "family" at this level, besides her dressers, pages, physicians, and an occasional equerry. This, along with the Crown's chronic financial problems, helps to explain why only 87, or 16 percent, of her middling household servants were able to turn their access into some tangible evidence of extraordinary royal favor (Table 5.1), almost certainly a lower proportion than in previous reigns. Nearly all of those who were able to do so either came from one of the above societies or had some other, special relationship to the royal family. Thus, most of the twenty middling officers holding pensions concurrently with their household places were former servants to Prince George.[115] Agneta Cooper, a dresser, received £71 14*s.* 6*d.* in royal bounty in order to discharge the debts of her late sister Dorothy, who had been a laundress to Prince George.[116] Similarly, the ever-attendant equerry Peter Wentworth received £500 out of the property of a foreigner who died intestate.[117] Nonmonetary gifts also went to those whom the Queen knew best, as in the case of the Greek Septuagint and New Testament she presented to her faithful Arbuthnot.[118] The Queen also spent amounts of up to £130 on furniture and alterations to his lodgings as well as those of the physician Sir Edward Hannes, her dressers Alice Hill and Abigail Masham, and her "yeowoman" of the robes, Rachel Thomas.[119]

Clearly, in both breadth and depth, Queen Anne's generosity to her middling servants fell short of the largesse of her uncle, Charles II, to his "little people." Nor do the above amounts stand comparison with the sums spent by William III or George I on their favorites.[120] The one possible exception to the overall picture of royal frugality and moderation at this level is the case of Abigail Masham. But even here the unreliable accusations of Whig politicians and historians combine with the Queen's native discretion to cloud the issue. It is a matter for speculation whether the 2,000 guineas requested by Anne out of the privy purse in June 1707 was, as Sarah suspected, for Abigail's dowry.[121] The supposed grant of a pension of £1,500 per annum late in the reign has proved equally untraceable in treasury records.[122] Abigail did secure military preferment and promotion for her brother John and her husband, Samuel. She was no doubt equally instrumental in procuring a pension of £1,000 out of the post office for the former in 1710 and a reversion to the post of Queen's remembrancer for the latter in 1713.[123] But there is no evidence for Vicary Gibbs's assertion, "She made money by selling commissions in the army 'to the most undeserving and most incompetent of persons.'"[124] While Lady Masham's percentage in the notorious Asiento contract would undoubtedly have provided a lucrative, if indirect, result of royal favor if it had materialized, there is again no evidence that Queen Anne allowed her to skim vast sums out of the privy purse or secret service funds as some have alleged.[125] Admittedly, this lack of evidence may owe more to the Queen's discretion than to her frugality. It was characteristic of Anne that she gave her faithful nurse a ring worth £1,000 in private, but moved to scotch the more public gift of a set of coach horses from Louis XIV.[126] Even if all the Whig accusations prove to be true, then Abigail Masham becomes, like her great rival at a higher level of officeholding, the Duchess of Marlborough, an anomaly, the last old-fashioned middling courtier left out of the many who had turned access to profit under the Stuarts.

The rest of the Queen's middling servants, prevented from frequent contact with her by her invalidism and shyness, with little hope of promotion, pluralism, or the benefits of royal largesse, were left dependent upon the wages, boardwages, fees, and perquisites of their single places. Middling household office could no longer, therefore, appeal to gentry families with great political or financial ambitions, particularly in a period during which the professions of law, medicine, government service, and the military were becoming increasingly attractive to this very group.[127] Nor could it, in most cases, provide enough income to maintain a member of the gentry in an appropriate style. Only the four clerkships of the greencloth and the groom porter's place, paid at around £1,000 per annum,[128] and the keepership of Whitehall, paid at £550 per annum, approached the figure of £650 to £800 that most contemporaries thought necessary to maintain a landed knight for a year. A very few more clerkships, gentlemen waiterships, and dresser's places came close to the figure of £400 to £450 per annum commonly held to be necessary to maintain the family of a gentleman or an esquire.[129]

Rather, middling household office was for the gentleman of established means looking for a little prestige and a supplementary income that did not have to be too regular in payment, in return for a moderate investment in time and (sometimes) money. For example, someone like Sir Edward Lawrence, knight and, afterwards, baronet, with his estate at St. Ives, Huntingdonshire, would not have been entirely or even primarily dependent upon his salary of £200 per annum as a gentleman usher of the privy chamber. But this sum, paid on time at least through mid-reign, plus about £40 per annum in additional fees, free meals when in attendance, lodgings at Whitehall (which he sublet), and his customs sinecure at Shoreham, would probably have enabled him to recoup within a few years of the Queen's accession the £800 he originally paid for the place in 1700. Even with the slowing down of payments at the end of the reign and occasional dry periods under George I, the rest of Lawrence's 39-year court career should have provided him with almost pure gain for only a quarter of a year's attendance.[130]

But for those who lacked a good estate and who were entirely dependent upon their household emoluments, their uncertain payment combined with the expense of middling office could be crushing. There were fees to pay upon being sworn into office and receipt of salary at similar rates to those paid by the great department heads.[131] Moreover, any middling officer serving in public view, such as a gentleman usher or an equerry, incurred the added expense of having to maintain "ye grandure of an Officer," that is, a gentle appearance in his clothes and lifestyle.[132] The annals of the court are full of the sad stories of men like Peter Wentworth, the younger son of an old Royalist family who lacked a good clear estate of his own and who squandered his time and money in the uncertain pursuit of royal favor.[133] It may be that service at the later Stuart court was as destructive of the fortunes of poor but respectable Royalist families as anything they had experienced during the Interregnum.

Worse, a lack of capital, initiative, ability, or an influential patron often kept middling servants and their families at court for generations. Thus, the matriarch of the Wentworth clan, Isabella, though herself an impoverished relic from previous Stuart courts and fully cognizant of the plight of her son, Peter, spent most of Anne's reign hoping that her daughter, Isabella Arundell, might be preferred as a dresser. When that hope was finally realized, in April 1713, Mrs. Wentworth was "hartely glad of it": "She will have near fowerteen hundred a year

& Lodgins, & in her power to doe somthing for her children. . . . Bell . . . has now all she can wish for, but Long Life to y Queen her self & children. . . . She will groe as Ritch as Lady Roysten."[134]

Such high hopes were not always dashed: the scion of the family, Thomas Wentworth, had risen from the position of page of honor to William III to be Earl of Strafford and one of the plenipotentiaries for the peace of 1713. But the respective fates of Strafford's two siblings were far more typical. The younger Isabella lost her royal employer, her salary, her lodgings, and the opportunity "to doe somthing for her children" within a little over a year. Her brother, Peter, was seemingly more fortunate, surviving the change of reign in 1714 as well as the next one in 1727. He died, still an equerry, in 1739, a pathetic figure of decayed gentility, trotting after the royal family, toadying to any potential patron, and driven to drink. Of his death, which occurred at court while dancing a quadrille, Lady Strafford was moved to write, "'Twas a mercy it pleased God to take him."[135] Before his death, Peter strove mightily to get his son, William, into the army or the law, eloquent testimony of the superior attractiveness of those professions even to the son of an old court family. But Peter, lacking the necessary capital, was eventually forced to beg his more powerful elder brother, Strafford, to find the youth a place as a gentleman usher to Prince Frederick. This outcome appears to have pleased no one, least of all young William. In 1736, with his father's fate undoubtedly in mind, he begged his uncle to find him some other employment, "that I may not Dye a Poor Gentleman Usher."[136]

Emoluments: Lower Officers

Still, however dire their situation, most of the Queen's middling servants could fall back on some other means, however small. Dr. Arbuthnot acknowledged that his situation was "not half so deplorable" at Anne's death as that of her menial servants, whom he likened to "so many poor Orphans, exposed in the very streets."[137] Indeed, the circumstances of inferior household servants were, on average, far more difficult (even allowing for their lower rank) than those of their superiors. First, their established salaries were generally small, sometimes pitifully so, as in the case of the £10 per annum allowed to the youngest breadbearer. More typically, annual stipends in the catering subdepartments below stairs began at £40 to the children of the kitchen, rising to £50 to grooms, £60 to yeomen, and between £120 and £150 to master cooks. Fortunately, the "Ancient Order of Succession" was still in operation at this level of officeholding. Consequently, it was possible for an individual such as Claud Arnaud senior to rise from the lowest of these positions to the highest between 1692 and his death in 1734. His son, Claud junior, who entered household service as a child of the kitchen in 1709, was even more fortunate, rising to a clerkship in that department before his death in 1748.

By contrast, there was little promotion among the inferior officers of the stables, whose established annual allowances ranged from £30 to helpers and postilions to £53 to footmen. In the chamber, payment of inferior servants went from £3 2*s*. 6*d*. per annum to the royal watermen up to £45 per annum to the messengers of the chamber. Most such officers had but slim hopes of becoming the master or clerk of their respective societies, each of whom made about £100 per annum. It was only in such inferior masterships or menial bedchamber posts (seamstress, starcher, laundress, necessary woman), paying between £100 and £200 per annum, that annual stipends at this level approached those of the Queen's middling servants. The rest were left with established incomes worthy, according to Edward Chamberlayne, of a "very ordinary" yeoman, at best.[138]

Moreover, it was the Queen's inferior servants who bore the brunt of her civil-list shortages from 1706, if not earlier.[139] Since 75 percent of those inferior servants preferred in 1702 were left over from William's household, most had begun her reign already laboring under arrears of one to two years' duration, most of which were never paid.[140] Nor were the majority of Anne's own debts to her family paid quickly or fully after her death.[141] Middling officers with landed estates might have been able to weather a year or two without payment, but those of the Queen's inferior servants who lacked outside employment must have been far more dependent upon the regular payment of their established allowances.

This dependence was rendered more complete by a general lack of perquisites and fees to fall back on at this level. Only the yeomen of the guard, pages of the bedchamber, and some of the inferior servants below stairs were allowed diet when in attendance.[142] After the destruction of Whitehall, an equally small number of inferior officers of the bedchamber, vestry, and below stairs were allowed permanent palace lodgings. However, when residing outside of London the court did provide temporary shared accommodation for the pages of the presence, grooms of the great chamber, yeomen of the guard, and kitchen staff in attendance.[143] For the rest, there were riding wages. These could run as high as £35 per annum for inferior bedchamber servants, but averaged around £15 per annum for most everyone else.[144] Livery, or a cash payment in lieu thereof, had been discontinued to most of the inferior tradesmen in 1667. For others, it could range from a payment of £10 6s. to the Queen's laundress, up to a full suit of clothes worth as much as £80 for her watermen, yeomen of the guard, trumpeters, and drummers.[145] It must again be remembered, however, that these last two emoluments were, in effect, compensation for necessary expenses, and were in any case often as infrequently paid as the wages and boardwages they supplemented.

Those monetary fees that did not pass through the exchequer were of negligible value. For example, fees of honor yielded an average of only £1 to £5 per annum at this level, assuming they were collected in full.[146] Unlike their superiors, a number of the Queen's menial servants still received New Year's gifts out of the privy purse, but these generally amounted to only a fraction of a pound to each recipient.[147] Finally, a number of department heads allowed menials to give tours of royal palaces, a source of income the annual value of which is impossible to estimate.[148]

Because of the distance from the Queen at which most inferior servants waited and the facelessness of the tasks they performed, the opportunities to cultivate royal favor enjoyed by their superiors were denied them. Table 5.1 indicates that only 88 of 926, or fewer than 10 percent, of her menial servants were the beneficiaries of royal largesse. These few were generally individuals with a special relationship to the royal family, such as servants with concurrent pensions as former retainers of Prince George. Others had some distinguishing talent, such as the singers John Gostling and Richard Elford, who received additional allowances of 50 guineas and £100 per annum, respectively, in recognition of their vocal abilities, both past and present.[149] It was virtually impossible for a pankeeper of the kitchen or a yeoman of the guard to distinguish himself in royal eyes.

Barred from the Queen's favor, paid erratically and often inadequately, and lacking a set of legal and flexible fees to fall back on, it was probably inevitable that many inferior household servants chose to abuse the rights of wastage that remained to them, particularly below stairs.[150] In 1707 the board of greencloth discovered a series of "very scandalous & notorious frauds" by which the officers of the acatry, larder, and scaldinghouse routinely took in provisions far in excess of what was needed, yet served inferior dishes and cuts of meat to the royal tables, in order to claim and sell, or perhaps eat, the "waste."[151] Additional evidence suggests that such practices were so longstanding and widespread below stairs that most servants were probably incapable of distinguishing legitimate perquisites from illegitimate. For example, in December 1686 the board of greencloth lifted the suspension of David Lloyd, gentleman and yeoman of the buttery, who had been accused of abuses similar to those described above; the board explained, "It doth appear that he found those practices in Use when he was lately admitted into ye Buttry and knew not but that it was an allowable proceeding."[152]

An alternative to corruption was the pursuit of a supplementary career in the service of a nobleman or the general public. As indicated previously, light work, duplication of office, rotation of attendance, and sometimes-illegal deputization made an outside career possible for over a third of the Queen's menial servants (see Table 4.3). Indeed, the court's refusal to make more demands upon, and its inability to pay, its artists and craftsmen in particular probably did much to foster the beginnings of public patronage of the arts in Britain.[153] For those without a noble patron, a talent to sell to the public, or the opportunity to defraud the Crown, there was only poverty, which many of Anne's servants appear to have fallen into after mid-reign.[154]

In summary, the emoluments of household posts varied greatly in form and value, the latter roughly corresponding to a particular office's place in the court's administrative and social hierarchy. At all levels, but especially at the top, established emoluments (wages and boardwages) increased or maintained their apparent value as nonestablished fees and perquisites (poundage, diet, lodgings, New Year's gifts, etc.) were eliminated or reduced at the end of the seventeenth century. But this resulted in a decrease in the real value of such places because the chronic financial difficulties of later Stuart monarchs made payment uncertain. While Anne's circumstances, and therefore those of her servants, were never so serious as those of Charles II or William III, payment of salaries fell steadily behind as her reign progressed, until arrears of one and a quarter years to three years became common.

As a result of the reductions in nonestablished fees and perquisites and the delays in paying established ones, household office was not capable of providing great wealth. Nor could it, at any level, maintain its holders in the style appropriate to the social rank from which that level was drawn. On the other hand, for those not entirely dependent on it, court office could provide a useful, if by no means reliable, supplementary income, especially for those of great and middle rank. Great officers in particular could double or treble the monetary value of their places to several thousands per annum through the exploitation of their remaining fees, lodgings, plate, and access to royal largesse. Middling officers had fewer fees and perquisites to exploit, and opportunities to cultivate royal favor were limited to those individuals with direct access to the Queen. Most inferior servants lacked all such opportunities to supplement their wages. Since these were generally the least well and regularly paid of Anne's "family," many turned to corruption or outside careers to stave off penury.

Tenure and Pensions

Fear of losing old arrears must have kept many a disgruntled servant in harness. No doubt equally persuasive was the lack of any comprehensive scheme of superannuation. Despite Queen Anne's generosity to the former servants of her sister, husband, and son, when it came time for her own servants to retire (mostly long after her death), room could be found on the household establishments for only 42 pensions at half pay (Table 5.1).[155] The Queen's servants were apparently expected to provide for their own retirement in the course of their careers. This explains the considerable number of household servants allowed to stay on into old age (and, occasionally, to name a deputy), despite obvious incapacity.[156] It also explains the preferment of the offspring of deceased servants even when the former were too young to do the work: these children were, in effect, serving out their parents' time.[157] In addition, the Crown provided 46 widows and other dependents not suitable for eventual preferment with pensions at half pay (Table 5.1).[158] The total number of pensions to the Queen's former servants and their dependents would undoubtedly have been higher but for the policy, instituted at the beginning of George II's reign, of making a single payment of a year's salary at the retirement or death of a servant, in place of a permanent annuity.[159] Since many of Anne's "family" came to retirement age or died under the second Hanoverian, this policy was to have dire consequences for them and their families. Some individual societies, most notably the yeomen of the guard, gentlemen of the chapel, and messengers of the chamber, originated their own contributory schemes during the first half of the eighteenth century. But these generally did little more than provide a colleague's widow and children with a small lump sum at his death.[160] It was as beyond the meager resources of such officers to provide a continuous income for their survivors as it was to provide for their own retirement.

Fortunately, a position for life was one thing that most of the Queen's servants could depend on. Officially, offices held for life or during good behavior had always been a small minority in the royal household, and the reforms of the later Stuarts reduced their number still further.[161] However, because many household officers had purchased their places, the tradition that office was a freehold, subject to the same rights as any other form of property, was particularly strong at the Stuart court. Thus when, in 1678, Charles II attempted to displace two grooms of the confectionery with an outsider whose work he preferred, he was persuaded to desist by Sir Stephen Fox, who argued, "No man will presume to dispute your power, but your goodness has been hitherto such as that never any sworn servant hath been put away since your happy restoration, nor can there hardly be found a precedent in any of your predecessors' times."[162] This policy dovetailed nicely with Anne's characteristic attitude of affection and loyalty toward her "family" and her more specific desire to keep them free from political pressures. Thus, as Princess, she observed to Sarah, "Who ever I take I reckon tis for ones whole life."[163]

Table 5.2 indicates that, as Queen, Anne was as good as her word:

TABLE 5.2
Average Length of Career of Anne's Household Officers

Rank of officer	Average length of career (in yrs.)	No. of officers for whom length of career is known (sample)	Sample as a % of the total no. of household officers[a]
High	12.1	55	100
Middle	20.3	515	94.7
Low	23.2	822	88.8
Total	21.7	1,392	91.3

SOURCES: LC 3/5–6; LC 3/53; LC 3/62; LS 13/11; LS 13/43; LS 13/199; LS 13/258–59; E. Chamberlayne and (from 1704) J. Chamberlayne, *Anglia Notitia*; J. Chamberlayne, *Magnae Britanniae Notitia*; G. Miege, *New State of England*; idem, *Present State of Great Britain*; and sources cited in Appendix B.

[a]I.e., 55 high officers, 544 middling officers, 926 low officers = 1,525 total household officers.

TABLE 5.3
Service of Anne's Household Officers by Number of Reigns

Rank of officer	No. of officers serving in a total of											
	1 Reign		2 Reigns		3 Reigns		4 Reigns		5 Reigns		6 Reigns	
	No.	%[a]	No.	%[a]	No.	%[a]	No.	%[a]	No.	%[a]	No.	%[a]
High	30	54.5	13	23.6	6	10.9	5	9.1	1	1.8		
Middle	127	23.3	202	37.1	142	26.1	57	10.5	15	2.8	1	0.2
Low	208	22.5	322	34.8	250	27.0	116	12.5	21	2.3	9	1.0
Total	365	23.9	537	35.2	398	26.1	178	11.7	37	2.4	10	0.7

SOURCES: As for Table 5.2.

NOTE: The numbers in the above columns are exclusive. Those officers who served in 6 reigns are not counted among those who served in 1–5; those who served in 5 are not counted in 1–4, etc. To find the total number of officers who served in one or more reigns, all the columns must be added from left to right, etc.

[a]I.e., % of 55 high officers, 544 middling officers, 926 low officers = 1,525 total officers.

the average length of career among her servants was almost 22 years, well over the span of her reign. Figure 5.1 indicates that though a 10 to 20 year career was most common—a function of Anne's 12 years on the throne—service of 40, 50, and even 60 years was not unknown. The extreme example of such longevity at the later Stuart and early Hanoverian courts was provided by Dr. William Turner, the celebrated countertenor. He was sworn a gentleman of the chapel royal in October 1669 and continued to hold that post until his death in December 1740, a career of 71 years.[164] Few of Queen Anne's "family" served in six reigns as he did, but according to Table 5.3 (adding columns together)

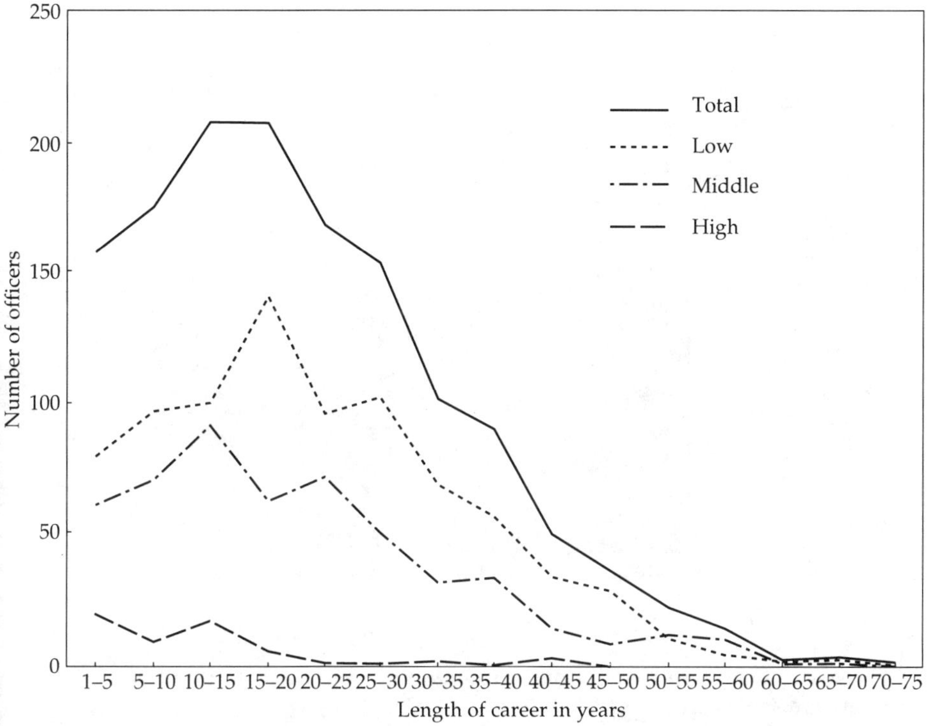

Fig. 5.1. Length of career: frequency distribution by rank (sample of 1,392 officers). Data from sources cited in Table 5.2.

fully three quarters could expect to serve in two or more and two fifths served in three or more. Some 141 of the Queen's servants had begun their careers at the court of Charles II. Four of her "family" served into the reign of George III. The last of these, a messenger named John Bill, died still in harness in 1770. Whether out of fear that retirement would bring poverty or simply because the work was light and the service honorable, 36 of Queen Anne's household officers served into their seventies, 15 into their eighties, and 5 into their nineties. The longest lived of her active servants would appear to have been a page of the presence chamber named Edward Wills, who retired—or was expelled—from the royal service in 1744 at the ripe old age of 96.[165]

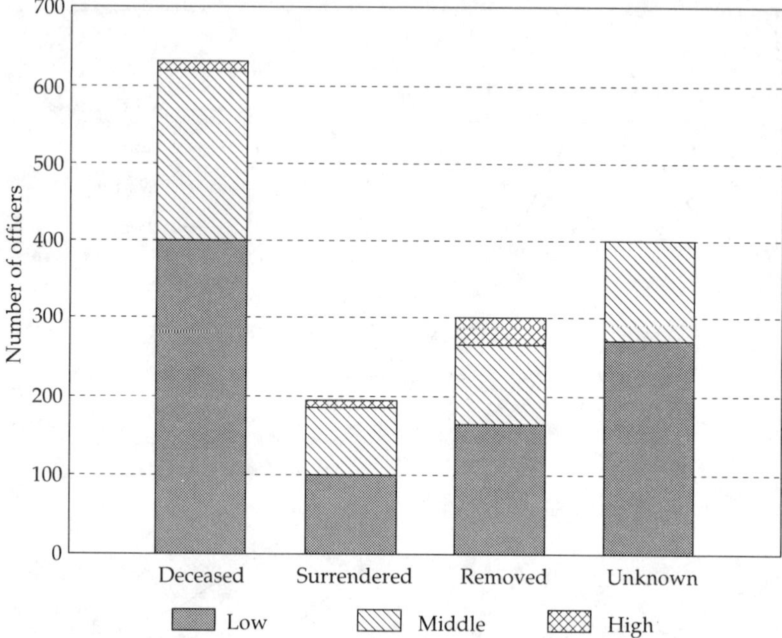

Fig. 5.2. Reasons for leaving office (sample of 1,525 officers). Data from sources cited in Table 5.2.

Clearly, the degree of continuity among individual court officers was at least as impressive as it was for families.

This evidence of continuity, stability, and security of tenure is qualified only by the figures for those at the very top of the court hierarchy. While long careers were not unheard of at this level, they were much less common.[166] According to Table 5.2 and Figures 5.1 and 5.2, great household officers tended to serve for a shorter period of time (12 years) and to be removed from office, rather than die in or voluntarily resign it, like the vast majority of their subordinates. This was the only group of incumbents to be purged almost completely in 1714. Admittedly, some of these removals were inevitable, given that about a third of the Queen's great officers were ladies in and about her bedchamber who could not have had any expectation of serving her male successor. But increasingly in the years preceding Anne's death, the attractiveness of high-ranking places outside the royal bedchamber and the lack of specific requirements for them had made many of them the prizes in the great political struggle that gripped the ruling class. Despite the Queen's otherwise successful endeavor to keep her household above politics, her three successive lords chamberlain, two of her four lords steward, ten of thirteen officers at the upper greencloth, two captains of the yeomen of the guard and one of the gentlemen pensioners, two masters each of the buckhounds and jewel house, and, finally, her first groom of the stole, mistress of the robes, and keeper of the privy purse all found themselves the sacrificial victims to political necessity, either during the reign or at the commencement of the next one.[167] It is thus perhaps understandable that Lady Portland, reflecting upon her husband's "forty years experience of a court," remarked to the Duchess of Marlborough, "Y^e changes, & uncertaintys of y^t life, has never made me envy it any body."[168]

Why did members of the nobility and gentry serve at court? Clearly, upper-class women could reap substantial material and social rewards from court service. These included high-paying office, pensions, gifts, favors, and, as demonstrated in the previous chapter, advantageous marriages. To some extent, such opportunities had always been available to the noblewomen and gentlewomen who attended the consorts and daughters of Stuart sovereigns. But Anne's status as sovereign herself magnified them and probably simplified the process of securing them. Moreover, her ladies in waiting had less male competition than those of previous Stuart queens thanks to her frail constitution, heavy personality, and sense of propriety. As these factors limited her contact with male courtiers, they increased her reliance upon, and time with, female servants. While her generosity never rivaled that of her male predecessors to their mistresses, it nevertheless provided an important means of material and social advancement for a small group of women in an age when their alternatives were few.

By contrast, the alternatives available to ambitious upper-class males were many, increasing, and generally superior in value. The stocks, the professions (including nonhousehold government service), the two political parties, and the new urban world of clubs, coffee houses, taverns, and theaters all promised greater opportunities for wealth, power, and (as shall be demonstrated) entertainment.[169] As a result, household office was not the means for a younger son or a budding financier, politician, or socialite to improve his lot in the world. Rather, a post in the upper or middle reaches of the royal household was for the man secure of his economic and social position, either devoid of political ambition or able to satisfy it in other ways, and desirous of the honor and prestige that still attached to the royal service in the opinion of many contemporaries. As suggested in Chapter 4, a place in the first household of England was, for those who viewed the world through traditional eyes, the clearest possible recognition of one's or one's family's place in it. This perhaps goes farthest to explain why a man such as Philip Ryley, holding numerous government offices and land all over England, should have chosen to continue to bear a mace as sergeant at arms to the lord treasurer for 42 years. Even at the lowest levels of the household, the prestige attached to a place in the royal service appears to have been a powerful attraction, particularly among artists and tradesmen.[170]

For those, at all levels, of more modest pretensions, it may be that some families found it convenient to have one of their number near the center of affairs, as much for business as for political purposes.[171] For a few, the privilege still allowed court servants against being imprisoned for debt or pricked for local office may have been crucial.[172] Finally, we must not dismiss the possibility that the great evidence of continuity among individuals and families at court owed as much to a lack of ability, education, or courage to do something else, as it did to job satisfaction or a deeply felt loyalty to the Stuarts.

Despite its relative stability in terms of personnel, the court of Queen Anne, as described in the preceding four chapters, was an institution in transition. It had taken the first steps away from the widespread sinecurism, deputization, venality, and fee taking that characterized the administrative system of the early Stuart court. But in the absence of a realistic financial settlement, such reforms were premature. Without adequate and regularly paid salaries and a comprehensive pension plan, some tolerance of such "abuses," as well as de facto life tenure, had to continue. Even assuming an adequate financial base, the total elimination of such practices, together with the nepotism that Anne made no attempt to stifle, was incompatible with the political needs of Augustan government, specifically the need to promote a compliant

Court party and generally keep the court attractive to the nobility and gentry. There is evidence that these abuses, if abuses they were, actually increased under the Hanoverians, a development that probably contributed as much to the stability of the 1720s and 1730s as it did to the movement for economical reform of the 1780s.[173] In attempting to eliminate or restrain the most "corrupt" features of court life, Anne often did away with what was necessary or attractive as well. In failing to compensate her servants by making their good husbandry more lucrative, she failed, except in the case of a few great officers, to attract, hold, and enrich the most greedy or ambitious members of the ruling class and London professional and artistic communities. The last two chapters of this work explore the political and social consequences of this state of affairs.

CHAPTER VI

Court Politics

The preceding chapters have examined the history, administration, finances, personnel, and material rewards of court service, all natural preoccupations for the twentieth-century historian, not least because of their susceptibility to the techniques of modern scholarship. But with rare, albeit significant, exceptions, these were not the aspects of court life that interested most contemporaries, for they were peripheral to its essential and altogether unique nature. In the words of John Larner, "While the court had institutional aspects it was not simply an institution. Administrative formalization indeed came rather late to it and, at any time, what was subject to it (in Household-Ordinances, Books of Ceremonies, etc.) was much less important than that business it carried out informally and through personal contact in a sphere unamenable to written regulation."[1]

It was "that business," in terms of politics and culture, which was, to judge from the amount of correspondence it generated, the most interesting feature of court life to Anne's subjects, and to which the remainder of this work will turn. The present chapter examines the court first as a forum for the transaction of political business, and second as a focus for the loyalty of those of its servants who sat in that other, greater political forum, parliament. While the parliamentary arena has received the attention of most of the best recent scholarship, it was the politics of the court, in particular the potential for favored courtiers to influence royal policy and patronage, that most excited the imaginations of Anne's subjects. Even if we must conclude, as Geoffrey Holmes does, that contemporary assessments of court influence were largely delusive, then the causes, proportions, and consequences of that delusion, as well as the reality it served to obscure, are worth investigating.

Access

Personal contact with the monarch was regulated on the basis of venue, a visitor's office, and social rank. Out of doors, virtually anyone could approach the Queen as she entered or alighted from her coach, or while it was stationary.[2] Within doors, any person capable of putting on a gentle appearance could get into the public rooms (guard, presence, and privy chambers; privy gallery; and withdrawing room) of a royal residence.[3] But, apart from great ceremonial events and the occasional drawing room, access to the public rooms did not necessarily mean access to Queen Anne. The previous two centuries had witnessed a gradual royal retreat from these rooms into the relative privacy of the royal bedchamber and closet.[4] This process culminated in the bedchamber ordinances drawn up for William III in 1689 and adopted, with minimal changes, by Anne in 1702. These limited bedchamber access to the personnel of that department and the following additional officers:

> The Master of Our Roabes, . . . the Keeper of Our Privy-Purse, . . . the Keeper of Our Closet . . . All Our Physitians & Our Chirurgeons, . . . the Lord Steward, Lord Chamberlaine, the Secretaries of State, the rest of the Lords and others of Our Privy-Councill & such other persons as Our Groome of the Stole shall, with Our leave, mention in a List under his hand, left with the Pages, or appoint to be hung up in any of the Roomes belonging to Our Bedchamber.[5]

In practice, the Queen's circle of daily contact was further restricted by contemporary expectations of her sex and marital status, her notorious shyness, and her fragile health. The latter in particular reduced her mobility and, later in the reign, often confined her within her private apartments for days at a time. Thus, apart from rare public ceremonial and social occasions, Queen Anne was isolated from the vast majority of her subjects and even her courtiers. Most of her life as Queen was spent within a narrow circle of individuals comprising Prince George, her chief ministers, her medical staff, and, above all, her female bedchamber attendants.

In the absence of a daily morning *levée*, the only major exceptions to this generalization were her daily attendance at the chapel royal and thrice weekly public drawing rooms during the court season, when her health permitted.[6] Even here the Queen's relative immobility and shyness and the presence of her ladies in waiting made access difficult.[7] Very occasionally, when the summer crowds at Windsor were thin, she might receive visitors in the relative convenience and intimacy of the private apartments—as she did at a drawing room in 1711 that attracted "so few company," according to Jonathan Swift, "that the queen sent for us into her bedchamber."[8] However, even this breach of form did not necessarily enable one to speak to the monarch. Court etiquette required formal presentation to kiss the Queen's hands, either by the groom of the stole or, in her absence, by some other great officer or lady of the bedchamber. Swift himself never spoke to the lady upon whom his hopes for ecclesiastical preferment depended for, despite Harley's promises, he was never presented to "kiss hands." Some idea of the seriousness with which this custom was viewed in general, and its necessity prior to any solicitation for royal favor in particular, is conveyed by the newly wed Bridget, Countess of Plymouth in a letter to Robert Harley written in 1706:

> The Duchess of Marlborough did me the honour yesterday to introduce me to the Queen in a very obliging manner, and . . . Her Majesty had the goodness to receive me very graciously. I hope, Sir, you will approve of my making this step, which I imagined necessary since the declaring of our marriage, before any application could well be made to her Majesty in favour of Dr. Bisse.[9]

The household ordinances and other contemporary evidence indicate that even after initial introduction it was still necessary for all visitors but the groom of the stole to "send in" via the groom or, in her absence, one of the ladies, women, or pages of the bedchamber to see whether the Queen would receive them.[10] The potential for these servants to facilitate, hinder, or otherwise manipulate access to the monarch for political purposes should be obvious. The groom of the stole in particular, with unlimited access herself and the positive right to limit the access of others, was entrusted with considerable power. That power was symbolized by the wearing of a gold key that opened the doors of "Our Bedchamber . . . every door of all Our Gardens, galleries & privy-lodgings and of all other Roomes of State & honour."[11]

During her tenure as groom of the stole, the Duchess of Marlborough was accused by the Tories of using her power to isolate Anne from their persons and opinions. For example, early in the reign the Tory James Johnston was compelled to abandon an attempt to pay his respects to the Queen at Hampton Court: "Observing the Duchess of Marlborough to look upon him with anger, he retired to his country seat and fine gardens."[12] Later, during the ministerial crisis of 1710, Swift charged Sarah with "watching all the avenues to the back-stairs" so that the Queen was "hemmed in, and as it were imprisoned, by the Duchess of Marlborough and her creatures."[13] In fact this view was exaggerated. Despite the obvious pride with which she wears the gold key in one contemporary portrait, and the constant urgings of Arthur Maynwaring and other Whig friends, the Duchess more or less abdicated her power by frequent and protracted absences from court after the death of her only son, the Marquess of Blandford, in February 1703.[14] As a result, the responsibility for regulating access to the monarch and the political power that this regulation implied devolved upon Anne's remaining bedchamber attendants, of whom Abigail Masham was, by mid-reign, the most assiduous. As is well known, she used her position during the fateful year 1710 to provide Robert Harley with access that was not only frequent but remarkably discreet. For all their accusations, and despite the existence of something like a Churchill court spy ring, neither contemporary Whig politicians nor subsequent Whig historians could point to much eyewitness testimony of Harley's visits. This is a tribute to the discretion and usefulness of which the Queen's servants were capable.[15]

With the accession of the Tory ministry in 1710, the Whigs, in their turn, began to charge that they were being kept from the Queen by Mrs. Masham, her sister Alice Hill, and assorted other High Church bedchamber attendants (Ladies Frescheville, Ormonde, and the two Hydes, Jane and Katherine). In the words of Anne's Whiggish physician, Sir David Hamilton, "By Management few were admitted to give Her a Contrary Account to what was habitually Sounding In Her Ears."[16] However, this view, too, was exaggerated. Masham's frequent pregnancies and illnesses, and the continuance of a number of Whig bedchamber ladies (Ladies Devonshire, Scarborough, Somerset, and probably the dressers Beata and Isabella Danvers) ensured that the Tories by no means monopolized the Queen's ear.[17] Indeed, the appointment of the Duchess of Somerset as groom of the stole in January 1711 gave the Church party equal cause for complaint when she was in attendance, and sometimes when she was not, if the following story, overheard by Peter Wentworth, is true: "A Gentleman desired to speak to the Queen, and the Dutchess of Ormond being in waiting wou'd have introduced him, but she was told by the page of the back stairs, that the Dutchess of Sommerset was just gone and had left orders that nobody shou'd be permitted to speak to the Queen till she came again."[18] Wentworth, with the prudence of a courtier, was careful to point out to his correspondent that this story was unconfirmed. Most such partisan allegations prove to be equally third-hand or otherwise unverifiable.[19] The best evidence indicates that Anne was able to maintain personal contact with elements of both parties for most of the reign, but with difficulty. According to Hamilton's eye-witness testimony, "If some Persons had been in waiting, however Her Majesty inclin'd to speak to me, yet either the Door must be left Open, or if that shut, I to stay no more than a Minute; whereas if others who had a Personal regard for me, had been then in waiting the door might be Shut, and I stay without her Concern."[20]

Clearly, to have the Queen's ear with any regularity, privacy, or ease it was necessary to cultivate those who stood outside the bedchamber door. In particular, Anne's gender and relative isolation from her male subjects dictated that the women who did so would have a political significance exceeded among representatives of their sex only by the mistresses of Charles II. Under Queen Anne it was the wives and mothers, sisters and daughters of male politicians who provided the greatest barrier or the surest approach to the royal ear. It must now be determined whether the Queen's ladies in waiting played an even greater role: as the source, not merely the vehicle, of political influence.

Influence

The ability of great court ladies to help others influence the Queen or prevent them from doing so was important. It was, however, the influence that they themselves were supposed to wield which most interested contemporaries. In the words of Daniel Defoe, "The nacion is perticularly jealous of Favourites."[21] Three ladies above all enjoyed that status, and aroused corresponding jealousy at the court of Queen Anne: Sarah Churchill, Duchess of Marlborough; Abigail Hill, afterwards Mrs. and then Lady Masham; and Elizabeth Seymour, Duchess of Somerset. Each had a considerable reputation. Of the Duchess of Marlborough, her friend Bishop Burnet wrote: "There never was a more absolute favourite in a court."[22] On the other side of the political fence, William Bromley, only slightly less impressed, compared her influence to that of Alice Perrers under Edward III; "indeed," in Burnet's analysis, "she was looked upon by the whole party, as the person who had reconciled the whigs to the queen, from whom she was naturally very averse."[23]

Even more extreme than Tory anxieties over Sarah's influence was the Whigs' "almost pathological" fear of what the Duke of Marlborough called "the absolute power of 256 [Mrs. Masham]."[24] Though he probably did not believe it himself, the Duke of Shrewsbury knew that he was touching a raw nerve when he informed a group of Whigs that Abigail "could make the queen stand upon her head if she chose." This view received equal credit and caused commensurate joy among the Tories.[25] They, in turn, blamed the Whig Duchess of Somerset for many of their troubles during the reign's last years. For example, Swift believed the Queen's equivocal behavior during the crisis over "No Peace Without Spain" in December 1711 to have been "all your d——d duchess of Somerset's doings."[26]

Each of these women was continually urged by the members of her party to attend the Queen as often as possible, as a matter of the highest importance. The first two, at least, were showered with petitions for pensions, gifts, and offices in the central government, the Church, and the military as well as the royal household. All of this moved one historian to conclude of Anne's reign: "No period in the British history presents . . . such a picture of corruption, venality, unconstitutional influence, court-intrigue, unbounded ambition in favourites, and of extensive abuse of popularity and power. . . . It is throughout, in a great measure, a scene of artifice and delusion."[27]

Behind this exalted view of the significance of bedchamber influence lies a much less exalted interpretation of Anne's own abilities and independence. As noted previously, her shyness, taciturnity, and fear of exposure combined with ill health and, sometimes, the machinations of her bedchamber staff to isolate her from the vast majority of her subjects. This left ample room for speculation about her character and competence. Into this vacuum stepped the Duchess of Marlborough. Sarah was for contemporaries and later historians the most pervasive and prolific source on Anne's personality. First in her conversations and correspondence with friends, then in her magisterial *Conduct of the Dowager Duchess of Marlborough* for posterity, she enshrined a picture of her one-time friend and mistress as a woman who "wou'd not go to take the air unless somebody advised her to it," who "loved fawning and adoration and hated plain dealing," and who "had a soul that nothing could so effectually move as flattery or fear." Of Anne's administration, Sarah wrote that her friend, Lord Treasurer Godolphin, "conducted the Queen with the care and tenderness of a father or a guardian through a state of helpless ignorance" until she "came to be flattered" by Mrs. Masham and Robert Harley into preferring a new ministry.[28] Out of print, Mrs. Freeman was even harsher, complaining to one friend of the Queen's "own stupid understanding."[29] To Lord Cowper, she summed up Mrs. Morley's character as follows: "Her Opinion, that Q. has no Original Thoughts on any Subject; is neither good nor bad, but as put into: that she has much Love & Passion, while pleas'd, for those who please; & can write pretty affectionate L$^{rs.}$; but do nothing else well."[30]

This picture of the last reigning Stuart was by no means universally accepted even in Sarah's own day.[31] But it was inevitable, given the forcefulness of the Duchess's personality and the vastness of her acquaintance, the subsequent Whig ascendancy, and the lack of any other readily available account of court life under Anne for over two centuries, that this was the picture that would stick, especially among historians whose own prejudices might be characterized as "Whig."[32] Only in this century has this interpretation of Anne's character been questioned and, in the recent biography by Edward Gregg, finally overturned.[33]

However, the corresponding emphasis placed by contemporaries upon the political significance of bedchamber influence has not been similarly scrutinized.[34] Objective analysis of it is difficult, for successful bedchamber intrigue was, by its very nature, secret, verbal, and so unamenable to conventional historical documentation. What evidence has survived is fragmentary and biased. Thus, it must be addressed critically and resourcefully.

If anyone could legitimately claim the status of absolute court favorite under Anne, it was Sarah, Duchess of Marlborough. Her domination of household patronage and weighty reputation in other areas have already been noted. Yet in the various drafts of her *Conduct* Sarah is quite equivocal about her ability to influence her mistress outside the household sphere. She admits that, despite the great favor shown her at the beginning of the reign, "the first important step which her Majesty took after her accession to the Government," namely the replacement of a number of Whig officeholders with Tories, "was against my wishes and inclination." In response, Mrs. Freeman resolved, as she put it, "to try whether I could not by degrees make impressions in her mind more favourable to the Whigs; and though my instances with her had not at first any considerable effect, I believe I may venture to say it was in some measure owing to them that her Majesty did against her own inclinations continue several of this party in office."[35] Elsewhere, she asserts that the Whigs' credit with Mrs. Morley would have remained virtually nonexistent "but for the zeal and diligence with which I seized every opportunity to raise and establish it," a view which was readily accepted by members of both parties.[36]

However, it has already been established that neither Anne nor her ministers had any intention of purging all or even most Whigs from office at the beginning of the reign.[37] Moreover, the Duchess's frequent absences from court after February 1703 left her with few face-to-face opportunities to "raise and establish" the Whig cause with her mistress. In lieu of more such opportunities, Mrs. Freeman began an intensive correspondence with Mrs. Morley "upon the subject of Whig and Tory."[38] Those letters that have survived do indeed demonstrate the "zeal and diligence" of the Duchess, but equally the stubbornness and tenacity of opinion of the Queen.[39] Sarah herself admitted of Anne's eventual softening toward her party: "It appears by these letters that the Queen was not hitherto inwardly converted to the Whigs, neither by all that I had been able to say nor even by the mad conduct of the tacking Tories, yet . . . their behaviour in the affair of the Invitation occasioned something like a change in her."[40] That it was indeed the parliamentary behavior of the Tories, culminating in the insulting and insensitive motion to invite the Electress Sophia to England in November 1705, not the importunities of a bedchamber favorite, that moved the Queen is confirmed by a letter she wrote to the Duchess in the wake of this affair: "I believe dear Mrs Freeman and I shall not disagree as we have formerly done, for I am sensible of the services those people have done me that you have a good opinion of, and will countenance them, and am thoroughly convinced of the malice and insolence of them that you have always been speaking against."[41] There is here a certain amount of the flattery that Mrs. Morley was always willing to use on the susceptible Freeman, as well as an acknowledgment of the latter's efforts on her party's behalf. But there is no indication that it was anything but the "services" of the Whigs in supporting the war, and the "malice and insolence" of the Tories in obstructing the Queen's measures, that caused her change of heart.

Anne's tentative rapprochement with the Whigs in the middle years of the reign is the one major policy initiative commonly attributed to the Duchess's influence.[42] She made no claim to any other and, indeed, complained in later years of her mistress continually sending her "to ask Mr Mountgomery [Godolphin] & Mr Freeman's [the Duke of Marlborough] opinion."[43] Nevertheless, in an age when men and measures were often inseparable, it was still possible for Sarah to exert an indirect but significant influence on royal policy through advice on the distribution of government patronage beyond her accustomed household sphere. Here, too, the Duchess was somewhat equivocal about her power. To begin with cabinet-level posts, she claimed to have procured the removal of Sir Nathan Wright from his lord keepership and the disposal of the great seal to William Cowper in 1705; the promotion of Lord Somers to the lord presidency of the council in 1708; that of the Earl of Orford to the first lordship of the admiralty in 1709; and that of Robert Walpole to the treasurership of the navy in 1710.[44] On the other hand, she confessed to being unable to procure a secretaryship for her son-in-law, Sunderland, in 1706, despite having spoken for him "with as much earnestness as if he had been my friend . . . this twenty year." Four years later, her protests against his removal were to prove equally unavailing.[45]

Even Sarah's claimed successes at this level are called into question by the direct testimony of Anne herself. According to Sir David Hamilton, "The Queen told me that the putting out of Wright, and putting in Cowper, made no difference between the Duchess and her, for the Duchess had never spoke but once to her of it; and once of Lord Sommers. . . . The Duchess never spoke to her of Lord Orford, but if in printing all this be said, it makes her mightilly in favour with the other Side."[46] Admittedly, it was as much in the Queen's interest to deny "all this" while she was attempting to free herself from the Duchess, as it was in the Duchess's interest to assert it. But it is surely significant that neither Godolphin nor the Duke was very enthusiastic about Sarah's efforts in this direction.[47] After her fall, in a rare moment of self-doubt, she was forced to admit, "[For all my attempts] to get honest men into the service . . . I never, or very rarely succeeded . . . till the ministers themselves came into it at last."[48]

In assessing her influence upon the disposition of places below cabinet level, as well as pensions and other favors in the Queen's gift, Sarah grew more sanguine. From the beginning of the reign, she recollected in her *Conduct*, "I began to be looked upon as a person of consequence, without whose approbation at least neither places nor pensions nor honours were bestowed by the Crown."[49] Evidence of this reputation is provided by the numerous petitions for places, pensions, and favors that she received, many of which still survive in the Blenheim manuscripts and elsewhere.[50] As with purely household petitions, this evidence shows Sarah exercising a real, if largely negative, power—in effect, a right of first refusal—over a wide variety of matters. More often than not, she cast herself in the role of guardian of limited royal resources. Thus, she refused a request from her importunate in-law, the Duke of Montagu, by informing him, "Every body as well as my lord treasurer are of the opinion that [the] queen gives pentions enough already."[51] With equal brusqueness she warned Lady Wentworth, an old retired servant of the Stuarts, that she should expect to lose her lodgings, "for it was but resonable that the Queen's own famely should be provyded for before strangers."[52] The imperious and self-righteous tone of most of Sarah's replies undoubtedly exacerbated the natural resentment felt by disappointed applicants. Still, by taking that resentment upon herself, Mrs. Freeman screened her mistress, and performed perhaps her greatest service for Mrs. Morley.[53]

Mrs. Freeman's power to exert a positive influence upon the distribution of nonhousehold places, large pensions, and honors is less in evidence. Her only known successes in these areas included an army appointment for John Hill, a seat on the commission of prizes for Emmanuel Scroop Howe, and a peerage for John Hervey.[54] Rather, her special province appears to have been the distribution of minor royal charity, an area in which she infringed upon the jurisdiction of Lord Almoner Sharp.[55] Sharp more than got his own back through his domination of ecclesiastical patronage, an area in which Sarah admitted to having "less opinion" of her "solicitations . . . than [in] any other."[56] That her doubts were well-founded is indicated by the Queen's response to one such solicitation in the spring of 1704:

> As to ye liveing you writt about, you may easily emagin I will do any thing you desire, but intending to be always Carefull in disposing of any thing of this nature, I hope you will not take it ill, if I desire you would enquire where this gentleman lives y^{t} . . . I may [get] ye Arch Bishop of York to inform him self if he be proper for it, & if he finds him to be soe, he shall be sure to have it.[57]

Once again, Mrs. Morley's flattery and tact do little to disguise her real lack of regard for Mrs. Freeman's opinion—which is to be subject to Sharp's veto—in "any thing of this nature."

Apart from her negative role in screening petitions, the Duchess's real influence was confined to the traditionally feminine spheres of the household and charity. Indeed, Anne's ready compliance with Sarah's wishes in these areas, her almost fawning tone in doing so, and the juxtaposition of this behavior with their frequent, bitter arguments over larger issues suggest that Morley was consciously giving Freeman her head in these "womanly" concerns in order to occupy or placate her for her lack of influence over more important, traditionally masculine ones. With hindsight, and in the relative privacy of personal correspondence, the Duchess herself admitted in later years, "In the late queens time, tho I was a favourit, without the help of the Duke of Marlborough and Lord Godolphin I should not have been able to do any thing of any consiquence and the things that are worth naming will ever bee don from the influence of men."[58]

Surprisingly in light of this statement, the Duchess far more commonly attributed her lack of influence to the machinations of another female, her kinswoman and one-time dependent, Abigail Masham, née Hill. Indeed, from Sarah's first discovery in the summer of 1707 that her "cousin was become an absolute favourite," it was the Duchess herself who almost single-handedly created her rival's reputation by accusing her, first to the Duke, then to those friends and acquaintances who could be persuaded to listen, and finally to present and future generations in her *Conduct* of 1742.[59] Fortunately, there exists a more direct source for evaluating Mrs. Masham's influence: a now-fragmentary but nevertheless revealing series of letters she wrote to her cousin and friend, Robert Harley, mostly during the period just prior to his return to power in 1710.[60] Split among the various deposits of the Portland papers, these letters form one of only two sources documenting the face-to-face working of bedchamber influence.[61] Like Sarah's attempts at persuasion through correspondence, they fully demonstrate the persistence of their author and the stubbornness of the Queen. But unlike the frank exchanges between Freeman and Morley, Masham's testimony reveals a marked reluctance on Anne's part even to discuss matters of high politics with a woman whom she could not but regard as a menial. For example, Abigail complained to Harley in September 1709:

> I can't tell you what use my friend has made of the advice was given her in your letter, but she heard it over and over. She keeps me in ignorance and is very reserved, does not care to tell me any thing. I asked her if she had gratified my Lord R [?Rivers] in what he desired; she answered, yes, he was very well satisfied but told me no more.[62]

That this was more or less a standing policy with the Queen even after she no longer had to fear a grilling from Sarah is indicated by Abigail's failure to know her mistress's mind during the crisis over "No Peace Without Spain" in December 1711. On the 6th of that month, before the opening of the new session, Mrs. Masham assured Swift, "The queen is stout" (i.e., committed to the peace), though he thought he detected some uneasiness in the favorite. On the 8th, after the disastrous vote in the Lords, wrote Swift, Masham "gave me some lights to suspect the queen is changed."[63] However, the one example of those "lights" related by Swift—that the Queen chose to be escorted from the house by the Duke of Somerset, who had spoken for the Whig measure—is external, physical, and subject to interpretation. There is no evidence that Abigail had any direct knowledge of a change of royal heart. In fact, on 10 December Anne defended her opening speech, which had called for a peace, to Sir David Hamilton. This indicates that, whatever her private doubts, her public position had not altered.[64] As Edward Gregg points out, it was perfectly natural for minor Tory functionaries to lose heart over the Queen's equivocal behavior on this crucial issue.[65] That her principal favorite and would-be adviser could do so does not suggest any great confidence between them.

Indeed, it is significant that in the letter quoted above, Mrs. Masham writes of giving the Queen Harley's advice, not her own. On 27 July 1708 she requested that he provide her with that advice on a regular basis: "I shall be very glad to have your opinion upon things that I may lay it before her."[66] That Abigail reported back to her Tory cousin so regularly indicates her subservient role. In the last analysis, she was little more than a conduit of his messages and opinions, just as later, beginning early in 1710, she would be a conveyor of his person into the royal presence.[67] Later still, after she had broken with her one-time friend, she performed the same function for Viscount Bolingbroke, his ally Lord Trevor, and, possibly, the Jacobite Earl of Mar.[68]

Nevertheless, Mrs. Masham's usefulness to Harley (and his would-be successors) in this capacity should not be underestimated. Her gender, free access, assiduous attendance, and discretion all enabled the future Earl of Oxford to cultivate nearly as complete a relationship with the Queen as the various members of the Churchill circle had once enjoyed, even while he was officially out of favor. Nor did Oxford stop paying court to his cousin after his restoration to power in the summer of 1710, despite the fact that pregnancies and ill health had begun to limit her attendance, and thus her usefulness to him.[69] Though signs of tension between the minister and the favorite appeared as early as March 1712, a certain amount of personal business passed between the Queen and Oxford through Abigail almost to the end of the reign.[70] Indeed, the lord treasurer continued to be a frequent guest at the Mashams's dinner parties through mid-1712. If Swift's suspicions were correct, political business was transacted on those occasions: "Mrs. Masham was with him when I came; and they are never disturbed: 'tis well she is not very handsome: they sit alone together, settling the nation."[71] Swift was one of Abigail's admirers, full of her importance to the kingdom, convinced that her constant attendance was absolutely necessary to maintain royal confidence in the Oxford ministry.[72] While this was patently not the case, it is hardly likely that so astute a politician as "the Dragon" (Oxford) would have spent any time cultivating his cousin if he had not considered her to be of some importance, albeit a secondary one.

In matters of appointment Masham's role was likewise secondary. The various petitions she received for offices in the treasury and revenue, the military, the Church, and elsewhere indicate that she was thought influential.[73] However, neither their number (which may be a matter of historical accident) nor her manner of handling them suggests that she assumed the Duchess of Marlborough's role as a clearinghouse for applications when she supplanted her in favor. Rather, the Queen is said by Lord Dartmouth to have been reluctant "that any body should apply to her."[74] In the spring of 1712 Lady Strafford reported what may have been an overt attempt on Anne's part to discourage such applications: "Lady Massam has not been with any body or receaved any visits at home this six weeks, and som says the Queen has order'd her to live very privatly that she may not get the envy of the Peaple, like the Duchess of Marlborough."[75] This rumor is consistent with the Queen's active discouragement of ostentatious gifts to Abigail, and her initial reluctance to elevate Samuel Masham to the peerage.[76] Anne did not merely wish to avoid creating another Mrs. Freeman. The Queen, so concerned with status and propriety, could not bring herself to see past Abigail's obvious social disadvantages and utility in her current station. As Anne confessed to Dartmouth, "She never had any design to make a great lady of her, and should lose a useful servant about her person: for it would give offence to have a peeress lie upon the floor, and do several other inferior offices."[77]

Mrs. Masham's correspondence does not reveal the self-confidence of "a great lady" in dealing with those petitions that came her way. She appears to have made few recommendations to the Queen directly or on her own, preferring instead to go through the lord treasurer or some other minister. Thus, her one documented attempt to influence the disposal of a cabinet-level post other than the treasurership, that on behalf of the Earl of Jersey to be lord privy seal, was made in conjunction with Harley, and was nevertheless resisted by Anne for months.[78] The ministry likewise supported her more immediately successful solicitation on Swift's behalf for the deanery of St. Patrick's.[79] Her subordinate position and need for ministerial support are made explicit in a deferential letter she wrote to Oxford concerning one Colonel Clayton, who had petitioned her for a regiment: "He alsoe begs your Lordships favour in it; I shall write to the Queen about it and I hope you will not disapprove."[80] When Abigail did engage the Queen directly, alone and face to face, on matters of patronage, Anne was every bit as stubborn and noncommittal as she was on matters of policy:

Last night I had a great deal of discourse with my aunt [the Queen] and much of it about the two men that are named for bishops. I told her what a wild character Bertan [Burton] had, and that her father never made a worse man one than he is. She said very little to me, but by what she did say, I suspect from it she has promised he shall be one as well as Bradford. . . . Now nobody can serve her if she goes on privately doing these things every day, when she has had so much said to her as I know she has, both from myself and other people; and because I am still with her people think I am able to persuade her to anything I have a mind to have her do, but they will be convinced to the contrary one time or other.[81]

A number of those close to Lady Masham were "convinced to the contrary" before the Queen's death. As early as January 1711 the usually prescient Abbé Gaultier doubted her usefulness on the issue of the peace: "Ne pouvait rendre aucun service dans une affaire de cette conséquence."[82] At the time of Abigail's final break with Oxford in April 1714, the latter informed her, "You cannot set any one up; you can pull any one downe."[83] The lord treasurer's assessment was seemingly fulfilled when, in the final days of the reign, he lost his staff, but not to Abigail's new ally, Bolingbroke. However, even this negative view of her powers was probably inflated. Dr. Arbuthnot, an observant and assiduous courtier in his own right and an intimate of all the principals, offered a more plausible analysis: "The fall of the Dragon [Oxford] dos not proceed alltogether from his old friend [Lady Masham] but from the Great person [the Queen], whom I perceave to be highly offended by little hints that I have receav'd."[84]

And yet, despite "the Dragon's" cool-headed assessment of Lady Masham's influence, during the period just before his fall he apparently sought to enlist the aid of yet another female bedchamber attendant. In his notes for an interview with the Queen dated 8 June 1714 is the phrase "Send for the D^{chs} of Somerset—no body else can save us."[85] Sarah seems to have been taken by surprise by the favor shown her fellow Duchess, and never thought it anything but a screen for Anne's real passion for Abigail.[86] But the Tories were in no doubt of the Queen's sincerity, or Somerset's power over her. Lord Dartmouth thought her "by much the greatest favourite, when the queen died," and others in the lord treasurer's circle appear to have been obsessed with her supposed intrigues.[87] The Whigs were naturally only too happy to exacerbate Tory fears by spreading rumors like the following, relayed by Lady Strafford in the summer of 1712: "The Whiggs say Ld Treasurer went down of his knees to the Queen to beg her to put the Duchess of Sumerset from her & told her, her person was not Safe while she was there, but the Queen refus'd it."[88] Assessment of the Duchess of Somerset's influence with the Queen is, unfortunately, almost entirely dependent on such hostile, and sometimes hysterical, evidence. Certainly, she possessed decided advantages over each of her rivals. The upstart Lady Masham could not match her excellent pedigree: she was a Percy and married to one of the first peers of the realm in order of precedence. Neither Masham nor the Duchess of Marlborough possessed anything like her calm disposition and courteous nature, which were remarked upon even by her political enemies.[89] In the opinion of her friend Hamilton, the Queen's friendship for the Duchess stemmed from "a suitableness of Quality, of Temper calm, and of breeding and Natural Affection," an analysis that Anne herself endorsed upon several occasions.[90]

Ironically for Hamilton and his Whig colleagues, these very attributes, namely her family and mild disposition, ultimately prevented her from exercising much influence on their behalf. It is true that about mid-reign she began to step up her attendance, along with her husband, the Duke, in support of his ministerial pretensions. But there is little evidence that she engaged in overt political intrigue, as he did.[91] After his fall from office in January 1712, it was only with great difficulty that he could be persuaded to allow his wife to continue as groom of the stole.[92] From that time on he frequently called the Duchess from the Queen's side. Anne, fearing to lose her friend's attendance altogether, apparently grew resigned to this arrangement. In August 1713 she charged Hamilton "to say nothing of the Duchess of Somerset's being gone to Petwith [*sic*], and said it must be so, sometimes, He will have it so."[93] Hamilton, like Maynwaring and Swift before him, was not so easily resigned. Hoping to counteract what he perceived to be the pervasive influence of Lady Masham, he remonstrated with the Duchess. Her reply makes clear that she, like Masham, held her familial responsibilities to be as important as those to her royal mistress and political party: "She said she ow'd a Duty to the Duke, and her Family, and that all her Spare time, that she had from her duty to the Queen, she must use it that way. But to Spend all Her Time with the Queen, was impossible."[94] Her role as a wife and mother, combined with occasional periods of ill health,[95] ensured that she no more monopolized the Queen's ear during her tenure of office than had her two rivals toward the end of their court careers.

When the Duchess was in attendance upon her royal mistress, her natural reticence and good breeding, that very "calmness" that was such a pleasant contrast to Sarah's hectoring and Abigail's importuning, prevented her from soliciting the Queen on her party's behalf to anything like the extent of those two ladies. Despite Tory rumors that "the Duchess of Somerset . . . [was] more publick in espousing the Whig intrest then ever" in the wake of her husband's fall, Sir David Hamilton observed: "She never press'd the Queen Hard, nothing makes the Queen more Uneasie than that."[96] Indeed, Hamilton apparently felt that she did not press the Queen hard enough, for an earlier version of his *Diary*, now lost, contained a section headed "The Dutchess of Somerset too reserv'd."[97] Certainly, for all the claims made on her behalf by the Tories, the Whigs had very little to show for her supposed influence, as Professor Holmes has pointed out.[98] Ultimately, the Duchess's virtues inhibited her from excelling at, and perhaps even from attempting, the sort of court in-fighting and bedchamber intrigue that came naturally, if not in the end successfully, to the Duchess of Marlborough and Lady Masham.

Discounting rumor and invective and relying upon eyewitness testimony and demonstrable results as much as possible, one can only conclude that the influence of female bedchamber favorites upon royal policy and patronage was vastly overrated by contemporaries. Indeed, the real significance of bedchamber intrigue for Augustan politics lay not so much in what it accomplished as in what it was thought capable of accomplishing. Being a largely unknown quantity, it tended to make governments and political parties, especially those in the ascendant, nervous and insecure. The most dramatic instance of this occurred in the months leading up to the "Queen's revenge" of 1710, when a successful ministry with a solid parliamentary majority in support of the greatest military commander of the age lost its collective nerve, in part because it thought that "the unreasonable passion of a bedchamber woman" had deprived it of royal favor.[99] In fact, the actions and opinions of Abigail Masham had far less to do with that development than did those of Robert Harley, the Whigs, and the ministry itself. But in an age used to looking for a power behind the throne, it was sometimes as important to be thought to have the monarch's ear as actually to have it.

Why did the Queen's subjects look so avidly for a power behind her throne? Why did they attribute so much significance to the influence of female bedchamber favorites upon so little evidence? The explanation is to be found in contemporary attitudes about the later Stuarts, the psychological makeup of the principal actors, the nature of Augustan party politics, and, perhaps, traditional views about women. First, there was the experience of the recent past, namely the reigns of Anne's uncle, father, and brother-in-law. According to much received opinion, each of these monarchs had been dominated, or at least unduly influenced, by favorites and courtiers. Since Anne was a Stuart, it was only to be expected that she, too, would be so dominated. Her characteristic shyness and taciturnity (which no one appears to have interpreted as evidence of a politic sense of discretion), combined with her apparently slavish devotion as Princess to the relatively scintillating Sarah Churchill, could only have confirmed this expectation in the minds of contemporaries. If, early in the reign, the throne did screen the power of a favorite, then Sarah, who took care of so much of the Queen's public business, was the logical, and undenying, candidate.

Sarah herself, a courtier since her teens, should have known better. She was instead so confident of her power and Anne's weakness that, as we have seen, she came to presume upon both.[100] Once it became apparent that Mrs. Freeman's power did not exist, her firm belief in Morley's weakness, combined with her almost pathological incapacity to admit either blame or the validity of another point of view,[101] dictated in her mind that some other, more powerful, favorite had to be poisoning the royal mind against her and her party. As early as the spring of 1704, long before she lighted on Abigail, Sarah accused the Queen of listening to the opinions of the Earl of Jersey and Sir Charles Hedges—a most unlikely pair, given Anne's positive dislike of the former and the political discretion of the latter.[102] During the debacle over Sunderland's appointment in 1706, both Sarah and Godolphin suggested the equally unpromising duo of Prince George and George Churchill for the role of ministers behind the curtain. Sarah explained her reasoning in the following accusing letter to her mistress and former friend:

> The only fear I have is that there is sombody artfull that takes pains to mislead Mrs. Morley for otherwise how is it possible that one who I have formerly heard say, she was not fond of her own Judgment, could persist in such a thing soe very contrary to the advise of two men that has certainly don more services both to the Crown & Country than can be found in any history.[103]

Once the Duchess found her cousin Masham, "It became easy," in Sarah's words, "now to decipher many particulars which had hitherto remained mysterious."[104] The Whigs, never great respecters of the Queen's person nor, by and large, experienced courtiers themselves, eagerly latched onto the idea that the flattery and secret advice of Abigail and "Robin the Trickster" were the real cause of the Queen's resisting policies and persons self-evidently in her and the nation's best interest. Indeed, party ideology was so powerful that bedchamber influence, rather than the possibility of an honest difference of opinion, became the standard explanation on both sides of the political fence for royal conduct one did not agree with. Thus, Hamilton frequently attributes non-Whig opinions and behavior to the influence of certain unnamed members of "the family"—undoubtedly Lady Masham and her associates—while the Tories, deprived of their hated "Alice Perrers" by Sarah's fall in January 1711, were left to blame "your d——d duchess of Somerset's doings."[105] Conversely, it was believed that all one needed to do to produce the royal behavior one desired was to get the right lady into the royal presence as often as possible, as Maynwaring tried to do with the Duchess of Marlborough, Swift with Lady Masham, and Hamilton with the Duchess of Somerset.

Anne herself was quite conscious of this notion: "Everything I say is imputed either to partiality, or being imposed upon by knaves and fools."[106] On at least one occasion she lost her patience with Hamilton after one of his periodic hints that she was being duped by those who were secretly plotting to bring in the Pretender: "Oh fye says she, there is no such thing. What, do they think I'm a Child, and to be imposed upon, and that I have only Integrity?"[107] But this outburst is uncharacteristic. The Queen's more customary reserve and isolation meant that few knew her mind. This in turn ensured that, outside the closet, Hamilton's mechanistic view of bedchamber politics would prevail, and with it a low estimate of royal independence. Thus, the specter of female bedchamber influence was conjured up in the party mind by the reputed history of the recent past; the Queen's isolation, apparent lack of initiative, and (in party terms) inconsistency; and each party's own insecurities.

Finally, there may have been a simpler, subtler underlying assumption among contemporaries that a female monarch would be more susceptible than a male to the whisperings of other females.[108] Certainly, the Queen's gender and that of her closest personal attendants was important, but not necessarily in the ways that her subjects may have assumed them to be. As with her predecessor, Queen Elizabeth, Anne's sex dictated that her primary personal attendants and body servants would be female. But, as Simon Adams has shown, this was not in itself enough to preclude male influence or ensure female sway over policy or patronage. As is well known, the Virgin Queen had frequent political and social interaction with male officers, courtiers, and subjects generally.[109] It was Anne's poor health, shyness, and strict morality which ensured that, apart from her husband, her chief ministers, and medical staff, she would be surrounded, even guarded, by other women.[110]

As noted above, this situation created opportunity for those on the inside and mystery for nearly everyone else. Almost uniquely among court offices (and opportunities for women generally at this time), bedchamber service often led to significant financial and social advancement. It also conferred real political significance upon those who regulated access to the Queen, whether that access was face to face or through verbal or written messages. Moreover, the Duchess of Marlborough in particular was given a wide initiative in the areas of household patronage and royal charity. Finally, there was the Queen's apparent friendship with and trust in Ladies Marlborough, Masham, and Somerset. It was only natural to assume that a woman so obviously conventional as Anne (a devoted wife and mother, a good housekeeper, quiet, dignified, etc.) would turn to such women for advice on running the kingdom.

But such an interpretation ignores just how conventional, how bound by contemporary attitudes toward gender, these four women really were. It should be noted that, in the case of the first three, family responsibilities and maternal feelings consistently took precedence over political opportunity. Sarah's grief, Abigail's pregnancies, and Somerset's wifely duties all interfered with their respective attempts to monopolize the Queen's attention and favor. As for Anne herself, she gave every indication of having embraced the traditional social and familial hierarchy promoted by her beloved Anglican Church. Such a woman might be the Queen God called her to be; but she could never trust a fellow, yet still "mere," woman with matters of state.

If Queen Anne was susceptible to the influence of any of her servants, it was to that of the men who surrounded her, not the women. As noted previously, she frequently used the latter to solicit the opinions of the Duke of Marlborough and Lords Treasurer Godolphin and Oxford. Sarah was quite correct when she noted that Godolphin in particular "had been an old Nurse to her" during the early years of the reign.[111] Such influence with the monarch was entirely consistent with ministerial office. When the Queen was separated from each of these men either by distance or by opinion for most of 1708, it was equally appropriate that she turn for advice to her husband and prince consort, George of Denmark.[112] None of this would or should have surprised contemporaries, nor will it concern us here, for it was in the very nature of their stations in life that these men should have the Queen's ear.

Of more immediate interest are the careers of three male courtiers who wielded or sought to wield a comparable influence, not through ministerial office or a family tie, but through the daily access afforded them by household posts: Lord Almoner Sharp, Master of the Horse Somerset, and Lord Chamberlain Shrewsbury. Each had qualities guaranteed to recommend him to royal favor: the first, his staunch Anglicanism and good judgment; the second, his excellent pedigree; and the third, varying degrees of all three. Each man had a long association with Anne from before her accession and each had a sufficiently equivocal attitude to party to serve her at crucial moments in her attempts to govern without it. For these and other reasons, each had some success within a limited sphere of influence.

Of these three, John Sharp, Archbishop of York and lord almoner from 1703 until his death in February 1714, had perhaps the greatest contemporary reputation for influence with Queen Anne. Observers as diverse in their politics as the Duchess of Marlborough and the Earl of Nottingham noted her regard for Sharp, and she herself admitted in reference to him, "There is but one of all our Bishops y^t I have any Opinion of."[113] His descendant and first biographer, Thomas Sharp, working from an extensive private diary, now lost, noted that she allowed him a "constant and free access to her person," "admitted him to an intimate participation in her counsels," and treated him, even in matters of great political significance, as "her confident; one to whom she could disclose her thoughts at all times, and in whose faithfulness and friendship she could entirely trust; though she could not always depend upon his judgment in those matters."[114]

In fact Sharp, like the Duchess of Somerset, probably won the Queen's trust in large measure by positively refusing to meddle in "those matters"; according to Thomas Sharp, the Archbishop "would have nothing to do with the struggles of the other courtiers and great men."[115] Rather, he largely confined his efforts to his one area of expertise and concern, the Church. In matters of ecclesiastical policy his opinion was consistently sought, invariably offered, and often followed. This was the case, for example, when he persuaded the Queen to make overtures to the nonjuring Bishop Ken at the beginning of the reign, and to revive convocation in 1710.[116] On other occasions, however, the Anglican Princess demonstrated a mind that was not only her own, but fully attuned to political realities. Thus, she followed Sharp's advice in granting Queen Anne's Bounty in 1704, but did so partially in compensation for not supporting another Occasional Conformity Bill that session, which he had also requested.[117] Similarly, he was able to secure some measure of royal charity for the Scottish bishops, but no royal support for the restoration of episcopacy north of the border, which they so dearly wished. He was equally powerless to arouse the

Queen's enthusiasm over a plan to convert the Catholic Irish to Anglicanism.[118]

Sharp really came into his own in the area of ecclesiastical patronage. Anne consulted him on these matters from the first: it was he who, at her accession, persuaded her to retain all of William's chaplains.[119] Not only did he continue to appoint those who preached before the Queen, but he also decisively influenced the disposal of at least eight bishoprics and a wide variety of smaller livings.[120] During the Bishoprics Crisis of 1707 he prevailed over the ministry itself in procuring the see of Exeter for Offspring Blackall and the see of Chester for William Dawes. He bested the next ministry in the appointment of one Mr. Drake to a living in Yorkshire and, from beyond the grave, in the naming of his own successor, Dawes, at York.[121] His word could also be damaging to a prelate's career, as in the case of Jonathan Swift's dashed hopes for the deanery of Wells in 1712.[122] All of this is not to say that Sharp's word was law, even in this area.[123] Outside it, he was far less sure of himself, generally making recommendations for civil posts through the Queen's ministers, and with only moderate success overall.[124] Nevertheless, to have beaten successive ministries as often as he did in those matters closest to his heart is a tribute to what access to the monarch could accomplish when married to prudence and mutual respect.

Sharp thus presents a marked contrast to the Duke of Somerset, who appears to have combined mediocre gifts with vaulting ambition and ridiculous pride. Nevertheless, Sarah's comment, "The Queen always thought the Duke of Somerset to be a fool," is probably unduly harsh.[125] It must be recalled that Anne's friendship with Somerset was of long standing and was apparently quite sincere. It was he who offered her the use of Syon House during her quarrel with Queen Mary, when most of the rest of the peerage had abandoned her. In return, upon her accession she named him master of the horse—a post generally reserved for a favorite—albeit after having first offered it to the Duke of Shrewsbury.[126] Twice, in 1703–4 and again in 1710–12, she refused to remove him from that post after he had fallen out with a predominantly Tory cabinet, in the last instance despite "constant Tory sniping."[127]

Admittedly, a number of practical considerations probably contributed to the Queen's support. In the first instance, she undoubtedly wished to avoid losing one of the few allies of Marlborough and Godolphin in the cabinet. In the second, she feared to lose her friend the Duchess along with the Duke. There were, too, Somerset's social prestige and electoral interest to consider, factors that figured prominently in the calculations made by all sides during the ministerial crises of 1708 and 1710. But against this, it hardly seems likely, given the example of the Earl of Jersey in 1704,[128] that Anne would have screened a servant so long in opposition if she also happened to dislike him. It is significant that Somerset only fell after he attempted to deceive her regarding his vote on the Hamilton peerage, and misrepresented her opinion to other peers prior to the vote on "No Peace Without Spain," acts of *lèse-majesté* worthy of the Duchess of Marlborough.[129] Finally, it has already been noted that Anne never filled the vacancy left by his removal, as she did that left by Sarah's.

The Queen's regard for Somerset and the access afforded by his place did confer a certain political significance, but they do not appear to have translated into outright influence with her or her ministers. From about mid-reign he began to press the latter on the disposal of a wide variety of posts, mostly in the military and mostly without success.[130] This, together with his failure to receive more useful employment after standing by Marlborough and Godolphin during the attempted coup of 1708, led him to step up his and his wife's attendance on the Queen herself. By the spring of 1710 he was reported to be "more hours in the day with 42 [the Queen] than Abigail." Godolphin, for one, was in no doubt about the reason: "'Tis hardly imaginable how farr 13's [Somerset's] malice and inveterary [*sic*] has wrought up 42's [the Queen's] displeasure to 240 [the Duchess of Marlborough], and to all those who will not forsake her."[131] In fact, Somerset later claimed to have put out Lord Chamberlain Kent in April 1710, then Godolphin himself in August of that year.[132] Just before the latter event Peter Wentworth asserted, "The Duke of Summerset is a great favourite, and is said to govern in concert with th' other Duke [Shrewsbury] and Harley."[133] However, there is no firm evidence with which to disentangle his strand from the very thick rope woven that summer by Harley and the Queen in order to hang the Godolphin ministry. For once, Sarah may have offered the shrewdest guess when she wrote to Arthur Maynwaring: "I am still of the opinion that 13 [Somerset] can only doe people mischeif & tell lyes, & that hee is not relyed on for advise any more than the bug [Kent] was that is turned out."[134]

As with Abigail Masham's, Somerset's real significance was as a conduit of information to the Queen from Harley and the Tories. During the summer of 1710 he was employed to run persons and messages into the royal presence whose arrival there had to be kept secret. A typical example of the sort of intrigue engaged in by Somerset at this time is the subject of the following letter to Harley, dated 30 July: "The Queen hath commanded me to write to you to come this night to the Duke of Shrewsbury's lodgings and from thence you are to be conveyed to ——— by me."[135] Somerset's ex officio access and well-known favor with the Queen made him a convenient ally for any politician lacking one or both of these advantages. However, they were not, in themselves, sufficient to make up for the lack of political judgment noted by contemporaries and of which Anne must have been aware. As a result, real influence over even a limited area, such as that enjoyed by Archbishop Sharp, eluded "the proud Duke."

Somerset's attendance began to drop off in the fall of 1710, once the dissolution of parliament made it clear that a more or less Tory game was afoot, and that he would play no more significant a role in the new ministry than he had in the old.[136] In fact, several of the most observant Whigs noted as early as the previous June that he was being eclipsed by a politician and potential favorite of an altogether superior caliber: Charles Talbot, Duke of Shrewsbury.[137] Even Shrewsbury's sharpest critics, such as the Duchess of Marlborough among the Whigs and Lord Dartmouth among the Tories, were compelled to admit his many good qualities. According to Dartmouth, "The duke of Shrewsbury was a man of a very noble family, a clear understanding, had an education that qualified him for any employment, extremely agreeable in his person, and of a very lively conversation."[138] Shrewsbury was much more than the perfect ornament to a court. His prominent role in the Revolution, his nevertheless ambiguous attitude to party, and his longtime friendship with both Anne and the Churchills all served to recommend him to royal favor. Indeed, the Queen and her ministers' regard for him was such that at her accession she offered him the mastership of horse, which he declined in order to go abroad for his health.[139]

When Shrewsbury did finally enter royal service, in April 1710, it was as Anne's lord chamberlain. This post gave him an ex officio right to constant, daily access to the monarch, while at the same time entailing none of the responsibilities and public scrutiny of ministerial office. This arrangement suited perfectly the Duke's well-known timorousness and fear of exposure. Its advantages were shrewdly noted by Godolphin soon after the new chamberlain's appointment: "I incline to think he may soon come to have as much influence with 42 [the Queen] as 38 [Godolphin] used to have heretofore, with this difference, that 38's post did necessarily create more occasions of shewing it to the world."[140] The lord treasurer's analysis proved highly prophetic. Shrewsbury did use his place as an excuse to attend and, presumably, to cultivate the Queen as assiduously as his health and (later) his other offices permitted. According to Sarah's best information (probably gathered from her informal court spy ring), Anne responded favorably: "The Queen sent for him perpetually, & kept him two hours together with her."[141] With the accession of the Oxford ministry he made himself almost indispensable by acting as a liaison between that body and the monarch when the two were physically separated, as during Harley's convalescence after the assassination attempt in the spring of 1711, or when the Queen was at Windsor.[142]

Above all, Shrewsbury used his access to influence the Queen, though not, as Sharp and Somerset attempted to do, in matters of appointment. The cautious Duke rarely made interest for places on behalf of others. When he did so, he generally went through or joined with the ministers, even for places in his own gift.[143] To a relative whose suit he did agree to support, he was careful to stress "the little interest" he had.[144] Rather, Shrewsbury generally reserved that "little interest" for matters of high policy. Thus, in September 1711 the Queen wrote to Oxford, "Lord Chamberlain has talked a good deale to me about the Peace."[145] In June 1714 he and Bolingbroke are supposed to have convinced her to issue the proclamation putting a price of £5,000 on the head of the Pretender.[146] Anne herself confessed to Oxford the greatest confidence in her apparently insecure lord chamberlain: "I am sorry the Duke of Shrewsbury should make complaints of me, I am sure I do not deserve them, for I speak to him of everything, and advise with him on all occasions and will continue doing soe."[147]

Edward Gregg has suggested that Oxford's relation to the Queen of Shrewsbury's supposed complaints was really a clever ruse to damage the Duke's credit with her.[148] Though Shrewsbury was a decidedly junior partner in the ministry, Oxford seems to have appreciated the danger posed by this potential rival for the Queen's ear, for he grew increasingly careful to keep the lord chamberlain in the dark about important affairs such as the peace negotiations.[149] Eventually, he sought to separate the Duke from his mistress entirely by sending him first to Paris as ambassador to the court of Louis XIV from January to September 1713 and then, after a brief respite in London, to Dublin as lord lieutenant of Ireland from September 1713 to June 1714. Nevertheless, upon his return from this exile the Duke's credit with the Queen was still sufficient to help tip the balance between Oxford and Bolingbroke, wrest the treasurer's staff out of the hand of the former, and, in a move that must have surprised even Shrewsbury, propel it into his own hand at her death.[150] While these developments were undoubtedly the culmination of many forces, they leave no doubt of Anne's great regard for her chamberlain's person and opinions. Surely, no other of her household servants could show so much for his trouble and attendance.

Most of the Queen's servants could show very little. Vice Chamberlain Coke received numerous petitions from relatives, friends, and constituents for the Queen's favor, which was often granted. But this had equally been the case before his household appointment, when he had merely been knight of the shire for Derbyshire and a teller of the exchequer.[151] Despite the relatively free access that every great officer was entitled to, most could boast no more than one or two such successes, usually won through the ministry rather than their own attendance.[152] Even an old and assiduous lady of the bedchamber like Frescheville thought it best to route petitions through the Duke of Somerset: "Having no interest any where else, I durst not presume to speak" to the Queen directly.[153] Well might the poor malodorous "Bugg," Lord Chamberlain Kent, complain, "Dey never let me into any of Deir Politicks"; but he was hardly unique among the great household officers in his lack of influence.[154]

Finally, contemporaries sometimes attributed great influence to middling and inferior household servants other than Mrs. Masham.[155]

However, apart from their importance in regulating access to the royal bedchamber and closet, there is little evidence to suggest that Anne's ministers had any need to cultivate the "little people" in the way that Charles II's had. Rather, Mary Stanhope's complaint that, as a maid of honor, she "had very little encouragement to ask any favours at court" would appear to be typical.[156] Even Dr. Arbuthnot, who was commonly thought to advise the Queen, left evidence only of his influence on minor appointments, virtually none on matters of policy, despite Anne's real regard for him and his constant attendance upon her during the last years of the reign.[157]

Arbuthnot's great Whig rival, Sir David Hamilton, did leave the evidence upon which to evaluate his influence in the form of his *Diary*, but it does not reveal Anne to have been any more susceptible to the intrigues of middling male attendants than she was to those of females like Mrs. Masham. Hamilton claimed that he had "no by End" in his attendance "but her Majesty's honour, health and quiet of Mind,"[158] but his *Diary* is, in fact, full of his subtle and not so subtle attempts to build up the Whigs and plant seeds of doubt about the Tory ministry in the Queen's mind. For example, he took every opportunity to promote the interests first of Sarah and the Churchills, then of the Duchess of Somerset, in the Queen's presence.[159] Equally forthright were his discussions with her in October 1710 concerning "the bill of Comprehensions, wishing she would begin it," and in December 1711 concerning his wish that "my Lord Cowper was in."[160] More subtle, if ultimately transparent, were his attempts to veil would-be influence under the guise of information, as when, in July 1710, he "acquainted her that it was said to be Mr. Wards opinion, that the Tories could not answer the Funds, if the Bank would not," or when, in September of that year, he showed her a number of Whig pamphlets.[161] There is little evidence that this "information" produced the desired effect; certainly the Whigs would have been hard pressed to point to any concrete advantages they derived from the physician's attendance.

Information

Nevertheless, it was clearly important to both the Queen and her nominally loyal opposition that she continue to hear their point of view. Not only did she put up with the insistent partisanship of servants like Hamilton and Masham, but she often used their attendance and the relative privacy of the backstairs to solicit the opinions of prominent members of the opposition. The most famous example of this was the attendance and advice given by Robert Harley in the months preceding his return to power in 1710. It is less well known that during this period and its immediate aftermath she likewise requested Cowper, Somers, and even Bishop Burnet to come to her via the backstairs: "During this winter I was encouraged by the queen to speak more freely to her of her affairs, than I had ever ventured to do formerly."[162]

As the political situation grew more tense and divisions over the peace and the succession more prominent, the once "moderate" Oxford ministry sought to prevent this sort of interaction between the Queen and its enemies, using the methods complained of by Hamilton.[163] Describing a rare three-hour visit to the royal closet in September 1713 by Christian Siegfried von Plessen, the Prince's former Danish secretary and a diplomat with ties to Hanover, Peter Wentworth observed: "He nick't his opportunity when none of the Ministry was here."[164] When the ministry was "here," the Queen was entirely dependent upon her Whig servants to keep her informed of what her Tory ministers would not. Thus, it was the Duchess of Somerset who, in December 1711, showed her Bothmer's printed memorial containing the Elector's formal condemnation of the peace, which the ministry had been anxious to keep from her.[165] It was the Duchess's friend Hamilton who, in July 1714, informed the Queen that Oxford had not been writing to General Schulenberg, his supposed contact with Hanover, as promised.[166]

Naturally, the Tories had earlier charged the Godolphin ministry with a similar policy of keeping the Queen in the dark, thus necessitating Masham's role as a conveyor of information and persons from their side of the political divide.[167] In each case the ministry ultimately failed in its attempt to isolate the Queen from alternate points of view because, while it could hinder the access of opponents *sans* office, it was never allowed to purge the Queen's own immediate "family."[168] Anne resisted the few attempts to do so not only because they struck at her right to choose her own servants, but because those servants were her only sources for certain kinds of information and her only links to certain shades of opinion. Those connections had to be maintained if she were to have any hope of remaining a free agent, or any claim to being the Queen of all her people. Burnet thought that his advice "had no effect upon her," and indeed, if judged according to the standards for measuring influence established in the previous section, it did not.[169] But on a subtler level, his views, as well as those of all who came into the royal presence, along with genuine news such as that provided by Somerset and Hamilton as mentioned above, undoubtedly colored Anne's own view of her ministry. At the very least, such information enabled her to maintain some sort of perspective on what it was telling her. Since she was a prisoner of her physical infirmities as well as of her ministers, the backstairs and closet were not only the most discreet venue for the receipt of such intelligence, but indeed the only one, and were thus of some constitutional significance. Finally, from her subjects' point of view, the knowledge that such information was being heard (for recurrent backstairs attendance could rarely be kept entirely secret) might tend to limit, if only slightly, the violence of an opposition party, while serving notice to its rival that the favor it enjoyed could not be presumed upon.

Of equal significance to Anne's solicitation of differing views was the way in which she used the relative privacy of the court to make her own opinions known, either to individuals or to the political nation as a whole. The most famous examples of this were her "closetings" of various peers in an attempt to influence their behavior in parliament. Before 1710 she seems to have confined her efforts almost exclusively to conversations with Archbishop Sharp, who she hoped would act as something of a government whip for the episcopal bench, but who proved to be distressingly independent on more than one occasion.[170] It was the impending Whig address calling for the removal of Mrs. Masham in January 1710 that caused her to broaden her efforts. Convinced that her prerogative and independence were as much under attack as was a faithful servant, Anne canvassed a wide variety of peers "with tears in her eyes." It is a measure of the Queen's continued personal prestige that she successfully averted what must have seemed the inevitable, given the Whig predominance in both houses.[171] According to one contemporary, "Observers say they never saw such a turn in their lives, & Lady Fretchvill says in 30 years she has served she never saw the like."[172] Subsequently, Oxford's precarious situation in the Lords forced the Queen to resort to this method fairly frequently, though with mixed results.[173]

In addition to personal canvassing, Queen Anne often made use of household servants to advertise her position on parliamentary issues. Not only Sharp, but also Thomas Coke, Shrewsbury, and, in particular, the Duke of Somerset sometimes acted as royal spokesmen.[174] The latter was joined by Devonshire in explaining the Queen's actions to the Whigs during the Bishoprics Crisis of 1707, and by Queensberry during the Whig offensive against Masham at the beginning of 1710.[175] Weeks later, during the Sacheverell trial, he acted alone but, according to Godolphin, with great effectiveness: "13 [Somerset] labours hard against us, and makes use of 42's [the Queen's] name to South and North Brittains with a good deal of freedom. I doubt he is pretty sure of not being disavowd and I believe him entirely linked with the opposite party, upon the foot of knowing 42's inclinations and flattering them."[176] The advantage of this arrangement from the Queen's point of view was that it enabled her to influence votes on sensitive issues without exposing her own position directly. This was especially useful when her position did not happen to coincide with that of her current ministry, as was the case, to varying degrees, in all of the above examples.[177] However, the tactic could backfire. Somerset's reputation for "knowing 42's inclinations" was so considerable that during the debate over the peace in December 1711—when Anne's position did coincide with that of her ministry—he persuaded a number of Court Whigs "to vote against the Ministry, by assuring them it was the Queen's Pleasure."[178]

The final way in which the Queen could release information through her servants was by employing them as messengers to individuals. She generally preferred to bypass the official household messengers (the messengers of the chamber and grooms of the great chamber) for a wide variety of personal servants, from the lord chamberlain and master of the horse down to pages and footmen.[179] For secret political correspondence, however, she relied almost exclusively upon trusted middling servants like Hamilton or Masham. Anne's faith in and reliance upon these members of her "family" are illustrated by the uses to which she put Abigail between 1707 and 1710, and by an even more remarkable initiative involving the Whig physician in the closing days of the reign. At the end of July 1714 Hamilton was instructed by the Queen to begin a secret correspondence and series of meetings on her behalf, through General Schulenberg, with the Elector himself. This undertaking, necessitated by Oxford's equivocal behavior over the succession and the ministerial crisis precipitated by his fall, was itself forestalled by the Queen's death on 1 August. It thus represents her last attempt to break out of the virtual captivity within which successive ministries of varying complexion had held her. If implemented, it would also have been the most remarkable use to which she ever put a royal servant. In the Queen's mind desperate measures were necessary, for, as Sir David reports her confidence to him, "she had none to trust, she would give me a proof of what Trust she put in me."[180]

And yet, as with so many of her "family," that trust was not entirely warranted. Throughout the Queen's last years Hamilton, truer to his party principles than to his royal mistress, was secretly sending information about her health and activities to Hanover through none other than George Frideric Handel, newly arrived in London.[181] At the same time she was beginning to suspect that Lady Masham and her sister Alice Hill were spying on her for the Tories.[182] While Anne's suspicions must remain a matter for speculation, her fears were understandable. As Princess, she had found herself the object of spying by some of her closest friends and attendants during the quarrel with William and Mary.[183] When she became Queen, information about her continued to be readily available from servants and courtiers whether she liked it or not. The Duchess of Marlborough in particular had a great number of court contacts who kept her informed about the slanders supposedly being conveyed about her to the Queen, of Abigail Masham's activities, of Lord Somers's secret access, and so on.[184] Sarah sometimes identifies the source of her information straightforwardly, by naming a friend at court or an old family retainer whom the Duchess had preferred into the household, but more often she is cryptic, citing the likes of "very good hands."[185] Given the breadth of acquaintance Sarah had built up at court over the years and the high proportion of royal servants who were Churchills themselves or clients of that family, it is clear that she had at her disposal nothing short of a fully fledged spy network. It is little wonder that, in the wake of her fall in January

1711, the Queen and the Duchess of Somerset purged some of the old Churchill servants at the lower echelons of the bedchamber and robes.[186]

Nevertheless, a court spy ring was not necessary in order to keep abreast of the Queen's activities. Such information was there for the asking, from women of the bedchamber, pages of the backstairs, or any other royal servant who maintained an assiduous and observant attendance.[187] The correspondence of Peter Wentworth shows him to have been just such a servant: as he assured his brother, the Earl of Strafford, in September 1713, "You may depend on't I'll have my eyes about me & refrain my tongue from speaking."[188] Wentworth's discreet watchfulness enabled him to keep Strafford informed about the court's daily activities, from the reception of ambassadors to hunting excursions.[189] More interesting was the political information he provided, much of which would have been available only to the vigilant courtier. In this category are his accounts of the crowds of people from both parties flocking to pay court to Mrs. Masham during the second half of 1710; of the Duke of Somerset's declining attendance over the same period; and, most importantly, of Whig and Tory politicians going up the backstairs to visit the Queen.[190] Finally, and perhaps most interestingly for his correspondent on the continent, Wentworth avidly reported court rumor, albeit carefully labeling it as such. Thus, he relayed speculation regarding the Whig attempt to dislodge Abigail and have the Duke of Marlborough named captain general for life in January 1710; the negotiations concerning the Duke and Duchess of Somerset in January 1712; and the quarrel between Oxford and Lady Masham in April 1714.[191] Similar information was available to and disseminated by the London diplomatic community.[192]

However, the most important subject upon which court servants and other observers could provide information was the Queen's health, for upon this frail reed hung the peace and, later, the succession.[193] The most reliable method of ascertaining the current state of the royal constitution was to make an evaluation based on face-to-face contact. But in the absence of a daily morning public *levée*, such opportunities were limited to a closed circle of trusted female bedchamber attendants. Only the occasional drawing room allowed for the widening of that circle. Indeed, L'Hermitage noted to his superiors that one such occasion had been scheduled in the spring of 1714 for the precise purpose of publicly demonstrating an improvement in the Queen's state of health after her near-fatal illness of the previous winter.[194] By the same token, the diagnostic opportunities afforded by these events seem to have been their main attraction for some observers, particularly during the last few, precarious months of Anne's life. Thus the French ambassador, d'Iberville, reported to his master at the end of 1713, "J'irey demain a Windsor pour scavoir moy mesme l'estat de sa santé a l'example de tous les Ministres étrangers."[195]

Unfortunately, drawing rooms were sometimes scheduled rather haphazardly under Anne and were in any case especially scarce at precisely those times when her condition was most in doubt.[196] At such times, the most authoritative source on the royal constitution should have been the royal physicians. Certainly, they broadcast their opinions freely, both in conversation and correspondence.[197] But political partisanship or personal loyalty often prevented them from giving out accurate information about their patient's condition. For example, in March 1711 Wentworth reported a recent royal illness during which "they keept it a secreet till the danger was past how many fitt she had had."[198] The Queen's friend Arbuthnot in particular pursued a conscious policy of denying or minimizing the seriousness of Anne's illnesses. He did so with such consistency that Wentworth (who had other sources) was forced to conclude: "What Doctor Alburtunote & Dicken & Blundel the surgeons say as to the Queen's State of health is not to be minded for God knows they have often said she was very well, when it has been known to be otherwise, but those are pious frauds & very allowable."[199]

Arbuthnot's duplicity and Wentworth's indulgence of it owed at least as much to their Tory sympathies as to their loyalty as servants. Each was a natural response to the concurrent Whig attempt, born of the impending crisis over the succession, to publicize and exaggerate the Queen's health problems. There is evidence to support Daniel Defoe's contention concerning the Whigs: "They discover in their very faces a secret satisfaction at any indisposition her Majesty may suffer, eagerly enlarge the account, and report every trifle of that kind to be fatal."[200] In an attempt to nip such rumors in the bud, Arbuthnot sought on a number of occasions to limit the attendance of his compatriots, just as the ministry sought to limit that of its rivals.[201] Though his attempt at a monopoly of information (in this case about, rather than for, the Queen) likewise failed, his undoubted popularity with Anne, and his possession, unique among her medical staff, of lodgings in all of her principal residences, left him with powerful tools with which to manage it.[202]

This fact, along with the misinformation that they themselves had done so much to disseminate, left the Whig leadership all the more dependent upon physicians of their own persuasion for accurate news of the Queen's condition. When Sir David Hamilton, a Dissenter, contemplated resignation in the event of passage of the Occasional Conformity Bill of 1711, Lord Cowper dissuaded him "by saying that then they should hav not a faithful servant of her health."[203] The political and constitutional significance of such information was stressed by the Whig Dr. Shadwell in a petition for royal favor submitted at the beginning of the next reign: "In the Queen's last illness he declared, in opposition to the opinion of the rest of his brethren, the true state of her case to the Lords of the Council, that they might take the necessary precautions for the security of the Protestant succession."[204]

For those with a more casual interest in the Queen's state of health, information of variable accuracy was probably always available from her servants, who thus acquired a certain kudos at the coffeehouse or tavern. It was also common to inquire about the Queen's condition at the backstairs from the lady in waiting: according to Lady Strafford, this "is what Every body dos now She has the Gout."[205] It is highly unlikely that the information thus received was any more reliable than that dispensed by the royal physicians, since bedchamber attendants were equally susceptible to feelings of loyalty or partisanship. But it was a good piece of courtier's wisdom to be seen to be inquiring about the monarch's health, especially given the Whigs' positive delight in disparaging it. Thus, Lady Strafford noted to her husband in January 1712, "I went two days Agoe to know how the Queen did Lady Rochester was in waiting she told me she allways told the Queen when I had been there & the Queen bid her tell me if I had any Business she wou'd see me her self."[206]

Finally, the activities, opinions, and ailments of the royal invalid were by no means the only subjects to be studied at court by the observant servant or the alert courtier *sans* office. Jonathan Swift found the court an excellent place, possibly second only to parliament itself, to gauge the disposition and health of the ministry. For example, he notes that when the news arrived of Stanhope's defeat at Brihuega in December 1710, "it was odd to see the whole countenances of the Court changed so in two hours."[207] A year later, in the days following the momentous vote on "No Peace Without Spain," he and the rest of the political world were drawn to court by the same impulse: "I took courage to-day, and went to Court with a very chearful countenance. It was mightily crowded; both parties coming to observe each other's faces."[208]

Swift's career at Anne's court, as chronicled in the *Journal to Stella* and his correspondence, demonstrates that the royal household provided access to and information about the Queen's ministers as well as the monarch herself. It is true that Godolphin, Marlborough, and, later, Oxford held *levées* at their London residences, but the relatively cramped quarters tended to make these affairs overcrowded and unpleasant.[209] The court could provide a more spacious and convenient point of contact between petitioners and potential patrons. Swift records that while he was at court, drawing rooms were held three times a week during the court season, at which could be found "all her Ministers, Foreignrs & Persons of Quality."[210] It is clear from his and other testimony that these were business as well as social occasions. For example, Peter Wentworth writes to his brother in 1713 concerning the latter's impending installation as a knight of the garter: "To morrow is another Court & if theres any thing stiring about this business, I shall know Lord Treasurer says he dispatches more business in one of these mornings then he us'd to do at home in a week."[211]

As noted at the beginning of this chapter, anyone capable of assuming a gentle appearance could go to court and try his luck, either by putting himself "in view" or by accosting a minister directly. To avoid the crowds, it was best simply to go to the backstairs and wait, hoping to catch one of the ministers entering or leaving a meeting with the Queen or of the cabinet. This was Wentworth's method on another occasion when he was called upon to run an errand for his absent sibling: "To night I went to the Back stairs to the waiting room before the Counsel, were [*sic*] I knew I shou'd see all the Great men, wch I thought wou'd be enough to put them in mind, without speaking."[212] Indeed, the backstairs seems to have been the place to meet anybody who was anybody at court, which helps to explain why the pages stationed there knew so much.[213] Ultimately, it was not bedchamber influence and backstairs intrigue but information—to, from, and about the monarch and her ministers—which was the real "cash nexus" of politics at the court of Queen Anne.

Household Officers in Parliament

As the preceding discussion shows, the court was an important forum for the transaction of political business. Nevertheless, by the date of Anne's accession it was a decidedly secondary one to parliament. It is therefore necessary to turn to the court as a focus for loyalty in politics as carried on within the palace of Westminster. The following does not examine the whole of what contemporaries sometimes referred to as "the Court party," but, rather, the parliamentary careers of the 30 peers and 52 M.P.s who, sometime during Anne's reign, held household office (see Appendix C).[214] During any given session there were, on average, only 11 such peers and 14 commoners, who thus formed only a small proportion of the total number of government members in each house (Table 6.1).[215] Nevertheless, this group was potentially of much significance to the viability of any "Court" or "government" party. To understand that significance fully, it is necessary to examine briefly the reputation and actuality of the government interest as a whole.

The Country vision of the government interest in parliament made it seem an impressive, if not invincible, machine for the passage of government-backed legislation. It was regarded as vast, comprising all civil and military officers, pensioners, and anyone else in parliament with like ambitions. All told, something like a third of the House of Commons and an even higher proportion of the Lords were supposed to be in the ministry's pocket. Moreover, it was often asserted that these proportions were rising as a result of the general expansion in the size of the central administration caused by the war.[216] In their quest for place and profit, "Court" members were said to follow the government of the day slavishly, irrespective of personal or party principles. Thus, in the pamphlet *Faults on Both Sides* the Tory failure to pass the

TABLE 6.1
Household Officers in Parliament, 1702–1714

	House of Lords	House of Commons
Avg. no. of household officers per session, 1702–14	11	14
Highest no. of household officers in a session	14[a]	18[b]
Lowest no. of household officers in a session	8[c]	9[d]
Total no. of household officers in Parliament, 1702–14	30	52

SOURCES: Cokayne, *Peerage*; information provided by Eveline Cruickshanks and David Hayton.
[a]Sessions of 1711–12, 1714.
[b]Session of 1709–10.
[c]Session of 1702.
[d]Session of 1713.

Tack in November 1704 is explained as follows: "Several of the most considerable men of that side having been taken off by the ministers, and gratified with good places, they left their party in the lurch, and voted against the tack."[217] Nor did the political nation have much hope of tossing the bounders out, for the government was supposed to have a powerful electoral interest at its disposal, capable of ensuring that landless, rapacious, and by definition unqualified and unscrupulous placemen could be returned at will. Thus, one Whig commentator complained just before the 1710 election, "Both parties talk very confidently of a majority, but the times are so corrupt they must know very little that don't think a Court can give either side a majority."[218] The only resort left to honest country gentlemen was the pursuit of place legislation, most of which either failed to achieve passage or was so watered down in execution as to be virtually meaningless.[219]

Recent scholarship has done much to undermine, if not outright demolish, this picture of the Augustan political world. Geoffrey Holmes and Clyve Jones have demonstrated that the Country claim of a rise in the number of placemen because of the war was exaggerated, and that at any given time the ministry could call on only about 60 members in the lower house. The proportion was somewhat higher in the Lords, but never the majority alleged by Country propaganda.[220] William

TABLE 6.2
Attendance and Participation in Business of Peers in Household Office (per Session), 1702–1714

	Over total parliamentary career	During period in household office
Avg. no. of days in attendance	45.9	42.2
Avg. no. of committees served on	12.1	10.8
Avg. no. of instances named as a manager w/ the Commons	0.3	0.2
Avg. no. of instances of reporting to the House	0.5	0.4

SOURCE: *Lords Journals* XVII–XIX.

NOTE: One peer whose household service did not coincide with that in the Lords (Francis, Earl of Godolphin), as well as a number of bishops who had been chaplains under Anne, have not been counted in Table 6.2.

Speck has cast serious doubt upon the number of government boroughs, the amounts of government money spent on elections, and the effectiveness of government influence in returning favored individuals generally. He argues that, in fact, most M.P.s were returned on their own interests.[221] Finally, Holmes, Jones, Speck, and most recently Clayton Roberts have argued that insofar as a Court party could be said to have existed at all under the later Stuarts, it was at best only intermittently effective in parliament, largely because the pull of party principle and organization was much stronger.[222]

An examination of the parliamentary behavior of the Queen's household servants fully bears out these more recent findings. Tables 6.2 and 6.3 attempt to measure the impact of household office upon the attendance and participation in parliamentary business of those peers and M.P.s who possessed it. They do so by comparing the average number of days in attendance or instances of participation per session of these two groups while in household office (column 2), with averages calculated for the whole of their parliamentary careers (column 1).[223] The results of this comparison indicate that receipt of a place at court had almost no effect upon the parliamentary behavior of either subpopulation. Specifically, the average amount of attendance, committee work, and participation in other forms of business per session stayed the same or declined slightly when the members of either group were in household office. Moreover, the low absolute values of the averages in either column suggest that household peers and M.P.s not only failed to grow more assiduous on taking office, but were in general a fairly lackadaisical bunch throughout their parliamentary careers. In short, it would appear that on the whole these members were not preferred to court office on the basis of a previously demonstrated parliamentary utility; nor were they expected to become more useful upon preferment.[224]

Naturally, these composite averages conceal individuals in both houses who were exceptional in their attendance to business. Lord Delawarr, for example, excelled as a reporter to the upper house, performing this function an average of 4.9 times per session, 7.0 when in household office.[225] Delawarr also had an outstanding record of attendance (averaging 66.8 days per session, 69.0 when in office) and committee work (sitting on an average of 21 committees per session, in or out of office). What makes Delawarr particularly unusual is that he was a diehard courtier who once described his place as "a blessing farr more valewable, then life it self."[226] The most active household members of either house were more typically prominent party politicians whose court places implied little change in behavior. For example, in the Lords the most regular attenders besides Delawarr were Buckingham and

TABLE 6.3
Participation in Business of M.P.s in Household Office (per Session), 1702–1714

	Over total parliamentary career	During period in household office
Avg. no. of committees served on	4.2	4.0
Avg. no. of committees chaired	0.2	0.2
Avg. no. of instances of reporting to the House	0.1	0.1
Avg. no. of instances of telling on divisions	0.5	0.4

SOURCE: *Commons Journals* XIII–XVII.

NOTE: Five M.P.s whose household service did not coincide with that in the Commons (Conyers Darcy, John Granville, George Granville, Robert Harley, and Crewe Offley) have not been counted in Table 6.3.

Mansell (each of whom turned up an average of over 65 days per session), the most frequent managers between the houses Bradford, the first Duke of Devonshire, Poulett, Somerset, and Townshend. In the Commons, the most frequent chairmen of select committees among the household members were the Marquess of Hartington, a committed and eventually Junto Whig; and Sir William Wyndham, an equally committed and probably Jacobite Tory. Likewise, the most active tellers in this group, Heneage Finch, Sir John Holland, Sir William Pole, William Walsh, and the above-named Wyndham, were all active party men of some importance.[227]

The dichotomy between a large group of more or less inactive household peers and M.P.s and a small core of active party men who did not modify their behavior in office is most clearly visible when one turns to the admittedly fragmentary data on parliamentary speaking. The evidence provided by the *Parliamentary History*, extant correspondence, and the few members' diaries in existence indicates that most of the Queen's "family" who sat in parliament were silent. Those few who were not tended to speak along party lines irrespective of place. They might do so subtly, as when Wyndham and his friend William Collier promoted the divisive Schism Bill in May 1714. Or they might do so overtly, as in the case of Seymour's opposition activities prior to April 1704; Compton's and Sharp's suggestion that the Church was in danger in 1705 and defense of Sacheverell in 1710; Somerset's speech, "louder than any in the house for the clause against Peace," in December 1711; or Montagu's opposition to the address of thanks for the Queen's speech at the opening of parliament in April 1713.[228] All supported their party's position against the current ministry despite holding household office at the time. Sometimes, the failure of a courtier to speak could be just as embarrassing to the government as a speech in opposition. It was widely noted during the debate over "No Peace Without Spain" that both Lord President Buckingham and Lord Chamberlain Shrewsbury remained silent, their reticence implying a crisis of ministerial conscience and solidarity on this issue.[229]

While the party politicians named to household office under Queen Anne obviously remained true to their partisan loyalties rather than assume government ones, the silent majority might still be made to fit with the Country image of an ill-suited and undistinguished assortment of flunkies sitting only to provide fodder for government majorities. The ultimate test of this charge, and of court office as a factor in parliamentary politics generally, is to be found in the voting record of household members insofar as it is recorded in the surviving division lists for each house. In recent years, a phalanx of historians led by Geoffrey Holmes have used these lists to demonstrate that the vast majority of Augustan peers and M.P.s were consistently loyal to one or the other of the two great political parties, rarely, if ever, crossing to vote with those who sat on the other side of the house. Since government under Queen Anne was not, by and large, straight party government, it was inevitable that even the most obscure household member would, sooner or later, have to choose between the course of unvarying party loyalty as described by Professor Holmes, and the slavish devotion to the hand that fed him alleged by Country apologists.

Before examining the evidence provided by the lists, it should be noted that they are very few, and almost exclusively concerned with great, that is to say party, issues.[230] On most such issues, it is impossible to separate the natural government position from that of the party currently in favor, or the opposition position from that of the party without it. Few lists survive for the period prior to the fall of the Tories in April 1704.[231] Most votes between that event and the disintegration of the Godolphin ministry in the summer of 1710 divided along Whig-government versus Tory-opposition lines. With the change of ministry, the picture blurs because of Oxford's reluctance to govern by party and, later, the fragmentation of his own administration.[232] However, most of the issues for which lists survive from this period united the Tory position with that of the government.[233] None of the surviving lists for Anne's reign is of a strict government/opposition vote devoid of party significance,[234] nor did the two parties often unite against the ministry. The only apparent example of the latter is the division of 21 January 1709 over whether to allow Scots peers with British titles to vote in the election of the sixteen representative peers, upon which issue most Whig and Tory peers opposed the government, for a variety of reasons.[235] In the absence of more lists recounting such divisions, the most direct way to assess "government" versus "party" loyalties will be to pay particular attention to the voting records of "government" Tories (mostly Harleyites) for the period 1704–10, and "government" Whigs

TABLE 6.4

Voting Record of Peers in Household Office, 1702–1714

% of recorded divisions	No. voting Whig or Tory over total career: Whig	Tory	No. voting w/ govt. or opposition over total career: Govt.	Opp.	No. voting w/ govt. or opposition while in household office: Govt.	Opp.
100%	11	13	6	5	7	3
76–99%	0	2	2	0	2	0
51–75%	1	2	7	3	4	1
50%	1	1	4	4	3	3
Total	13	18	19	12	16	7
Total no. of peers in sample[a]	30		27		20	

SOURCES: See Appendix D.

[a]I.e., members who left records of their votes on issues fitting the above categories (omits one peer and several bishops whose terms of household office and service in the Lords did not coincide).

during the subsequent four years, when the members of each of these groups would have had to make a choice.

Tables 6.4 and 6.5 characterize household peers and M.P.s according to the consistency with which they voted along, first, party lines (column 1); second, government or opposition lines (column 2); and third, government or opposition lines while in household office (column 3).[236] Turning first to the 30 household peers, Table 6.4 indicates that significantly more voted either Whig (11) or Tory (13) 100 percent of the time than voted for the government position (6) with equal consistency over the span of their parliamentary careers under Anne (column 1 compared to column 2). Limiting the inquiry to the period of household service yields only seven peers who always voted with the government, though another six did so most of the time (i.e., in 51–99 percent of their recorded votes) while in office (column 3). Only two peers, the nominally Tory Earl of Cardigan and the nominally Whig Duke of Kent, were more consistent government voters than party voters, while nine peers were more consistent party men than government men even when in office. Five peers voted against the government in every recorded division, though only the two Dukes of Montagu and Lord Townshend did so while in office. Opposition was a luxury the Montagus, at least, could well afford since they held their successive masterships of the great wardrobe by patent, for life.

TABLE 6.5
Voting Record of M.P.s in Household Office, 1702–1714

% of recorded divisions	No. voting Whig or Tory over total career		No. voting w/ govt. or opposition over total career		No. voting w/ govt. or opposition while in household office	
	Whig	Tory	Govt.	Opp.	Govt.	Opp.
100%	20	15	18	4	23	2
76–99%	3	2	3	0	1	0
51–75%	1	0	3	3	3	1
50%	2	2	3	3	1	1
Total	26	19	27	10	28	4
Total no. of M.P.s in sample[a]	43		34		31	

SOURCES: See Appendix D.
[a]I.e., members who left records of their votes on issues fitting the above categories (omits five M.P.s whose terms of household office and service in the Commons did not coincide).

An examination of individual divisions that involved a definite clash between government and party loyalties reveals only a few instances in which the former won out among peers in household office. It did so for Compton and Sharp on the Union in 1706; for Cholmondeley in the debates about the war in Spain in January 1711; for Cholmondeley and Shrewsbury in December 1711 in the Hamilton affair; and for Shrewsbury again in June 1713 on the Commercial Treaty.[237] But it was more common for household peers to follow the dictates of party, as Compton and Sharp did over applying the Test Act to Scotland in 1707; Northumberland did over the Scots peers; Northumberland and Sharp did in March 1710 in the Sacheverell affair; Cholmondeley did in February 1711 over government inquiries; Montagu, St. Albans, and Somerset did in December 1711 on "No Peace Without Spain"; Montagu did again on the Hamilton peerage; and Montagu and the irresolute Cholmondeley did on the Commercial Treaty. Thus, even the Earl of Cholmondeley's haphazard voting record ended with him firmly back in the Whig fold—and bereft of his treasurership of the household. Clearly, there is little evidence to support the charge that household peers slavishly followed the government of the day.[238]

Table 6.5 indicates a somewhat more favorable picture for the ministry in the lower house. On the one hand, 35 (20 Whigs, 15 Tories) of 43, or 81 percent, of the household M.P.s who left a record of their votes on Whig/Tory issues voted with one of those two parties without exception over the span of their parliamentary careers under Anne (column 1). On the other hand, 23 of 31, or 74 percent, of those who left a record of their votes on government/opposition issues always voted with the ministry *when in office* (column 3). That both of these percentages could be so high is explained by the congruency between the government's position and that of the currently ascendant party on the issues for which lists survive, and by the tendency of household vacancies to be filled as they occurred by members of that party.[239]

In short, the loyalty of household M.P.s was rarely tested, at least in the divisions for which we have evidence. When it was tested, it tended to crack as readily as it did among the household peers. It is true that Comptroller Mansell and Yeoman of the Jewel House Pauncefort, both moderate Tories, opposed the Tack in 1704 and that a Whig clerk of the greencloth, Charles Godfrey, defied his party in voting for the Commercial Treaty in 1713. But these appear to have been isolated cases. More typical was the behavior of William and Charles Seymour, of the gentlemen pensioners and the Prince's bedchamber, respectively, who followed their father, Sir Edward, in voting for the Tack. Similarly, in the Speaker's election of 1705 the Tory carver George Morley voted for his party's candidate, not the government's, while Jeffrey Palmer, gentleman of the privy chamber, voted against the government in the Sacheverell affair in the spring of 1710. Apart from Godfrey's defection in 1713—for which he was to pay dearly—Whig M.P.s in household office proved to be equally disciplined party men when forced to choose. Thus, Godfrey, Master of the Household Dunch, and the Queen's bookseller, William Churchill, all voted against the government on "No Peace Without Spain" in December 1711; Sir Thomas Read risked his place in the privy chamber by voting against the expulsion of Richard Steele in March 1714.[240]

Marshaling this admittedly meager evidence as best we can, it appears that household office did not, in general, determine the votes of its holders in parliament, any more than it did their attendance or participation in business. Why should this have been so? Professors Holmes, Horwitz, Roberts, Snyder, and Speck have argued in numerous publications that the fundamental issues dividing Whig from Tory were so intimately bound up with the most basic interests of the

Augustan ruling class that sheer ideological conviction explains the unprecedented appeal and solidity of the two parties, overriding ties of kinship, local interests, or the attractions of office.[241] While there is undoubtedly much merit to this argument, there were other, more immediately practical reasons where household servants were concerned.

The most obvious of these reasons was that the threat of removal from household office for opposition behavior was never clearly or consistently enforced by either of Queen Anne's lords treasurer.[242] For instance, of the two Seymour brothers who voted for the Tack in November 1704, William was left undisturbed in the enjoyment of his lieutenancy of the gentlemen pensioners. Though his brother Charles was one of those "pitched upon to bee made examples" of by the Godolphin ministry, he did not actually lose his post in the Prince's bedchamber until August 1706.[243] Similarly, George Morley's vote against the ministry's candidate for speaker in October 1705 cost him his places, but not until the following May in the case of his seat on the commission of prizes and June in the case of his carvership.[244] In the Lords, Anne's "faithful" Archbishop Sharp is listed as opposing the Godolphin ministry in two out of three recorded votes. The Duke of Northumberland, who is supposed by one historian to have displayed "so marked a deference for the Queen," was three for three in opposition to her first government, according to extant division lists.[245] Yet both of these men retained their places.

The government's position was weaker and its discipline correspondingly laxer under the Oxford ministry. Despite the lord treasurer's reported boast, "There shou'd not be a Whig in place by Lady-day," which followed the disastrous vote on "No Peace Without Spain," he only managed to remove one of three household M.P.s who voted for the measure, Edmund Dunch, and that not until June 1712.[246] Among the three household peers who supported the motion, the Earl of Cholmondeley had been granted virtual royal permission to vote his conscience beforehand.[247] The Dukes of St. Albans and Somerset did lose their places, but in the latter case only after much hesitation on Anne's part.[248] Cholmondeley eventually lost his household post for voting his Whig conscience, without permission, on the Commercial Treaty of 1713, but the Tory Lord Paget, who also opposed the measure, did not.

Indeed, the last session of the reign saw Paget, Bishops Robinson and Smalridge, and the commoner Sir Thomas Read oppose the ministry on a variety of issues, all without forfeiting their places.[249]

The government's failure to hold its household members responsible for their parliamentary behavior goes a long way toward explaining why it could not consistently count upon their support. There are several reasons, in turn, for this apparent failure of royal and ministerial nerve. First, there was the ancient idea that office was a freehold, possessed independently of politics. Allied to this was the Queen's characteristic loyalty to her "family," her refusal to politicize offices attendant upon her person, and her reluctance, often shared by her ministers, to be dictated to by the ascendant party. Further, the often moderate and uncertain nature of household emoluments, as described in the previous chapter, undoubtedly blunted the "threat" of removal for many royal servants. Indeed, on more than one occasion Lord Treasurer Oxford dangled the possibility of prompt payment of salaries, pensions, and old arrears before impoverished or dissatisfied courtiers in an effort to win some measure of their loyalty, if only for the moment.[250] To do so consistently would have required a permanent augmentation of the civil-list revenue, which was beyond Oxford's grasp unless he could secure the sort of substantial majority that these temporary measures had no hope of winning.[251]

The government's inability to break this vicious cycle of circumstance ensured that, for much of the reign, the ministry of the day needed its placemen, household and otherwise, far more than they needed their places. This was most obviously the case from 1711 to 1714, when Oxford's precarious position in the Lords forced him to put up with much equivocal behavior from "Court" Whig peers (not to mention incessant criticism from his own party for doing so) in order to have a working majority on most occasions.[252] As noted previously, he sometimes tolerated similar behavior even from his ministerial colleagues, Buckingham and Shrewsbury. Presumably, he did so in order to secure the parliamentary expertise of the former and the great personal prestige of the latter for the government.[253] Finally, the government needed more than the votes, expertise, or ornamental value of its household members in parliament; it needed their electoral interest beyond Westminster as well. At least five household servants who sat

TABLE 6.6
Primary Type of Interest upon Which M.P.s in Household Office Sat, 1702–1714

Type of interest	No. of constituencies	% of total
Government	5	7.4
Personal	21	30.9
Family	26	38.2
Patron or party	12	17.6
Unknown	4	5.9
Total	68	100

SOURCES: *History of Parliament 1715–1754*, ed. Sedgwick; Speck, *Tory & Whig*; Walcott, *English Politics*.

in parliament under Queen Anne had great multicounty and sometimes multiregional interests: the Dukes of Beaufort and Somerset; Lord Granville and his successor to the family interest, George Granville, Lord Lansdowne; and Sir Edward Seymour.[254] Another seven men had considerable countywide interests, often in alliance with others: the two Dukes of Devonshire; Sir Thomas (afterwards Lord) Mansell; Robert Harley (afterwards Earl of Oxford); Henry (afterwards Lord) Paget; the Earl Poulett; and Viscount Townshend.[255] Such men could dictate the votes of only a handful of M.P.s, but their interest could be of great use in returning party men who were at least moderately congenial to the government of the day. This begins to explain why individuals of such doubtful abilities and odd dispositions as the Dukes of Beaufort and Somerset not only acquired great household office, but managed to keep it despite occasional disloyalty and, in the latter case, incessant and often unreasonable demands on the ministry.

Just how useful and necessary the great electoral magnates could be to the favorable composition of the lower house is suggested by the data in Table 6.6. Out of the 68 constituencies represented by household officers under Queen Anne, only 5, or 7.4 percent, involved a government interest. Twenty-one, or just under 31 percent, of these seats were won on a personal interest; 26, or just over 38 percent, on a family interest; and 12, or almost 18 percent, on the interest of a nonfamilial patron, usually of a similar party or ideological persuasion. In short, only a fraction of the M.P.s in household office owed their seats primarily to the influence of the government.

The implications of this for a would-be "Court party" are clear. Those household M.P.s who sat upon their own or their family's interest thereby acquired a measure of independence in their dealings with the ministry. Those who sat on a patron's interest obviously owed their allegiance elsewhere. When Charles Godfrey opted for his government loyalties over Whig principles in his vote on the Commercial Treaty in 1713, his patron at Chipping Wycombe for 23 years, the arch-Whig Earl of Wharton, promptly withdrew his electoral patronage. Godfrey was unable to find a safe government seat in the subsequent election, despite its being an overall triumph for the ministry and the Tories.[256] This suggests that there were few such seats to go around. Nor was government backing necessarily of much use to those who received it. During the election of 1705 Lord Treasurer Godolphin campaigned hard to get his son, Francis (who was already cofferer of the household), elected one of the members for Cambridge. Despite extraordinary efforts, including a royal visit, two Tackers were elected; hence the treasurer had to resort to the family borough at Helston to get his son into parliament.[257]

It is little wonder that most household M.P.s and their noble patrons should have felt themselves more beholden to their own or their party's interest than to that of "the Court." From a practical point of view Godfrey made the wrong decision when he chose his responsibilities to the Queen and ministry over those to his party and borough patron. Having done so in an age characterized by "the rage of party," his fate was sealed. Others found that a choice of party over place did not necessarily result in the loss of the latter. This, combined with the sometimes dubious attractions of household office, provided a perfectly practical reason for the weakness of "Court" loyalties and the general political unreliability of household officers under Queen Anne.

There was one further, less tangible, but possibly even more important reason for this state of affairs, and for the general decline in the political significance of the court from the heady days of Charles II. Just as party ideology and organization were growing in scope and sophistication at the beginning of the eighteenth century, permeating the social and cultural life of the nation via political clubs, coffeehouses, taverns, and the milieu of the great country house, the royal household was declining as a place where the ruling class came to meet, eat, sleep, play, plot, and be entertained or overawed with majesty. Such a shift in the attentions of the political nation, the disposition of its leisure time, the focus of its culture, and the arena of its politics could only contribute to the more obvious shift in its loyalties, already described. It is to this more subtle and fundamental shift, the decline of court culture under the last of the Stuarts, that the final chapter turns.

CHAPTER VII

Court Life and Culture

When modern commentators discuss the social and cultural life of Anne's court, they tend to echo the negative verdict of that connoisseur of courts, Lord Chesterfield, who wrote: "Queen Anne had always been devout, chaste, and formal; in short, a prude. She discouraged, as much as she could, the usual and even the most pardonable vices of Courts. Her Drawing Rooms were more respectable than agreeable, and had more the air of solemn places of worship than the gaiety of a Court."[1] Admittedly, Chesterfield was barely out of adolescence by the time of Anne's death and was, moreover, a Whig who rejoiced at the Hanoverian succession.[2] He can hardly be considered an impartial eyewitness. Nevertheless, examination of the accounts left by observers as diverse in their backgrounds and politics as the Duc d'Aumont, the Duchess of Marlborough, the Countess of Orkney, Bishop Burnet, Sir John Clerk of Penicuik, Conrad von Uffenbach, and Jonathan Swift amply confirms that the court of Queen Anne was dull, at least in the view of contemporaries reared on the experience or reputation of the Restoration court.[3]

As noted in the introductory chapter, the social and cultural standards of the later Stuart court had, in fact, begun to decline long before the accession of Queen Anne. It will be argued here that the court's continuing decline under the last Stuart was due as much to the political and financial circumstances of postrevolutionary monarchy and to Anne's precarious health as to some defect of her personality. Whatever its cause, the relative social and cultural failure of her court had a profound significance not only for the life of her own household, but for Augustan politics and society in general.

Ceremony

Paradoxically, Anne began her reign with every intention of reviving the social and symbolic life of the court and of combining regal splendor and hospitality with good husbandry, piety, and virtue. The result, if successful, would have been a pattern for the nation as a whole and a natural focus for the loyalty of her most important subjects in particular. The most visible and popular element in this ambitious undertaking was the new Queen's revival of royal ceremony and etiquette. It is well known that Anne was, like her father and grandfather, a stickler for ceremony. Her almost obsessive interest in and extensive knowledge of courtly ritual and custom were much commented on by observers whose place it was to know, such as her groom of the stole, the Duchess of Marlborough, and her master of the ceremonies, Sir Clement Cotterell.[4] In the words of Jonathan Swift (probably based on the testimony of Abigail Masham), "This princess was so exact an observer of forms, that she seemed to have made it her study, and would often descend so low as to observe, in her domestics of either sex who came into her presence, whether a ruffle, a periwig, or the lining of a coat, were unsuitable upon certain times."[5] There exist several stories about her indignation at some mistake in court etiquette or dress, and numerous examples of her settling a point of ceremony or precedence.[6] At her very darkest hour, Prince George's death, she appears to have found some consolation in busying herself with the details of his funeral.[7]

Anne's almost legendary punctiliousness was not a function of personal vanity. Even the Duchess of Marlborough, her most uncompromising critic, acquits her of this vice, noting that, in private, unlike her father, Mrs. Morley liked to dispense with ceremony.[8] There seems to have been very little daily monarchical ritual, such as a morning *levée* or dining in state, at Anne's court, even early in the reign, when her physical maladies were not yet so far advanced as to preclude them. It may also be significant that, unlike her immediate predecessors, Anne does not appear to have possessed a single copy of her own state portrait.[9]

The Duchess explained the Queen's insistence on the proper forms as simply the bugbear of a small mind. Writing of the royal memory,

Mrs. Freeman found it "exceeding great, almost to a wonder," but charged that Anne "chose to retain in it very little besides ceremonies and customs of courts and suchlike insignificant trifles."[10] Such an interpretation of the Queen's punctiliousness is virtually impossible to disprove. However, it can be reasonably argued that Anne had better and more significant reasons for attaching such importance to court ritual. First, it should be remembered that most contemporaries were far more likely to share her attitude in such things than that of the iconoclastic Sarah.[11] Secondly, it must be recalled that, as Princess, Anne had undergone a series of calculated and galling slights at the hands of William and Mary. These included their prohibiting their servants from acknowledging her presence; the withdrawal of her guards; the curtailment of the usual civic honors upon her arrival at Bath in 1692; and, the final indignity, the King's refusal to allow her to put her own household at St. James's into mourning at her father's death in 1701.[12] Even to a woman devoid of personal vanity, these actions must have seemed a scandalous disregard of the respect due a princess and heir designate. It was only natural that, as Queen, Anne would attempt to redress the balance.

Finally, it is clear that, from the first, Anne Stuart had an acute sense of the practical political significance of royal ceremony and etiquette. This was first noticeable in her ostentatious attendance at the Anglican chapel royal and her insistence upon the full royal treatment there during her father's reign.[13] Nor could the young Princess have been ignorant of the political consequences when, under William and Mary, she appeared at one of her sister's drawing rooms accompanied by the wife of the disgraced Earl of Marlborough.[14] It was noted previously that on two occasions in her own reign Anne made overt political points by means of ceremony: when, in 1702, she handed the Whig Earl of Wharton's staff as comptroller of the household to the Tory Sir Edward Seymour in the presence of the former; and when, in 1711, she chose to be escorted out of the House of Lords by the Whig Duke of Somerset rather than a more assiduous government supporter after the debate on "No Peace Without Spain."[15]

Both of these examples show Anne using court ceremony to demonstrate partisanship or displeasure. It was more characteristic of her, and consistent with her own conception of monarchy and avowed government policy (for most of the reign, at least), to use public appearances and the ritual that accompanied them to demonstrate her aloofness from party bickering. Indeed, Anne sought to use the big public occasions of her reign as a means to unite a divided nation under her impartial rule. Her desire to be Queen of all her people was evident in the way she accepted the compliments of the nobility on the first "Sunshine Day" of the reign, 8 March 1702. According to Bishop Burnet, "She received all that came to her in so gracious a manner, that they went from her highly satisfied with her goodness, and her obliging deportment; for she hearkened with attention to every thing that was said to her."[16]

Three days later the new Queen created an equally favorable impression before a wider audience with her first address to parliament. According to one eyewitness, "Never any woman spoke more audibly or with better grace."[17] Anne's melodious speaking voice was one of her chief assets. Years before, Charles II was so taken with it that he commissioned the celebrated actress, Elizabeth Barry, to coach the young Princess. As a result, Lord Dartmouth later recalled, "it was a real pleasure to hear her; though she had a bashfulness that made it very uneasy to herself to say much in public."[18] On this occasion even that bashfulness, which manifested itself in the form of blushing, worked to Anne's advantage: while "some compared her to the sign of the Rose and Crown," others found in it "a sort of charm."[19]

If the new Queen's manner seemed disarmingly uncontrived, her appearance was, in the words of one modern commentator, "a masterpiece of stage management," fully illustrating an ability to rise to great ceremonial occasions that she was to demonstrate repeatedly in the years to come.[20] Only a few days before, Godolphin had feared Anne too "unwieldy and lame" to go to the House because of the gout.[21] Yet she not only went, but was, by all accounts, resplendent. She wore the crown, the star and garter, and a magnificent gown of red velvet lined with ermine and edged with gold galloon. It was not lost on her audience that this ensemble resembled that worn in a well-known portrait of Queen Elizabeth.[22]

Indeed, the very words spoken by Anne on this occasion, specifically her assertion, "I know my own heart to be entirely English," though usually interpreted as an insult to William's memory, may equally be taken as an evocation of Elizabeth's.[23] The phrase is redolent with Elizabethan association: for example, Gloriana's assertion of pride in being "mere English"; or the speech at Tilbury, in which she boasts of having "the heart and stomach of a king, and of a king of England too."[24] The appropriateness of the Elizabethan parallel was apparent to contemporaries, and goes well beyond the obvious fact that both were female sovereigns. Anne was the first Stuart, and therefore the first monarch since Elizabeth, who could legitimately revel in her Englishness, for she was the first of her house born in England of an English mother and raised for virtually the whole of her youth there. Like Elizabeth, Anne was confronted with the formidable task of rallying a divided nation in the midst of a dangerous international situation, after succeeding an unpopular predecessor. Finally, like Elizabeth, Anne was a Protestant queen about to stand up to the most powerful Catholic king on earth, an image that could not fail to arouse the gallantry and loyalty of the gentlemen of England.

As every schoolboy knows, Elizabeth I found it politically expedient to play upon this image of feminine vulnerability as well as upon the related image of a "Virgin Queen" wedded to her first love, the people of England. The latter was hardly an appropriate metaphor for the happily married and naturally maternal Anne. The new Queen, who had sacrificed her bodily health in a vain attempt to give her people an heir, aspired instead to be their common mother. Her coronation sermon was preached on Isaiah 49:23: "And kings shall be thy nursing fathers, and their queens thy nursing mothers."[25] Clearly, from the first days of the reign, Anne's actions and demeanor amply fulfilled what G. R. Elton, writing of her great female predecessor, calls "the first duty of monarchy—to appear as the symbol of the nation and the sum of all earthly allegiance."[26]

Throughout the first year of her reign, Anne continued to invoke the memory of her illustrious Tudor forebear. In December 1702 she chose Elizabeth's motto, *Semper Eadem*, as her own.[27] Earlier in the year she revived two other mainstays of Elizabethan court life, both of which brought her closer to her people. From 22 August to 10 October the Queen, Prince George, and the rest of the court went on progress to Bath via Oxford and Cirencester, it was said in the hope that the waters might have a beneficial effect upon the Prince's asthma.[28] On 12 November the Queen, again accompanied by the Prince and their respective households, became the first sovereign since Elizabeth to attend a service of thanksgiving in St. Paul's Cathedral, appropriately enough, to commemorate the naval victory at Vigo Bay. The Elizabethan parallel was self-evident to the anonymous author of the verses tacked onto the Ludgate monument that day: "As threatning Spain did to Eliza bow, / So France and Spain shall do to ANNA now."[29]

Whatever their ostensible medical or spiritual significance, these excursions beyond St. James's had a definite political meaning as well. On the most obvious level, thanksgivings and progresses, as well as the coronation, garter ceremonies, military reviews and parades, gave the political classes an excuse, even an obligation, to attend the monarch and her court, to participate in and so validate royal and national ritual.[30] Thanksgiving days began with the Queen's reception of the compliments of the nobility at St. James's. This was followed by a procession to St. Paul's led by the great officers, the judges and masters in Chancery, and the members of both houses.[31] On progress, the royal party was met at the border of each county it passed through by the lord lieutenant and principal gentlemen. Like Elizabeth, Anne occasionally partook of the hospitality of some great noble house, early in the reign dividing her favor equally among leading Tories and Whigs.[32] Finally, it was said of her first visit to Bath that she attracted "a great court," including "most of the foreign ministers and many persons of the best quality."[33] Indeed, this and a subsequent visit in the fall of 1703 are generally credited with helping to launch Bath as a fashionable resort.[34]

Though initiated by the court and supported by the landed aristocracy, thanksgivings and progresses equally served to inspire civic expressions of loyalty to or sympathy with the royal family in reply, a process Malcolm Smuts has called "ceremonial dialogue."[35] At the very least, these involved an obligatory greeting by the mayor and corporation at the gates of the city or, in London, at Temple Bar; the surrender of the city sword; and, in the words of one optimistic observer, "a short, but pithy and loyal Speech." On thanksgiving days the route to St. Paul's was lined up to Temple Bar by the Westminster Militia, the route from it by the city's trained bands. Behind the latter stood "the several Companies in their Gowns, with their respective Flags, Streamers and Musick."[36]

Provincial communities through which the court progressed spared no expense to prove that they were every bit as loyal as the capital. The corporation of Bath was particularly anxious to do so after the slights of the previous reign. As a result, the Queen's entry in 1702 had something of Tudor pageantry and exuberance about it. She was met on the outskirts of the city by

> a fine Company of the Citizens, all clad like Grenadiers, and about 200 Virgins richly attired, many of them like Amazons, with Bows and Arrows, and others with gilt Scepters, and other Ensigns of the Regalia in their Hands. All of them with a Set of Dancers, who danc'd by the Sides of her Majesty's Coach, and waited upon her Majesty to the West-gate of the City.[37]

The symbolic program pursued here seems to be fairly straightforward. If Smuts is correct that such occasions contained a vestigial element of the popular acclamation that used to guarantee succession,[38] then the "gilt Scepters, and other Ensigns of the Regalia" reaffirmed Anne's royal status and Bath's acknowledgment of it. The latter was especially significant in light of her previous experience of the city. The "200 Virgins" probably amounted to a general acknowledgment of her sex and her role as a defender of virtue, as evidenced by her proclamation of 26 March 1702.[39] Any more specific feminine symbolism might have proved awkward given the Queen's status as a mother who had lost her children. Finally, the equally safe feminine image of Amazons, along with those of grenadiers, bows and arrows, and so forth, recalled and, seemingly, approved her martial foreign policy. When the Queen visited Bristol later on the same progress the imagery was equally martial, including a triumphal arch, flags, the ringing of church bells, and the firing of cannon from harbor and marsh.[40] At Cambridge in 1705 the festivities combined learned gravity with undergraduate revelry: while the scholars of St. John's greeted the royal visitor with shouts of "Vivat Regina," the rest of the city was "strowed with Flowers; the Bells rung, and the Conduits run with Wine."[41] In each entry, therefore, local history (Bath's earlier treatment of Anne) or function (Bristol as a seaport, Cambridge as a university town) played a role in how the Queen's person and politics were greeted.

Nor was the Queen's physical presence necessary to provoke an orgy of municipally sponsored loyalism. Her accession, coronation, and birthday anniversaries, the proclamations of war and peace, and the news of and thanksgivings for military victory all gave excuse for deployment of the full panoply of civic ritual—processions, maypoles, bells, bonfires, illuminations, fireworks, loyal healths from the corporation and local gentlemen, food and drink for the masses, extraordinary displays of charity, and more—in towns large and small throughout England.[42] Even where no such demonstrations appear to have taken place, milestones such as the victory at Blenheim or the passage of the Act of Union called forth scores of loyal addresses in which the Queen was frequently referred to as the new Elizabeth or the nursing mother of her people.[43] While the spontaneity and even the sincerity of these productions is open to question, their producers clearly felt compelled, for whatever reason, to respond to the ceremonial cues being dropped by the court in London. Moreover, many did so in the Queen's chosen noumenal language, her preferred medium for describing herself and her reign.

However, all of this sound and fury would have signified little had not the general populace also joined in with "all Demonstrations imaginable." As Elizabeth knew well, and so many of her Stuart successors apparently did not, the greatest single virtue of public thanksgivings, progresses, and processions was that they exposed the spectacle of the Queen and her court to the widest possible audience. Thanksgiving processions down the Strand and up Ludgate Hill were always observed by "great Numbers of Spectators" from balconies and windows.[44] We are told of "great Crowds" at the Queen's entry into Bath in 1702. At her dining in state upon a return visit the following year, "such a crowd of country-people came in, there was no stirring."[45] While one must beware of obviously "official" accounts, contemporaries seem to be unanimous about the Queen's reception when she went out amongst her people in these early years. For example, the Whig Abel Boyer reports that when Anne and her consort went to the Guildhall to be fêted by the Lord Mayor in October 1702, she "was receiv'd as she pass'd along with the loud Acclamations of the People, and as great Demonstrations of Joy as have been known in the Memory of Man upon the like Occasion."[46]

Even allowing for Augustan hyperbole, the people obviously took to their nursing mother. Such occasions served to unite them, however briefly, with the Queen, her court, the aristocracy, gentry, clergy, and armed forces in truly national celebration of military victory, in the case of thanksgivings; or, more generally, of the benefits of Anne's rule. They juxtaposed the elements of "structure" and "communitas" detected by Victor Turner in other, similar ceremonies.[47] One can see, too, the vestigial remains of acclamation, whereby a ruler was accepted and approved by the general populace, which Malcolm Smuts has found in early Stuart entries. His suggestion that such occasions contained an element of benediction, of mutual blessing between prince and people, also seems appropriate.[48] However we interpret them, the importance of such widespread participation and apparent popular approval to a regime fighting an expensive war financed by a divided and often reluctant ruling class should not be underestimated. It was no mere accident of the Prince's health that led the Queen to progress through the West Country, among the most recalcitrantly Tory and least bellicose regions of England. Anne and her ministers made this connection explicit in her opening speech to the parliament that met at the end of 1702. Noting her recent progress, she observed: "I have met with so many Expressions of Joy, and Satisfaction in all the Countreys, thro' which I have lately had Occasion to pass, that I cannot but look upon them as true Measures of the Duty and Affection of the rest of my Subjects." This remark was immediately followed by the Queen's request for supply for the coming year; specifically, for the Earl of Marlborough's next campaign.[49] Clearly, Anne and her ministers regarded such popular expressions of, in Boyer's words, "Affection to her Majesty's Person, and Zeal for her Government" as a virtual mandate for current policy.[50]

Unfortunately, the Duke's military prowess could provide excuse for no more than about one thanksgiving per year, on average, before his fall in January 1712 (Table 7.1). Nor would the Queen's responsibilities or health allow more than one or two progresses a year through 1707 (Table 7.2). If Anne was to be an effective national mother figure she would need more frequent contact with her subjects. It may be this, and not a nostalgic longing for divine right (which she repudiated on several occasions),[51] which explains her revival of the practice of touch-

TABLE 7.1
Thanksgiving Services, 1702–1714

Year	Date	Occasion	Location	Comment
1702	12 Nov.	Success of Her Majesty's forces (Vigo Bay, Flanders, etc.)	St. Paul's	Queen present[1]
1704	7 Sept.	Blenheim	St. Paul's	Queen present[2]
1705	23 Aug.	Forcing of the French lines	St. Paul's	Queen present[3]
1706	27 June	Brabant (Ramillies)	St. Paul's	Queen present[4]
1706	31 Dec.	Successes of year	St. Paul's	Queen present[5]
1707	1 May	Act of Union w/ Scotland	St. Paul's	Queen present[6]
1708	19 Aug.	Success against Pretender; Oudenarde	St. Paul's	Queen present[7]
1709	17 Feb.	Success of last campaign	Chapel royal, St. James's	Queen at chapel royal[8]
1709	22 Nov.	Victory at Blaregnies, near Mons	Chapel royal, St. James's	Queen at chapel royal[9]
1710	7 Nov.	Success of campaign; victory in Spain	Chapel royal, St. James's	Queen at chapel royal[10]
1713	7 July	Peace	St. Paul's	Queen at chapel royal[11]

SOURCES: Based in part on Burrows, "Handel," chap. 2, Table 1, "Thanksgiving Services During Queen Anne's Reign." Other sources as follows. (1) Luttrell, *Brief Relation* V: 232, 235; Sheppard, *St. James's* I: 232–33; *Daily Courant*, no. 181, 14 Nov. 1702. (2) Luttrell, *Brief Relation* V: 442, 458, 460, 461, 462–63; Boyer, *Annals* III: 96–99; Add. MSS 6307, ff. 42–43; Bodl. Lister MSS 37, f. 80; *Evelyn Diary* V: 578 (7 Sept. 1704). (3) Luttrell, *Brief Relation* V: 575, 579–80, 585; Add. MSS 6307, f. 43 verso. (4) Luttrell, *Brief Relation* VI: 49, 61; Boyer, *Annals* V: 150–54; Sheppard, *St. James's* I: 235–36; Add. MSS 61417, f. 3. (5) Boyer, *Annals* V: 398; Luttrell, *Brief Relation* VI: 109, 118, 122–23. (6) Luttrell, *Brief Relation* VI: 166–67; Boyer, *Annals* VI: 223–24. (7) Luttrell, *Brief Relation* VI: 326, 328, 340; Boyer, *Annals* VII: 243. (8) Luttrell, *Brief Relation* VI: 409; Boyer, *Annals* VII: 297–98. (9) Luttrell, *Brief Relation* VI: 496, 514. (10) Ibid., pp. 628, 651; Boyer, *Annals* IX: 253; *British Apollo* III, no. 98, 8–10 Nov. 1710. (11) Burrows, "Handel" I: 101–6; Add. MSS 22226, f. 85 verso; *Hamilton Diary*, p. 56; *British Mercury*, no. 418, 8 July 1713.

ing for scrofula or King's Evil. It is also possible that the devout Queen actually believed in the sacramental efficacy of her touch as anointed monarch and supreme head of the Church of England.[52] In any case, there is more of motherly concern than Stuart imperiousness in her promise to Sarah in the spring of 1704 "to touch as many poor people as I can before hott weather coms."[53] For their part, enough "poor people" believed in her powers to force Lord Almoner Sharp to turn many away. He noted to the representative of one disappointed applicant, "There are now in London several thousands of people, some of them ready to perish, come out of the country waiting for her Healing."[54] In an attempt to satisfy this demand, Anne regularly touched

TABLE 7.2
Progresses, 1702–1714

Year	Dates	Destination	Stops	Comment
1702	22 Aug.–10 Oct.	Bath	Oxford Cirencester Badminton Bristol Marlborough	"To take the waters"[1]
1703	Easter week	Newmarket		"To see the horse raceing, &c"[2] (progress canceled)
1703	18 Aug.–9 Oct.	Bath	Marlborough	Waters[3]
1704	late May	Bath		(Canceled)[4]
1704	mid Sept.–early Oct.	Winchester		(Canceled)[5]
1705	10–20 Apr.	Newmarket	Cambridge Earl of Orford's	Horseracing[6]
1705	28 Aug.–8 Sept.	Winchester	Duke of Bolton's	Hunting[7]
1706	Easter week	Newmarket		(Canceled)[8]
1706	2–12 Oct.	Newmarket		Horseracing[9]
1707	Easter week	Newmarket		(Canceled)[10]
1707	30 Sept.–17 Oct.	Newmarket		Horseracing[11]
1708	5 Oct.–?	Newmarket		(Canceled)[12]
1711	? late July	Bath		(Canceled)[13]

SOURCES: (1) Luttrell, *Brief Relation* V: 197, 204, 205, 207, 210, 218, 223; Boyer, *Annals* I: 75–79, 99–101; Warner, *History of Bath*, p. 209; H.M.C., *Fifteenth Report*, App. IV, pp. 44, 46, 48; Melville, *Bath Under Beau Nash*, p. 118. (2) Luttrell, *Brief Relation* V: 274, 281. (3) Ibid., pp. 310, 314, 315, 319–20, 323, 330, 337, 339, 343, 347; Aitken, *Arbuthnot*, p. 28; D. Green, *Anne*, p. 118; Boyer, *Annals* II: 160; *London Gazette*, no. 3942, 19–23 Aug. 1703; no. 3956, 7–11 Oct. 1703. (4) Luttrell, *Brief Relation* V: 414. (5) Ibid., pp. 447–48. (6) Ibid., pp. 536, 537, 539, 542, 544; Speck, *Tory & Whig*, pp. 100–101; H.M.C., *Fifteenth Report*, App. IV, p. 178; Green, *Anne*, pp. 140–41; Boyer, *Annals* IV: 10–14; *London Gazette*, nos. 4115–16, 16–23 Apr. 1705; *Seafield Correspondence*, p. 395. (7) Luttrell, *Brief Relation* V: 578, 586, 589; Boyer, *Annals* IV: 178–79; Green, *Anne*, p. 141; *London Gazette*, nos. 4154–55, 30 Aug.–6 Sept. 1705. (8) Luttrell, *Brief Relation* VI: 29. (9) Ibid., pp. 82, 91, 96; Gregg, *Anne*, p. 150. (10) Luttrell, *Brief Relation* VI: 148. (11) Ibid., pp. 207, 215, 218, 224; Add. MSS 22225, f. 47; *Marlborough-Godolphin Correspondence*, pp. 922, 923, 931, 933, 934–35. (12) Luttrell, *Brief Relation* VI: 352, 357. (13) H.M.C., *Portland MSS* V: 15.

one to two hundred sufferers at a time twice weekly during the court season.[55] Over the years she must have touched literally thousands of her subjects, an act of benediction that brought them together from all parts of the realm under her nursing hand.

Healing ceremonies undoubtedly inspired popular devotion to the monarch: one merely has to consider Samuel Johnson's "solemn recollection of a lady in diamonds" and his lifelong attachment to the Stuarts, or the tenacity of popular belief in the thaumaturgic powers of royal healing-medals and even coins with Stuart effigies on them to see this.[56] But healing ceremonies admitted of little in the way of aristocratic participation. That requirement was fulfilled by the round of court festivals outlined in Table 7.3. As befitted an Anglican princess, the backbone of her court calendar was the series of twelve collardays, fourteen saint's days, and most Sundays during the court season when the Queen, her great officers, household servants, and assiduous courtiers might be seen processing through the privy gallery to services in the chapel royal at St. James's. Conrad von Uffenbach, a German tourist, availed himself of such an opportunity in 1710: "The Queen walked with great ceremony up the centre aisle into a seat near the altar, that was like a pew. Most of her retinue preceded her, a sword and four great sceptres with crowns being carried in front of her. Then came the Queen with her 'dames d'honneur' behind her."[57]

However, apart from these processions, Anne does not appear to have made much of Church holidays. Above all, she studiously avoided any ostentatious celebration of the great—but increasingly partisan—political anniversaries of Augustan England, that is, those of the Royal Martyr (30 January), the Restoration (29 May), the Gunpowder Plot (5 November), or even Queen Elizabeth's accession (17 November).[58] Rather, Anne chose to emphasize those anniversaries personal to her and her rule, in particular that of the royal birth on 6 February. Annually upon that date she received the compliments of the nobility and attended chapel in the morning; heard an ode in her praise in the afternoon or evening; and then presided over a drawing room at which the nobility and gentry appeared in splendid new clothes, especially tailored for the occasion.[59] This routine predated Anne's reign, but she appears to have given it new life and significance. It was said of the first such celebration of the reign, in 1703, "There had not been such a Magnificent Appearance at Court for Twenty Years past."[60] Subsequent celebrations in these early years were expanded to include gambling, dancing, concerts, and, often, a play or an opera (Table 7.4). Nor was the popular element slighted, the evening generally concluding with "Ringing of Bells, Bonefires [*sic*], and other Demonstrations of publick Joy."[61] Similar, if less elaborate, festivities took place on New Year's Day, the Queen's Accession Day (8 March), Prince George's birthday (29 February), and the Queen's Coronation Day, which coincided with the feast of St. George (23 April) (Table 7.3). As noted previously, each of these anniversaries was commemorated with parallel celebrations in the countryside.

TABLE 7.3
Queen Anne's Court Calendar

Date	Occasion	How celebrated	Known celebrations
1 Jan.	New Year's Day	Collarday[a] Drawing room Ode	1703–8;[1] (omitted 1709);[2] prob. 1710;[3] 1711;[4] 1712;[5] 1713;[6] (prob. omitted 1714)
6 Jan.	Twelfth Day	Collarday Queen attends chapel royal and offers gifts of gold, frankincense, and myrrh Gambling in evening[7]	1709[8]
30 Jan.	Royal Martyr	Sermon	1703–14
2 Feb.	Candlemas	Collarday	
6 Feb.	Queen's birthday	Drawing room Ode Sometimes a ball or play Bonfires, illuminations, and fireworks	1703–14 (see Table 7.4)
24 Feb.	St. Matthias	Attend chapel royal	
29 Feb.	Prince George's birthday	Drawing room Play	1704;[9] ?1708[10]
8 Mar.	Queen's accession	Drawing room Song (1703)[11] Bonfires and illuminations;[12] Inspection of troops (1703)[13]	1703;[14] 1706;[15] 1707;[16] 1708;[17] 1710;[18] 1711;[19] 1712;[20] 1713[21]
25 Mar.	Lady Day	Collarday	
Easter week	Palm Sunday	Attend chapel royal	
	Maundy Thursday	Queen's Maundy[22]	1704[23]
	Good Friday	Attend chapel royal ?	
	Easter Sunday	Collarday	1709[24]
23 Apr.	St. George	Attend chapel royal	
	Queen's coronation	Drawing room Dancing (1704)[25] Play (1704)[26]	1703;[27] 1704;[28] 1705;[29] 1706;[30] 1711;[31] 1712;[32] 1713;[33] 1714[34]
25 Apr.	St. Mark	Attend chapel royal	
1 May	Sts. Philip and Jacob		
40 days after Easter	Ascension	Collarday	
Whitsun week	Whit Sunday	"	
	Ember Day (Wed.)	Attend chapel royal	
	" (Fri.)	"	
	" (Sat.)	"	

TABLE 7.3 *(continued)*

Date	Occasion	How celebrated	Known celebrations
1 week after Pentecost	Trinity Sunday	Collarday	
29 May	Restoration	Sermon	1703–14
24 June	St. John the Baptist	Collarday	
29 June	St. Peter	Attend chapel royal	
25 July	St. James	"	
24 Aug.	St. Bartholomew	"	
21 Sept.	St. Matthew	"	
29 Sept.	St. Michael Arc.	Collarday	
18 Oct.	St. Luke	Attend chapel royal	
28 Oct.	Sts. Simon and Jude	"	1705[35]
1 Nov.	All Saints	Collarday	
5 Nov.	Gunpowder Plot	Sermon	1703–13
30 Nov.	St. Andrew	Attend chapel royal	
21 Dec.	St. Thomas	"	
25 Dec.	Christmas	Collarday	1705;[36] 1710;[37] 1713[38]

SOURCES: Based on a list of "Collar Days and Offering Days" dated 1702 contained in a copy of the Chamber Establishment ("A List of Her Majesty's Officers Sworn by the Lord Chamberlain of her Maj[ts] Household on His Order"), Melbourne Hall, Derbyshire, Melbourne Hall MSS, box marked "London and Court." Other sources as follows. (1) Burrows, "Handel" I: 141; *Nicolson Diaries*, pp. 156, 345, 406; *Post Man*, no. 1069, 31 Dec. 1702–2 Jan. 1703; no. 1362, 30 Dec. 1704–2 Jan. 1705; no. 1565, 1–3 Jan. 1706; Add. MSS 17677 BBB, f. 36 verso; *Daily Courant*, no. 1208, 28 Feb. 1706. (2) Luttrell, *Brief Relation* VI: 390. (3) Ibid., p. 529. (4) *Nicolson Diaries*, p. 527. (5) *Wentworth Papers*, p. 235; *Nicolson Diaries*, p. 575. (6) Green, *Anne*, p. 280; *Wentworth Papers*, p. 312; *Post Boy*, no. 2754, 1–3 Jan. 1712/13. (7) See Boulton, *Amusements of Old London* I: 131–33, 137–38; *Post Boy*, no. 2130, 6–8 Jan. 1708/09; Add. MSS 17677 GGG, f. 29 verso. (8) *Post Boy*, no. 2130, 6–8 Jan. 1708/09: "[It] being Twelfth-Day, the Queen went to St. James's Chappel, but did not play in the Evening, as usual, by reason of the Mourning." (9) Luttrell, *Brief Relation* V: 396; H.M.C., *Twelfth Report*, App. III, p. 163; *London Stage* II: 59. (10) See *Nicolson Diaries*, p. 457. (11) *London Stage* II: 36; *Cal. Ref. Mus.*, p. 50. (12) Luttrell, *Brief Relation* V: 275; *Post Boy*, no. 2312, 7–9 Mar. 1709/10; no. 2782, 7–10 Mar. 1712/13. (13) Luttrell, *Brief Relation* V: 275. (14) Ibid.; *London Stage* II: 36. (15) *Post Man*, no. 1586, 7–9 Mar. 1706. (16) *Nicolson Diaries*, p. 423. (17) Add. MSS 17677 CCC, f. 353 recto and verso. (18) *Post Boy*, no. 2312, 7–9 Mar. 1709/10; *Post Man*, no. 1856, 7–9 Mar. 1710. (19) Luttrell, *Brief Relation* VI: 699; *Swift Correspondence* I: 214; *Nicolson Diaries*, pp. 556–57; *British Mercury*, no. 150, 7–9 Mar. 1711. (20) Add. MSS 22226, ff. 89–90, 95; *Nicolson Diaries*, p. 593; *British Mercury*, no. 308, 10–12 Mar. 1712. (21) Swift, *Journal*, p. 635; *Evening Post*, no. 559, 7–10 Mar. 1713; *Post Boy*, no. 2782, 7–10 Mar. 1713; Add. MSS 17677 GGG, f. 97. (22) See D. G. Spicer, *Yearbook of English Festivals* (New York, 1954), p. 209; Wright, *British Calendar Customs*, pp. 64–65; Luttrell, *Brief Relation* V: 413. (23) Luttrell, *Brief Relation* V: 413. (24) *Post Boy*, no. 2176, 23–26 Apr. 1709. (25) *London Stage* II: 65. (26) Mitchell, "Command Performances . . . Anne," pp. 114, 116. (27) *Post Man*, no. 1119, 22–24 Apr. 1703. (28) *London Stage* II: 65; Mitchell, "Command Performances . . . Anne," p. 116. (29) *Post Man*, no. 1396, 21–24 Apr. 1705. (30) Ibid., no. 1604, 23–25 Apr. 1706; Add. MSS 17677 BBB, ff. 244, 248. (31) LC 5/3, f. 7; *Evening Post*, no. 265, 21–24 Apr. 1711. (32) *British Mercury*, no. 327, 23–25 Apr. 1712; *London Gazette*, no. 4995, 22–24 Apr. 1712. (33) *Evening Post*, no. 579, 23–25 Apr. 1713. (34) H.M.C., *Portland MSS* V: 430; *Nicolson Diaries*, p. 609; Add. MSS 17677 HHH, f. 200 verso. (35) *Post Man*, no. 1556, 24–27 Nov. 1705. (36) Luttrell, *Brief Relation* V: 627. (37) *British Apollo* III, no. 129, 25–27 Dec. 1710. (38) Add. MSS 17677 GGG, f. 20.

[a]Collarday: "Twelve days in the year, being high and principal Festivals, His Majesty after Divine Service, attended with his principal Nobility, adorned with their Collars of Esses, in a grave solemn manner at the Altar offers a sum of Gold to God, in Signum Specialis dominii, that by his Grace he is King, and holdeth all of him." E. Chamberlayne, *Anglia Notitia* (1669), p. 237; see also Add. MSS 31143, f. 486 verso.

TABLE 7.4
Royal Birthday Celebrations, 1702–1714

Entertainment	Comments
1703	
Ode by Wall, set Abell[1] Song by Motteux, set Eccles[2] Dances by Mr. Isaacks[3] Ball[4]	"Great Preparations are made for celebrating the same with much Splendour at the Royal Pallace of St. James's."[5] "Extraordinary Rejoycings throughout the whole Kingdom; and it was remark'd, That there had not been such a Magnificent Appearance at Court for Twenty Years past."[6]
1704	
Ode by Eccles[7] Play, Dryden's *All for Love*[8] "A Dialogue which was Sung before Her Majesty"[9] "Several new Entertainments" performed by the dancers du Ruel, Cherrier, and Mrs. Mayers[10] Dance by Mr. Isaacks[11] Gambling[12]	Celebrated on the 7th, "the 6th . . . being Sunday . . . the Court . . . was very Numerous and Splendid."[13] Re the Play: "And the Court very well pleas'd."[14] "They say there was great order in the play room, but some difficulty to get to it."[15]
1705	
Ode by Eccles[16] Concert "of Vocal and Instrumental Musick"[17] Opera, Clayton's *Arsinoe*[18] Dance, "The Marlborough," by Mr. Isaacks[19] "Several Entertainments of Dancing" performed by Mr. and Mrs. du Ruel[20]	"Yesterday thear was great rejoysing, all the Ladys & Gentlemen in thear Birthday cloaths. But the Queen would not giv them a Baul, nor Play."[21] "Was observed with great Solemnity. There was an extraordinary Appearance at Court of the Nobility and Gentry, as well for their number as the Magnificence of their Habits."[22]
1706	
Ode by Eccles[23] Play, Ravenscroft's *The Anatomist*[24] Concert by Mrs. de l'Epine and other soloists[25] Dance by Mr. Isaacks[26] Dancing by l'Abbé, du Ruel, and others[27] Ball[28]	Celebrated on the 5th, "Her Majesty's Birth-day falling on Ash-Wednesday . . . the Court was very numerous, and extreamly magnificent."[29] Anne was ill with gout; the next morning Prince George fell seriously ill.[30]

TABLE 7.4 *(continued)*

Entertainment	Comments
1707	
Ode by Eccles[31] Dance "by du Ruel and others"[32] Dance, "The Union," by Mr. Isaacks[33] Ball[34] Opera, Haym's *Camilla*[35]	"The Court was extraordinarily numerous and magnificent."[36]
1708	
Ode by Eccles[37] Possibly a dance, "The Saltarella," performed by de Legarde and Miss Santlow[38]	Celebrated at Kensington: "There has been a great appearance at Kensington, and will be a greater this evening. Her Majesty did not come to town, and has not ordered any ball or comedy, which they say will be reserved for H.R.H.'s birthday."[39] Anne was ill: "The Queen, lame and Indisposed, and Prince, complimented by a Numerous Court."[40]
1709	
? (See comment; however, there is some evidence that Eccles was paid for an ode)[41]	Anne did appear despite Prince George's recent death: "The court for that day will putt off their mourning, but no song as usual, nor any other publick entertainments."[42] "Last Night there was a Drawing-Room at Her Majesty's Palace at St. James's, where abundance of the Nobility and Gentry made their Appearance."[43]
1710	
No ode[44]	Anne attended the Chapel Royal in the morning; "there was a drawing room at night, but every body in as deep morning as ever."[45]

(continued)

TABLE 7.4 *(continued)*
Royal Birthday Celebrations, 1702–1714

Entertainment	Comments
1711	
Ode by Eccles[46] Dialogue in Italian in praise of the Queen by Handel, sung by Grimaldi "and the other Celebrated Voices of the Italian Opera: With which Her Majesty was extreamly well pleas'd."[47] Play, George Granville's *The Jew of Venice*[48] Ball[49]	"The nobility and gentry went to compliment her majestie at St. James's in richer habits than has been known since 1660; the ladies appeared with jewels very glorious . . . and the evening concluded with bonefires [*sic*], illuminations, &c."[50] "There has not been so fine nor so full a court since King Charles's time. The common people are very much pleased that so much respect is shewn to the Queen."[51]
1712	
No ode Concert of Italian opera selections performed by Grimaldi "and the other best Voices"[52]	There was much speculation, most of it Whig, that the Queen would be forced to cancel or postpone the festivities because of a recent attack of the gout; but on the night, Wentworth reports, "there was as much fine cloaths as ever, and I thank God the Queen appear'd both morning and afternoon as usual . . . the Guards were doubled, some people affirm there was no accation for't."[53] Lady Strafford reports, "There was a very Great Croud."[54] Prince Eugene attended and was presented with a diamond-studded sword.[55]
1713	
? Ode by Handel[56] Ball[57] Gambling[58]	"The Queen is not well enough to see the Lady's in the morning but at Seven A Clock she dos . . . there will be a great Crowd."[59] Because of her gout, the Queen had to be carried into the Great Presence Chamber in the evening.[60] Nevertheless Swift "never saw it [the Birthday] celebrated with so much Luxry, and fine Cloaths."[61]

TABLE 7.4 *(continued)*

Entertainment	Comments
	1714
? Ode by Eccles[62] Ball and a "splendid entertainment" in the evening[63]	Celebrated at Windsor, where the Queen had been seriously ill all winter; nevertheless she "on Her Birthday entertaind Company above 3 hours."[64] "There was a numerous Court at Windsor; and the same was observed in the Cities of London and Westminster, with the usual Solemnity, as, Ringing of Bells, Bonfires, Illuminations, and other Demonstrations of Joy."[65]

SOURCES: (1) *Cal. Ref. Mus.*, p. 47. (2) Ibid.; Burrows, "Handel" 1: 141, quoting LC 5/152–54. (3) *Post Man*, no. 1088, 9–11 Feb. 1703. (4) *English Post*, no. 363, 3–5 Feb. 1702[/03]. (5) Ibid. (6) Boyer, *Annals* I: 215; see also Luttrell, *Brief Relation* V: 266. (7) Burrows, "Handel" I: 141. (8) *London Stage* II: 56; LC 5/153, pp. 440–41. (9) *London Stage* II: 58. (10) Ibid., p. 56. (11) *Post Man*, no. 1245, 24–26 Feb. 1704. (12) H.M.C., *Twelfth Report*, App. V, p. 180. (13) Boyer, *Annals* II: 219. (14) [J. Downes], *Roscius Anglicanus, or An Historical Review of the Stage* (1708), p. 47. (15) H.M.C., *Twelfth Report* App. V, p. 180: Lady Russell to Lady Granby at Belvoir, 8 Feb. 1703/04. (16) Burrows, "Handel" I: 141. (17) *London Gazette*, no. 4095, 5–8 Feb. 1704[/05]. (18) Ibid. (19) *Post Man*, no. 1372, 10–13 Feb. 1705. (20) *London Stage* II: 87. (21) Add. MSS 31143, f. 22 verso: Lady Wentworth to Lord Raby, 9 Mar. 1704/05; see also Add. MSS 31144, f. 141; Luttrell, *Brief Relation* V: 516–17. (22) *London Gazette*, no. 4095, 5–8 Feb. 1704[/05]. (23) Burrows, "Handel" I: 141; Boyer, *Annals* IV: 219. (24) *London Stage* II: 116; Boyer, *Annals* IV: 219. (25) *London Stage* II: 116. (26) *Post Man*, no. 1586, 2–5 Mar. 1706. (27) *London Stage* II: 116. (28) Ewald, *Newsmen*, p. 43. (29) Boyer, *Annals* IV: 219; see also Luttrell, *Brief Relation* VI: 13; Ewald, *Newsmen*, p. 43; *London Gazette*, no. 4199, 4–7 Feb. 1705[/06]. (30) Green, *Anne*, p. 150. (31) Burrows, "Handel" I: 141. (32) *London Stage* II: 141. (33) *Daily Courant*, no. 1502, 6 Feb. 1707. (34) Boyer, *Annals* V: 492. (35) *London Stage* II: 139. (36) Boyer, *Annals* V: 492. (37) Burrows, "Handel" I: 141. (38) *London Stage* II: 166. (39) Manchester, *Court and Society* II: 275: Joseph Addison to the Earl of Manchester, Cock Pit, 6 Feb. 1707/08. (40) *Nicolson Diaries*, pp. 448–49; Gregg, *Anne*, p. 258. (41) Burrows, "Handel" I: 141. (42) Luttrell, *Brief Relation* VI: 390, 403. (43) *Post Boy*, no. 2143, 5–8 Feb. 1708/09. (44) Burrows, "Handel" I: 141. (45) *Wentworth Papers*, p. 108: Peter Wentworth to Lord Raby, 14 Feb. 1710. See *Post Man*, no. 1844, 7–9 Feb. 1710, for a dance—"The Royal Galliard"—choreographed for, but apparently not performed on, the birthday. (46) Burrows, "Handel" I: 141. (47) Boyer, *Annals* IX: 335. (48) *London Stage* II: 255. (49) British Mercury, no. 139, 9–12 Feb. 1711. (50) Luttrell, *Brief Relation* VI: 688. (51) H.M.C., *Fifteenth Report*, App. IV, p. 657: [Edward Harley] to Abigail Harley, at Eywood, 6 Feb. 1710/11. For the extensive preparations made for this birthday by the court, see Add. MSS 31143, f. 613; Swift, *Journal*, p. 181; *Lady Mary Wortley Montagu Letters* I: 70–71. (52) Boyer, *Annals* X, 344. (53) *Wentworth Papers*, pp. 247–48: Peter Wentworth to the Earl of Strafford, London, 12 Jan. 1712. See also H.M.C., *Twelfth Report*, App. III, pp. 99–100. (54) Add. MSS 22226, f. 87 verso: Lady Strafford to the Earl of Strafford, 25 Feb. 1712; see also *Nicolson Diaries*, p. 584. (55) *Wentworth Papers*, pp. 247–48. (56) Burrows, "Handel" I: 142–43. (57) Ibid., p. 142; *British Mercury*, no. 397, 11 Feb. 1712/13; *Daily Courant*, no. 3534, 9 Feb. 1713; Add. MSS 17677 GGG, f. 67 verso. (58) Add. MSS 17677 GGG, f. 67 verso; D. Green, *Anne*, p. 281. (59) Add. MSS 22226, f. 288 verso: Lady Strafford to the Earl of Strafford, 6 Feb. 1712/13. (60) Burrows, "Handel" I: 142; D. Green, *Anne*, p. 281. (61) Swift, *Journal*, p. 615. (62) Burrows, "Handel" I: 141–43. (63) Ibid., p. 142, quoting A. Boyer, *The Political State of Great Britain* (1711–40), VII: 184. See also Add. MSS 17677 HHH, f. 71 verso. (64) *Swift Correspondence* II: 11: Jonathan Swift to Joshua Dawson, London, 11 Feb. 1713/14. (65) *British Mercury*, no. 449, 3–10 Feb. 1713/14.

As with Anne's administrative reforms, the "Sunshine Day" of revived royal ritual and court ceremony did not last. As early as Easter week 1703 she canceled a projected progress to Newmarket.[62] The last such excursion, to Newmarket, occurred in the fall of 1707 (Table 7.2). Her last appearance at a public thanksgiving service in St. Paul's Cathedral took place in August 1708 (Table 7.1). The middle years of the reign saw but one notable celebration of her Accession Day, none of her Coronation Day or Prince George's birthday (Table 7.3). Even the royal birth does not appear to have been commemorated with quite the same gusto after 1707. In 1708 the Queen not only failed to order a ball or a play; she did not even come to town, preferring to remain at Kensington instead.[63]

The ostensible reason for the subdued tone in 1708 was royal illness. As noted previously, the gout had already rendered Anne periodically lame by 1702. Though she managed to walk at her going to parliament on 11 March, she had to be carried to the door of Westminster Abbey on 23 April.[64] By mid-reign, she had lost most of the use of her limbs and was often too ill to participate in regular or elaborate public ceremony.[65] Worse, her visible physical decline could not help but undermine, for those with access to her person, the very image of monarchy such ceremony was supposed to promote. As described, for example, by Sir John Clerk of Penicuik, Anne emerges as a pathetic figure. Clerk found her at Kensington "labouring under a fit of the Gout, and in extrem pain and agony," her face "red and spotted," her dress "negligent," her gouty foot "tied up with a pultis and some nasty bandages," her surroundings "in the same disorder as about the meanest of her subjects." The irony that this pitiable creature aspired to be the nursing mother of those subjects was not lost on Clerk: "I was much affected at this sight, and the more when she had occasion to mention her people of Scotland. . . . What are you, poor mean like Mortal, thought I, who talks in the style of a Soveraign? Nature seems to be inverted when a poor infirm Woman becomes one of the Rulers of the World."[66]

Prince George's health was also a concern from the beginning of the reign, and several royal progresses were canceled because of his periodic bouts with asthma and gout.[67] After his death from respiratory failure on 28 October 1708, Anne retreated from the social and ceremonial life of the court and nation almost as completely as Victoria was to do a century and a half later. Mourning for the Prince was observed from 7 November 1708 to Christmas Day 1710.[68] Though the Queen began to receive visitors again as early as mid-December 1708, she declined to receive the New Year's compliments of the nobility in 1709.[69] The following month she put in an appearance at her birthday celebration, but Luttrell reports "no song as usual, nor any other publick entertainments." One year later, on 6 February 1710, there was a drawing room, "but," according to Peter Wentworth, "every body in as deep morning [*sic*] as ever."[70]

Genuine as the Queen's physical ailments and wifely grief undoubtedly were, they were also remarkably convenient in light of her political situation by mid-reign. Despite her palpable personal popularity with the masses, it must have been obvious to her, as the Whigs stormed the closet and the Tories attacked royal policy in parliament, that the attempt to unite the political nation through a revival of court ceremony and monarchical sentiment was failing where it mattered most, among the ruling class. Worse, far from being allowed to retire into peaceful impotence, the monarchy and its ritual began to be appropriated by the ascendant party for its own ends. Thus, during the electoral spring and summer of 1705 the Queen was persuaded to undertake two progresses, one to Newmarket and Cambridge, the other to Winchester (Table 7.2). These were ostensibly to take the diversions of horseracing and hunting, respectively, but their real purpose was to show favor to the Whigs.[71] Nor could Anne have long deceived herself that Whig participation in court ceremonial had anything to do with veneration for her person or crown, for they chose to exploit their new royal connection without regard for her personal feelings. For example, in February 1710, while she and the court were still in mourning, the Whiggish Beefsteak Club celebrated the royal birthday as follows: "From Dinner till Evening a curious Collection of Musick was perform'd, and at Night a Firework illuminated Covent-Garden."[72] Behavior such as this gave Anne cause, her poor health and widowhood excuse, for not undertaking more progresses on behalf of Whig candidates; for not receiving the compliments of an increasingly Whig court on her Accession or Coronation days; and for not going to St. Paul's Cathedral to give thanks for the victories of a Whig general in a war for which neither she nor the nation could any longer muster enthusiasm.

Such considerations go far to explain her uncharacteristic behavior at the opening of an overwhelmingly Whig parliament in November 1709: "The Queen's Speech was very well liked, but it was observ'd that she spoke it in a much fainter voyce than she used to have; & her manner was more careless, & less moving, than it has been upon other occasions."[73] This was a sorry contrast to the triumphant demeanor of the matriarch in Elizabethan dress who had so charmed parliament seven years earlier with her melodious voice and disarming blush.

With the fall of the Whigs in 1710 and the rise of a ministry under Robert Harley that achieved power on a platform of moderation and national unity, there came a corresponding revival of the Queen's ceremonial role. The first significant manifestation of this after the timely lifting of mourning for Prince George at Christmas 1710 was the 1711 birthday celebration. Preparations among what proved to be Anne's predominantly Tory courtiers appear to have been well in hand by the end of the previous year.[74] On the day, the court was reported to be "extream numerous and magnificent," its adherents going to compliment the Queen "in richer habits than has been known since 1660."[75] Anne herself broke with personal custom and also purchased a new gown, of flowered satin embroidered with gold, for the occasion.[76] The entertainment provided for this magnificent assemblage consisted of the usual ode set by the master of the Queen's musick, John Eccles; a play, Granville's *Jew of Venice*; and, most spectacular of all, a concert: "Between One and Two in the Afternoon, was perform'd a fine Consort, being a Dialogue in Italian, in Her Majesty's Praise, set to excellent Musick by the famous Mr. Hendel . . . and sung by Signior Cavaliew [*sic*] Nicolini Grimaldi, and the other Celebrated Voices of the Italian Opera: With which Her Majesty was extreamly well pleas'd."[77] The evening concluded with the usual bonfires, illuminations, and other popular demonstrations, on the evidence of which one ministerial supporter remarked, "The common people are very much pleased that so much respect is shewn to the Queen."[78]

The remainder of 1711 saw the first noteworthy celebrations of Anne's Accession and Coronation days in several years, though illness and security concerns following Guiscard's attempt on Harley's life prevented her from actually appearing on the former occasion (Table 7.3).[79] Drawing-room nights, which do not appear to have been a regular feature of court life for several years, were held twice a week during the London season and often attracted large crowds. The Abbé Gaultier, reporting to the Marquis de Torcy, noted the change: "Sa court, auparavent deserté etait remplait tous le jour."[80] When the court retired to Windsor that summer, the Queen sponsored gambling and dancing, and there was even talk of a progress to Bath.[81]

Despite increasingly precarious health and a delicate political situation, Anne and her advisers did their best to maintain the accelerated tempo of court ceremonial and social life to the very end of the reign. Attacks of the gout and Whig rumors to the contrary notwithstanding, she appeared at each of her subsequent birthdays.[82] The high standards of entertainment set in 1711 were maintained on those occasions with gambling, balls, and the music of Eccles, Handel, and the Italian opera (Table 7.4). The Queen also managed to attend celebrations of her Accession Day in 1712 and 1713, and of her Coronation Day, just three months before her death, in 1714 (Table 7.3). On the other hand, doctor's orders and fear of a political disturbance did prevent her at the last minute from attending the thanksgiving for the peace of Utrecht at St. Paul's in 1713. Drawing rooms were also occasionally canceled because of royal illness.[83] This may explain a number of well-publicized social and artistic soirees hosted by the Duke and Duchess of Shrewsbury, the Duke of Ormonde, and other prominent Tory courtiers during the last years of the reign.[84] Even the round of masquerades, water parties, and "splendid Entertainments" sponsored by the French and Spanish ambassadors in 1712 and 1713 may be seen as complementary to those of the court, whose peace policy had, of course, made them possible.[85]

While the Shrewsburys and others helped to entertain people of quality, there was a parallel attempt in the last years of the reign to convince the general public that the Queen's health held firm. It has already been noted that the Whigs were anxious to portray her health, and by implication that of her dynasty and ministry, in the opposite light.[86] In response, and particularly after her nearly fatal illness in the winter of 1713–14, government newsletters and supporters frequently and avidly reported her to be taking the air in her coach, engaged in healing, and so on.[87] Ironically, these efforts appear to have taxed the healer far more than they cured the scrofulous. According to one observer, "The Queen disorders herself by preparing herself to touch, . . . noe one about her cares she should doe it; for she fasts the day before and abstains severall days, which they think does her hurt."[88] Despite the concern of her personal servants, the government was clearly anxious that Anne continue to appear in public and look well when doing so. As late as 1 May 1714 a government newsletter reported that during the previous week she had taken the air as far as Kensington and touched for the Evil. The anonymous author could not resist adding, smugly, "And it is observed that she never was better."[89]

Within a quarter, the Queen was dead. It is therefore reasonable to ask whether the extraordinary efforts she expended in reviving the ceremonial and social life of the court during the last four years of her reign justified the obvious strain on her health. Insofar as those efforts were aimed at uniting the country in common allegiance to the sovereign, they were most successful among those who mattered least: the common people. From the first, Anne was, like Elizabeth, a popular monarch. As with the latter, this had much to do with her Englishness, her Anglicanism, and her sex.[90] But of equal significance was Anne's Elizabethan ability to rise to a great occasion despite her miserable health. One need only compare Clerk's description of her private appearance to contemporary accounts of her public self to see this. For example, though Anne had to be carried to her coronation, Celia Fiennes's most vivid memories about that occasion were of the regal bearing with which she walked in the Abbey; her "obligeing lookes and bows to all that saluted her"; and how the diamonds in her hair "at the least motion brill'd and flamed."[91] Even Sarah had to admit that there was "something of majesty in her look," and, indeed, she always seems to have created an impressive aura in public.[92]

And yet, the Queen's majesty was never perceived as aloofness. The very fact that, like Elizabeth but unlike Dutch William or German George, she was willing to go out among her subjects seems to have elicited their sympathy, loyalty, and good will. The anonymous author of one history of her reign may have had these other monarchs in mind when, writing in 1721, he looked back on Anne's 1706 progress to Newmarket:

> Crouds of people from all parts of the Country came to see her Majesty, and wish her a long Life and happy Reign; and, indeed, thus it was in whatever part of England she was pleased to appear amongst them. Nor was their sin-

cerity, I believe, ever doubted, for . . . they ever look'd upon her as their common Parent. She found no necessity of following the Turkish Maxim of immuring her self for fear of being assassinated, the affections of the people were her surest Guard, and she was never safer than when she was surrounded by them.[93]

Only at the very end of the reign, as the issue of the succession grew more prominent and her ministry's perceived equivocal position less acceptable to many, is there evidence that some of that unpopularity began to rub off on the Queen herself.[94] However, the majority of these reports concern individuals, not mobs, and words, not deeds, as in the case of Watts, noted above in Chapter 2. Nevertheless, her advisers feared for her safety on occasion and took the appropriate precautions, doubling the guards at the later birthday celebrations and urging her to avoid crowds during politically sensitive periods.[95] Anne seems never to have shared their fears.[96] If she acquiesced in their precautions, it was probably as much out of reluctance to be the excuse for and center of a popular partisan demonstration as out of a sense of self-preservation.[97] While her suspected Jacobite sympathies undoubtedly offended certain groups within the lower classes, she appears to have retained her general personal popularity to the very end. After Dr. Radcliffe refused to attend her on her deathbed, he was threatened by "the mob as well as Quality," who, he was informed by a friend, "expresst so much Resentment that if your new House had stood at London or Kensington they would scarce be restrain'd from pulling it down."[98]

Despite implied aristocratic participation in the demonstration just referred to, it was at this most important level of Augustan society that Anne's revival of royal ceremony and symbolism failed most dramatically to promote unity and moderation. It failed in large part because, for all her talk of these virtues, the Queen's version of unity and moderation ultimately had very little to offer Dissenters and Junto Whigs. Nor did it please the most aggressive members of the High Church party.[99] In other words, it was a victim of the rise of party issues, party loyalties, and party divisions that no amount of courtly ritual and monarchical sentiment could smooth over. Indeed, as noted previously, successive ministries sought to appropriate royal ceremony and even the royal person for their own partisan ends. Consequently, Tories grew increasingly scarce at court during the Whig ascendancy of the middle years of the reign.[100] Conversely, after the Tory resurgence of 1710 the Whigs not only boycotted the court, but did their best to spoil its various ceremonial and social activities by spreading rumors of royal illness, cancellations, and poor attendance.[101]

Indeed, they went even further, attempting to set up an alternate Whig ceremonial and social life centering on the very party and partisan symbolism that the Queen so studiously avoided. As early as November 1703, during the first period of Tory dominance, the Whig Kit-Cat Club is reported to have gone all out in celebrating the birthday of William III on the 4th: "At the Kitcat 'twas very great. Lord Hartington, Duke of Somersett &c. were there. The glass sent down was to the immortal memory of King William. They had all new cloaths &c."[102] The celebration of a royal birthday, the attendance of the nobility (both Hartington and Somerset held household office), and the wearing of new clothes in honor of the occasion—all were supposed to be the prerogative of the court. At mid-reign, during the Queen's retreat from public life, her apparent refusal to support an increasingly Whig ministry with courtly ritual sometimes forced that ministry and its allies to improvise. For example, Lord Treasurer Godolphin compensated for her absence from the November 1709 thanksgiving by afterwards fêting the Duke of Marlborough and other notables at his own expense, while the Dutch ambassador provided a ball for "the Ladies" in the evening.[103]

After the fall of the Godolphin ministry in the summer of 1710, the Whig attempt to appropriate national ritual accelerated in keeping with a general intensification of political animosities during the last years of the reign. In the fall of 1711 various members of the Kit-Cat (including Master of the Great Wardrobe Montagu) subscribed a total of £1,000 toward a pope-burning on 17 November, Queen Elizabeth's Accession Day. There were to have been additional figures representing the Devil (made up to look like Robert Harley), the Pretender, Dr. Sacheverell, and an assortment of cardinals, Jesuits, and Franciscans. In effect, Anne's evocation of Elizabeth as a symbol of national unity was to be usurped by one that associated Gloriana exclusively with Whig principles in order to promote a popular demonstration against the Queen's own government. Though that government discovered the figures and suppressed the demonstration well before the day in question,[104] Whig politicians continued to sponsor public celebration of an alternative, Whig political calendar in the period 1712–14. These years saw boisterous celebrations of the birthdays of the Electoral Prince (17 May), the Electress Sophia (3 October), William III, and (independent of the court) Anne; as well as Elizabeth's Accession Day and even Princess Anne's flight from London in 1688 (25 November).[105] Indeed, the whole business of political anniversaries threatened to get out of hand as the Whig *Flying Post* urged public commemoration of James II's flight on 11 December, William and Mary's proclamation on 13 February, and the handing down of the Sacheverell verdict on 23 March.[106] In contrast to the Queen's attempt to heal division through the bipartisan commemoration of the glories of her reign, the public celebration of this calendar could only have served to open old wounds. Indeed, those celebrations that did take place were often marked by violence. This, the government's hostility, and a latent conviction that state ritual was still the Queen's may explain why, according to the most recent examination of London politics during the period, the Whig attempt to upstage the court's ceremonial calendar was largely unsuccessful.[107]

If the court's monopoly of national ritual and symbolism could not be broken, perhaps its social preeminence might be challenged. After her dismissal from office in January 1711, that old courtier the Duchess of Marlborough attempted to set up something of a Whig anti-court at Marlborough House, which just happened to overlook the gardens of St. James's Palace. In November of that year, at the beginning of the next court season, she was rumored to be planning regular assemblies "to out do the Duchess of Shrewsberry's," which were, as suggested earlier, supplementary to those of the court.[108] Early in 1712, just after the fall of the Duke and two of the Churchill daughters from royal service, there were even plans to hold an "opposition" ball on the night of the Queen's birthday. Several prospective guests actually "made cloath for that day that had not for the birthday." This caused much adverse comment, representing the affair as "a sort of vying with the Court" and even as "a design to sett up for themselves." This was too much for the Duke, who prudently canceled the ball, though a number of Whig ladies were informed that "the Dutchess wou'd be at home."[109]

That winter, the Whigs did sponsor a number of successful entertainments in honor of the visit of Prince Eugene of Savoy.[110] Nevertheless, there was clearly a limit to how far the court's ceremonial and social role could be usurped. In the end, "King John" had to content himself with celebrating Blenheim Day in August 1712 by feasting a number of Whig notables in a tent erected for that purpose on the grounds of Holywell House. As a concession to popularity, the acquisitive Duke permitted the locals to inspect the tent, which was made of "Arras work and very curious of its kind," for a fee of 6*d*. apiece.[111] By November, Marlborough had taken up his self-imposed exile on the continent and nothing more is heard of the Kit-Cat Club. That the Whig attempt to set up an alternate source for national ritual and symbol ultimately failed is a tribute to the authority the Queen and her court still possessed in these areas. However, that such an attempt was made at all reveals the limitations of mere ritual and symbol, even of the authentic variety, as a force for uniting the political nation. In the following two sections it will be argued that court occasions under Queen Anne had, unfortunately, little else to recommend them.

Art

The provision of an entertaining and culturally refined court life, as under Charles II, or a court art with an overt Royalist message, as Louis XIV was fostering across the Channel, offered an alternate means of attracting aristocratic support. It was not, however, one that Anne pursued with any vigor. One of her more moderate critics has written of the arts in her reign, "Some of them at least shone well without her."[112] Others are less restrained: "Of patronage in the sense of sympathetic understanding from this fat, dull and persevering lady, there was none."[113] Indeed, the popular attribution of the designation "Queen Anne" to particular styles in a number of the decorative arts is mistaken. Apart from a few examples noted below, neither Anne nor any of her courtiers promoted a specifically "court" aesthetic, in the sense of art that reflected the court's daily life or some idealized picture of its mistress. This is not to deny the significance of courtiers who were also either artists—such as Arbuthnot, Swift, Gay, and others in their circle—or patrons, such as the Dukes of Marlborough, Montagu, Shrewsbury, and Somerset. It is simply to recognize that relatively little of their art was directly inspired by Queen Anne, her taste, or the specific experience of being at her court. Even Pope's *Rape of the Lock,* the most famous literary depiction of that experience, gives every appearance of being an idealization owing less to the reality of the Augustan court than to the memory of its Restoration predecessor.[114] Since there was little attempt to produce art for the purpose of glorifying the monarch, there was little need to centralize and regulate its production. The handful of artistic academies and societies founded under Anne were invariably a substitute for her patronage, not a consequence of it. In short, most of the great artistic commissions of the period had little to do with the woman after whom it is often named.

This state of affairs has generally been attributed to the Queen's reputed indifference to culture. In fact, Anne was neither wholly insensitive to the arts nor entirely neglectful of them. As a child of the Restoration court, she appears to have had a respectable artistic training. Growing up at Richmond, St. James's, and Whitehall, she was familiar with one of the great art collections of Europe.[115] She had acted with her sister, Mary, in amateur court theatricals and, as noted previously, received training in speech from one of the great actresses of the day.[116] But it was at music that the young Princess truly excelled. She was said to have had a fine ear as a girl, and her father, the Duke of York, hired a small army of teachers and musicians to cultivate it. At various times prior to her marriage in 1683 the Princess was under the tutelage of a dancing master, a singing master, a teacher of music, a teacher of the harpsichord, and a guitar man. Lest all of this instruction make Anne a dull girl, her establishment included a musician to provide entertainment.[117]

These efforts appear to have paid off, for music was one major art form in which Anne took an active interest from the first. For example, during her father's reign she insisted that anthems in the Anglican chapel royal continue to receive orchestral accompaniment, as they had under Charles II. Throughout the reigns of James II and William III, while the court was, for the most part, neglecting the work of the choir and allowing its numbers to dwindle, Princess Anne continued to patronize individual members, such as Henry Purcell and William Turner, for birthday odes and occasional pieces. Her association with the cause of English church music was acknowledged by John Blow in

1700 with the dedication of the anthology *Amphion Anglicus*.[118] Blow's appreciation was not misplaced. Once on the throne, though Anne did not restore the orchestral accompaniment of anthems discontinued by William in 1689, she did bring the choir back up to strength and gave pensions to deserving prospects such as Richard Elford.[119] Above all, by reviving the custom of attending public thanksgivings at St. Paul's, she gave the musicians of the chapel choir a public showcase for their work, as both composers and performers. According to Tudway, the anthems and *Te Deums* of Blow, Clarke, Croft, Handel, and Weldon "made upon the great events of her Majesty's reign" in turn inspired a revival of sacred music in the country at large.[120]

While Anne's patronage of church music might be attributed to her staunch Anglicanism and love of ceremony, these do not explain her equally strong interest in secular music. As Princess, she had a band of her own musicians, danced at court balls, and occasionally attended public concerts and operas, including Purcell's *Fairy Queen*.[121] That she did so only occasionally had less to do with indifference than with physical indisposition, as indicated in the following letter to Sarah from the early 1690s: "I fancy now you are in Town you will be tempted to See the Opera which I shall not wonder at for I should be so to if I were able to Stir but when that will be God knows for my feavor is not quite [*sic*]."[122]As Queen, Anne was prevented by poor health and resultant immobility from attending the opera or concert hall, but on her birthdays in 1705, 1707, 1711, and 1712, the opera came to her (Table 7.4). Her own instrumental musicians frequently attended at Windsor early in the reign.[123] Throughout the reign, birthdays, New Year's days, progresses, the coronation in 1702, the visit of the King of Spain in 1703, and the passage of the Act of Union in 1707 all provided the impetus or inspiration for odes, songs, or full concerts by Abell, Conti, Eccles, Gasparini, Handel, Hughes, Paisible, and other noted musicians of the day (Table 7.5). On 25 May 1704, for example, the Queen and her "family" were the guests of honor at a musical water party the equal of that in any other reign: "Thursday evening, the earl of Kent, lord chamberlain, treated her majestie and the court upon the river Thames, where were near 1000 barges and boats, with all sorts of musick and eatables."[124] More characteristic, if less well documented, were the occasional private concerts held in the royal bedchamber or closet

TABLE 7.5
Balls, Plays, Concerts, and Entertainments, 1702–1714

Date	Occasion	Event and comment
	1702	
22 Aug.–10 Oct.	Bath progress	Plays (incl. *The Innocent Lampoon*) performed by Drury Lane Theatre Company[1] Dances by "Mr. J.B."[2]
	1703	
1 Jan.	New Year's Day	Song by Tate, set Eccles[3]
6 Feb.	Queen's birthday	Song by Motteux, set Eccles[4] Ode by Wall, set Abell[5] Dance by Isaacks[6] Ball[7]
? 8 Mar.	Queen's accession	Song, set Hughes[8]
By 23 Apr.		? Concert by Margarita de l'Epine[9]
Fortnightly in summer	Court at Windsor	Balls: "All the beaus, & Beles, that are heare, have desired me to lett them have a ball once in a week, or once a fortnight. I have consented to the last part of ye request, & they are to dance a Wednesday."[10]
30 Dec.	Visit of King of Spain	Concert, ball, and dancing, including music by Paisible[11]
	1704	
1 Jan.	New Year's Day	Ode, set Eccles[12]
7 Feb.	Queen's birthday (6 Feb.)	Ode, set Eccles[13] Dance by Isaacks[14] Dancing by du Ruel, Cherrier, and others[15] "A Dialogue which was Sung before Her Majesty on Her Birthday at St. James's."[16] Play: Dryden's *All for Love*, "being exactly done, and the Court very well pleas'd."[17]
29 Feb.	Prince George's birthday	Play: Caryll's *Sir Solomon Single*: "There was a play last night at Court, as it was said there would be. It was Solomon Jingle: they say the Queen and Prince was both extremely diverted with it."[18] Entertainments by du Ruel, Cherrier, Mrs. Mayers, and "Devonshire Girl."[19]

(continued)

TABLE 7.5 *(continued)*
Balls, Plays, Concerts, and Entertainments, 1702–1714

Date	Occasion	Event and comment
		1704 *(continued)*
24 Apr.	Anniversary of Queen's coronation (23 Apr.)	Play: Shakespeare's *Merry Wives of Windsor*[20] Dancing by du Ruel, Cherrier, and Mrs. du Ruel[21]
25 May		Water party: "Thursday evening, the earl of Kent, lord chamberlain, treated her majestie and the court upon the river Thames, where were near 1000 barges and boats, with all sorts of musick and eatables."[22]
		1705
1 Jan.	New Year's Day	Ode, set Eccles[23]
6 Feb.	Queen's birthday	Ode (three-part songs), set Eccles[24] Opera: Clayton's *Arsinoe*[25] Concert "of Vocal & Instrumental Musick"[26] Dance, "The Marlborough," by Isaacks[27] Dancing by du Ruel and Mrs. du Ruel[28]
		1706
1 Jan.	New Year's Day	Ode, set Eccles[29] Music "by the Italian Masters"[30] Music by Jeremiah Clarke[31]
5 Feb.	Queen's birthday (6 Feb.)	Play: Ravenscroft's *The Anatomist*[32] Ode, set Eccles[33] Concert by Mrs. de l'Epine and others[34] Dance by Isaacks[35] Dancing by l'Abbé, du Ruel, and others[36] Ball[37]
July		? Concert by a boy soloist[38]
By mid-Aug.		? Concert by "the Barroness"[39]

TABLE 7.5 *(continued)*

Date	Occasion	Event and comment
	1707	
1 Jan.	New Year's Day	Ode, set Eccles[40]
6 Feb.	Queen's birthday	Ode, set Eccles[41]
		Opera: Haym's *Camilla*[42]
		Dance, "The Union," by Isaacks[43]
		Dance by du Ruel and others[44]
		Ball[45]
6 Mar.	Union Day	Concert "of Musick compos'd" by Sir Francisco Conti "which he had the Honour to perform at Court upon the Union day."[46]
		"Union Dance" performed by Mrs. Santlow and Mons. du Bargues[47]
	1708	
1 Jan.	New Year's Day	Ode, set Eccles[48]
6 Feb.	Queen's birthday	Ode, set Eccles[49]
		Possibly a dance, "The Saltarella," performed by de Legarde and Miss Santlow[50]
By 26 Mar.		? Concert featuring "That celebrated Sonata for a Violin and Flute, made by the famous Signor Gasperini, and play'd by him and Paisable often before her Majesty."[51]
Biweekly	Court at Windsor	Concerts: "A Scheme, now preparing by my Ld Chamb: and Others, to have Concerts of Musick in the Summer at Windsor, twice a Week in the Apartment."[52] (This scheme was probably abortive.)
	1709	
1 Jan.	New Year's Day	No ode[53]
6 Feb.	Queen's birthday	? No ode[54]
	1710	
1 Jan.	New Year's Day	Ode, set Eccles[55]
6 Feb.	Queen's birthday	? no ode[56]

(continued)

TABLE 7.5 *(continued)*
Balls, Plays, Concerts, and Entertainments, 1702–1714

Date	Occasion	Event and comment
	1711	
1 Jan.	New Year's Day	Ode, set Eccles[57]
6 Feb.	Queen's birthday	Ode, set Eccles[58]
		Concert: "Between One and Two in the Afternoon, was perform'd a fine Consort, being a Dialogue in Italian, in Her Majesty's Praise, set to excellent Musick by the famous Mr. Hendel . . . and sung by Signior Cavaliew [*sic*] Nicolini Grimaldi, and the other Celebrated Voices of the Italian Opera: With which Her Majesty was extreamly well pleas'd."[59]
		Play: Granville's *The Jew of Venice*[60]
		Ball[61]
After 19 Sept.	Court at Windsor	"Dancing" (ball?): "The queen designs to have cards and dancing here next week."[62]
	1712	
1 Jan.	New Year's Day	? No ode[63]
6 Feb.	Queen's birthday	? No ode[64]
		Concert: "An excellent Consort collected out of several Italian Operas, by Signior Cavaliero Nicolini Grimaldi and perform'd by him, and the other best Voices."[65]
11 Aug.	?	Ball involving just seven couples[66]
	1713	
1 Jan.	New Year's Day	? No ode[67]
6 Feb.	Queen's birthday	? Ode, set Handel[68]
		Dancing[69]
		Ball[70]
	1714	
1 Jan.	New Year's Day	? No ode[71]
6 Feb.	Queen's birthday	? Ode, set Eccles[72]
		Ball[73]

SOURCES: (1) Melville, *Bath Under Beau Nash*, p. 118; *Post Man*, no. 1050, 17–19 Nov. 1702. (2) *Post Man*, no. 1080, 21–23 Jan. 1703. (3) *Cal. Ref. Mus.*, p. 16. (4) Ibid., p. 47. (5) Ibid. (6) *Post Man*, no. 1088, 9–11 Feb. 1703. (7) *English Post*, no. 363, 3–5 Feb. 1702[/03]. (8) *Cal. Ref. Mus.*, p. 50. (9) See Add. MSS 61420 (Privy Purse Accounts) for a payment of £32 5*s*. "to ye Italien wooman for Singing before

where an Italian opera star, a boy soloist, or a celebrated instrumentalist would entertain the Queen for a few pounds out of the privy purse (Table 7.5). Finally, her gout permitting, she might entertain herself on what Hawkins called "the loudest and perhaps the finest" harpsichord "that ever was heard."[125]

Clearly, Anne was not entirely devoid of aesthetic sense. Her failure to be a more enthusiastic patron of music's sister arts is more plausibly explained by lack of time, shortage of money, and poor health than by the dullness of soul usually alleged by critics. The Duchess of Marlborough once discouraged a request for royal patronage for some Italian musicians by claiming, "The queen has so little time that she never heard any of her own music, among which she has some that is very good."[126] While this is undoubtedly an exaggeration, it contains an element of truth. Between the death of Charles II and the accession of Anne, the amount of government business had expanded enormously and with it the demands upon the time and energy of a conscientious monarch. Anne was by any definition such a monarch. Her day usually began with a morning chapel service and always included private

---

ye Queen." See also *Marlborough-Godolphin Correspondence*, p. 181 n. 4. (10) Add. MSS 61416, f. 104 recto and verso: Anne to Sarah, Windsor, 29 June [?1703]. (11) Luttrell, *Brief Relation* V: 375; Price, *Music in Restoration Theatre*, p. 241; Add. MSS 61420, f. 13; *Daily Courant*, no. 535, 3 Jan. 1704. (12) Burrows, "Handel" I: 141. (13) Ibid. (14) LC 5/153, pp. 440–41; *Post Man*, no. 1245, 24–26 Feb. 1704. (15) *London Stage* II: 56. (16) Ibid., p. 58. (17) Ibid., p. 56, quoting [Downes], *Roscius Anglicanus*, p. 47. (18) H.M.C., *Twelfth Report*, App. III, p. 163: Elizabeth Coke to Thomas Coke, London, [1704]. (19) *London Stage* II: 59. (20) Mitchell, "Command Performances . . . Anne," pp. 114, 116. (21) *London Stage* II: 65. (22) Luttrell, *Brief Relation* V: 429. (23) Burrows, "Handel" I: 141. (24) Ibid.; *Cal. Ref. Mus.*, p. 62; *London Stage* II: 98, 102. (25) Mitchell, "Command Performances . . . Anne," p. 114. (26) *London Gazette*, no. 4095, 5–8 Feb. 1704[/05]. (27) *Post Man*, no. 1372, 10–13 Feb. 1705. (28) *London Stage* II: 87. (29) Burrows, "Handel" I: 141. (30) *Cal. Ref. Mus.*, p. 63. See also Add. MSS 17677 BBB, f. 36 verso. (31) *Cal. Ref. Mus.*, p. 64. (32) Mitchell, "Command Performances . . . Anne," pp. 114, 117. (33) Burrows, "Handel" I: 141; D. Green, *Anne*, p. 150. (34) *London Stage* II: 116. (35) *Post Man*, no. 1586, 2–5 Mar. 1706. (36) *London Stage* II: 116. (37) Ewald, *Newsmen*, p. 43. (38) Eg. MSS 2678, f. 10. (39) See ibid., f. 7, for a privy purse payment of £10 15s. to "the Barroness" for singing before the Queen. (40) Burrows, "Handel" I: 141. (41) Ibid. (42) Mitchell, "Command Performances . . . Anne," p. 115; Add. MSS 61420, f. 31. (43) *Daily Courant*, no. 1502, 6 Feb. 1707. (44) *London Stage* II: 141. (45) Boyer, *Annals* V: 492. (46) *Cal. Ref. Mus.*, p. 68. (47) *Daily Courant*, no. 1602, 2 Apr. 1707. (48) Burrows, "Handel" I: 141. (49) Ibid. (50) *London Stage* II: 166. (51) Ibid., p. 169. (52) *Coke's Theatrical Papers*, p. 107: J. Vanbrugh to the Earl of Manchester, [11 May 1708]. (53) Luttrell, *Brief Relation* VI: 390. (54) According to Burrows, "Handel" I: 141, Eccles was paid for an ode, but Luttrell, *Brief Relation* VI: 403, reports, "No song as usual, nor any other publick entertainments." (55) Luttrell, *Brief Relation* VI: 529. (56) See Burrows, "Handel" I: 141. (57) Ibid. (58) Ibid. (59) Boyer, *Annals* IX: 335. (60) *London Stage* II: 255. (61) *British Mercury*, no. 139, 9–12 Feb. 1711. (62) Swift, *Journal*, p. 363. (63) Burrows, "Handel" I: 141. (64) Ibid. (65) Boyer, *Annals* X: 344. (66) *Wentworth Papers*, pp. 296–97. (67) Burrows, "Handel" I: 141. (68) Ibid., pp. 142–43. (69) D. Green, *Anne*, p. 281. (70) Burrows, "Handel" I: 142. (71) Ibid., p. 141. (72) Ibid., pp. 141–42. (73) Ibid., p. 142.

conferences with important ministers. Twice a week, more than any other monarch in British history, she attended long cabinet meetings. Often, as noted previously, she attended the treasury and the House of Lords as well. Finally, there was a steady stream of ambassadors to receive, peers to closet, petitions to answer, and warrants, orders, diplomatic instructions, and letters to sign.[127] If, as she confessed to Archbishop Sharp, "she was really so taken up with business that she had not time to say her prayers," it is hardly surprising that she spent no more time in the theater or concert hall.[128]

The Crown's straitened financial situation was also a limiting factor. Whereas Charles II or even William III might have been willing to run up large debts in pursuit of artistic glory, the daughter of James II was made of sterner stuff. Her predilection for housewifely thrift over queenly grandeur is clearly evident in her attitude to the most conspicuous form of royal consumption, architecture. In Sarah's admiring phrase, "She was never expensive, nor made any foolish buildings."[129] In fact, the destruction of Whitehall in 1698 had left the Crown bereft of a palace large or grand enough for its ceremonial needs. In keeping with the Queen's revival of royal ceremony, there was talk in the first years of the reign of rebuilding Whitehall and finishing Winchester. However, at an estimated cost of £600,000 and £18,000 respectively, such fancies soon passed.[130]

Instead, the new Queen made do with refurbishing St. James's. Even here, Wren's original plans had to be scaled down to merely enlarging the existing council chamber, drawing room, and chapel, at a cost of under £4,000.[131] Years later, as part of her last attempt at household reform in February 1714, Anne approved an enlargement of the privy gallery at her main residence. Though the cost was a mere £315, the warrant authorizing this work was endorsed by her financially pressed lord treasurer: "Let this work be performed, taking care her Maty be eased in the Expense thereof as much as may be, but in no case to exceed the Estimate."[132] Similarly, Anne's most characteristic building project, the charming and intimate Orangery at Kensington, is thought to have been planned as a much more elaborate state reception suite, probably abandoned out of thrift.[133] Some work was done at Hampton Court and Windsor, but this almost invariably involved the completion of projects begun by her predecessors.[134] Her refusal to be expensive, while undoubtedly good for her parlous financial situation, left the Crown without the facilities necessary for a brilliant court life. In particular, the lack of a theater capable of handling balls and plays helps to explain their relative infrequency between 1702 and 1714 (Table 7.5). Worse, neither the rambling maze of St. James's nor the rustic simplicity of Kensington did anything for the prestige of the British monarchy in foreign or domestic eyes.[135]

Anne's reign did see the continuation of two great royal commissions, St. Paul's Cathedral and Greenwich Hospital; and the initiation of two others, Blenheim Palace (1706) and the Fifty London Churches (1711). Clearly, she was willing to build to the glory of God or of the nation, if not to her own person or Crown. There was, however, a personal element in each of these projects: her love of the Church, her charitable nature, her generosity to a friend. Moreover, the net result for architects like Archer, Hawksmoor, Vanbrugh, and Wren and for fine craftsmen like Gibbons, Thornhill, Vanderbanks, and Verrio was materially little different from the great days of Charles II, in that there was a steady stream of court-sponsored work to be done and paid for. What was missing was the conscious Royalist purposefulness and intellectual stimulation that Charles had often provided. It is said that after approving the model for her greatest and most expensive commission, Blenheim Palace, Anne lost all interest in its progress.[136]

Indeed throughout her reign, the Queen, ever the nursing mother of her subjects, showed less interest in art than in the material welfare of artists. Despite her own financial difficulties, she always managed to find money for truly needy artists, though more in a spirit of charity than connoisseurship. When the ceiling painter Verrio finished his work in the great drawing room at Hampton Court, he asked the Queen for a new assignment. Her reply was characteristically generous yet pragmatic: "Her Majesty was pleased to say though there was no haste of any more painting, yet her Majesty would take care of him." True to her word, the treasury-board minute that records Anne's decision to award him a pension of £200 per annum concludes with a condition: "but no more charge for painting."[137] This was consistent with her policy of reducing bills and fees to set allowances. But, as with her decision to pay the arrears of the late John Dryden, it also represents an act of generosity to an old servant to the Stuarts.[138] Anne also gave financial support to the musicians Richard Bradley, Richard Elford, Bernard Gates, John Gostling, and George Frideric Handel and the actress Mary Betterton.[139] In addition, she found honorary places on her establishment for the scholar John Chamberlayne, the painter Sir Godfrey Kneller, the historian James Tyrrel, and the poet William Walsh.[140] While most of these places demanded little or no work, artistic or otherwise, the income, privilege, or prestige they provided helped in varying degrees to make work possible; and for this Anne deserves some credit.

Nor was art always a casualty to thrift or a hostage to charity. The Queen's support of budding chapel singers and music in general has already been noted. Both her own correspondence and the writings of her master gardener, Henry Wise, reveal a royal interest in his area of expertise. Just after her accession Anne wrote to Sarah, "Since I saw you I went to Kensington to walk in y[e] garden w[ch] would be a very prety place if it weare well kept but nothing can be wors, it is a great deal of pity & indeed a great shame that there should be no better use made of soe great an alowance, for I have bin told the King alowed four hundred pound a year for y[t] one garden."[141] These sentiments were also conveyed to Wise, who, despite Anne's avowed intention of retrenching her gardens' expenses, was allowed to spend £26,000 in four years in remodeling the gardens at Kensington alone.[142] The Queen also authorized him to lay out the Little Canal at Hampton Court, the Maestricht Garden at Windsor, and innumerable chaise ridings and roads, and to maintain St. James's Park and Mall at her expense.[143] All gave Londoners and others pleasure during her reign and immediately after. Those that survive remain her most lasting and popular artistic legacy.

Though hardly great patrons of painting or literature, Anne and George did supply notable commissions to the miniaturist Charles Boit and to Kneller for his distinguished series of admirals.[144] On a somewhat more esoteric plane, while it is highly unlikely that Anne ever read Elstob's *Homilies* (1709), Flamsteed's *Tables* (1706–12), Hill's *Present State of Aethiopia, Egypt, &c* (1708), Rymer's *Foedera* (1704–32), the final edition of Nahum Tate's translation of the *Psalms* (1703), or Johan Ernst

Grabe's translation of the Alexandrine manuscript of the *Septuagint* (1707–20), all saw the light of day, wholly or in part, because of her financial assistance or that of Prince George.[145] She was also persuaded to purchase Cotton House and its library (1706), which later became part of the nucleus of the British Museum.[146]

Occupational and financial constraints apart, the Queen's ambivalent attitude to literature, the theater, architecture, and painting may have had a medical explanation. Since the age of three she had suffered from a "defluxion" of the eyes, and she was to complain of eye trouble all her life. The nature of her ailment is obscure, but it appears to have involved both nearsightedness and difficulty in reading, resulting in a permanent squint.[147] Obviously, any art form with an important visual element posed considerable difficulties for enjoyment, hence few paintings and fewer plays. Her gout likewise limited her attendance at the theater and concert hall, and it affected her relationship to dress and fashion.

The issue of royal clothing was not trivial. Like the more costly forms of royal advertisement, architecture, music, painting, and the theater, fine clothes emphasized the monarch's importance, enhanced her physical majesty, and influenced high society. Anne seems to have had a certain amount of fashion sense and, as might be expected, was a keen observer of what was being worn and what was not.[148] Her public appearance was, as has been shown, expressly and often successfully calculated to impress. Nor was Mrs. Morley entirely free of personal vanity, as she reveals in a letter to Mrs. Freeman in the latter's capacity as mistress of the robes, written just prior to the Oudenarde thanksgiving in 1708: "I had a mind to be fine too & in order to be soe I intended to have two diamond buttens & loops upon each sleeve." However, in the same letter, Anne admits the impracticality of these plans: "Heavy clôths are soe uneasy to me."[149] Sarah explains in one of the preliminary drafts of her *Conduct*, "Her limbs were so weakned with the goute for many years, that she cou'd not endure heavy clothes."[150] This in turn helps to explain why Anne's private appearance could be so uninspiring.

The Queen's inclination toward good husbandry, seconded by Sarah, contributed to her lack of style. By various economies, including the elimination of poundage and the cleaning and reusing of old

TABLE 7.6
Periods of Mourning, 1702–1714

Year	Dates[a]	Type	Deceased
1702	8 Mar.–23 May	Full, 1st	King William III[1]
	Begun 24 May	Full, 2nd	King William III[2]
	Begun 18 Oct.	Court	Duke of Holstein[3]
1703	Noted 18 May	"	Daughter of the Emperor[4]
	Begun 15 Aug.	"	Prince of Hanover[5]
1704	5 Nov.–18 Feb. 1705	"	Duchess of Holstein[6]
1705	Noted 6 Feb.–19 May	"	Queen of Prussia[7]
	Begun 3 June	"	Emperor[8]
	Begun 16 Sept.	"	Duke of Zell[9]
	Noted 4 Dec.	"	Prince William of Denmark[10]
1706	Begun 10 Feb.	"	Queen Catherine[11]
	Begun 5 May	(6 mos.)	Princess of Newburgh[12]
1708	Noted 21 May	Court	Prince of Orange[13]
	Begun 23 May	"	Prince of Prussia[14]
	7 Nov.–Xmas 1710	Full	Prince George of Denmark (Prince Consort)[15]
1711	Begun 29 Apr.	Court	Emperor[16]
1712	c. 10 Apr.	?	? (Lady Strafford reports the court to be in mourning)[17]
1713	Begun 15 Mar.	(6 mos.)	King of Prussia[18]
	Noted 25 Nov.	(3 wks.)	Prince of Tuscany[19]
1714	c. 8 Apr.	Court	Queen of Denmark[20]

SOURCES: (1) Luttrell, *Brief Relation* V: 154. (2) Ibid., p. 176. (3) Ibid., pp. 215, 227. (4) Ibid., p. 299. (5) Ibid., p. 328; *Daily Courant*, no. 415, 16 Aug. 1703. (6) Luttrell, *Brief Relation* V: 481; Boyer, *Annals* III: 192; *Post Man*, no. 1338, 2–4 Nov. 1704. (7) Boyer, *Annals* III: 192; Luttrell, *Brief Relation* V: 553; H.M.C., *Fifteenth Report*, App. IV, p. 161. (8) Luttrell, *Brief Relation* V: 550, 555, 559; Boyer, *Annals* IV: 19; Add. MSS 17677 AAA, f. 311. (9) Luttrell, *Brief Relation* V: 591. (10) *Post Man*, no. 1556, 1–4 Dec. 1705. (11) Boyer, *Annals* IV: 19–20; *London Gazette*, no. 4200, 7–11 Feb. 1705[/06]. (12) Luttrell, *Brief Relation* VI: 42–43; *London Gazette*, no. 4224, 2–6 May 1706; Add. MSS 17677 BBB, f. 262 verso. (13) H.M.C., *Eighth Report*, App. I, p. 34. (14) *London Gazette*, no. 4439, 24–27 May 1708. (15) Luttrell, *Brief Relation* VI: 368, 382, 390; *Wentworth Papers*, pp. 82, 104, 154; Uffenbach, *London in 1710*, pp. 35, 132. (16) Boyer, *Annals* IX: 363; *British Mercury*, no. 170, 23–25 Apr. 1711; *Post Boy*, no. 2490, 26–28 Apr. 1711. (17) Add. MSS 22226, f. 137 recto and verso. (18) *British Mercury*, no. 401, 11 Mar. 1712/13; *Evening Post*, no. 558, 5–7 Mar. 1713; Add. MSS 17677 GGG, f. 102; B. L. Stowe MSS 225, f. 65. (19) *British Mercury*, no. 438, 25 Nov. 1713; *Post Boy*, no. 2892, 19–21 Nov. 1713. (20) H.M.C., *Portland MSS* V: 412.

[a]Generally, full mourning would last for one year, court mourning for six to twelve weeks.

gowns, the expenses of the robes were significantly reduced.[151] Unfortunately, this did more for Anne's reputation as a housekeeper than for her role as a setter of fashion trends. Moreover, growing international commitments, combined with the Queen's punctiliousness, dictated that long periods of court mourning had to be observed at the death of any allied prince or princeling (Table 7.6). For anywhere from six weeks to six months (longer in the case of Prince George) any man coming to court was expected to "wear black Cloth, with plain Linnen, black

Swords, and white Gloves." Ladies were required to dress themselves in "black Silk, laune Linnen, and white Gloves," without exception.[152] Nor was this attire confined solely to those who went to court. There is evidence from Anne's reign to suggest that, as one midcentury observer wrote, "everybody that thinks themselves anybody wear deep mourning" at such times as a mark of social distinction.[153] While purveyors of plain black cloth consequently did well out of court mournings, numerous contemporary petitions from milliners, weavers, hosiers, silk-men, lace-men, ribbon makers, and makers of gold and silver thread indicate that the overall effect on the fashion industry was ruinous. One correspondent noted in 1705, "On Sunday her Majesty will go into mourning for the Queen of Prussia, to the great mortification of the shopkeepers by reason it will spoil their spring trade."[154]

The combination of factors outlined above left the London fashion industry without effective court patronage, and thus the fashionable world without a court lead. There is almost no evidence that Anne or her courtiers introduced or popularized a single new style in dress, coiffure, jewelry, makeup, or other aspect of habiliment, as had been commonly done under Charles II.[155] Rather, it seems to have been during this period that court fashions began to be a law unto themselves, studied by professional courtiers, but irrelevant to the world of high fashion beyond St. James's. It was from about 1710 that court dress alone featured heavily embroidered gold vests and small swords for men; flounced petticoats, long trains, red shoes, and small artificial flowers for women.[156] The court under Queen Anne did not merely abdicate its leadership of the fashionable world; it became an isolated and esoteric corner of it.

The court's uneven record of artistic patronage under Anne led practitioners and connoisseurs in fields other than fashion to pursue alternate sources of entertainment. Many artists turned to the patronage of the nobility, seeking work in the great country houses as architects, painters, and craftsmen had always done, or performing in the theater or concert hall "at the command of several persons of Quality," as actors and musicians began to do in this reign.[157] Much patronage was distributed through that ultimate expression of Augustan aristocratic values, the political club. It is characteristic of the age that the one great cycle of portraits it has left us is not a parade of court beauties, such as

Lely painted under Charles II, but the gallery of party politicians painted by Kneller for the Kit-Cat Club. The Kit-Cat in particular acted very much like a court, bringing artists, patrons, and middlemen together and commissioning in its own right pamphlets, poems, plays, and even a theater in the Haymarket—dubbed, ironically—"The Queen's."[158] While political clubs like the Kit-Cat provided the means, the worlds of parliamentary politics and the war increasingly provided the subject matter and ideals, the events and heroes for artists to commemorate, as monarchy once had done.[159]

Finally, the ambitious artist starved of royal patronage could turn to the ever-growing public patronage being dispensed beyond the walls of St. James's.[160] Just as the Queen ceased attending thanksgiving services in St. Paul's Cathedral, the gentlemen of the chapel royal found an equally public showcase for their work in the festivals of the Sons of the Clergy.[161] Similarly, Kneller and his fellow painters founded an academy in 1711, which was, according to his most recent critic, "privately sponsored, entirely unofficial, and governed as democratically as a joint-stock company."[162] This period also saw a proliferation of music rooms in London.[163] In 1708 an entrepreneur named Heidegger filled another void left by Anne's declining court when he began to sponsor public masquerade balls during the London season.[164] The continued vitality of the public theater is well known; Anne's reign is also associated with the rise of the professional writer, able to make his way in the world without courtly or even aristocratic patronage. The significance of these developments was not merely aesthetic. In failing to attract and patronize artists, in forcing them to look elsewhere for their employment, the court simultaneously drove away those members of the aristocracy and gentry who formed their accustomed audience.

Social Life

As George I demonstrated from 1717 to 1720, an otherwise lively and sociable court might have attracted the aristocracy and gentry even if its ceremony was dull and its artistic standards undistinguished.[165] As a young woman at the courts of her uncle and father, Anne had maintained a social schedule as full and as frivolous as any self-respecting courtier could wish.[166] As Queen, she did her best to maintain the two great outdoor traditions of the Stuart court, hunting and horseracing. The demands of her office, her health, and the weather permitting, she frequently called upon the court to attend her as she hunted—or, more precisely, pursued and observed the hunt from a two-wheeled cart—down specially constructed chaise ridings at Hampton Court and Windsor, or on the Winchester progress of 1705.[167] Despite her inability to ride, a function of her gout and ever-increasing size, Swift was writing only half in jest when he described her to Stella as hunting "furiously, like Jehu."[168] As he testifies elsewhere, "hunting days" not only involved strenuous activity on the part of the Queen, but must have been a sore trial for her courtiers as well: "The queen was hunting the stag till four this afternoon, and she drove in her chaise above forty miles, and it was five before we went to dinner."[169]

She probably attracted a wider aristocratic audience by her patronage of the turf. Between 1705 and 1707 the Queen, her court, and a significant portion of the nobility, gentry, and foreign ministers descended annually upon Newmarket for the racing (Table 7.2).[170] When at Windsor, she often attended the races at Datchet, and in July 1711, she founded Royal Ascot.[171] She encouraged race meetings she did not attend, at Datchet, at Doncaster, and at York, by giving gold cups.[172] Finally, like her immediate predecessors, she kept a stud and trained horses, at a cost of £1,000 per annum, under the direction of Tregonwell Frampton.[173] No doubt this sum was considered well spent, for Frampton trained several winners for her. This characteristically formal woman showed her appreciation by calling him "Governor" and allowing him to treat her with the sort of familiarity that Charles II had accepted from artists. Thus, Anne set a pattern, not unknown in later reigns, of royal appreciation of horseflesh over culture.[174]

Indoor entertainment, the traditional focus of court society, proved disappointing in quality. For much of the reign, and especially toward its end, drawing rooms were held twice or thrice weekly, in the afternoon or early evening, in the royal apartments.[175] In theory, anyone of gentle appearance could attend and see or be seen by the sovereign and her court. During the Queen's last years she supplemented these assemblies by receiving ladies of quality in her bedchamber or closet after Sunday chapel services.[176] However, a number of factors conspired to limit the effectiveness of these assemblies as a means of attracting aristocratic support. The most important was the Queen's uncertain health. As early as November 1703 it was reported that she was receiving no company because of her gout. At mid-reign, Clerk gave this as one reason for the rarity of drawing room days. Even during the Queen's last years, when she was intent upon recreating a more splendid court life, functions were occasionally canceled because of her illness.[177] Indeed, even when they were held, the expectation of cancellation or royal indisposition was sometimes so strong as to keep attendance down.[178] Another reason given by Clerk for the dearth of assemblies during the summer of 1707 was the distance of the Queen's residence at Kensington from London.[179] Her preference for Kensington and Windsor over St. James's must often have made participation in drawing rooms inconvenient for their intended clientele. Writing from Windsor in the summer of 1711, Jonathan Swift noted of one such occasion, "There was a drawing-room to-day at Court; but so few company, that the queen sent for us into her bedchamber, where we made our bows, and stood about twenty of us round the room."[180] Between the frequent cancellations and relative inaccessibility of such assemblies, it must have been difficult for potential courtiers to develop any rhythm or routine to their attendance. This was a far cry from the unremitting hospitality provided by the "Merry Monarch" in his heyday, when the palace of Whitehall seems always to have been open and where, according to the French ambassador, "There is a ball and a comedy every other day."[181]

Even if a drawing room was held at a convenient time and place, there was little hope of actually speaking to its royal hostess. First, a visitor to court had to run the gauntlet of gentlemen ushers, yeomen ushers, and grooms who guarded not only the doors but the social and sartorial standards of the public rooms.[182] Upon reaching the "withdrawing room" itself, an aspirant had to overcome its own peculiar physical and social arrangements in order to make contact with the Queen. Because of her lameness, Anne could not circulate about the room, sauntering, gossiping, favoring with conversation, or snubbing with inattention as Charles II (or, later, George II) were wont to do.[183] She was instead forced to remain seated on a raised chair of state at the far end of the room, distant and aloof, surrounded by a phalanx of ladies in waiting, as shown in several contemporary paintings.[184] Sarah reports that even at the bassett table, virtually the only concession to informality and amusement on these occasions, "the Ladys [sat] on both sides of the Queen so close sometimes, that the Queen cou'd hardly put her hand in her pocket."[185] Nor was she any more accessible when she received visitors in the seemingly more intimate surroundings of her bedchamber. According to Celia Fiennes, she was, even here, set apart from her guests by a "screen round the bed."[186]

Finally, having braved all these obstacles and prevailed upon one of the Queen's ladies to perform the formal introduction without which informal acknowledgment and conversation were impossible,[187] the assiduous courtier had still to overcome her native shyness. Unlike her witty uncle or giddy sister, Queen Anne was notoriously lacking in conversation. According to Sarah:

> It was a sort of unhappiness to her that she naturally loved to have a great crowd come to her; for when they were come to Court, she never cared to have them come in to her nor to go out herself to them, having little to say to them but that it was either hot or cold, and little to enquire of them, but how long they had been in town or the like weighty matters. She never discovered any readiness of parts, either in asking questions or in giving answers. In matters of ordinary moment her discourse had nothing of brightness or wit; and in weightier matters she never spoke but in a road.[188]

While this passage contains plenty of Mrs. Freeman's characteristic venom, its essential accuracy is borne out by the record of Anne's conversations with Bishop Nicolson, Abigail Masham, and Sir David Hamilton. The Queen herself admitted to Lady Bathurst, "I am a very ill Speaker."[189] Indeed, Sarah's depiction of her mistress's lack of social skills is confirmed almost word for word by Swift's account of the drawing room at Windsor in 1711 noted previously: "She looked at us round with her fan in her mouth, and once a minute said about three words to some that were nearest her, and then she was told dinner was ready, and went out."[190] It is hardly surprising that the shy Mrs. Morley retreated into the security of formality, etiquette, and protocol, or that her best-bred subjects sometimes attributed that retreat to aloofness, dullness, or prudery.[191] Thus, Anne's bashfulness, so disarming from a distance, combined in the intimate surroundings of her own house with her punctiliousness, frugality, and poor health to stifle the sort of open and convivial relationship with noble and gentle subjects that Charles II had fostered and enjoyed.

Worse, the Queen's apparent dullness and formality seem to have permeated her court and infected her courtiers as well. Thus, in the summer of 1707 the Duchess of Somerset wrote to her fellow lady of the bedchamber, the Duchess of Devonshire, "Wee have not much divertion" apart from gambling.[192] In 1710 Conrad von Uffenbach was advised to avoid drawing rooms: "They say that there is nothing special to be seen, but that a quantity of foreign Ministers and ladies sit round the Queen for a quarter of an hour and no one says a word."[193] That Uffenbach's information was essentially correct is indicated by the experience of Elizabeth, Countess of Orkney, as conveyed in a letter to Henrietta, Lady Holles:

> I don't make you a compliment to say you are wanted at Windsor, for after the respectful thoughts seeing the Queen gives there is nothing but ceremony, no manner of conversation! my Lady Burlington in good earnest and imitated in perfection; the Duke of Somerset sitting at a little table by, that the ladies and most of them his own daughters might have room, without one bit of meat upon it till the other table had done; the Duke of St. Albans a jesting, Lord Arran sleeping, my Lord Burlington eating with his eyes. We played after dinner, drank tea, bowed extremely and so returned. Reflection, how vain is ambition if these are the ornaments of Courts.[194]

The Countess's impressions are especially valuable because, like Chesterfield, she had an extensive knowledge of courts. She was descended from one of the most distinguished court families in England (the Villiers) and had herself been the mistress of William III.[195] Admittedly, this deliciously drawn scene took place at Windsor, probably during the summer, when attendance at court tended to be sparse. But there is no evidence, certainly nothing like the wealth of eyewitness testimony available for Charles II's reign, to suggest that her experience would have been significantly more agreeable had she attended a drawing room at St. James's during the height of the court season. One need only compare this passage with John Evelyn's equally eloquent account of the last days of life at Whitehall under the "Merry Monarch," quoted in Chapter 1, to see why Anne's most important subjects stayed away from her court in droves.

Or did they? The surprising fact is that, despite the veritable epiphany of dullness described above, the Countess of Orkney was not alone in going to court. Jonathan Swift, when he is not railing at the vanity, triviality, and tedium of life at court, is bragging to Stella about whom he has met there, about the eminences with whom he has dined, and in general about what a splendid and important figure he cuts there.[196] Indeed, he goes further: "The Court serves me for a Coffee-house, once a week I meet acquaintance there that I should not otherwise see in a quarter"[197] Throughout the *Journal to Stella* he frequently repeats the idea that the court was a useful place to make and meet friends.[198] Even so unlikely a courtier as the future Lady Mary Wortley Montagu turned up at drawing rooms and chapel services in order to rendezvous with friends, including her prospective husband.[199] The court's convenience as a place where one could see ministers and hear news was noted earlier.[200] As a consequence, dull or not, drawing rooms are reported to have been full more often than not during the Queen's last four years on the throne.[201]

But whom were drawing rooms full of? If the names Swift chooses to drop are scrutinized, they are not spectacular. They naturally include government ministers, such as Oxford and Bolingbroke, and household servants, such as Lady Burlington and Dr. Arbuthnot, as well as relatively minor peers and commoners, such as Lord Winchilsea or Sir Edmund Bacon.[202] A brighter light, such as the Duke of Buckingham or Lord Berkeley of Stratton, also turns up on occasion.[203] But there are few Whigs and even fewer parliamentary politicians, moneyed men, artists, rakes, or toasts such as might have been encountered at the court of Charles II.[204] What remained were either diehard Tories or political neutrals with little parliamentary interest, financial clout, or social prestige, solid citizens cut from the same socioeconomic cloth as the Queen's sworn servants. Most probably attended court assemblies out of a sense of obligation, or in fond hopes of maximizing their personal importance through association: as Chesterfield implies, worshiping at a shrine that could no longer answer their prayers. If Swift seems a big fish among this company, it is because the court had become such a little and isolated pond.[205]

Already by 1714, London offered other, larger, more exciting and more lucrative opportunities to the big political, cultural, and social fish of the Augustan Age. The great aristocractic houses in town and country provided their own brand of hospitality and culture, which frequently stole the royal thunder. Increasingly, entertainment and companionship could be more easily procured at the theater, the concert hall, or pleasure garden than at Anne's staid and even soporific court. There were, too, hundreds of taverns, coffeehouses, and clubs offering all that the royal household could offer and more, including food, drink, news, gossip, conversation, and companionship, all day, every day. Political clubs, the Kit-Cat in particular, operated like small, kingless courts, banishing those who lost favor and toasting those whose favors they sought. Above all, it was increasingly here and not at court that art was commissioned, business transacted, political plots laid, and the beau monde displayed. Just as the constitutional sovereignty of the monarch had been challenged and—in some areas—usurped, so had the sovereignty of her court in the worlds of art, fashion, business, and politics. What remained was "nothing but ceremony, no manner of conversation!" In spite of its brief moment of reflective glory under George II and Caroline, the British court was well on its way to the highly symbolic, sober, secluded, and slightly strange institution it has since become.

Conclusion

In the age of Castiglione's courtier, the prince's household was the logical primary arena for the pursuit of ambition. The key to success for any young man (and, often, a certain type of young woman) was to gain first access to the prince, and then his favor. This would lead in turn to employment, wealth, social standing, political power, and even, perhaps, influence over fashions in art, music, literature, dress, and decorum. As we have seen, this remained more or less the case during the early years of the reign of Charles II. But as the seventeenth century came to an end, as the monarchy became a constitutional one, as factions coalesced into parties, as new economic, social, and cultural opportunities proliferated in London, the pattern of initiative shifted. It became gradually more necessary and at the same time more difficult for that monarchy to compete with these new institutions and opportunities for the time, the attention, and ultimately the loyalty of the ruling class. By the time of Anne's accession in 1702, it was incumbent upon the new Queen to prove to her most powerful and wealthy subjects that the royal household remained the fount of opportunity and entertainment in the broadest sense, as well as that of honor and state ritual.

It is a moot point whether Anne simply failed to realize this or, having realized it, was prevented from entering the competition more aggressively by her poor finances, poorer health, sober disposition, or increasing reluctance to enrich or empower any single individual or group of courtiers. Whatever the reason, she made little attempt to draw her most important subjects to her side, either physically or figuratively. Her one endeavor to do so, the revival of royal ceremony and symbol, was a popular success, but failed with this crucial segment of society. In a stimulating article dealing with the image of monarchy at the end of the eighteenth century, Linda Colley suggests that this failure occurred because the later Stuart monarchs were still too heavily involved in the day-to-day political battle to be effective national symbols, as the doddering George III was to be.[1] This is true, but it is only part of the story. If the institution of monarchy was changing at the beginning of the eighteenth century, so were the nature and interests of the English ruling class. In the brave new political world of postrevolutionary England, ritual, symbol, and personal allegiance were coming to mean less and less to an increasingly cosmopolitan, venal, and partisan ruling class. It is true, as J. C. D. Clark has pointed out, that the members of this class continued to favor monarchy as a form of government and continued to mouth Royalist sentiments on appropriate occasions, but this rarely seems to have translated into a feeling of personal loyalty to the monarch, or an increase in her area of initiative.

Indeed, for those members of the ruling class who, like Sir John Clerk, actually went to court, the contrast between Anne's splendid public appearance and her pitiable private self could only emphasize the gap between the monarchical ideal and her realization of it. Whereas under the Tudors, contemporaries often seem to have conflated or confused the monarch's two bodies—one symbolic of the power of the state, the other physical[2]—under the last Stuart the difference was painfully obvious. As a result, it was easy for her most important subjects to venerate the idea of monarchy without feeling any particular attachment to its current representative. Having failed to conjure such sentiments of veneration and loyalty among the English nobility and gentry through the splendor of her person and court, Anne's concurrent failure to appeal to their mercenary or fun-loving instincts left her and her "family" still further isolated, even as it contributed to the proliferation and growth of alternative opportunities beyond St. James's Palace.

In this context, Anne's palpable popularity with the masses was almost irrelevant, despite the cynical attempts of both parties to appropriate and exploit it. Her refusal to cooperate was understandable but, like the refusal to embrace single-party government with which it was consistent, it was also reactionary. In the end, she and her court reveal themselves to have been doubly anachronistic. On the one hand, her rather naive appeal to monarchical sentiment, her faith in the importance of forms and symbols, her desperate attempt to hold together the Queen's two bodies reveal her to have been even more "Elizabethan" than she or her subjects perhaps realized. On the other hand, in attempting to keep the monarchy above partisan politics, in attempting to make herself into a sort of national mother figure, and in presiding over a court that embodied the middle-class virtues of thrift, sobriety, moderation, and decorum, she also anticipated a time when the monarch's greatest service to the state would be to represent it, and when the perpetuation of even that limited role would depend upon popularity with the masses in general and with a politically significant middle class in particular. Thus, in entirely unintended ways, the Augustan court and its mistress were at once a throwback to the past and a harbinger of the future.

Appendixes

APPENDIX A

Household Offices Divided According to Rank

High

(High offices are defined as those that could be held by a peer.)

Chamber and bedchamber: lord chamberlain; vice chamberlain; treasurer of the chamber; masters of the great wardrobe, jewel house, robes, and buckhounds; groom of the stole; ladies of the bedchamber; captain of the gentlemen pensioners; captain of the yeomen of the guard; dean of the chapel royal; lord almoner; keeper of the privy purse.

Household below stairs: lord steward; treasurer of the household; comptroller of the household; cofferer of the household; master of the household.

Stables: master of the horse.

Middle

(Middle offices are defined as those that, in effect, conferred courtesy esquire status upon their holders. All holders of these offices who were not of a superior social rank are habitually referred to in official household documents as "esquire," no matter how low their actual rank in society. For example, the warrant of 1 March 1708/09 appointing John Faveral to be a master cook identifies him as "esq.," the rank borne by all other master cooks. However, in all previous documentation, as well as in the warrant appointing him to the inferior place of yeoman of the pastry on 2 March, he bears no such designation [LS 13/258–59].)

Chamber and bedchamber: maids of honor, women, and pages of the bedchamber; secretaries and clerks to the lord chamberlain; gentlemen, gentlemen ushers, and grooms of the privy chamber; cupbearers, carvers, sewers, gentlemen ushers (daily waiters, quarter waiters, and assistant to the gentlemen ushers) in the presence chamber; master, assistant master, and marshal of the ceremonies; master, yeoman, and comptroller of the revels; yeomen, grooms, pages, clerks, housekeepers, and wardrobe keepers in the removing wardrobe; deputy master and clerks of the great wardrobe; yeomen, groom, and clerk of the jewel house; yeomen, grooms, and waiters of the robes; all officers and the band of gentlemen pensioners; all officers of the yeomen of the guard; sergeants at arms; poet laureate; historiographer; groom porter; knight harbinger; physicians; apothecaries; surgeons; goldsmith; jeweler; clock and watch maker; principal painter; master of the barges; master of the tennis courts; sergeant skinner; master of the musick; sergeant trumpeter; printer; keeper of the private armory; keeper of the lions in the Tower; keeper, surveyor, and repairer of pictures; drum major; library keeper; Latin secretary; clerk of the closet, closet keeper, chaplains, subalmoner, and subdean of the chapel.

Household below stairs: clerks of the greencloth; all other gentlemen, sergeants, clerks, and master cooks; the knight marshal.

Stables: gentleman of the horse; avenor and clerk martial; equerries; pages; governor to the pages; surveyor general of the highways; surveyor of the stables; riding surveyor; clerks of the avery; clerk of the stables; master of the stud; purveyors.

Low

(Low offices are defined as all those that are not high or middle.)

Chamber and Bedchamber: laundress, seamstress, starcher, cofferbearers, necessary woman, and surveyor of the dresser in the bedchamber; sewers of the chamber; pages of the presence; chamber keepers; grooms of the great chamber; yeomen of the guard; messengers; watermen; musicians; trumpeters; drummers; all other tradesmen, including those to the great wardrobe and robes; gentlemen and children of the choir; sergeant, yeoman, and groom of the vestry; huntsmen.

Household below stairs: yeomen; grooms; pages; children; turnbroaches; scourers; doorkeepers; soil carriers; table waiters and dressers; wine porters; cartakers; pankeepers; breadbearers; harbingers; marshal's men; clerk and coroner of the verge; porters and watchmen.

Stables: footmen; coachmen; postilions; helpers; grooms; chairmen; bottlegroom; saddlers; farriers; riders; mews and stable keepers; messenger.

APPENDIX B

Biographical and Genealogical Sources Used in This Study

General

Burke, J., *A Genealogical and Heraldic Dictionary of the Landed Gentry of Great Britain and Ireland* (1850–51 and subsequent editions).

———, *A Genealogical and Heraldic History of the Commoners of Great Britain and Ireland*, 4 vols. (1833–38).

Cokayne, G. E., *Complete Baronetage*, 6 vols. (Exeter, 1900–1909).

———, *Complete Peerage of England, Scotland, Ireland, Great Britain and the United Kingdom*, ed. V. Gibbs, H. A. Doubleday, et al., 14 vols. (1910–59).

The Dictionary of National Biography, ed. L. Stephen and S. Lee, 22 vols. (1908–9).

The Knights of England: A Complete Record . . . of all the Orders of Chivalry in England, Scotland, Ireland, and of Knights Bachelors, ed. W. A. Shaw, 2 vols. (1906).

Le Neve, J., *Monumenta Anglicana*, 5 vols. (1717–19).

List of Sheriffs for England and Wales from the Earliest Times to A.D. 1831, ed. A. Hughes and J. Jennings (P.R.O. Lists and Indexes IX, 1898).

Memoirs British and Foreign of the Lives . . . of the Most Illustrious Persons Who Dye'd in . . . 1711 (1712).

Memoirs British and Foreign . . . 1712 (1714).

Professional, Scholastic, and Other Lists

Admiralty Officials, 1660–1870, ed. J. C. Sainty (1975).

Alumni Cantabriensis, pt. I [to 1751], ed. J. Venn and J. A. Venn, 4 vols. (Cambridge, 1927).

Alumni Oxoniensis, Being the Matriculation Register of the University 1500–1714, ed. J. Foster, 4 vols. (Oxford, 1891–92).

Biographia Navalis or Impartial Memoirs of the Lives and Characters of Officers of the Navy . . . from . . . 1660 to the Present Time, ed. J. Charnock, 6 vols. (1794–98).

A Biographical Dictionary of Actors, Actresses, Musicians . . . in London, 1660–1800, ed. P. Highfill, Jr.; K. Burnim; and E. Langhans (Carbondale, Ill., 1973+).

British Diplomatic Representatives, 1689–1789, ed. D. B. Horn (Camden Society, 1932).

Chamberlayne, E. (from 1704, Chamberlayne, J.), *Anglia Notitia: or, The Present State of England*, 22 editions (1669–1707).
Chamberlayne, J., *Magnae Britanniae Notitia*, 16 editions (1708–55).
English Army Lists and Commission Registers 1661–1714, ed. C. Dalton, 6 vols. (1892–1904).
History of Parliament: The House of Commons, 1660–1690, ed. B. D. Henning (1983).
History of Parliament: The House of Commons, 1715–1754, ed. R. Sedgwick (1970).
Letters of Denization and Acts of Naturalization for Aliens in England and Ireland, 1603–1800, ed. W. A. Shaw, 2 vols. (1911 and 1923).
Miege, G., *The New State of England*, 6 editions (1691–1707).
———, *The Present State of Great Britain*, 11 editions (1707–48).
Munk, W. R., *The Roll of the Royal College of Physicians of London, Comprising Biographical Sketches of All the Eminent Physicians*, 3 vols. (1878.)
The New Grove Dictionary of Music and Musicians, ed. S. Sadie, 20 vols. (1980).
Officers of the Exchequer, ed. J. C. Sainty (1983).
Officials of the Boards of Trade, 1660–1870, ed. J. C. Sainty (1974).
Officials of the Secretaries of State, 1660–1782, ed. J. C. Sainty (1973).
Treasury Officials, 1660–1870, ed. J. C. Sainty (1972).

Genealogy

(The following should be consulted in conjunction with *The Genealogist's Guide to Printed Pedigrees*, ed. G. W. Marshall, 4th ed. [Guildford, 1905], and *A Genealogical Guide*, ed. J. B. Whitmore [1948].)

The Ancestor, 12 numbers (1902–5).
Collecteana Topographia et Genealogica, 8 vols. (1834–43).
The Genealogist, 45 vols. (1877–1922).
Harleian Society Publications:
  no. 8: *Le Neve's Pedigrees of the Knights*.
  no. 14: *Visitations of Essex* ii (including *Berry's Essex Pedigrees*).
  no. 17: *Visitation of London* ii.
  no. 18: *London Marriage Licenses 1611–1828*.
  nos. 37–40: *Familiae Minorum Gentium*.
  nos. 44–49: *Musgrave's Obituary*.
  nos. 50–52 & 55: *Lincolnshire Pedigrees*.
  no. 60: *Visitation of Surrey 1662–68*.
  no. 61: *Visitation of Suffolk 1664–68*.
  no. 62: *Visitation of Warwickshire 1682–83*.
  no. 63: *Staffordshire Pedigrees 1664–1700*.
  no. 73: *Visitation of Rutland 1682–83*.
  nos. 85–86: *Visitation of Norfolk 1664*.
  no. 87: *Visitation of Northamptonshire 1681*.
  no. 88: *Hunter's Pedigrees*.

no. 89: *Visitation of Sussex 1662.*
nos. 91, 97: *East Anglian Pedigrees.*
no. 92: *London Visitation Pedigrees.*
no. 93: *Cheshire Visitation Pedigrees.*
nos. 94–96: *Yorkshire Pedigrees.*
Miscellanea Genealogica et Heraldica, 31 vols. (1868–1938).
Topographer and Genealogist, 3 vols. (1846–58).

Local History

(In addition to the publications of the various local record societies and the *Victoria County History*, the following older works were most useful.)

Baker, G., *History and Antiquities of the County of Northampton*, 2 vols. (1822–41).
Blore, T., *History and Antiquities of the County of Rutland*, 1 vol. printed (Stamford, 1811).
Bridges, J., *History and Antiquities of Northamptonshire Compiled from the Manuscript Collections of Sir Peter Whalley*, 2 vols. (1791).
Clutterbuck, R., *History and Antiquities of the County of Hertford*, 3 vols. (1815–27).
Collinson, J., *History and Antiquities of the County of Somerset*, 3 vols. (Bath, 1791).
Cussans, J. E., *History of Hertfordshire*, 3 vols. (1870–81).
Hoare, R. C., et al., *Modern History of Wiltshire*, 6 vols. (1822–45).
Hutchins, J., *History and Antiquities of the County of Dorset*, 4 vols. (Westminster, 1861–70).
Lipscomb, G., *The History and Antiquities of the County of Buckingham*, 4 vols. (1831–47).
Maclean, J., *The Parochial and Family History of the Deanery of Trig Minor*, 3 vols. (Bodmin, 1863–79).
Manning, O., and Bray, W., *History and Antiquities of the County of Surrey*, 3 vols. (1804–14).
Morant, P., *History and Antiquities of the County of Essex*, 2 vols. (1768; repr., Chelmsford, 1816).
Nichols, J., *History and Antiquities of the County of Leicester*, 4 vols. in 8 parts (1795–1815).
Ormerod, G., *History of the County Palatine and City of Chester*, rev. T. Helsby, 3 vols. (1875–82).
Surtees, R., *The History and Antiquities of the County Palatine of Durham* (Sunderland, 1908+).
Thoroton, R., *The Antiquities of Nottinghamshire*, with additions by J. Throsby, 3 vols. (1797).
Whitaker, T. D., *A History of Richmondshire . . .*, 2 vols. (1823).

APPENDIX C

Household Officers in Parliament, 1702–1714

(A plus [+] before or after a period of service indicates continuous service from before 1702 or after 1714. Service in previous or subsequent reigns that was not continuous with service under Anne has not been noted.)

House of Lords

Peer	Service in Lords	Household Service
Henry, Duke of Beaufort	+1702–May 1714	Housekeeper of St. James's, May 1708–May 1714 Captain of the gentlemen pensioners, Jan. 1712 –May 1714
Francis, Earl of Bradford	+1702–Sept. 1708	Treasurer of the household, +1702–Sept. 1708
John, Duke of Buckingham	+1702–1714+	Lord steward, Oct. 1710–June 1711
George, Earl of Cardigan	Jan. 1709–1714+	Master of the buckhounds, June 1712–1714+
Hugh, Earl of Cholmondeley	+1702–1714+	Comptroller of the household, Apr.–Nov. 1708 Treasurer of the household, Nov. 1708–Aug. 1713
Henry Compton, Bishop of London	+1702–July 1713	Dean of the chapel royal, +1702–July 1713
John, Lord Delawarr	+1702–1714+	Treasurer of the chamber, Sept. 1713–1714
William, first Duke of Devonshire	+1702–Aug. 1707	Lord steward, +1702–Aug. 1707
William, second Duke of Devonshire	Aug. 1707–1714+	Captain of the Yeomen of the Guard, +1702–Aug. 1707 Lord steward, Aug. 1707–Oct. 1710
Francis, Earl of Godolphin	Sept. 1712–1714+	Cofferer of the household, May 1704–May 1711
John, Lord Granville	Mar. 1703–Dec. 1707	Housekeeper of St. James's, Mar. 1703–Dec. 1707
Edward, Earl of Jersey	+1702–Aug. 1711	Lord chamberlain, +1702–Apr. 1704
Henry, Duke of Kent	Aug. 1702–1714+	Lord chamberlain, Apr. 1704–Apr. 1710

Peer	Service in Lords	Household Service
George, Lord Lansdowne	Jan. 1712–1714+	Comptroller of the household, July 1712–Aug. 1713 Treasurer of the household, Aug. 1713–1714
William Lloyd, Bishop of Worcester	+1702–1714+	Lord almoner, +1702–Nov. 1702
Thomas, Lord Mansell	Jan. 1712–1714+	Comptroller of the household, Apr. 1704–Feb. 1708; June 1711–July 1712
Samuel, Lord Masham	Jan. 1712–1714+	Cofferer of the household, May 1711–1714
John, second Duke of Montagu	Mar. 1709–1714+	Master of the great wardrobe, Mar. 1709–1714+
Ralph, first Duke of Montagu	+1702–Mar. 1709	Master of the great wardrobe, +1702–Mar. 1709
George, Duke of Northumberland	+1702–1714+	Housekeeper of Hampton Court, ?1702–1714
Robert, Earl of Oxford	May 1711–1714+	Housekeeper of St. James's, May 1714+
Henry, Lord Paget	Jan. 1712–1714+	Captain of the yeomen of the guard, June 1711–1714+
John, Earl Poulett	+1702–1714+	Lord steward, June 1711–1714
John Robinson, Bishop of London	Nov. 1710–1714+	Dean of the chapel royal, July 1713–1714+
Charles, Duke of St. Albans	+1702–1714+	Captain of the gentlemen pensioners, +1702–Jan. 1712
John Sharp, Archbishop of York	+1702–Feb. 1714	Lord almoner, Feb. 1703–Feb. 1714
Charles, Duke of Shrewsbury	+1702–1714+	Lord chamberlain, Apr. 1710–1714+
George Smalridge, Bishop of Bristol	Apr. 1714+	Lord almoner, Apr. 1714+
Charles, Duke of Somerset	+1702–1714+	Master of the horse, 1702–Jan. 1712
Charles, Viscount Townshend	+1702–1714+	Captain of the yeomen of the guard, Sept. 1707–June 1711

House of Commons

M.P.	Constituency and Dates	Household Service
Sir Benjamin Bathurst, knight	New Romney, 1702–Apr. 1704	Cofferer of the household, 1702–Apr. 1704
Peregrine Bertie	Boston, +1702–1705, 1708–July 1711 Truro, 1705–1708	Vice chamberlain, +1702–Dec. 1706
Robert Bulkeley	Beaumaris, +1702–Dec. 1702	Equerry, 1702–Dec. 1702
James Chase	Marlow, +1702–1710	Apothecary, +1702–1714+

M.P.	Constituency and Dates	Household Service
Walter Chetwynd	Stafford, 1702–Jan. 1711, Jan. 1712–1714+	Master of the buckhounds, June 1709–June 1711
William Churchill	Ipswich, Nov. 1707–Apr. 1714	Bookseller, bookbinder, and stationer, +1702–1714+
Thomas Coke	Derbyshire, +1702–1710 Grampound, 1710–1714+	Vice chamberlain, Dec. 1706–1714+
William Collier	Truro, 1713–1714+	Gentleman of the privy chamber, ?–1714
Conyers Darcy	Yorkshire, 1707–1708	Gentleman of the horse, Dec. 1710–1714+ Avenor and clerk martial, June 1711–1714+ Commissioner for the master of the horse, July 1712–1714
Edmund Dunch	Cricklade, 1705–1713 Boroughbridge, 1713–1714+	Master of the household, Nov. 1708–June 1712
William Feilding	Castle Rising, Nov. 1705–1714+	Lieutenant of the yeomen of the guard, Apr. 1704–June 1708
Sir Thomas Felton, baronet	Bury St. Edmunds, +1702–Mar. 1709	Master of the household, +1702–Nov. 1708 Comptroller of the household, Nov. 1708–Mar. 1709
Heneage Finch	Maidstone, 1704–1705 Surrey, 1710–1714+	Master of the jewel house, June 1711–1714+
John, Viscount Fitzharding	New Windsor, +1702–1710	Treasurer of the chamber, 1702–Dec. 1712
Sir William Forrester, knight	Wenlock, +1702–1714+	Clerk of the greencloth, +1702–1714+
Charles Godfrey	Chipping Wycombe, +1702–1713	Master of the jewel house, +1702–Oct. 1704 Clerk of the greencloth, Oct. 1704–1714+
Francis Godolphin	Helston, +1702–1708 Oxfordshire, 1708–1710 Tregony, 1710–Sept. 1712	Cofferer of the household, May 1704–May 1711
Bernard Granville	Camelford, +1702–July 1711 Fowey, Feb. 1712–1713	Carver, 1702–1714
George Granville	Fowey, 1702–1710 Cornwall, 1710–Jan. 1712	Comptroller of the household, July 1712–Aug. 1713 Treasurer of the household, Aug. 1713–1714

M.P.	Constituency and Dates	Household Service
John Granville	Cornwall, +1702–Mar. 1703	Housekeeper of St. James's, Mar. 1703–Dec. 1707
Robert Harley	New Radnor, +1702–May 1711	Housekeeper of St. James's, May 1714+
William, Marquess of Hartington	Castle Rising, +May 1702	Captain of the yeomen of the guard, +1702–Aug. 1707
	Yorkshire, 1702–Aug. 1707	Lord steward, Aug. 1707–Oct. 1710
Sir John Holland, baronet	Norfolk, +1702–1710	Comptroller of the household, Mar. 1709–June 1711
Sir Edward Lawrence, knight	Stockbridge, 1705–1710	Gentleman usher of the privy chamber, +1702–1714+
		Gentleman of the privy chamber, 1702–1714+
Richard Lockwood	Hindon, 1713–1714+	Gentleman of the privy chamber, May 1711–1714+
William Lowther	Pontefract, +1702–Jan. 1712	Gentleman of the privy chamber, c. 1704–?
Sir Thomas Mansell, baronet	Glamorgan, +1702–Jan. 1712	Comptroller of the household, Apr. 1704–Feb. 1708; June 1711–July 1712
Samuel Masham	Ilchester, 1710–May 1711	Cofferer of the household, May 1711–1714
	New Windsor, May 1711–Jan. 1712	
Sir Philip Meadows, knight	Truro, 1702–1705	Knight marshal, +1702–1714+
	Tregony, 1705–1708	
Thomas Meredith	Medhurst, Mar. 1709–1710	Equerry, Nov. 1704–Jan. 1708
		Gentleman of the horse, Mar. 1708–Dec. 1710
Carew Mildmay	Harwich, 1713–1714+	Gentleman of the privy chamber, Dec. 1710–1714
George Morley	Hindon, +May 1702; 1705–1708; Dec. 1710–May 1711	Sewer, +1702–July 1704
		Carver, July 1704–June 1706
Sir Nathaniel Napier, baronet	Dorchester, +1702–1705	Gentleman of the privy chamber, Feb. 1704–Jan. 1709
Crewe Offley	Newcastle-under-Lyme, Feb. 1706–1708; Feb. 1709–1710	Gentleman of the privy chamber, July 1714+
Lewis Oglethorpe	Haslemere, 1702–Oct. 1704	Equerry, 1702–Oct. 1704
Wyriott Owen	Pembrokeshire, 1705–1710	Gentleman of the privy chamber, Jan. 1710–1713
Henry Paget	Staffordshire, +1702–Jan. 1712	Captain of the yeomen of the guard, June 1711–1714+
Jeffery Palmer	Leicestershire, 1708–1710, 1714	Gentleman of the privy chamber, ?1702–1714

M.P.	Constituency and Dates	Household Service
Edward Pauncefort	Malmesbury, +1702–1705	Yeoman of the jewel house, +1702–1714+
Sir William Pole, baronet	Camelford, Jan. 1704–1708 Newport, 1708–1710 Devonshire, 1710–June 1712 Bossiney, 1713–1714+	Master of the household, June 1712–1714
Sir Thomas Read, baronet	Cricklade, 1713–1714+	Gentleman of the privy chamber, 1702–1714+
Sir Edward Seymour, baronet	Exeter, +1702–Feb. 1708	Comptroller of the household, 1702–Apr. 1704
William Seymour	Cockermouth, +May 1702 Totnes, 1702–1705 Newport, Dec. 1710–1713	Lieutenant of the gentlemen pensioners, 1702–1714+
Philip Sherrard	Rutland, 1708–1710	Gentleman of the privy chamber, Jan. 1705–1714+
Sir John Statham, knight	Mitchell, 1713–1714+	Gentleman of the privy chamber, May 1714+
Sir John Stonehouse, baronet	Berkshire, +1702–1714+	Comptroller of the household, Aug. 1713–1714
Sir Anthony Sturt, knight	London, 1713–1714+	Gentleman of the privy chamber, Aug. 1704–1714+
Horatio Walpole	Lostwithiel, Jan.–Sept. 1710 Castle Rising, 1713–1714+	Corporal of the yeomen of the guard, Apr. 1710–May 1712
William Walsh	Worcestershire, 1702–1705	Gentleman of the horse, 1702–Mar. 1708
Sir John Walter, baronet	Oxford, Dec. 1706–1714+	Clerk of the greencloth, Feb. 1711–1714+
John Weston	Surrey, +May 1702	Gentleman of the privy chamber, +1702–1712
Sir William Wyndham, baronet	Somerset, April 1710–1714+	Master of the buckhounds, June 1711–June 1712

APPENDIX D

Parliamentary Lists Used in This Study

Marginal numbers and descriptions are taken from *A Register of Parliamentary Lists 1660–1761*, ed. D. Hayton and C. Jones (Leicester, 1979); and *A Register of Parliamentary Lists 1660–1761: A supplement*, ed. D. Hayton and C. Jones (Leicester, 1982).

I wish to thank Drs. Eveline Cruickshanks and David Hayton for allowing me to consult copies of unprinted lists in their possession. I also wish to thank Clyve Jones for supplying me with advance copies and offprints of a number of his articles analyzing and printing such lists.

House of Lords Lists

50. c. Jan. 1703, Lord Nottingham's estimate of support for and opposition to the Occasional Conformity Bill, described in Snyder, "Occasional Conformity," p. 87 n. 1.

51. 16 Jan. 1703, those for and those against the "penalties amendment" to the Occasional Conformity Bill, printed in Snyder, "Occasional Conformity," pp. 188–90.

52. c. Nov. 1703, forecast by Lord Sunderland for the second Occasional Conformity Bill, described in Snyder, "Occasional Conformity," pp. 188–91.

53. c. 26 Nov.–8 Dec. 1703, Sunderland's second forecast for the second Occasional Conformity Bill, described in Snyder, "Occasional Conformity," pp. 175–76 and n.

54. 14 Dec. 1703, those for and those against the second Occasional Conformity Bill, printed in *Parl. Hist.* VI: 170–71.

59. c. May 1708, marked copy of a printed list of the First Parliament of Great Britain, with the returns of the 1708 election added in MS, printed as *A True List of the Lords Spiritual and Temporal, Together with the Members of the House of Commons constituting the First Parliament of Great Britain . . . What Alterations have been since made to the 30th of March 1708 are here Corrected*, in the possession of Mr. R. B. Freeman, Department of Zoology and Comparative Anatomy, University College, London; photocopy in the possession of the History of Parliament Trust.

60. 21 Jan. 1709, those for and those against allowing Scots peers with British titles the right to vote in the election of the representative peers, printed in C. Jones, "Godolphin," pp. 172–74.

61. 20 Mar. 1710, those voting Dr. Sacheverell guilty or not guilty of high crimes and misdemeanors, and those abstaining, printed in G. S. Holmes, *British Politics*, pp. 425–35.
63. 3 Oct. 1710, analysis of the English lords by Robert Harley: those expected to support the ministry; court Whigs and others doubtful; those considered certain to oppose, printed in C. Jones, "Scheme Lords," pp. 152–60.
67. 1710–11, list of Tories in the first session of this Parliament, described in Snyder, "New Parliament List," pp. 185–93.
68. c. Dec. 1711, list, partly in the hand of Lord Oxford; perhaps a calculation of support, printed in C. Jones, "Scheme Lords," pp. 152–60.
70A. 8 Dec. 1711, an assessment of those against presenting the Address (vote confirming that of 7 Dec. on the "No Peace Without Spain" motion) in an abandoned division, printed in C. Jones, "Division That Never Was," pp. 196–99.
71. 10 Dec. 1711, list in Oxford's hand of officeholders and pensioners who had voted against the ministry on the "No Peace Without Spain" motion, 7/8 Dec., with some suggested replacements, and a separate list, apparently of loyal peers to be gratified, printed in C. Jones, "Scheme Lords," pp. 152–60.
73. 19 Dec. 1711, list compiled by Oxford, possibly a second forecast for the Hamilton peerage division, printed in C. Jones, "Scheme Lords," pp. 152–60.
74. 20 Dec. 1711, those for and those against disabling Hamilton from sitting as a hereditary British peer, and those abstaining, printed in G. S. Holmes, *British Politics*, pp. 425–35.
79. c. 13 June 1713, Oxford's estimate of voting on the French Commerce Bill, printed in G. S. Holmes, *British Politics*, pp. 425–35.
82. Apr.–June 1714, Lord Nottingham's forecast for the Schism Bill, printed in G. S. Holmes, *British Politics*, pp. 425–35.

House of Commons Lists

78. 20 Oct. 1702, marked copy of a printed list of the Parliament, perhaps a forecast for the Tack, Nov. 1704, in B.L. Eg. MSS 3359, ff. 45–46.
79. 13 Feb. 1703, those for and those against agreeing with the Lords' amendments to the Bill Extending the Time for Taking the Abjuration, printed in R. R. Walcott, "Division-Lists of the House of Commons, 1689–1715," *B.I.H.R.* XIV (1936–37): 27–28.
Unnumbered. c. 25 Nov. 1703, Nottingham's forecast of supporters of the Occasional Conformity Bill, moved for that day.
80. 30 Oct. 1704, forecast for the Tack, B.L. Loan 29/35/12.
82. 28 Nov. 1704, those for and those against the Tack, printed in Walcott, "Division-Lists," pp. 28–29.
84. c. June 1705, list of the election returns, annotated by Lord Sunderland, printed in Snyder, "Party Configurations," pp. 59–63.

87. 25 Oct. 1705, the division on the Speaker, printed in Speck, "Choice of a Speaker," pp. 38–46.
88. Feb. 1706, those supporting the court over the "place clause" in the Regency Bill, printed in Walcott, "Division-Lists," pp. 30–33.
92. c. Jan. 1708, analysis of the House into Whigs and Tories, in Cambridge Univ. Library, MS Mm. VI 42, ff. 14–20.
93. See House of Lords list no. 59.
94. c. May 1708, list of election returns, annotated by Lord Sunderland, printed in Snyder, "Party Configurations," pp. 63–66.
95. Feb.–Mar. 1709, those in favor of the Bill for Naturalizing Foreign Protestants, printed in Walcott, "Division-Lists," p. 33.
96. Feb.–Mar. 1710, those for and those against the impeachment of Dr. Sacheverell, printed in Walcott, "Division-Lists," pp. 33–35.
97. c. Nov. 1710, analysis of the new House into Whigs, Tories, and those "doubtful," in B.L. Stowe MSS 223, ff. 453–56.
99. 1710–11, list of Tories in the first session of this Parliament, described in Snyder, "New Parliament List," pp. 185–93.
101. 25 May 1711, those supporting the amendments to the South Sea Bill, printed in Sperling, "Division of 25 May 1711," p. 193.
102. 7 Dec. 1711, those supporting the motion of "No Peace Without Spain," printed in G. S. Holmes, "Commons' Division on 'No Peace Without Spain,'" pp. 233–34.
106. 18 June 1713, those for and those against the French Commerce Treaty, printed in Walcott, "Division-Lists," pp. 35–36.
110. 18 Mar. 1714, those opposed to the expulsion of Steele, printed in Walcott, "Division-Lists," p. 36.

Reference Matter

Notes

Chapter I

Place of publication is London unless otherwise indicated.

1. N. Elias, *Die höfische Gesellschaft* (Darmstadt and Neuwied, 1969), trans. E. Jephcott as *The Court Society* (New York, 1983). For the "courtly" character of early modern European society, see ibid., pp. 36–37.

2. For example, see E. S. Turner, *The Court of St. James's* (1959); P. Erlanger, *The Age of Courts and Kings: Manners and Morals 1558–1715* (New York, 1967); G. Masson, *Courtesans of the Italian Renaissance* (New York, 1975); D. Seward, *Prince of the Renaissance: The Golden Life of Francis I* (New York, 1973); R. Burnand, *La cour des Valois* (Paris, 1938); K. A. Patmore, *The Court of Louis XIII* (1910); J. Levron, *Les courtesans* (n.d.); P. Heuzé, *La cour intime de Louis XIV* (Paris, 1902); N. Mitford, *The Sun King: Louis XIV at Versailles* (1966); I. Saint-Amand, *The Court of Louis XV*, trans. E. G. Martin (New York, 1900); P. La Fue, *La vie quotidienne des cours allemandes au XVIIIe siècle* (Paris, 1963); G. Maugras, *La cour de Lunéville au XVIIIe siècle* (Paris, 1925); idem, *Dernières années de la cour de Lunéville* (Paris, 1925); N. Williams, *Henry VIII and His Court* (New York, 1971); D. Mathew, *The Courtiers of Henry VIII* (1970). For an example of popular court history that is also scholarly, see A. Somerset, *Ladies in Waiting: From the Tudors to the Present Day* (New York, 1984).

3. However, honorable mention should be made of L. Batiffol, *Marie de Médicis and the French Court in the XVIIth Century*, trans. M. King (1908); F. Arnheim, *Geschichte des preussischen Hofes: Herausgegeben von Archivrat Dr. Georg Schuster vol. II: Der Hof Friedrichs des Grossen* (Berlin, 1912); W. Koch, *Hof und Regierungsverfassung: König Friedrich I. von Preussen (1697–1710)* (Breslau, 1926); I., Ritter von Zolger, *Der Hofstaat des Hauses Österreich* (Vienna, 1917); L. Dorez, *La cour du Pape Paul III d'après les registres de la trésorerie secrète* (Paris, 1932); C. E. von Malortie, *Der Hannoversche Hof unter dem Kurfürsten Ernst August und der Kurfürstin Sophie* (Hanover, 1847); and the Introduction to E. K. Chambers, *The Elizabethan Stage* (Oxford, 1923).

4. In the author's experience, this sentiment is more often expressed verbally and informally than in print.

5. See W. A. Speck, *Stability and Strife: England, 1714–1760* (Cambridge, Mass., 1979), pp. 4–5; P. Zagorin, *The Court and the Country: The Beginning of the English Revolution* (1969), p. 41.

6. Specifically, for the purposes of Chapters 2–5 of the present work, the court is defined as the sworn servants of the royal household (excluding the heralds and officers of the works), regardless of form of payment, work, or rank (see Appendix A). In Chapters 1, 6, and 7, the focus expands to include courtiers and habitués *sans* household office as well as the physical environment they inhabited.

7. The best recent discussion of the reality and role of a "Court party" in later Stuart England is C. Roberts, "Party and Patronage in Later Stuart England," in *England's Rise to Greatness, 1663–1763*, ed. S. B. Baxter (Berkeley, Calif., 1983), pp. 185–212.

8. This point is recognized by R. E. Mousnier, *The Institutions of France Under the Absolute Monarchy: 1598–1789*, trans. A. Goldhammer (Chicago, 1984), II: 121–23.

9. For the best recent work on art, literature, and pageantry at court, see below under the discussion of various national "schools" of court history.

10. Elias, *Court Society*, pp. 28–29, 35–36.

11. Ibid., pp. 32, 80, 104, and chaps. 6–7.

12. Ibid., chaps. 3, 5.

13. Such translations appeared in 1983, 1974, and 1987, respectively. For an appraisal of the overall significance of Elias's work to sociologists, see the review article by D. Smith, "Norbert Elias—Established or Outsider?," *The Sociological Review* XXXII (1984): 367–89.

14. A. G. Dickens, ed., *The Courts of Europe: Politics, Patronage and Royalty 1400–1800* (New York, 1977). See also *Europäische Hofkultur im 16. und 17. Jahrhundert*, ed. A. Buck, G. Kauffmann, B. L. Spahr, and C. Wiedemann, 3 vols. (Hamburg, 1981). This collection, emerging from a conference held at the Herzog-August-Bibliothek in Wolfenbüttel in 1979, contains numerous brief articles on courts and language, art and theater, the role of women in court culture, and the court and public opinion. Finally, H. M. Baillie, "Etiquette and the Planning of the State Apartments in Baroque Palaces," *Archaeologia* CI (1967): 169–99 is a seminal article that covers ceremonial, social, and architectural developments at the English, French, and German courts.

15. For an explanation of the work of the Centro Studi and a compelling review of some of its publications, see J. Larner, "Europe of the Courts," *Journal of Modern History* LV (1983): 669–81. Among the Centro Studi's publications are *Le corti farnesiane di Parma e Piacenza (1545–1622)*, ed. M. A. Romani and A. Quondam, 2 vols. (Rome, 1978); D. A. Franchini, R. Margonari, G. Olmi, R. Signorini, A. Zanca, and C. T. Perina, *La scienza a corte* (Rome, 1979); *La corte e il "Cortegiano,"* ed. C. Ossola and A. Prosperi, 2 vols. (Rome, 1980); *La corte e lo spazio: Ferrara estense*, ed. G. Papagno and A. Quondam, 3 vols. (Rome, 1982); and *La corte nella cultura e nella storiografia: Immagini e posizioni tra Otte- e Novecento*, ed. C. Mozzarelli and G. Olmi (Rome, 1983). For other recent work on Italian courts, see below.

16. See, for example, H. G. Koenigsberger, "Republics and Courts in Italian

and European Culture in the Sixteenth and Seventeenth Centuries," *Past and Present*, no. 83 (1979): 32–56; F. Haskell, "The Market for Italian Art in the 17th Century," *Past and Present*, no. 15 (1959): 48–59; E. Borsook, "Art and Politics at the Medici Court I: The Funeral of Cosimo I de'Medici," *Mitteilungen des Kunsthistorischen Institutes in Florenz* XII (1965): 31–54; C. M. S. Johns, "Papal Patronage and Cultural Bureaucracy in Eighteenth-Century Rome: Clement XI and the Accademia di San Luca," *Eighteenth Century Studies* XXII (1988): 1–23; C. Vasoli, *La cultura delle corti* (Florence, 1980); *Le sedi della cultura nell' Emilia Romagna: L'epoca delle signorie le corti*, ed. G. Chittoloni (Milan, 1985); G. Ianziti, *Humanistic Historiography Under the Sforzas: Politics and Propaganda in Fifteenth-Century Milan* (Oxford, 1988); J. H. Bentley, *Politics and Culture in Renaissance Naples* (Princeton, N.J., 1987); *Il Rinascimento nelle corti padane: Società e cultura* (Bari, 1977); A. W. Atlas, *Music at the Aragonese Court of Naples* (Cambridge, Eng., 1985); and the beautifully illustrated S. Bertelli, F. Cardini, and E. Garbero Zorzi, *Le corti italiene del Rinascimento* (Milan, 1985).

17. For the papal court, see Dorez, *Cour du Pape Paul III*; P. J. Grisar, "Papstliche Finanzen, Nepotismus und Kirchenrecht unter Urban VIII," *Miscellanea Historiae Pontificae* VII (1943); P. Partner, *The Pope's Men: The Papal Civil Service in the Renaissance* (Oxford, 1990); idem, *Renaissance Rome 1500–1559: A Portrait of a Society* (Berkeley, Calif., 1976). For other, worthy exceptions to the above generalization, see A. F. C. Ryder, *The Kingdom of Naples Under Alphonso the Magnanimous: The Making of a Modern State* (Oxford, 1976), chap. 3; C. Stango, "La corte di Emanuele Filiberto: Organizzazione e gruppi sociali," *Bolletino Storico-bibliographico Subalpino* LXXXV (1987): 445–502; R. B. Litchfield, *Emergence of a Bureaucracy: The Florentine Patricians 1530–1790* (Princeton, N.J., 1986).

18. J.-F. Solnon, *La cour de France* (Paris, 1987).

19. R. J. Knecht, "The Court of Francis I," *European Studies Review* VIII (1978): 1–22; idem, "Francis I," in *Courts of Europe*, ed. Dickens, pp. 99–119; idem, *Francis I* (Cambridge, Eng., 1982), chaps. 6, 17. See also C. H. Clough, "Francis I and the Courtiers of Castiglione's *Courtier*," *European Studies Review* VIII (1978): 23–70.

20. For public ceremony and etiquette, see I. D. McFarlane, *The Entry of Henri II into Paris 16 June 1549* (Binghamton, N.Y., 1982); R. E. Giesey, *The Royal Funeral Ceremony in Renaissance France* (Geneva, 1960); idem, *Cérémonial et puissance souveraine: France XVe–XVIIe siècles* ([Paris], 1987); L. M. Bryant, *The King and the City in the Parisian Royal Entry Ceremony: Politics, Ritual, and Art in the Renaissance* (Geneva, 1986); idem, "Royal Ceremony and the Revolutionary Strategies of the Third Estate," *Eighteenth Century Studies* XXII (1989): 413–50; G. Antonetti, "Gloire dynastique et puissance nationale: Le mariage du Grand Dauphin (1680)," *Mémoire* V (1986): 91–105; O. Ranum, "Courtesy, Absolutism, and the Rise of the French State, 1630–1660," *Journal of Modern History* LII (1980): 426–51; J.-M. Apostolidès, *Le roi-machine: Spectacle et politique au temps de Louis XIV* (Paris, 1981); A.-C. Gruber, *Les grandes fêtes et leurs décors à l'époque de Louis XVI* (Paris, 1972); R. A. Jackson, *Vive le Roi! A History of the French Cor-*

onation from Charles V to Charles X (Chapel Hill, N.C., 1984); K. Mosenender, *Zeremoniell und Monumentale Poesie: Die Entrée solenelle Ludwig XIV 1660 en Paris* (Berlin, 1983); V. E. Graham and W. McAllister Johnson, eds., *The Royal Tour of France by Charles IX and Catherine de'Medici: Festivals and Entries 1564–66* (Toronto, 1979); idem, *The Paris Entries of Charles IX and Elizabeth of Austria 1571* (Toronto, 1974); M. C. Moine, *Les fêtes à la cour du Roi-Soleil* (Paris, 1984); S. Hanley, *The Lit de Justice of the Kings of France: Constitutional Ideology in Legend, Ritual and Discourse* (Princeton, N.J., 1983); H.-J. Martin, *Entrées royales et fêtes populaires à Lyon (XVe–XVIIIe siècles)* (Lyon, 1970). For art, music, ballet, etc., see W. L. Wiley, *The Formal French* (Cambridge, Mass., 1967); D. Maland, *Culture and Society in Seventeenth-Century France* (New York, 1970); D. Marrow, *The Art Patronage of Maria d'Medici* (Ann Arbor, Mich., 1982); P. Gaxotte, *The Age of Louis XIV*, trans. M. Shaw (New York, 1970); P. du Colombier, *Le style Henri IV–Louis XIII* (Paris, 1941); P. de Nolhac, *L'art à Versailles* (Paris, 1930); R. A. Weigert, *L'époque Louis XIV* (Paris, 1962); S. Béguin, *L'école de Fontainebleau: Le maniérisme à la cour de France* (Paris, 1960); A. Schnapper, "The King of France as Collector in the Seventeenth Century," *Journal of Interdisciplinary History* XVII (1986): 185–202; R. M. Isherwood, *Music in the Service of the King: France in the Seventeenth Century* (Ithaca, N.Y., 1973); M. Benoit, *Versailles et les musiciens du roi 1661–1733* (Paris, 1971); M. M. McGowan, *L'art du ballet de cour en France, 1581–1643* (Paris, 1963); M.-C. Canova-Green, "Ballet et comédie-ballet sous Louis XIV, ou l'illusion de la fête," *Papers on French Seventeenth Century Literature* XVII (1990): 253–62. For buildings and gardens, see J.-P. Babelon, "Les travaux de Henri IV au Louvre et aux Tuileries," *Paris et Ile de France* XXIX (1978): 55–130; F. Kimball and A. Marie, "Unknown Versailles: The Apartement du Roi 1678–1701," *Gazette des Beaux-Arts*, 6th ser., XXIX (1946): 85–112; J.-P. Néraudau, "La mythologie à Versailles au temps de Louis XIV. Architecture, jardins et musique," *Bulletin Association Guillaume Budé* I (1988): 72–85; B. Rosasco, "Masquerade and Enigma at the Court of Louis XIV," *Art Journal* XLVIII (1989): 144–49; G. Van der Kemp and J. Levron, *Versailles and the Trianons*, trans. E. Whitehorn (Fair Lawn, N.J., 1958); E. Guillou, *Versailles: Le palais du soleil* ([Paris], 1963); G. Lenôtre, *Versailles au temps des rois* (Paris, 1934); P. de Nolhac, *La création de Versailles* (Paris, 1925); idem, *Versailles: Résidence de Louis XIV* (Paris, 1925); idem, *Les jardins de Versailles* (Paris, 1906); R. Devismes, *La cour à Versailles* (Paris, 1974); P. Verlet, *Versailles* (Paris, 1961); Y. Bottineau, "Essais sur le Versailles de Louis XIV," *Gazette des Beaux-Arts* CXXX (1988): 77–97; idem, "La cour de Louis XIV à Fontainebleau," *XVIIe Siècle* XXIV (1959): 697–734.

21. A brief introduction to these concerns is provided by Mousnier, *Institutions* II: 112–29. A pioneering study of the structural development of the household is J. Boucher, "L'évolution de la maison du roi: Des derniers Valois aux premiers Bourbons," *XVIIe Siècle* XXXIV (1982): 359–79. More impressionistic but still useful studies of the household at Versailles include R. Hatton, "Louis XIV: At the Court of the Sun King," in *Courts of Europe*, ed. Dickens, pp. 232–61; J. Saint-Germain, *Louis XIV secret* ([Paris], 1970); J. Levron, *Daily*

Life at Versailles in the Seventeenth and Eighteenth Centuries, trans. C. E. Engel (New York, 1968). For the Queen's household, see Batiffol, *Marie de Médicis,* chaps. 3–4, 8; R. Kleinman, "Social Dynamics at the French Court: The Household of Anne of Austria," *French Historical Studies* XVI (1990): 517–35.

22. See, for example, Mousnier, *Institutions* II: 112–29; F. Bluché, *Louis XIV* (Paris, 1986); N. N. Burke, *Brother to the Sun King: Philippe, Duke of Orleans* (Baltimore, Md., 1989); F. Funck-Brentano, *The Old Regime in France,* trans. H. Wilson (1929); idem, *La cour du Roi Soleil* (Paris, 1937); Gaxotte, *Age of Louis XIV;* Levron, *Courtesans;* G. Mongrédien, *La vie privée de Louis XIV* ([Paris], 1938); Heuzé, *Cour intime;* A., duc de La Force, *Louis XIV et sa cour* (Paris, 1956); L. Hautecœur, *Louis XIV Roi Soleil* (Paris, 1953); Mitford, *The Sun King;* E. Le Roy Ladurie, "Auprès du roi, la cour," *Annales* XXXVIII (1983): 21–41; idem, "Versailles Observed: The Court of Louis XIV in 1709," in idem, *The Mind and Method of the Historian,* trans. S. Reynolds and B. Reynolds (Chicago, 1981), pp. 149–73.

23. See C. Hofmann, *Das spanische Hofzeremoniell von 1500–1700* (Frankfurt am Main, 1985); M. de Ferdinandy, "Die theatralische Bedeutung des spanischen Hofzeremoniells Kaiser Karls V," *Archiv für Kulturgeschichte* XLVII (1965): 306–20; idem, "La forma de vivir del monarca español: El ceremonial de la corte y su significación simbólica," *Eco* XXIX, no. 176 (1975): 113–33; L. Pfandl, "Philip II und die Einführung des burgundischen Hofzeremoniells in Spanien," *Historisches Jahrbuch* LVIII (1938): 1–33; J. E. Varey, "The Audience and the Play at Court Spectacles: The Role of the King," *Bulletin of Hispanic Studies* LXI (1984): 399–406; idem, "Processional Ceremonial of the Spanish Court in the Seventeenth Century," in *Studia Iberica: Festschrift für Hans Flasche,* ed. K. H. Körner and K. Rühl (Bern, 1973), pp. 643–52; A. Rodríguez Villa, *Etiquetas de la Casa de Austria* (Madrid, 1913); D. de la Válgoma y Díaz-Varela, *Norma y ceremonia de las reinas de la Casa de Austria* (Madrid, 1958); Y. Bottineau, "Aspects de la cour d'Espagne au XVIIe siècle: L'étiquette de la chambre du roi," *Bulletin Hispanique* LXXIV (1972): 138–57; L. Cortés Echánove, *Nacimiento y crianza de personas reales en la corte de España 1566–1886* (Madrid, 1958).

24. P. Williams, "Lerma, Old Castile and the Travels of Philip III of Spain," *History* LXXIII (1988): 379–97; F. Tomás y Valiente, *Los validos en la monarquía española del siglo XVII* (Madrid, 1982); J. H. Elliott, *The Count-Duke of Olivares: The Statesman in an Age of Decline* (New Haven, Conn., 1986); R. A. Stradling, *Philip IV and the Government of Spain 1621–1665* (Cambridge, Eng., 1988); G. Marañón, *El conde duque de Olivares* (Madrid, 1936).

25. A. Dominguez Ortiz, "Los gastos de corte en la España del siglo XVII," in idem, *Crisis y decadencia de la España de los Austrias* (Madrid, 1973), pp. 73–96.

26. S. N. Orso, *Philip IV and the Decoration of the Alcázar of Madrid* (Princeton, N.J., 1986); idem, *Art and Death at the Spanish Habsburg Court: The Royal Exequies for Philip IV* (Columbia, Mo., 1989); F. I. Almech, *Casas reales y jardines de Felipe II* ([Madrid], 1952); B. von Bargahn, *Philip IV and the "Golden House" of the Buen*

Retiro: In the Tradition of Caesar (New York, 1986); J. Brown, "Enemies of Flattery: Velázquez' Portraits of Philip IV," *Journal of Interdisciplinary History* XVII (1986): 137–54; Y. Bottineau, *L'art de cour dans l'Espagne de Philip V 1700–1746* (Bordeaux, 1960). For court life in general under Philip IV, see J. Deleito y Piñuela, *El Rey se Divierte* (Madrid, 1955).

27. J. Brown and J. H. Elliott, *A Palace for a King: The Buen Retiro and the Court of Philip IV* (New Haven, Conn., 1980). See also J. H. Elliott, "The Court of the Spanish Habsburgs: A Peculiar Institution?," in *Politics and Culture in Early Modern Europe*, ed. P. Mack and M. C. Jacob (Cambridge, Eng., 1987), pp. 5–24; idem, "Philip IV of Spain: Prisoner of Ceremony," in *Courts of Europe*, ed. Dickens, pp. 168–89; and Stradling, *Philip IV*, which draws upon a doctoral thesis in progress on the Spanish royal household by R. G. Trewinnard.

28. See the works noted above, n. 3.

29. T. Da Costa Kaufmann, *Variations on the Imperial Theme in the Age of Maximilian II and Rudolf II* (New York, 1978); W. Senn, *Musik und Theater am Hof zu Innsbruck; Geschichte der Hofkapelle vom 15. Jahrhundert bis zu deren Auflösung im Jahre 1748* (Innsbruck, 1954); H. Bethe, *Die Kunst am Hofe der pommerschen Herzöge* (Berlin, 1937); R. J. W. Evans, *Rudolf II and His World: A Study in Intellectual History 1576–1612* (Oxford, 1973); H. Pönicke, *August der Stärke (Ein Fürst des Barock)* (Zurich, 1972), pp. 61–74; I. Becker-Glauch, *Die Bedeutung der Musik für die Dresdener Hoffeste bis in die Zeit Augusts des Stärken* (Kassel, 1951); K. Vocelka, *Habsburgische Hochzeiten 1550–1600: Kulturgeschichtliche Studien zum Manieristischen Repräsentationsfest* (Vienna, 1976); E. Straub, *Repraesentatio Maiestatis oder churbayerische Freudenfeste: Die höfischen Feste in der Münchner Residenz vom 16. bis zum Ende des 18. Jahrhunderts* (Munich, 1969); R. Alewyn and K. Sälzle, *Das grosse Welttheater: Die Epoche der höfischen Feste in Dokument und Deutung* (Hamburg, 1959); *Kurfürst Max Emanuel: Bayern und Europa um 1700*, ed. H. Glaser (Munich, 1976); E. E. Helm, *Music at the Court of Frederick the Great* (Norman, Okla., 1960).

30. H. C. Ehalt, *Ausdrucksformen absolutistischer Herrschaft: Der Wiener Hof im 17. und 18. Jahrhundert* (Munich, 1980); J. Lampe, *Aristokratie, Hofadel und Staatspatriziat in Kurhannover: Die Lebenskreise der höheren Beamten an den kurhannoverschen Zentral-und Hofbehörden 1714–1760* (Göttingen, 1963); J., Freiherr von Kruedener, *Die Rolle des Hofes im Absolutismus* (Stuttgart, 1973).

31. G. R. Elton, *The Tudor Revolution in Government* (Cambridge, Eng., 1953); idem, "Tudor Government: The Points of Contact, III: The Court," *T.R.H.S.*, 5th ser., XXVI (1976), pp. 211–28; W. C. Richardson, *Tudor Chamber Administration, 1485–1547* (Baton Rouge, La., 1952).

32. The controversy is explained and continued in *Revolution Reassessed: Revisions in the History of Tudor Government and Administration*, ed. C. Coleman and D. Starkey (Oxford, 1986).

33. See esp. D. R. Starkey, "The King's Privy Chamber, 1485–1547" (Ph.D. diss., Cambridge University, 1973); idem, "Representation Through Intimacy: A Study in the Symbolism of Monarchy and Court Office in Early-Modern

England," in *Symbols and Sentiments: Cross-Cultural Studies in Symbolism*, ed. I. Lewis (1977), pp. 187–224; idem, "Court and Government," in *Revolution Reassessed*, ed. Coleman and Starkey, pp. 29–58; idem, "Court History in Perspective" and "Intimacy and Innovation: The Rise of the Privy Chamber, 1485–1547," in *The English Court: From the Wars of the Roses to the Civil War*, ed. D. R. Starkey (1987), pp. 1–24, 71–118.

34. S. L. Adams, "Eliza Enthroned? The Court and Its Politics," in *The Reign of Elizabeth I*, ed. C. Haigh (Athens, Ga., 1985), pp. 55–77; idem, "Faction, Clientage and Party: English Politics 1550–1603," *History Today* XXXII (Dec. 1982): 33–39; D. E. Hoak, "The King's Privy Chamber, 1547–1553," in *Tudor Rule and Revolution*, ed. D. J. Guth and J. W. McKenna (Cambridge, Eng., 1982), pp. 87–108. See also J. Murphy, "The Illusion of Decline: The Privy Chamber, 1547–1558," in *English Court*, ed. Starkey, pp. 119–46; P. Wright, "A Change in Direction: The Ramifications of a Female Household, 1558–1603," in *English Court*, ed. Starkey, pp. 147–72.

35. S. Anglo, *Spectacle, Pageantry, and Early Tudor Policy* (Oxford, 1969); R. C. Strong, *Holbein and Henry VIII* (1967); idem, *Portraits of Queen Elizabeth I* (Oxford, 1963); idem, *The Cult of Elizabeth: Elizabethan Portraiture and Pageantry* (1977). See also J. Stevens, *Music & Poetry in the Early Tudor Court* (1961).

36. D. M. Loades, *The Tudor Court* (Totowa, N.J., 1987).

37. This is more or less the view espoused by G. P. V. Akrigg, *Jacobean Pageant: The Court of King James I* (Cambridge, Mass., 1963).

38. The most sophisticated restatement of the old Whig view is L. Stone, *The Causes of the English Revolution 1529–1642* (1972). See also Zagorin, *Court and Country*, passim.

39. See R. C. Strong, *Splendour at Court: Renaissance Spectacle and Illusion* (1973), chap. 6; idem, *Van Dyck's Charles I on Horseback* (1972); J. Charlton, *The Banqueting House, Whitehall* (1964); J. Harris, S. Orgel, and R. C. Strong, *The King's Arcadia: Inigo Jones and the Stuart Court* (1973); O. Millar, *The Age of Charles I* (1972); S. Orgel, *The Jonsonian Masque* (Cambridge, Mass., 1965); idem, *The Illusion of Power: Political Theater in the English Renaissance* (Berkeley, Calif., 1975); S. Orgel and R. C. Strong, *Inigo Jones: The Theatre of the Stuart Court* (1973); G. Parry, *The Golden Age Restor'd: The Culture of the Stuart Court, 1603–42* (New York, 1981).

40. R. M. Smuts, *Court Culture and the Origins of a Royalist Tradition in Early Stuart England* (Philadelphia, 1987). See also idem, "The Political Failure of Stuart Cultural Patronage," in *Patronage in the Renaissance*, ed. G. F. Lytle and S. Orgel (Princeton, N.J., 1981), pp. 165–87; idem, "Public Ceremony and Royal Charisma: The English Royal Entry in London, 1485–1642," in *The First Modern Society*, ed. A. L. Beier, D. Cannadine, and J. M. Rosenheim (Cambridge, Eng., 1989), pp. 65–93.

41. For a short summary of the debate, written from a revisionist point of view, see K. Sharpe, "'Revisionism' Revisited," in *Faction and Parliament: Essays on Early Stuart History*, ed. K. Sharpe (1985), pp. ix–xvii.

42. N. Cuddy, "The Revival of the Entourage: The Bedchamber of James I, 1603–1625," in *English Court*, ed. Starkey, pp. 173–225; R. Lockyer, *Buckingham: The Life and Political Career of George Villiers, First Duke of Buckingham 1592–1628* (1981); K. Sharpe, "Faction at the Early Stuart Court," *History Today* XXXIII (Oct. 1983): 39–46; idem, "The Image of Virtue: The Court and Household of Charles I, 1625–1642," in *English Court*, ed. Starkey, pp. 226–60; idem, "The Earl of Arundel, His Circle and the Opposition to the Duke of Buckingham, 1618–1628," in *Faction and Parliament*, ed. K. Sharpe, pp. 209–44; L. L. Peck, *Northampton: Patronage and Policy at the Court of James I* (1982); idem, "Court Patronage and Government Policy: The Jacobean Dilemma," in *Patronage in the Renaissance*, ed. Lytle and Orgel, pp. 27–46. See also D. Hirst, "Court, Country, and Politics before 1629," in *Faction and Parliament*, ed. Sharpe, pp. 105–37.

43. C. Hibbard, *Charles I and the Popish Plot* (Chapel Hill, N.C., 1983).

44. G. E. Aylmer, *The King's Servants: The Civil Service of Charles I, 1625–1642*, 2nd ed. (1974). For the Interregnum, see idem, *The State's Servants: The Civil Service of the English Republic, 1649–1660* (1973); R. Sherwood, *The Court of Oliver Cromwell* (1977).

45. See especially D. Allen, "The Political Function of Charles II's Chiffinch," *H.L.Q.* XXXIX (1976): 277–90; J. R. Jones, *The Revolution of 1688 in England* (New York, 1972), pp. 18–35; J. P. Kenyon, *Robert Spencer, Earl of Sunderland, 1641–1702* (1958), passim; J. Miller, *James II: A Study in Kingship* (1978), passim. Finally, honorable mention should be made of J. M. Beattie, *The English Court in the Reign of George I* (Cambridge, Eng., 1967). This pioneering study examines definitively the administration, finances, working conditions, and politics of the court that succeeded Anne's. It lays much of the groundwork for the present study, in particular Chapters 2 and 5. However, Beattie's work deals less fully with the culture, social life, and chronological context of the first Hanoverian court. It is the contention of the present work that the respective characters of the court's administration, finances, politics, culture, and social life were interdependent, and that they are best understood in relation to what came before.

46. The following is a necessarily cursory and somewhat exploratory survey of the immediate historical background of Anne's court. It is, in part, a down payment on a projected longer work, currently in progress, dealing with the Restoration court.

47. Anthony Hamilton, Count de Grammont, *Memoirs of the Life of Count de Grammont . . .*, trans. A. Boyer (1714). For good examples of Grub Street memoirs, see David Jones, *The Secret History of White-hall from the Restoration of Charles II down to the Abdication of K. James*, 6 pts. (1697); and Anon., *Secret History of the Reigns of King Charles II and King James II* ([?London], 1690). For the continued notoriety of the Restoration court in general, see J. H. Wilson, *The Court Wits of the Restoration* (Princeton, N.J., 1948), p. 42.

48. *The Diary of John Evelyn*, ed. E. S. de Beer, 6 vols. (Oxford, 1955); *The Diary of Samuel Pepys*, ed. R. Latham and W. Matthews, 11 vols. (Berkeley, Calif.,

1970–83). Much Restoration correspondence is to be found in the H.M.C.; see also *Savile Correspondence*, ed. W. D. Cooper (Camd. Soc., 1858); *The Rochester-Savile Letters, 1671–1680*, ed. J. H. Wilson (Columbus, Ohio, 1941); *Martha, Lady Giffard: Her Life and Correspondence (1664–1722)*, ed. J. G. Longe (1911). For rakes and mistresses, see M. Petherick, *Restoration Rogues* (1951); E. B. Chancellor, *The Lives of the Rakes*, 6 vols. (1924–25); M. Gilmour, *The Great Lady: A Biography of Barbara Villiers, Mistress of Charles II* (1944); C. H. Hartmann, *Charles II and Madame* (1934); idem, *La Belle Stuart . . . Francis . . . Duchess of Richmond and Lennox* (1924); B. Bevan, *Nell Gwynn* (1969); idem, *Charles II's French Mistress* (1972); J. H. Wilson, *Nell Gwynn* (1952).

49. For the size of the main household, see LC 3/24 (Rough Establishment, Chamber, 1660–85); LS 13/31 (Establishment, Household Below Stairs, 1662); Staffordshire R.O., Dartmouth MSS D 1778/V, nos. 132–34 (Stables Establishments and Papers, temp. Charles II). For the side courts, see E. Chamberlayne, *Anglia Notitia* (edns. 1669, 1670, 1671, 1673, 1676, 1677, 1679, 1682, 1684); LS 13/32 (Establishment, Queen Consort, 1663); B.L. Add. MSS 15897, ff. 8–9 (Stables Establishment, Duke and Duchess of York). For supernumeraries and reversions, see LC 3/26 (Rough Establishment, 1660–[71]). For the King's granting of reversions, see B. L. Harl. MSS 1843, pp. 15–16; *C.T.B.* III: 1142; IV: 658, 744; V: 296.

50. See G. E. Aylmer, "From Office-holding to Civil Service: The Genesis of Modern Bureaucracy," *T.R.H.S.*, 5th ser., XXX (1980): 92.

51. H.M.C., *Ormonde MSS*, n.s. (1902–20), IV: 291: Fox to the Duke of Ormonde, Whitehall, 28 Dec. 1678; see also ibid., p. 139. For life tenures, see *C.T.B.* III: 381; IV: 692, 747; V: 296, 649, 653, 661, 668, 991.

52. H.M.C., *Ormonde MSS*, n.s., IV: 291.

53. See, for example, ibid., n.s., III: 43, 78, 252; IV: 291; V: 70, 79, 104–5, 122, 147; H.M.C., *Fifth Report* (1876), App., p. 186; H.M.C., *Seventh Report* (1879), App., pp. 371, 478, 491; H.M.C., *Twelfth Report*, App. V (1889), pp. 45, 52; App. VII (1890), p. 56; H.M.C., *Fourteenth Report*, App. IX (1895), p. 442; H.M.C., *Portland MSS* (1899–1931), VIII: 365; H.M.C., *Finch MSS* (1913–61), II: 62–63; H.M.C., *House of Lords MSS*, n.s. (1903–12), V: 155; S.P. Dom. 34/36, f. 304; *Letters Addressed from London to Sir Joseph Williamson While Plenipotentiary at the Congress of Cologne in the Years 1673 and 1674*, ed. W. D. Christie (Camd. Soc., 1874), I: 88, 104; A. Boyer, *The History of the Reign of Queen Anne, Digested into Annals* (1703–13), VIII: 369; John Macky, *Memoirs of the Secret Services of John Macky . . .*, 2nd edn. (1733), p. 43; Wilson, *Court Wits*, p. 48 and n. For the role of department heads, see LC 5/150, p. 366; Worcestershire R. O., Henning Papers, BA 2252/6 i, "An Account of the Lord Chamberlain's Office by Mr. Couling" and "Places in the Lord Chamberlains disposall."

54. *Calendar of State Papers and Manuscripts Relating to English Affairs . . . Venice*, ed. A. B. Hinds (1931), XXXII: 210: Francesco Giavarina to the Doge and Senate, London, 29 Oct. 1660.

55. See G. E. Aylmer, "The Last Years of Purveyance 1610–1660," *Economic History Review*, 2nd ser., X (1957); J. M. Beattie, *English Court*, pp. 17, 76–77, 196.

56. *D.N.B.*, sub "Fox"; see also C. Clay, *Public Finance and Private Wealth, the Career of Sir Stephen Fox, 1627–1716* (Oxford, 1978), pp. 85–87 for a listing of a number of well-heeled court officers who had financial dealings with Fox. It should be noted that Fox made the bulk of his fortune in land and as paymaster of the forces: see Clay, *Public Finance*, pp. 26, 38.

57. LC 5/2, pp. 18, 31–32, 38, 124; Michael Foss, *The Age of Patronage: The Arts in England 1660–1750* (Ithaca, N.Y., 1972), pp. 23–24. See also C. Jones, "Seating Problems in the House of Lords in the Early Eighteenth Century: The Evidence of the Manuscript Minutes," *B.I.H.R.* LI (1978): 137; J. Wildeblood, *The Polite World: A Guide to the Deportment of the English in Former Times* (1973), p. 101.

58. D. Allen, "Charles II's Chiffinch," pp. 279–80.

59. For Charles II's openness, see H.M.C., *Fourteenth Report*, App. II (1894), p. 255; D. Allen, "Charles II's Chiffinch," pp. 285–87; Foss, *Age of Patronage*, pp. 25–26; J. Sutherland, "The Impact of Charles II on Restoration Literature" in *Restoration and Eighteenth-Century Literature*, ed. C. Camden (Chicago, 1963), pp. 251, 253–54.

60. C. D. Chandaman, *The English Public Revenue 1660–1688* (Oxford, 1975), p. 270.

61. Stone, *Causes of the English Revolution*, p. 85, describing the pre–Civil War court. For grants of land or leases, see *C.T.B.* I: 88, 125, 300; III: 1252, 1279; IV: 151, 654–55, 819; V: 132, 230, 238, 239, 283, 301, 530, 1056; VII: 377–78, 464, 1129. For pensions paid directly out of the revenue, see *C.T.B.* IV: 500, 587. For payments out of the secret service, see *Moneys Received and Paid for Secret Services of Charles II. and James II.*, ed. J. Y. Ackerman (Camd. Soc., 1851), passim. There are no surviving privy-purse accounts for the early years of the reign of Charles II; for the period after 1668, see P.R.O. E 351/2795–96. For sinecures, etc., see D. Allen, "Charles II's Chiffinch," p. 289; *C.T.B.* III: 1159.

62. Petherick, *Restoration Rogues*, pp. 352–53, 356, 357, 360–62; Somerset, *Ladies in Waiting*, p. 152.

63. See, for example, *C.T.B.* I: 300, 354, 594; III: 306, 544, 843, 1252, 1254, 1279, 1280; IV: 151, 493, 523, 548, 560, 587, 702, 786, 819; V: 230, 238, 283, 301, 581, 693, 1056; VII: 465, 1129; D. Allen, "Charles II's Chiffinch," p. 289; L. G. Matthews, *The Royal Apothecaries* (1967), p. 105.

64. See, for example, H.M.C., *Tenth Report*, App. IV (1885), p. 151; H.M.C., *Eleventh Report*, App. V (1887), p. 59; H.M.C., *Twelfth Report*, App. VII (1890), p. 171; H.M.C., *Ormonde MSS*, n.s., IV: 586; D. Allen, "Charles II's Chiffinch," pp. 278, 279, 285–86; Petherick, *Restoration Rogues*, pp. 340–41, 347–48, 355, 357; J. Miller, "Faction in Later Stuart England, 1660–1714," *History Today* XXXIII (Dec. 1983): 8–9; Miller, *James II*, pp. 52, 77. However, the most recent scholarly examination of the early years of the reign seems to downplay the

role of bedchamber politics: see R. Hutton, *The Restoration: A Political and Religious History of England and Wales 1658–1667* (Oxford, 1985).

65. *The Lauderdale Papers*, ed. O. Airy (Camd. Soc., 1885), III: 141: Sir Andrew Forrester to the Duke of Lauderdale, Whitehall, 9 May 1678; see also D. Allen, "Charles II's Chiffinch," p. 278.

66. *Pepys Diary* III: 191 (7 Sept. 1662); see also Miller, *James II*, p. 38; D. Allen, "Charles II's Chiffinch," p. 280.

67. Calculation based on LC 5/201, pp. 79–89 ("Whitehall Lodgings: taken by S[r] Thomas Duppa. November. 1685").

68. LS 13/31; LS 13/32; calculation based on figures given in H.M.C., *Ormonde MSS*, n.s., III: 174. For the ease with which meals could be had, see R. J. Minney, *Hampton Court* (1972), p. 164.

69. J. J. Jusserand, *A French Ambassador at the Court of Charles II* (1892), p. 91: Cominges to Louis XIV, 25 Jan. 1663.

70. O. Millar, *The Queen's Pictures* (New York, 1977), pp. 66–67, 71, 73–76, 78–79, 81; idem, *The Tudor, Stuart and Early Georgian Pictures in the Collection of Her Majesty the Queen* (1963), I: 20–26; E. H. Fellows, *English Cathedral Music* (1948), p. 134; C. Dearnley, *English Church Music, 1650–1750* (New York, 1970), pp. 21–22, 25–26, 40–41, 48; R. Nash, *Hampton Court* (1983), pp. 108–9; D. Green, *Gardener to Queen Anne: Henry Wise (1653–1738) and the Formal Garden* (Oxford, 1956), pp. 14–16, 49–51; H. B. Wheatley, *London Past and Present: Its History, Associations and Traditions* (1891), II: 290–94; W. B. Boulton, *The Amusements of Old London* (New York, 1901; repr., 1969), II: 138–41; R. T. Wray, *Ancient Royal Palaces in and near London* (1902), p. 90.

71. Boulton, *Amusements* II: 138–44; Wheatley, *London Past and Present* II: 290–94; J. H. Plumb, *Georgian Delights* (Boston, 1980), p. 40.

72. Dearnley, *Church Music*, pp. 19–20, 42–43; Fellows, *Cathedral Music*, p. 115; J. A. Westrup, "Foreign Musicians in Stuart England," *Musical Quarterly* XXVII (1941): 74; T. Hughes, *Old English Furniture* (New York, 1969), p. 46; R. W. Symonds, "Charles II Couches, Chairs and Stools 1660–1670," *Connoisseur* XCIII (1934): 19; D. Green, *Gardener to Queen Anne*, pp. viii, 7, 14; M. Evans, *Costume Throughout the Ages* (Philadelphia, 1950), p. 144; E. S. de Beer, "King Charles II's Own Fashion," *Journal of the Warburg Courtauld Institute* II (1938): 106, 112; B. R. T. Hughes, *Three Centuries of English Domestic Silver 1500–1820* (New York, 1968), p. 125. For the rise of French taste in general, see C. Bastide, *The Anglo-French Entente in the Seventeenth Century* (New York, 1914), p. 24. In fact, French musical styles were first introduced into England by Henrietta Maria; see Smuts, *Court Culture*, p. 25.

73. J. Banister, *An Introduction to Old English Silver* (1965), p. 107; W. Gaunt, *Court Painting in England from Tudor to Victorian Times* (1980), p. 163; C. Oman, *English Silversmiths' Work, Civil and Domestic: An Introduction* (1965), p. 7; J. F. Hayward, *Huguenot Silver in England 1688–1727* (1959), p. 1.

74. Dearnley, *Church Music*, pp. 25–26, 40, 44, 49; J. Harley, *Music in Purcell's London: The Social Background* (1968), pp. 81–83.

75. J. Loftis, "The Court and the Stage," in *The Revels History of Drama in English V 1660–1750* (1976), pp. 5–7; A. H. Schouten, "Tragedy," in *Revels History V*, p. 259; A. Nicoll, *A History of English Drama 1660–1900* (1962–67), I: 9, 219; Sutherland, "Impact of Charles II," pp. 258–61.

76. D. C. Calthrop, *English Costume 1066–1820* (1963), pp. 373–76; Evans, *Costume Throughout the Ages*, p. 145; G. Squire, *Dress, Art and Society 1560–1970* (1974), p. 106; R. M. Green, *The Wearing of Costume* (1966), p. 92; but cf. de Beer, "King Charles II's Own Fashion," passim, and F. M. Kelly and R. Schwabe, *A Short History of Costume and Armour . . . 1066–1800* (1931), II: 38.

77. D. Yarwood, *English Costume from the Second Century B.C. to 1967* (1967), pp. 159–62.

78. Foss, *Age of Patronage*, p. 28.

79. A. Simon, *Drink* (New York, 1953), pp. 67–68.

80. J. Latham, *The Pleasure of Your Company: A History of Manners and Meals* (1972), p. 38; W. Andrews, *Bygone England: Social Studies in Its Historic Byways and Highways* (1892; repr., Washington, 1968), pp. 136–37.

81. G. Brett, *Dinner Is Served: A Study in Manners* (1939), p. 141.

82. For Blow, Humfrey, and Purcell, see Fellows, *Cathedral Music*, p. 134; Dearnley, *Church Music*, pp. 21–22, 25–26. For Gibbons, see D. Green, *Grinling Gibbons: His Work as Carver and Statuary 1648–1721* (1964), pp. 18, 31, 33–35, 41, 43. For Kneller, see M. Morris, Lord Killanin, *Sir Godfrey Kneller and His Times, 1646–1723* (1948), pp. 16–18; Millar, *Tudor, Stuart . . . Pictures* I: 141. For Riley, see J. D. Stewart, *Sir Godfrey Kneller and the English Baroque Portrait* (Oxford, 1983), pp. 31–32. For the wits at court, see Wilson, *Court Wits*, pp. 52–53.

83. Foss, *Age of Patronage*, pp. 21–22, 48; Sutherland, "Impact of Charles II," pp. 255–57.

84. H.M.C., *Heathcote MSS* (1899), p. 78: Samuel Boothhouse to Sir Richard Fanshaw, Whitehall, 12 Apr. 1663.

85. For evidence that both men and women went to court, and that their countrymen wished to hear about its activities, see H.M.C., *Seventh Report*, App., pp. 468, 479, 531, 536; H.M.C., *Twelfth Report*, App. V, pp. 11, 17, 21, 22–23, 27, 31–34, 37–38, 42–45, 52, 63; App. IX (1891), pp. 54–55, 65; H.M.C., *Fourteenth Report*, App. II, pp. 304, 311, 314; H.M.C., *Bath MSS* (1904–8), II: 160–61, 162–63; *Lady Giffard Correspondence*, pp. 98–100, 111, 113, 114, 118; *Letters to Williamson*, passim; *Correspondence of the Family of Hatton: Being Chiefly Letters Addressed to Christopher First Viscount Hatton A.D. 1601–1704*, ed. E. M. Thompson (Camd. Soc., 1878), passim.

86. Jusserand, *French Ambassador*, p. 89. For Charles II's frequent progresses, see H.M.C., *Sixth Report* (1877), App., p. 336; H.M.C., *Seventh Report*, App., p. 469; H.M.C., *Twelfth Report*, App. VII, pp. 62, 84–85; App. IX, p. 85; H.M.C., *Fourteenth Report*, App. II, pp. 311, 314, 337, 365; App. IV (1894), p. 89; H.M.C., *Fifteenth Report*, App. I (1896), pp. 122–24; App. VII (1898), pp. 170, 171, 173; H.M.C., *Ormonde MSS*, n.s., III: 69, 286; VI: 427, 429, 437, 438; VII:

274; H.M.C., *Buccleuch at Drumlanrig Castle MSS* (1903), pp. 123, 127; H.M.C., *Hastings MSS* II (1930), pp. 142–43; *Hatton Correspondence* I: 56, 146, 222; II: 18.

87. H.M.C., *Buccleuch at Drumlanrig Castle MSS*, pp. 123, 127; Minney, *Hampton Court*, p. 175; H.M.C., *Ormonde MSS*, n.s., VI: 438, 443; VII: 274.

88. Quoted in G. Curtis, *The Life and Times of Queen Anne* (1972), p. 43.

89. *The Life and Times of Anthony à Wood*, ed. L. Powys (Oxford, 1961), p. 154. See also G. Burnet, *History of His Own Time* (Oxford, 1833), I: 168; Hutton, *Restoration*, pp. 186–87, 195–96, 238–39, 258, 271–72; *Letters to Williamson* I: 109–10, 184; *Letters of Humphrey Prideaux, Sometime Dean of Norwich to John Ellis, Sometime Under-Secretary of State, 1674–1722*, ed. E. M. Thompson (Camd. Soc., 1875), p. 101.

90. Foss, *Age of Patronage*, pp. 42–44; Wilson, *Court Wits*, pp. 26–42.

91. Roger North, *The Lives of . . . Francis North, Baron Guilford . . . The Hon. Sir Dudley North . . . and the Hon. and Rev. Dr. John North* (1826), II: 164; III: 324.

92. Hutton, *Restoration*, p. 278; *C.T.B.* VIII: 658, 779; LC 5/143, pp. 191, 196; LS 13/172, f. 16; H.M.C., *Sixth Report*, App., p. 723; H.M.C., *Seventh Report*, App., p. 410; H.M.C., *Twelfth Report*, App. VII, p. 106; App. IX, pp. 74, 83; Harley, *Music in Purcell's London*, pp. 66, 157; Westrup, "Foreign Musicians," p. 80; *Letters to Williamson* II: 85.

93. Wilson, *Court Wits*, pp. 9–10, 171, 198–205.

94. Chandaman, *English Public Revenue*, pp. 262–64, 268, 270–73, and chap. 6 passim.

95. H.M.C., *Ormonde MSS*, n.s., III: 175. See also ibid., pp. 74, 78–79, 83, 85, 88, 91; H.M.C., *Finch MSS* I: 274; H.M.C., *Third Report* (1872), App., pp. 92, 93; Harl. MSS 1843, pp. 8–10.

96. *C.T.B.* II: 2, 52, 61, 79, 91, 97, 143, 225, 245, 271, 317, 325, 331, 565; III: 159, 163, 242, 533.

97. *C.T.B.* II: 56, 114, 377, 392, 395, 429; III: 153.

98. For tenure, see *C.T.B.* II: 392; III: 381. For salaries awarded in lieu of fees and perquisites, see ibid. II: 132, 237, 245, 383, 391–92. For declaration of accounts, see ibid. II: 127–28; III: 90, 153, 236. For weekly certificates of receipts and remains, see ibid. II: 12, 43 (the cofferer's certificate was to be monthly); III: 143–44.

99. Chandaman, *English Public Revenue*, pp. 251–53; *C.T.B.* VII: 753–54 and passim.

100. *Lady Giffard Correspondence*, p. 111.

101. H.M.C., *Ormonde MSS*, n.s., V: 541.

102. O. Hedley, *Windsor Castle* (1967), pp. 127–28.

103. Harley, *Music in Purcell's London*, pp. 81–83, 155, 157.

104. Chandaman, *English Public Revenue*, p. 252; *C. T. B.* I: 542; II: 223, 336; V: 116–18; H.M.C., *Fourteenth Report*, App. IX, p. 413; H.M.C., *Ormonde MSS*, n.s., V: 143, 147, 239; *Letters to Williamson* II: 104. For examples of lengthy arrears owed during the first half of the reign, see *C.T.B.* I: 619; II: 100, 135, 156,

158, 160, 566, 598, 601, 620, 622; III: 268, 635, 641, 650, 743, 898, 930, 980, 1124, 1136, 1156, 1164; IV: 133, 147, 170, 181, 372, 450, 476, 480, 593, 651; V: 57–63, 73–82, 168, 567, 602, 654, 805, 1341–42, 1382; H.M.C., *Ormonde MSS*, n.s., III: 257, 258; "The state of the Tre'r of the Chamber his office at Midsummer 1665," printed in *Secret Services of Charles II. and James II.*, pp. vi–viii.

105. See LS 13/172 (unpag.), entry of 28 Nov. 1682; and *C.T.B.* II: 18, 23, 413, 603; III: 646, 762, 772, 1193; IV: 512, 514; V: 579; VI: 684.

106. H.M.C., *Ormonde MSS*, n.s., III: 452; Foss, *Age of Patronage*, pp. 77–78.

107. See, for example, Petherick, *Restoration Rogues*, pp. 360–62, 377; *C.T.B.* I: 547, 579, 595, 608, 624, 628; II: 269, 287, 297, 334, 410, 415, 424, 429, 467, 468, 575, 578, 604–5; V: 118, 321, 766; VI: 460, 559; VII: 465.

108. *Wren Society VII* (Oxford, 1930), pp. 11, 20.

109. *Evelyn Diary* IV: 413–14 (6 Feb. 1685).

110. Calculation based on LC 3/39, ff. 33 recto–34 verso. The figure is an underestimate, for it omits arrears to servants paid at the exchequer.

111. S. Pegge, *Curialia: or An Historical Account of Some Branches of the Royal Household, &c.* (1791), I iii, 67; Miller, *James II*, pp. 121–22.

112. For the basis of this reputation, see H.M.C., *Eleventh Report*, App. V, p. 73; H.M.C., *Ormonde MSS*, n.s., VI: 442.

113. For James's reforms in general, see Miller, *James II*, p. 121. For the elimination of life tenures, see *C.T.B.* VIII: 308, 378–79, 430, 457, 475, 1110. For the restraint of fee taking, see J. R. Western, *Monarchy and Revolution: The English State in the 1680s* (1972), p. 88; *C.T.B.* VIII: 756, 827, 1096. For the increase in work load, see LC 5/145, pp. 212, 215; H.M.C., *Fifth Report*, pp. 344–45; *C.T.B.* VIII: 193. For the rise in salaries, see LS 13/38 (Establishment, 1685). Finally, there is no evidence of sale of household office under James II.

114. Quoted in J. R. Tanner, *Samuel Pepys and the Royal Navy* (Cambridge, Eng., 1920), p. 41.

115. H.M.C., *Downshire MSS* I i (1924), p. 79; LC 5/145, pp. 212, 215; LC 5/201, p. 189.

116. Miller, *James II*, p. 122.

117. H.M.C., *Russell Astley MSS* (1900), p. 60: Lord Fauconberg to Sir William Frankland, [?10 Mar. 1685].

118. H.M.C., *Fourteenth Report*, App. II, p. 393.

119. E. Boswell (Murrie), *The Restoration Court Stage* (Cambridge, Mass., 1932), pp. 54–55, 140; H.M.C., *Twelfth Report*, App. V, pp. 100, 102–6; V. Cowles, *The Great Marlborough and His Duchess* (1983), p. 96.

120. *Evelyn Diary* IV: 537 (30 Jan. 1687); *C.T.B.* VIII: 1442; LS 13/255, warrants of 26 Apr., 5 July, 26 Mar. 1687, 20 Feb. 1687/88.

121. J. A. Westrup, "The Chapel Royal Under James II," *Monthly Musical Record* LXX (1940): 219; H. C. de La Fontaine, *The King's Musick . . .* (1909), p. 383; D. J. Burrows, "Handel and the English Chapel Royal During the Reigns of Queen Anne and King George I" (Ph.D. diss., Open University, 1981), I: 22–23.

122. Millar, *Tudor, Stuart . . . Pictures* I: 21–22; idem, *Queen's Pictures*, p. 73; *Wren Society VII*, pp. 71–74; E. J. Sheppard, *The Old Royal Palace of Whitehall* (1902), pp. 28–29; LC 5/68, ff. 3, 32–33, 38 verso.

123. L. D. Mitchell, "Command Performances During the Reign of Queen Anne," *Theatre Notebook* XXIV (1970): 117; idem, "Command Performances During the Reign of George I," *Eighteenth Century Studies* VII (1974): 343, 348.

124. H.M.C., *Twelfth Report*, App. V, p. 120: [Newsletter] to the Countess of Rutland at Belvoir, 31 July 1688.

125. Quoted in Miller, *James II*, p. 173. For more evidence of the increasing isolation of James's court, see ibid., pp. 146, 174; idem, "Faction in Later Stuart England," p. 10; idem, "The Later Stuart Monarchy," in *The Restored Monarchy, 1660–1688*, ed. J. R. Jones (1979), p. 40; H.M.C., *Fourteenth Report*, App. II, p. 417; but cf. Kenyon, *Sunderland*, p. 220n.

126. C. Roberts, "The Constitutional Significance of the Financial Settlement of 1690," *H.J.* XX (1977): 59–76, esp. 62–65; see also E. A. Reitan, "From Revenue to Civil List, 1689–1702: The Revolution Settlement and the 'Mixed and Balanced' Constitution," *H.J.* XIII (1970): 571–88.

127. LC5/149, p. 273.

128. S. B. Baxter, *William III and the Defense of European Liberty 1650–1702* (New York, 1966), p. 248.

129. *Wren Society IV*, pp. 8, 16, 23, 29, 38; *Wren Society VII*, pp. 134, 138, 179–83.

130. Sources listed below in Appendix B; and H.M.C., *Stuart MSS* (1902–10), I: 42, 118, 128, 158, 162, 198 (warrants of appointment to the Jacobite court, 1689–1704).

131. See the case of Dennis Carney, gentleman usher, quarter waiter, in LS 13/198, warrant (appointing Henry Colinge) of 11 Mar. 1688[/9]; see also Add. MSS 61423, f. 160 verso.

132. See, for example, the case of John Fox, clerk comptroller of the greencloth and a nephew of Sir Stephen: LS 13/174, p. 29; Add. MSS 51324, f. 17 recto.

133. For the court service and interrelationships of these families, see below, Chapter 3, n. 22 and Chapter 4, n. 41.

134. About fifteen Dutchmen were also named grooms of the stables. For household appointments under William and Mary, see LC 3/3–4; LC 3/32; LC 3/61; LS 13/42; LS 13/256–57.

135. Copies in B.L. Stowe MSS 563; Add. MSS 50842 and 61419; and Worcestershire R.O., Henning Papers, BA 2252/2, pp. 58–70. For Portland's role in particular, see Baxter, *William III*, pp. 274–75; for William's reclusiveness and aversion to intrigue, see ibid., pp. 248–50.

136. See below, Chapter 4, n. 79.

137. For this relationship, see J. Swift, *Journal to Stella*, ed. H. Williams (Oxford, 1948), p. 272 and n. 13. For William's probable reasoning in appointing individuals of Republican background, see Baxter, *William III*, p. 250.

138. See Roberts, "Party and Patronage," pp. 192–205.

139. For example, Anthony Rowe, who handled some of William's early financial transactions, was made avenor and clerk martial; William Churchill, whose services were unspecified but probably financial, was made bookseller, bookbinder, and stationer. Information kindly provided by Drs. Eveline Cruickshanks and David Hayton, of the History of Parliament Trust.

140. Add. MSS 51324, ff. 44 verso, 50 recto and verso.

141. See, for example, H. Horwitz, *Parliament, Policy and Politics in the Reign of William III* (Manchester, 1977), p. 38; J. H. Plumb, *The Growth of Political Stability in England, 1675–1725* (1967), pp. 138–39; Baxter, *William III*, pp. 254, 285; J. S. Brewer, *The Sinews of Power: War, Money and the English State, 1688–1783* (New York, 1989), pp. 94, 139.

142. For sale of office, see N. Luttrell, *A Brief Historical Relation of State Affairs from September 1678 to April 1714* (Oxford, 1857), IV: 62, 280, 281; *C.S.P.D. 1700–02*, pp. 90, 143; S.P. Dom. 34/36, f. 260; H.M.C., *Buccleuch at Montagu House MSS* (1899–1903), II ii, 634; H.M.C., *Downshire MSS* I i, 312; Add. MSS 20101, f. 15; 61425, f. 7 verso; 61475, f. 74 verso; Bodl. MSS Locke C.22, f. 109. For life tenures, see *C.T.B.* XIII: 427; XIV: 125.

143. Add. MSS 51324, f. 17.

144. LC 3/53, pp. 14–15; *C.T.B.* IX: 367, 393, 686; X: 201; Add. MSS 5750, f. 13.

145. LS 13/174, f. 72; Horwitz, *William III*, p. 93.

146. LS 13/174, f. 99 recto and verso.

147. *C.T.B.* IX: 43–47, 1698, 1758, 1761, 1762, 1764, 1766, 1787, 1918, 1951; X: 21, 35, 44, 83, 124, 128, 200, 433, 507, 732, 817, 1071, 1194–95, 1329, 1354; XI: 138, 148, 150, 183, 184, 187, 189, 228; XII: 162, 209–10; LS 13/174, pp. 122–23, 128. For an explanation of tallies of fictitious loan, see P. G. M. Dickson, *The Financial Revolution in England: A Study in the Development of Public Credit* (1967), pp. 351–52.

148. *C.T.B.* XI: 261, 262, 283, 369; XII: 158, 184, 190.

149. LS 13/105, f. 85 verso: Devonshire and Wharton to Bradford, 10 Jan. 1696[/7].

150. Reitan, "From Revenue to Civil List," pp. 585–87.

151. *C.T.B.* XIII: 100–104. For later deliberations, see *C.T.B.* XIV: 45, 50–52; XV: 38, 49, 101; XVI: 63, 80–81, 112.

152. LS 13/41 (Establishment, Household Below Stairs, October 1701); *C.T.B.* XVII: 115–22 (Establishment, Chamber, December 1701).

153. Calculation based on *C.T.B.* XVII: 941–1078. I have added the totals of arrears paid to William's former servants, pp. 944–45, to those for the debt still outstanding in 1711. As in the case of Charles II's final household debt, this figure does not include arrears owed to servants paid at the exchequer.

154. Baxter, *William III*, pp. 276, 295; H.M.C., *Twelfth Report*, App. VII, p. 295; Worcestershire R.O., Henning Papers, BA 2252/2, [Privy Purse Account, n.d.], p. 127.

155. Baxter, *William III*, p. 279.

156. *Wren Society IV*, p. 19; Baxter, *William III*, p. 319.

157. Dearnley, *Church Music*, pp. 57–58 and n.; Green, *Gardener to Queen Anne*, pp. 30, 48, 60; Minney, *Hampton Court*, pp. 179–80; Add. MSS 34195, f. 100; LC 5/149, pp. 318, 364; LC 5/150, pp. 77, 306; LC 5/151, p. 369; Boswell, *Restoration Court Stage*, pp. 55–56, 292–93, 299.

158. M. Ede, *Arts and Society in England Under William and Mary* (1979), pp. 19–20, 42; A. F. Kendrick, *English Needlework* (1967), pp. 140–41; A. Ray, *English Delftware Pottery* . . . (Boston, 1968), p. 37; T. Hughes, *Old English Furniture*, pp. 26, 156; H. Van der Zee and B. Van der Zee, *William and Mary* (New York, 1973), p. 291.

159. For painting, see Stewart, *Kneller*, pp. 40, 44. For gardening, see Minney, *Hampton Court*, pp. 184–85; Green, *Gardener to Queen Anne*, pp. 59–60. For craftsmen, see Hayward, *Huguenot Silver*, pp. 10, 64; H. P. Fourest, *Delftware Faience Production at Delft*, trans. K. Watson (New York, 1980), pp. 40–42; F. P. Thomson, *Tapestry: Mirror of History* (New York, 1980), pp. 136, 142; R. Fastnedge, *English Furniture Styles from 1500 to 1830* (1962), p. 88; Foss, *Age of Patronage*, pp. 117–18; Ede, *Arts and Society*, p. 124; R. W. Symonds, *Thomas Tompion, His Life & Work* (1951), p. 43; H. A. Lloyd, *Old Clocks* (1970), pp. 63, 107.

160. *Evelyn Diary* IV: 624–25 (22 Feb. 1689); [N. Hooke], *An Account of the Conduct of the Dowager Duchess of Marlborough* . . . , reprinted in *Memoirs of the Duchess of Marlborough*, ed. W. King (1930), pp. 18–19.

161. *Evelyn Diary* IV: 625 (22 Feb. 1689).

162. Burnet, *History* III: 406–7; see also L. G. Schwoerer, "The Glorious Revolution as Spectacle: A New Perspective," in *England's Rise to Greatness*, ed. Baxter, pp. 109–49, esp. pp. 112, 134.

163. For these activities, see H.M.C., *Hastings MSS* II: 342; Boswell, *Restoration Court Stage*, pp. 55, 104, 292–93; LC 5/149, p. 364; LC 5/150, pp. 77, 156, 306; LC 5/151, p. 369; H.M.C., *Twelfth Report*, App. V, p. 152; *Hatton Correspondence* II: 171, 199.

164. Add. MSS 34195, f. 100: [Anonymous Newsletter], n.d. [?summer 1690].

165. Ibid., ff. 100–101.

166. Ibid., ff. 101–2.

167. *Observator* I, no. 2, 8 Apr. 1702.

168. Foss, *Age of Patronage*, pp. 111–12; LC 5/150, p. 279.

169. J. Ashton, *Social Life in the Reign of Queen Anne, Taken from Original Sources* (1883; repr., Detroit, 1968), p. 360.

170. H.M.C., *Thirteenth Report*, App. II (1893), p. 246: Nathaniel Harley to Sir Edward Harley, Aleppo, 14 May 1696; see also Burnet, *History* IV: 181–82, 239–41; W. P. Baker, "The Observance of Sunday," in *Englishmen at Rest and Play*, ed. R. Lennard (Oxford, 1931), pp. 138–39.

171. According to Paul Fritz, mourning for Queen Mary lasted over two years: "The Trade in Death: The Royal Funerals in England, 1685–1830," *Eighteenth Century Studies* XV (1982): 307 n. 42. However, cf. *Seafield Correspondence*

from 1685 to 1708, ed. J. Grant (Edinburgh, 1912), p. 191, for evidence that mourning for the Queen had ended by April 1696.

172. H.M.C., *Twelfth Report*, App. V, p. 166: Countess of Rutland "to her husband" [Earl of Rutland], "Thursday night" [Apr. 1701].

173. Add. MSS 61415, f. 135: Anne to Sarah, Countess of Marlborough, Windsor, 20 Oct. [dated 1696 by Edward Gregg: see *Queen Anne* (1980), p. 109 n. 26, quoting a later portion of the same letter].

174. H.M.C., *Twelfth Report* (1888–89), App. II, p. 365: Mary Fanshaw to Thomas Coke, Parslow, 9 Nov. 1696; see also ibid., Alice Coke to Thomas Coke, Parslow, 5 Nov. 1696.

175. T. B. Macaulay, *The History of England from the Accession of James the Second* (Longman's Popular Edn., 1895), II: 664–65 and n.

176. Baxter, *William III*, pp. 246, 255; G. S. de Krey, *A Fractured Society: The Politics of London in the First Age of Party, 1688–1715* (Oxford, 1985), pp. 58–60; Schwoerer, "Glorious Revolution," passim; *The Correspondence of Henry Hyde, Earl of Clarendon and of His Brother, Laurence Hyde, Earl of Rochester; with the Diary of Lord Clarendon from 1687 to 1690*, ed. S. W. Singer (1828), II: 264.

177. For the danger of assassination, see Baxter, *William III*, pp. 296, 300–301, 336–37, 354.

178. Ibid., p. 333; Van der Zee and Van der Zee, *William and Mary*, pp. 399–400; H.M.C., *Fourteenth Report*, App. VIII, pp. 112–14.

179. H.M.C., *Fourteenth Report*, App. II, p. 573: E. [Harley] to Sir Edward Harley, 12 Nov. [16]95.

180. Van der Zee and Van der Zee, *William and Mary*, pp. 399–400. William also undertook trips to Newmarket, of little propagandistic significance, in 1689 and 1699: Baxter, *William III*, pp. 255, 370.

181. Add. MSS 6283, ff. 1–5 verso; 6308, f. 50; L. Melville, *Bath Under Beau Nash* (1907), p. 10; Baxter, *William III*, p. 359.

182. Horwitz, *William III*, pp. 260, 283; Baxter, *William III*, pp. 383–84.

183. Nicoll, *English Drama* II: 281, quoting LC 5/153, warrant dated 17 Feb. 1701/02.

184. G. M. Trevelyan, *English Social History* (1942), p. 338. According to Steven Baxter, William retained his popularity with the common people to the end of the reign: Baxter, *William III*, pp. 263–64, 370, 401. At issue here is his relationship with the political classes.

185. Foss, *Age of Patronage*, p. 111.

Chapter II

1. Chamberlayne, *Anglia Notitia* (1684), pt. I, p. 220.

2. See LC 5/2 (Notebooks of Sir Charles Lodowick Cotterell, 1660–1710), passim, esp. pp. 1–3, 17–18, 37, 141, 147, 159–60; Add. MSS 51324, ff. 44 verso, 50 recto and verso. For the significance of usage vs. written instructions, see

H.M.C., *Ormonde MSS*, n.s., VII: 28–29; Worcestershire R.O., Henning Papers, BA 2252/5 i, p. 35; and LC 5/2, p. 37.

3. See Add. MSS 51324, ff. 17, 44 verso, 50 recto and verso, 52 recto and verso, 53.

4. The following series have been most important to the administrative portion of this study: LC 2/14–20 (Accounts of Royal Funerals and Coronations, 1700–1714); LC 3/5–6 (Chamber Establishments, 1702–14); LC 3/53 (Sign Manual Warrants for Appointments, 1689–1720); LC 3/62 (Appointment Books, Series 2, 1702–13); LC 5/2–3 (Masters of the Ceremonies, Bound Papers, 1660–1758 [The Notebooks of Sir Charles, Sir Charles Lodowick and Sir Clement Cotterell]); LC 5/70–71 (Great Wardrobe, Warrants Dormant, 1698–1714); LC 5/108–9 (Jewel Office Warrant Books, 1677–1731); LC 5/153–55 (Lord Chamberlain, Warrant Books, General, 1700–1714); LS 13/11 (Miscellaneous Books: Cheque Roll [Anne]); LS 13/43 (Establishment, 1702); LS 13/106 (Entry Book of Letters, 1702–10); LS 13/199 (Servants, Certificate Book of Admissions, 1702–14); LS 13/258–59 (Warrants of Appointment, 1702–14 [royal and lord steward's]).

5. LC 5/154, p. 339; LC 5/155, p. 306; LS 13/175, ff. 48 verso–50 recto.

6. Printed accurately in the introductions to *C.T.B.* XVII–XXVIII.

7. The following description of the household's administrative and financial structure, though modified in detail by my own research, is heavily indebted to the much more extended exposition in J. M. Beattie, *English Court*, chaps. 2–4. For the historical development of the early modern household, see also Aylmer, *King's Servants*, pp. 26–32; *English Court*, ed. Starkey, passim.

8. A "society" was a group of officers of the same type: the gentlemen pensioners; the gentlemen ushers, quarter waiters; and the messengers of the chamber each formed a "society."

9. Contained in LC 5/70–71 (Great Wardrobe, Warrants Dormant, 1698–1714) and LC 5/108–9 (Jewel Office Warrant Books, 1677–1731).

10. LC 5/201, pp. 9–47, 48, 51, 53, 157, 355–67, 456, 457.

11. See LC 5/201, pp. 9–47, 71–75, 456; H.M.C., *Ormonde MSS*, n.s., VII: 27–32; *Hatton Correspondence* II: 21–22.

12. Cf., however, LC 5/202, pp. 109–12.

13. LS 13/43 (Establishment, 1702).

14. See G. E. Aylmer, "Attempts at Administrative Reform, 1625–40," *E.H.R.* LXXII (1957): 229–59; idem, *King's Servants*, pp. 62–63; Sharpe, "Image of Virtue," pp. 235–39.

15. See above, Chapter 1, sub "Charles II."

16. For the chamber comptroller, see *C.T.B.* IX: 686; for the great wardrobe, see J.M. Beattie, *English Court*, p. 125.

17. *C.T.P. 1708–1714*, p. 394; *C.T.B.* XXVI: 44–45; B.L. Loan 29/34, n.d. [endorsed Oct. 1711], petition and related documents of the messengers of the chamber.

18. J. M. Beattie, *English Court*, p. 125.

19. Extracts of Cotterell's notebooks, 1710–58, copied in 1826 by B. Chester from original papers then in the possession of the Cotterell-Dormer family, are contained in LC 5/3.

20. See, for example, ibid., pp. 8, 15, 45, 67. For Anne's reforms, see below, sub "Finance."

21. LC 5/3, pp. 48–49. For a similar sentiment, expressed by a secretary of state, see *Letters and Correspondence, Public and Private, of the Right Honourable Henry St. John, Lord Visc. Bolingbroke; During the Time he was Secretary of State to Queen Anne*, ed. G. Parke (1798), II: 21.

22. Note the Queen's difficulties in trying to get one of her servants paid even by direct order: B.L. Loan 29/32, no. 44, "Petition of Charles Lucas," closet keeper, 4 Sept. 1710; and the delays suffered by the Duke of Marlborough in attempting to procure a picture of the Queen to give to Count Wratislaw: *The Marlborough-Godolphin Correspondence*, ed. H. L. Snyder (Oxford, 1975), p. 858: Marlborough to the Duchess, 24 July/4 Aug. 1707.

23. Sir Charles Lodowick Cotterell, master of the ceremonies 1686–1710, succeeded his father, Sir Charles, who had served in the office since 1641. Sir Charles Lodowick was succeeded by his son, Sir Clement Cotterell (afterwards Cotterell-Dormer), who was succeeded by *his* son, Sir Charles Cotterell-Dormer, in 1758. Charles Killigrew, master of the revels circa 1680–1725 and gentleman of the privy chamber circa 1670–1702, was the son of Thomas Killigrew, dramatist, master of the revels, and a groom of the bedchamber to Charles II. See Chapters 3 and 4 below for additional examples of household officers and administrators with long careers or a family tradition of household service.

24. Add. MSS 51324, f. 44 recto and verso.

25. Luttrell, *Brief Relation* V: 192.

26. Note, for example, H.M.C., *Portland MSS* V: 163, 245; and W. Sussex R.O., Petworth House Archives, Somerset Papers, P.H.A. 6306, "The Book of Receipts & Disbursements on Acco^{t}. of Her late Majesty Queen Anne's Stables, From Sept 19th 1709 to Janry 20th 1713/14," all of which show Somerset's care not to leave the department in debt at his removal in 1712. This care extended to his supply of £1,542 13*s*. 0 ½*d*. over and above what he received from the exchequer. See also Petworth House Archives, Somerset Papers, P.H.A. 322, letters between Somerset and the treasury dated 23 Feb. 1724/25, 16 June 1725, 16 Aug. 1728; no. 6330, letters between Henry Pigott and William Taylor dated 9 July, 19 Aug. 1702. For Somerset's poor contemporary and latter-day reputation, see G. S. Holmes, *British Politics in the Age of Anne* (1967), p. 226.

27. Coke's papers are preserved at Melbourne Hall by the Marquess of Lothian. Some were printed in H.M.C., *Twelfth Report*, App. III. Those dealing with the theater (most not at Melbourne Hall) are contained in *Vice Chamberlain Coke's Theatrical Papers, 1706–1715*, ed. J. Milhous and R. D. Hume (Carbondale, Ill., 1982).

28. For Coke's role, see S.P. Dom. 34/24, f. 220; Melbourne Hall, Derbyshire, Melbourne Hall MSS, old no. 64 / new no. 103; old n. 70 / new nos. 114–15; old no. 71 / new no. 116, passim; *Bolingbroke Correspondence* III: 350; IV: 339; P.R.O. 31/3/201, ff. 11, 67 verso; H.M.C., *Twelfth Report*, App. III, pp. 80–81, 97, 99–100, 106, 107–20, 181, 183–87; and *Coke's Theatrical Papers*, passim. For Stanley's role, see ibid.; S.P. Dom. 34/31, f. 101; H.M.C., *Twelfth Report*, App. III, pp. 78, 118, 185, 186; and (for the period 1699–1700) H.M.C., *Buccleuch at Montagu House MSS* II ii, 628–53. For Evans, see H.M.C., *Twelfth Report*, App. III, p. 109; B. L. Stowe MSS 750, f. 73; Add. MSS 4552, f. 206 recto and verso.

29. See H.M.C., *Twelfth Report*, App. III, pp. 84, 88–89, 93–95; Melbourne Hall, Derbyshire, Melbourne Hall MSS, old no. 97: Elizabeth Coke to Thomas Coke, 7 June 1710; same to same, 14 Aug. 1710; same to same, 9 Sept. 1710. In contrast, Stanley chose to accompany Shrewsbury to Ireland as his secretary from October 1713 to June 1714.

30. *C.T.B.* XXX: 290–91.

31. J. M. Beattie, *English Court*, chap. 4, esp. pp. 106–10. The following discussion is based, in large part, upon that of Professor Beattie.

32. 9 William c. 23.

33. Reitan, "From Revenue to Civil List," pp. 578–87; Roberts, "Constitutional Significance," p. 70.

34. 12 and 13 William c. 12; Reitan, "From Revenue to Civil List," p. 587.

35. See the civil-list accounts printed in the introductions to *C.T.B.* XVII–XXVIII; J. M. Beattie, *English Court*, p. 109.

36. Calculation based upon the only surviving civil establishment of the reign, dated 4 Feb. 1713/14, printed in *C.T.B.* XXVIII: viii–ix.

37. *Parl. Hist.* VI: 8–11; *C.T.B.* XVIII: v–xviii.

38. *C.T.B.* XVIII: vi.

39. 1 Anne c. 1; 2 and 3 Anne c. 3.

40. Burnet, *History* V: 4. See also the comment by Thomas Johnson in *The Norris Papers*, ed. T. Heywood (Chetham Soc., 1846), pp. 79–80.

41. See, for example, Burnet, *History* VI: 105–6, 173–74. See also Brewer, *Sinews of Power*, p. 40.

42. *Memoirs of the Duchess of Marlborough*, pp. 274–75; H.M.C., *Bathurst MSS* (1924), p. 4; Eg. MSS 1695, f. 7.

43. Boyer, *Annals* I: 20.

44. Ibid.; Burnet, *History* V: 4.

45. Calculation based upon "An account of what her Majesty has given out of the Civil List for the service of the public since her Majesty's accession to the Crown . . . ," dated 17 Jan. 1710–11 and printed in *C.T.B.* XXV: xxx–xxxiii. In 1710 a further £28,000 per annum was appropriated for public uses by act of parliament, 9 Anne c. 11. In 1713 another £35,000 per annum was taken away to pay the interest on the civil list lottery loan, 12 Anne c. 11. Finally, in 1714 the Queen promised a reward of £5,000 out of the civil list for the apprehension of the Pretender: D. Szechi, *Jacobitism and Tory Politics 1710–14* (Edinburgh, 1984), p. 172.

46. 2 and 3 Anne c. 20; J. M. Beattie, *English Court*, p. 107.
47. *C.T.B.* XXVIII: viii–ix.
48. For Fox, see Add. MSS 51324, ff. 44 recto and verso, 50 verso–51; for the Duchess of Marlborough, see below.
49. For the chamber establishment, see LC 5/202, pp. 125–32, summarized in *C.T.B.* XVII: 426–28; for the household below stairs, see LS 13/43.
50. These included one apothecary, four court drummers, five pensionary falconers, three grooms of the great chamber, ten messengers of the chamber, five house and wardrobe keepers, a page of the removing wardrobe, twelve pensionary watermen, and the keeper and repairer of pictures.
51. LS 13/258, p. 4; Burnet, *History* V: 63 n. Dartmouth.
52. LS 13/258, p. 17.
53. *C.T.B.* XVIII: 26; XIX: 64; LC 3/53, pp. 18, 47–48.
54. *C.T.B.* XVII: 34, 372–73; XVIII: 5, 26, 29, 272–74; XIX: 216; LC 5/108, warrants dated 23 May 1702, 19 May 1703.
55. *C.T.B.* XVIII: 313.
56. LS 13/43, f. 26 verso.
57. Add. MSS 61424, ff. 39 verso–40.
58. Add. MSS 61424, f. 17 verso. For a stronger statement, see Add. MSS 61425, f. 8 verso. For a more conservative one, see Add. MSS 61424, f. 29 verso.
59. Add. MSS 61420, ff. 103 verso–104; 61423, ff. 2 verso–3; *Memoirs of the Duchess of Marlborough*, p. 197.
60. Add. MSS 61424, ff. 39 verso–40; 61423, f. 3 verso.
61. See Add. MSS 61424, ff. 84, 112, for abstracts of Anne's robes expenses under Sarah and those of Queen Mary under Lady Derby: the average expense of the former was £2,199 13*s.* 0 ¾*d.* per annum, the latter £10,658 5*s.* 10 ½*d.*, for a savings of about £8,460 per annum, or £76,140 over nine years. Compare with the slightly different figures in *Memoirs of the Duchess of Marlborough*, pp. 195–97. In Add. MSS 61423, f. 164, Sarah estimates Mary of Modena's robes to have cost about £8,000 per annum, for an annual savings of about £5,800, or £52,200 over nine years.
62. See below, Chapter 6, sub "Influence."
63. See Gregg, *Anne*, p. 329; *Memoirs of the Duchess of Marlborough*, pp. 207–10.
64. Add. MSS 61416, f. 36 verso.
65. B.L. Loan 57/71, ff. 3, 5, 7 recto and verso, 13, 17, 19, 29 recto and verso; Add. MSS 61415, ff. 151–52; 61455, f. 62; *Clarendon Correspondence* II: 250, 314–16.
66. Add. MSS 61415, ff. 151–52.
67. Add. MSS 61418, f. 20: Anne to Sarah, n.d. [Apr. 1697] (copy by Sarah).
68. *C.T.B.* XVII: 21, 40, 56; XVIII: 25, 39, 49, 68; XIX: 31, 60; XX: 17, 80, and esp. 101.
69. Add. MSS 51324, f. 44.

70. Gregg, *Anne*, pp. 139, 157–58, 320.

71. See, for example, Add. MSS 61416, ff. 6, 111 verso–112 recto, 205 recto and verso; H.M.C., *Bathurst MSS*, pp. 8–9; H.M.C., *Bath MSS* I: 218, 225, 243; D. Green, *Gardener to Queen Anne*, pp. 65, 82, 89, 148–49; LC 5/154, p. 52.

72. *C.T.B.* XX: 101.

73. William's debts were to be paid out of the arrears that came in from his civil-list revenues. Since these were minuscule and subject to long delays, his servants were very much at Anne's mercy. At her accession she passed a privy seal intended to divert £20,000 out of her own revenue to her predecessor's debts, but her precarious financial position rendered this impossible to execute: see *C.T.B. 1695–1702*, Introduction, p. xli.

74. *C.T.B.* XVII: 42.

75. Ibid. XVIII: 50. For the identification of the painting, see Millar, *Tudor, Stuart . . . Pictures* I: 143.

76. *C.T.B.* XVIII: 50.

77. For Anne's generosity, see *Memoirs of the Duchess of Marlborough*, p. 275, and below, Chapter 5, sub "Tenure and Pensions." For her care of her establishments, see Add. MSS 61416, ff. 6, 205 recto and verso; H.M.C., *Bathurst MSS*, pp. 8–9; *C.T.B.* XVIII: 26, 40, 68; and above.

78. Most of the steady rise in civil expenditure through 1709–10 is explained by increased issues to the ambassadorial service (from £34,243 in 1702–3 to £56,542 in 1709–10); issues out of the civil revenues for "public uses" (over £31,000 annually from 1704 to 1708); and expenditure at Blenheim (over £34,000 annually from 1704 to 1710). A comparison of the civil-list revenue with issues to the civil departments (Table 2.1) shows that revenue, though averaging less than £700,000 per annum throughout the reign, was not exceeded by expenditure until exchequer year 1704–5. The civil-list accounts of income and expenditure printed in *C.T.B.* indicate that the surplus built up to Michaelmas 1704 was used to supply the shortfall from that date to Michaelmas 1705. Also, as early as exchequer year 1703–4, £33,300 from loans made on the security of the sale of the Queen's tin was applied to the civil list (*C.T.B.* XIX: clvii). In 1705–6, £76,987 16*s.* was applied (ibid. XXI: cxlii); in 1706–7, £107,689 5*s.* 4*d.* was applied (ibid. XXII: cxlix); and in 1709–10, £277,872 2*s.* 0 ½*d.* (ibid. XXIV: cxxiii). This source was supplemented in 1711–12 by tallies of anticipation and fictitious loan and, in 1713–14, by Oxford's civil-list lottery. Despite the apparent adequacy of these measures and the resultant neatness of the civil accounts as reproduced in *C.T.B.*, it should be understood that they took into account only money paid out, not wages or bills left unpaid (debt), for which we have only the various estimates and complaints noted in the present chapter.

79. *C.T.B.* XIX: 24; XX: 72.

80. LS 13/175, f. 37 verso.

81. Ibid., f. 47 recto.

82. *C.T.B.* XXIV: xxiv–vi.

83. LS 13/175, f. 69: Board of Greencloth to Lord Steward Devonshire, 29 May 1710.

84. Minney, *Hampton Court*, pp. 196–97.

85. T. Sharp, *The Life of John Sharp . . . Archbishop of York . . .* (1825), I: 325–26; A. T. Hart, *The Life and Times of John Sharp, Archbishop of York* (1949), pp. 222–23.

86. H.M.C., *Portland MSS* VIII: 292.

87. This impression derives from the relatively steady supply of the chamber in general (see Table 2.2); the absence of complaints by high-ranking chamber servants prior to 1710; and Hamilton's assertion, "There was but one half year owing me" at Godolphin's fall: *The Diary of Sir David Hamilton 1709–1714*, ed. P. Roberts (Oxford, 1975), p. 56.

88. See, for example, *C.T.B.* XVIII: 312, 414; XIX: 288–89, 373, 449; XX: 427–28, 528, 617, 694, 700; XXI: 61, 222, 332, 341; XXII: 301, 302; XXIII: 52, 242.

89. LS 13/175, ff. 48 verso–50 recto; 52–54.

90. *C.T.P. 1708–1714*, p. 394: William Vanbrugh to Secretary Lowndes, 12 June 1712.

91. *C.T.B.* XVIII: 26, 304–5, 316, 319.

92. LS 13/21.

93. See Add. MSS 22226, f. 158; 61416, f. 122 recto and verso; LS 13/176, f. 81; Luttrell, *Brief Relation* V: 423; VI: 155.

94. *C.T.B.* XIX: 34. Pensionary watermen continued to be paid to the end of the reign.

95. For specific instances of this, see ibid. XX: 553; LC 3/53, pp. 21, 45, 58–59, 62–63, 64.

96. LC 3/53, pp. 24–29, 33–34, 44, 46–47, 49–56, 78.

97. Calculation based on figures in Table 2.1.

98. Add. MSS 20101, f. 10.

99. *C.T.B.* XXVIII: viii–ix.

100. See *C.T.B.* XXIV: v–xxxviii; XXV: v–liii; A. McInnes, *Robert Harley, Puritan Politician* (1970), pp. 124–30.

101. *C.T.B.* XXIV: 36. For other instances of attendance by the Queen, see ibid., pp. 52, 67, 83, 106.

102. Ibid., p. 43.

103. Ibid., p. 45.

104. Ibid., pp. 47, 451.

105. J. M. Beattie, *English Court*, pp. 118–19.

106. For the most eloquent expression of the usual negative view of Oxford's treasurership, see William Shaw's comments in *C.T.B.* XXV: xxvii–xxxiv. For a corrective to this view, cf. B. W. Hill, *Robert Harley: Speaker, Secretary of State and Premier Minister* (New Haven, Conn., 1988), chaps. 10–14.

107. *C.T.B.* XXV: 110; XXVI: 126, 390, 398.

108. *London Gazette*, no. 4895, 1–4 Sept. 1711.

109. *C.T.B.* XXVI: 133, 155.

110. See J. M. Beattie, *English Court*, p. 124.

111. See LC 5/166, warrant of 20 Sept. 1712, which notes "her Majesty's leave" to Andrew Bertin to surrender—and, by implication, to sell—his messenger's place.

112. *C.T.B.* XXV: cxxxix.

113. LS 13/175, f. 85 verso: Board of Greencloth to the Lords of the Treasury, 3 Apr. 1711.

114. LS 13/175, f. 81 recto; *C.T.B.* XXV: 455. For tallies of fictitious loan, see Dickson, *Financial Revolution*, pp. 351–52.

115. LS 13/175, f. 99 recto and verso.

116. For another Whig view, see *Hamilton Diary*, p. 56; for that of the Tory Peter Wentworth, see Add. MSS 31144, f. 410 recto and verso. See also J. B. Curling, *Some Account of the Gentlemen at Arms* (1850), pp. 179–80; *Bolingbroke Correspondence* IV: 169, 233, 243–44.

117. *Hamilton Diary*, p. 56; Burnet, *History* VI: 105–6, 173–74; P. Wentworth et al., *The Wentworth Papers, 1705–1739*, ed. J. J. Cartwright (1883), p. 339. Oxford was certainly not above manipulating the shortage of funds for political purposes: see E. Gregg, *The Protestant Succession in International Politics, 1710–1716* (New York, 1986), p. 245; and below, Chapter 6, sub "Household Officers in Parliament."

118. *Hamilton Diary*, p. 56; H.M.C., *Bath MSS* I: 214, 218, 243; see also B.L. Loan 29/32, no. 44.

119. See esp. William Shaw's comments in *C.T.B.* XXVII: 492–94.

120. *Wentworth Papers*, p. 339; see also H.M.C., *Portland MSS* V: 467.

121. Printed in *C.T.B.* XXVIII: viii–ix.

122. Both figures include an estimated £20,000 for household officers paid at the exchequer.

123. LS 13/175, f. 104 recto: entry of 21 June 1714.

124. *C.T.B.* XXVII: 495–514.

125. See Dickson, *Financial Revolution*, pp. 74–75.

126. *C.T.B.* XXVIII: 101, 103, 106, 127–28.

127. H.M.C., *Portland MSS* V: 401: [Government Newsletter], 18 Mar. 1713/14.

128. Add. MSS 29267, f. 64. This figure includes the debt in the royal works but not that owed to servants paid at the exchequer; see also LS 13/175, f. 111 recto.

129. J. M. Beattie, *English Court*, p. 131.

130. For arrears owed to servants of Queen Anne under George I, see LS 13/176, pp. 27, 71, 86, 137, 163, 167, 168–70, 175; *C.T.B.* XXIX: 194, 195, 198, 211–18, 298, 333, 344–45, 423–24; XXX: 36, 240, 271, 415; XXXI: 34, 51, 129. For arrears still owed during the reign of George II, see W. Sussex R.O., Petworth House Archives, Somerset Papers, P.H.A. 322, 16 Aug. 1728, Duke of Somerset to the Lords of the Treasury (a statement of the debt owed to stables tradesmen

of Queen Anne); *C.T.B. & P. 1729–1730*, pp. 180, 181–83, 325; *C.T.B. & P. 1731–1734*, pp. 422, 600; *C.T.B & P. 1735–1738*, pp. 61, 328, 430.

Chapter III

1. T. F. Tout, "Literature and Learning in the English Civil Service in the Fourteenth Century," *Speculum* IV (1929): 366.

2. The biographical and genealogical information referred to in this and subsequent chapters and summarized in the various tables was obtained using the method pioneered (for modern English history, at least) by Sir Lewis Namier in *The Structure of Politics at the Accession of George III*, 2nd ed. (1957) (see esp. p. xiv), and Aylmer, *King's Servants* (see esp. p. 256). Briefly, it consists in tracing the household careers of Anne's servants through the court's departmental records and then tracing their lives outside the household through such standard publications as *D.N.B.*; the various peerages, baronetages, knightages, J. Burke's *Commoners* and *Gentry*; the admissions registers of Oxford and Cambridge; army, navy, and governmental departments' lists; and the wealth of printed genealogical material cited in the works of G. W. Marshall and his successors. For the most important of these sources, see below, Appendix B.

3. Add. MSS 61455, f. 69 recto; see also Add. MSS 17677 XX, f. 257. For Sarah's involvement in court patronage, see esp. Add. MSS 61474, passim; and below.

4. *Marlborough-Godolphin Correspondence*, p. 288: Godolphin to Sarah, "Wednesday Evening" [26 Apr. 1704]; see also ibid., p. 284.

5. H.M.C., *Downshire MSS* I ii, 867: Thomas Butler to Sir William Trumbull, 28 Dec. 1708.

6. *Marlborough-Godolphin Correspondence*, p. 887; Add. MSS 61417, f. 85.

7. H.M.C., *Portland MSS* V: 65: Lady Pye to Mrs. Abigail Harley, at Eywood, Derby, 28 July 1711; see also H.M.C., *Fifteenth Report*, App. IV (1897), p. 654.

8. See *Wentworth Papers*, pp. 118, 144, 150, 197, 225, 242, 249–50, 257, 262, 275, 280, 309; Add. MSS 22225, f. 220; 22226, ff. 52, 59, 79, 171. For d'Aumont's comment, see F. Salomon, *Geschichte des letzten Ministeriums Königin Annas von England (1710–1714) und der englischen Thronfolgefrage* (Gotha, 1894), p. 355.

9. See below, Chapter 4, sub "A Good Family."

10. LC 3/3 (unpag.), "Places in the Disposal of the Lord Chamberlain of His Ma[ts.] Household"; LC 3/4, p. 2; LS 13/199; LS 13/258–59; Add. MSS 61423, f. 163 verso; 61425, ff. 7 verso–8; Harl. MSS 1843, pp. 14–17; Curling, *Gentlemen at Arms*, pp. 132–35; J. M. Beattie, *English Court*, pp. 132–33, 166.

11. Add. MSS 61425, f. 7 [vacated].

12. Add. MSS 61415, f. 32 verso: Anne to Sarah, "Wed. night," n.d.; see also Add. MSS 61414, ff. 51, 57, 58, 66, 106; 61415, f. 152 verso.

13. See, for example, Add. MSS 61416, ff. 104 verso–105, 148, 150, 205 verso.

14. See Jonathan Swift's comment to John Gay, 12 June 1714, in *The Correspondence of Jonathan Swift*, ed. H. Williams (Oxford, 1963), II: 33.

15. See, for example, H.M.C., *Bathurst MSS*, p. 5; Add. MSS 61417, f. 85; 61425, f. 5; 61450, ff. 195–99 verso; Eg. MSS 1695, ff. 6–7. Sarah claimed in one version of her *Conduct*, "I did constantly write abundance of letters, in Answer to the Petitions and Applycations that were made, by which her Ma[ty] was pleased to say, I saved her a great deale of trouble" (Add. MSS 61423, ff. 183 verso–184).

16. See Add. MSS 61417, f. 186 verso; and below.

17. For reductions in the size of the royal household in 1702, see above, Chapter 2, sub "Finance."

18. See Gregg, *Anne*, pp. 85, 88.

19. Luttrell, *Brief Relation* V: 208.

20. LS 13/175, f. 24 verso (refers in passing to this order).

21. Gregg, *Anne*, pp. 78–79, 156.

22. Sir Benjamin Bathurst, named cofferer in 1702, had served as treasurer to the Duke of York and Princess Anne; he was married to Frances née Apsley, whose family had also been prominent at the courts of Charles II and James II. Dr. William Grahme, clerk of the closet 1702–13, was the brother of Richard Grahme, Viscount Preston, master of the great wardrobe 1686–88; and of James Grahme, keeper of the privy purse to James as Duke of York and as King 1679–88 and master of the buckhounds 1685–89. Col. Bernard Granville, carver 1702–14, was the son of Bernard Granville, groom of the bedchamber to Charles II; and nephew of the Earl of Bath, groom of the stole to the same. Lewis Oglethorpe, equerry 1702–4, was the son of Sir Theophilus Oglethorpe, equerry; and Eleanor née Wall, laundress; and nephew of Sutton, page of honor, to Charles II or James II. Rosamunda Yarborough, maid of honor 1702–4, was the daughter of Thomas Yarborough, groom of the bedchamber to Charles II and James II; and sister of Henrietta Maria Wyvill, maid of honor to Catherine of Braganza and Mary of Modena. The politics of each of the above families were demonstrably Tory. For sources, see Appendix B.

23. *The Old Cheque-Book, or Book of Remembrance, of the Chapel Royal, from 1561 to 1744*, ed. E. F. Rimbault (Camd. Soc., 1872), pp. 22, 24; LC 5/166, warrant dated 9 Nov. 1702.

24. *Memoirs of the Duchess of Marlborough*, p. 86.

25. For this policy, see G. S. Holmes, *British Politics*, pp. 191–92; H. L. Snyder, "Godolphin and Harley: A Study of Their Partnership in Politics," *H.L.Q.* XXX (1967): 245–46; for Anne's support of it, see Gregg, *Anne*, pp. 155–57.

26. *Memoirs of the Duchess of Marlborough*, p. 44; Gregg, *Anne*, pp. 66–67; *D.N.B.*, sub "William Cavendish, first Duke of Devonshire." It should be noted that the Duke hesitated to accept in the face of his friend Wharton's removal: see O. Klopp, *Der Fall des Hauses Stuart und die Succession des Hauses Hannover in Gross-Britannien und Irland* (Vienna, 1881–88), X: 38; Add. MSS 17677 XX, ff. 281–82.

27. See *Memoirs of the Duchess of Marlborough*, p. 44; *D.N.B.*, sub "Francis Newport, Earl of Bradford."

28. Information supplied by Eveline Cruickshanks and David Hayton; Add. MSS 61442, ff. 171–72 verso; Kenyon, *Sunderland*, pp. 326–27.

29. For Bigg , see *The History of Parliament: The House of Commons, 1660–1690*, ed. B. D. Henning (1983), sub "Walter Bigg"; *The History of Parliament: The House of Commons, 1715–1754*, ed. R. Sedgwick (1970), sub "John Bigg"; for Orme, see *C.T.P. 1702–1707*, p. 5; for Tyrrel, see *D.N.B.*, sub "James Tyrrel"; for Churchill, Evance, Lawrence, Meadows, and Rowe, information provided by Cruickshanks and Hayton.

30. Add. MSS 61425, f. 7 verso.

31. Add. MSS 61456, ff. 43 recto and verso, 46.

32. Add. MSS 61425, f. 7 verso.

33. See Gregg, *Anne*, p. 64, for Griffith's activities in 1688.

34. Add. MSS 61416, f. 205 verso: Anne to Sarah, Windsor, 3 Aug. [1705].

35. Gregg, *Anne*, pp. 87–88.

36. *Memoirs of the Duchess of Marlborough*, p. 50; Add. MSS 61456, ff. 10, 15, 20 recto and verso.

37. Add. MSS 61423, f. 162 verso.

38. Add. MSS 61474, f. 53 verso, for Ormonde; 61422, f. 158, for Somerset; 61463, f. 99, for Burlington; *Memoirs of the Duchess of Marlborough*, pp. 93–95, for Hyde; Add. MSS 61456, ff. 39–41, for Scarborough; 61416, f. 212, and *Memoirs of the Duchess of Marlborough*, p. 240, for Frescheville.

39. *Memoirs of the Duchess of Marlborough*, pp. 94–95, for Hyde; Add. MSS 61456, f. 41, for Scarborough. Neither the Duchess of Ormonde (Add. MSS 61474, ff. 52–53) nor the Duchess of Somerset (Add. MSS 61457, f. 1) in their letters of thanks to the Queen, conveyed through the Duchess of Marlborough, make the slightest mention of any obligation to Sarah except as a messenger.

40. See Add. MSS 61416, ff. 104–5, 205 recto and verso; 61456, f. 116; 61474, ff. 56 verso, 57, 185–86.

41. H.M.C., *Bathurst MSS*, pp. 7–8.

42. Add. MSS 61418, f. 40: Sarah to Anne, St. Albans, 29 Oct. 1709 (copy).

43. Add. MSS 31143, f. 328 verso: Wentworth to Lord Raby, London, 8 Apr. 1709.

44. Add. MSS 61443, f. 3; 61474, ff. 100, 104. Mansell was an associate of Robert Harley, who probably played a much greater role in his appointment.

45. Add. MSS 61449, f. 1; 61450, ff. 224–25 verso; 61451, f. 131.

46. H.M.C., *Buccleuch at Montagu House MSS* I: 352.

47. Add. MSS 61450, ff. 195–99 verso.

48. Add. MSS 61454, f. 133 recto and verso.

49. *Marlborough-Godolphin Correspondence*, p. 442: Godolphin to Sarah, "Munday at 2" [4 June 1705]. See also Add. MSS 61417, f. 186 verso.

50. *Memoirs of the Duchess of Marlborough*, p. 16.

51. See H.M.C., *Bathurst MSS*, pp. 8–9; Add. MSS 61417, ff. 173–74; 61454, f. 133 recto and verso.

52. *Marlborough-Godolphin Correspondence*, p. 887: Godolphin to Marlborough, Windsor, 19 Aug. 1707.

53. Ibid., p. 340: Marlborough to Sarah, "Aicha," [9]/20 July 1704. For the circumstances behind this promise, see ibid., pp. 60 n. 5, 162, 171, 310, 310 n. 3, 331.

54. See below, Chapter 4, sub "Politics."

55. Add. MSS 61425, f. 13 verso.

56. Add. MSS 61417, f. 186.

57. Add. MSS 61417, ff. 181–82. For Lady Scarborough's surprise that Mrs. Masham could be involved, see Add. MSS 61456, f. 58. The Whig Sir David Hamilton appears to have seen Danvers as an ally: *Hamilton Diary*, pp. 48, 62.

58. Add. MSS 61417, f. 183 verso: [Sarah] to Anne, 29 July 1709.

59. Ibid., ff. 187 verso–188 verso: [Sarah to Anne], St. James's, 6 Aug. 1709.

60. Add. MSS 61418, f. 11: [Sarah to Anne], St. Albans, 26 Oct. [1709].

61. Ibid., f. 14 recto and verso: [Anne to Sarah], Windsor, "Thurs." [27 Oct. 1709], rearranged to make Anne's argument clearer.

62. LC 3/4, p. 2; see also Worcestershire R.O., Henning Papers, BA 2252/2 (Bedchamber Ordinances of William III), p. 62.

63. H.M.C., *Ormonde MSS*, n.s., IV: 93, 139, 393–94; H.M.C., *Buccleuch at Montagu House MSS* II: 632; Harl. MSS 1843, pp. 15–16.

64. H.M.C., *Ormonde MSS*, n.s., IV: 93; V: 40, 610; Harl. MSS 1843, pp. 15–16.

65. LS 13/175, ff. 64 recto, 65 verso.

66. Ibid., f. 24 verso.

67. J. M. Beattie, *English Court*, pp. 135–38.

68. Add. MSS 61418, f. 26 verso: [Sarah to Anne], St. Albans, 29 Oct. 1709.

69. Add. MSS 61416, ff. 26–27 verso, 96 verso, 185 verso, 211; 61417, ff. 137–40, 182; 61418, ff. 40–41 verso; 61422, f. 156 recto and verso.

70. See J. Swift, "An Enquiry into the Behaviour of the Queen's Last Ministry," in idem, *Political Tracts 1713–19*, ed. H. Davis and I. Ehrenpreis (Oxford, 1953), p. 172n, for Swift's attribution of Mary Foysten's preferment, as starcher, to Mrs. Masham, the only such attribution I have been able to uncover.

71. See below, Chapter 6, sub "Information."

72. Burnet, *History* VI: 37 n. Dartmouth.

73. Eg. MSS 1695, f. 49: Shrewsbury to Viscountess Longueville, London, 21 Nov. 1711.

74. Swift, *Journal*, p. 206.

75. See below, Chapter 4, sub "Politics."

76. Gregg, *Anne*, p. 351; see also G. S. Holmes, *British Politics*, p. 390.

77. Add. MSS 22226, f. 171 recto and verso; Swift, *Journal*, pp. 206, 434, 435, 437, 443, 450, 451, 461, 467, 471, 482; *Wentworth Papers*, pp. 235, 270–71.

78. It should be noted that the Countess of Abingdon reluctantly resigned her place as a lady of the bedchamber in November 1705 at the instigation of

her husband, who had just been removed as constable of the Tower and lord lieutenant of Oxfordshire: H.M.C., *Fifteenth Report*, App. IV, p. 274. She was restored to her post in 1712.

79. *Swift Correspondence* I: 248: Swift to Archbishop King, [26 Aug. 1711].

80. *Wentworth Papers*, p. 311: Lord Berkeley of Stratton to the Earl of Strafford, 26 Dec. 1711.

81. Add. MSS 31144, f. 410 verso: Peter Wentworth to the Earl of Strafford, Windsor, 2 Sept. 1713. For evidence that Oxford was considering other candidates, see ibid., f. 408; B.L. Loan 29/311 m., f. 61 verso, Lansdowne to [Oxford], 18 Dec. 1712.

82. H.M.C., *Bath MSS* I: 237: Anne to Oxford, Windsor, 21 Aug. 1713.

83. For additional examples of such interference, see J. M. Rosenheim, *The Townshends of Raynham: Nobility in Transition in Restoration and Early Hanoverian England* (Middletown, Conn., 1989), p. 203 n. 57.

84. Add. MSS 61454, ff. 133, 196 verso; 61455, ff. 2 verso, 208 verso; 61457, ff. 4 verso, 6 verso; 61458, f. 136; 61463, f. 110; 61474, ff. 56 verso, 101, 150–51, 186; 61475, f. 11 verso.

85. Seven of Anne's bedchamber and robes servants can be traced to the Churchill household: Elizabeth Abrahall, starcher; William Lovegrove and Michael Woolrich, cofferbearers; George Curtis and William Forster, waiters to the robes; Charles Hodges, groom of the robes; and Rachel Thomas, "yeowoman" of the robes (Add. MSS 61425, f. 8). The Somersets preferred six servants into the bedchamber, robes, and stables: Nathaniel Bridgewater, cofferbearer and messenger of the avery; Edward Brockhurst, coachman: Henry Pigott, waiter; John Bowen, riding surveyor; Castleman Smith, stable keeper at Kensington; and Henry Stilbeck, groom (W. Sussex R.O., Petworth House Archives, Somerset Papers, P.H.A. 6322–25; 6329; 6330–31, passim). The Dukes of Devonshire preferred six servants into the household below stairs: Aaron Kenton, groom porter at gate; Henry Lowman, clerk of the kitchen; John Rivet, groom of the pantry; Thomas Rowe, gentleman harbinger; William Slatter, groom of the almonry; John Whildon, groom of the larder (Chatsworth House, Derbyshire, Whildon Collection, group B, v. 1–3; C, passim [esp. no. 44]; E, xciv, cix, cxix, cxxii, cxxix).

86. Add. MSS 61303, ff. 14–15; 61425, f. 3. For the term "yeowoman," see G. Miege, *The New State of England, Under Our Sovereign, Queen Anne* (1703), pt. III, p. 485.

87. See, for example, *Marlborough-Godolphin Correspondence*, pp. 1228, 1296, 1477, 1478, 1686; Add. MSS 61476, ff. 46–48; W. Sussex R.O., Petworth House Archives, Somerset Papers, P.H.A. 6329, passim; Chatsworth House, Derbyshire, Whildon Collection, group B, v. 1–35; C, passim; E, passim.

88. Add. MSS 61422, f. 159 verso.

89. H.M.C., *Buccleuch at Montagu House MSS* II ii, 628–53.

Chapter IV

1. Among the 62 officers who held clerical posts at court, only 11 had spent any time at university. Eight had attended an Inn of Court. (For the information contained in the tables and on specific individuals, see Appendix B, except where otherwise noted.)

2. For entrance examinations in the customs, see G. S. Holmes, *Augustan England: Professions, State and Society, 1680–1730* (1982), p. 252.

3. For the population and evidence for this analysis, see above, Chapter 3, nn. 2, 10.

4. For the "Ancient Order," see LS 13/171, pp. 270–71; J. M. Beattie, *English Court*, pp. 73, 168–71.

5. See below, sub "A Good Family."

6. Among the nineteen individuals who achieved the rank of sergeant, gentleman, or master cook under Queen Anne, eleven had risen from subordinate positions and five of these had begun their careers at the bottom of their subdepartments' hierarchies.

7. Among the gentlemen of the Queen's chapel who had been members of the choir as children were Jeremiah Clarke, William Croft, Thomas Edwards, Bernard Gates, and Samuel Wheeley.

8. The best-known example is Lord Monthermer's reversion to his father's mastership of the great wardrobe. This was a unique favor procured from the Queen by his mother-in-law, the Duchess of Marlborough, upon his marriage to her daughter, Mary, in 1705: *C.T.B.* XIX: 549; XX: 222. For evidence of another reversion granted by the board of greencloth, see LS 13/175, f. 58.

9. The usual justifications for naming servants to extraordinary or supernumerary positions were the possession of some distinguishing talent, the indisposition of an incumbent, or the early death of a relative in household office. See above, Chapter 1, n. 49, for Charles II's extraordinary servants. James II named about 100 of Charles's retrenched household and stables officers supernumerary at half pay until they could succeed to other posts on the establishment of 1685 (LS 13/38). William III named about 60 supernumerary or extraordinary officers during the course of his reign, including sewers and grooms of the chamber, messengers, watermen, and menials below stairs (see LS 13/256–57, passim; LC 3/3–4, 31–32, passim). Queen Anne named 17 extraordinary or supernumerary officers, including 2 physicians, 2 messengers, a clerk of the kitchen, a groom of the great chamber, a musician, a child of the scullery, and 9 gentlemen of the chapel (see LS 13/258–59, passim; LC 3/5–6, passim). For evidence of apprenticeship below stairs, see LS 13/175, f. 65 verso, and below, sub "Court Families."

10. See below, sub "Court Families."

11. *D.N.B.*, entries on John Adams, Henry Aldrich, Charles Ashton, Francis Atterbury, Thomas Bisse, Offspring Blackall, Samuel Bradford, Nicholas Brady,

Arthur Charlett, John Clarke, Sir William Dawes, Richard Duke, Jonathan Edwards, William Fleetwood, Robert Freind, Francis Gastrell, Edward Gee, Henry Hesketh, George Hooper, John Inett, William Jane, White Kennett, Thomas Manningham, John Mill, Robert Moss, John Potter, William Reeves, Nathaniell Resbury, Thomas Sherlock, William Sherlock, George Smalridge, Andrew Snape, George Stanhope, and William Wake. The sheer number of Anne's chaplains who appear in *D.N.B.* is itself evidence of the professional prominence required of those selected to preach before the Queen.

12. Sir Thomas Millington and Sir Hans Sloane, presidents; Millington, Sloane, John Arbuthnot, and Martin Lister, censors.

13. For publications, see *D.N.B.*, entries on John Arbuthnot, Sir David Hamilton, Martin Lister, and Sir Hans Sloane. For evidence of practice among the nobility, see ibid.; G. S. Holmes, *Augustan England*, p. 179; *Hamilton Diary*, pp. xx–xxi, xxvii–xxx; *Marlborough-Godolphin Correspondence*, pp. 150, 199; *The Private and Original Correspondence of Charles Talbot, Duke of Shrewsbury*, ed. W. Coxe (1821), p. 176; W. R. Munk, *The Roll of the Royal College of Physicians of London . . .* (1878), II: 37; H.M.C., *Twelfth Report*, App. II, p. 405; Add. MSS 61442, f. 60; E. L. Furdell, "The Medical Personnel at the Court of Queen Anne," *The Historian* XLVIII (1986): 415.

14. *Hamilton Diary*, pp. xx–xxi.

15. *D.N.B.*, sub "John Arbuthnot"; *London Gazette*, no. 4171, 29 Oct.–1 Nov. 1705.

16. *Marlborough-Godolphin Correspondence*, pp. 150–51, 199, 412; Luttrell, *Brief Relation* V: 413; Add. MSS 61346, passim; 61415, f. 120; 61475, f. 94. This reliance upon a candidate's "professional reputation"—or mere common fame—was not foolproof. Both of the Queen's oculists, Roger Grant and Sir William Read, were appointed on the strength of "having cured great Numbers in Her Majesty's Service, who have laboured under Distempers in the Eyes." However, both proved to be quacks: *London Gazette*, no. 4749, 26–28 Sept. 1710; *D.N.B.*, entries on Roger Grant and Sir William Read; G. S. Holmes, *Augustan England*, p. 7; *Remarks and Collections of Thomas Hearne*, ed. C. E. Doble (Oxford, 1885–1921), I: 54.

17. Gregg, *Anne*, p. 106; *Hamilton Diary*, p. xxvi; *The Epistolary Correspondence, Visitation Charges, Speeches, and Miscellanies, of the Right Reverend Francis Atterbury, D.D. Lord Bishop of Rochester* (1784), III: 81–82, 185–86n. Radcliffe also disapproved of the Revolution: see Furdell, "Medical Personnel," p. 415.

18. See R. I. Cook, *Sir Samuel Garth* (Boston, 1980), pp. 12–14, for Garth's politics and skepticism.

19. See J. Swift, *Historical and Political Tracts—English*, vol. 5 of *The Prose Works of Jonathan Swift D.D.*, ed. T. Scott (1911), p. 477; *Swift Correspondence* II: 62–63.

20. See below, Chapter 7, sub "Art"; and Burrows, "Handel," passim, esp. I: 60–71, 82–83, 415–16.

21. The medical personnel were Calverley Leigh, M.D. Oxon., gentleman

pensioner; John Stone senior, apothecary, groom of the great chamber; and Cornelius Tilburgh, M. D. Cantab., carver. The lawyers were William Collier, gentleman of the privy chamber; John Darley, gentleman pensioner; and George Morley, successively sewer, then carver, in ordinary.

22. H.M.C., *Portland MSS* V: 118.

23. *D.N.B.*, entry on his son, Andrew Snape.

24. H.M.C., *Eleventh Report*, App. V, p. 123; Staffordshire R.O., Dartmouth MSS D 1778, no. 132, petition of Walter Furnis, groom saddler, n.d.; W. Sussex R.O., Petworth House Archives, Somerset Papers, P.H.A. 6322, nos. 12, 22; 6323, no. 59a; 6330, passim; 6331, Henry Pigott to Samuel Taylor, 3 Aug. 1703.

25. H.M.C., *Buccleuch at Montagu House MSS* II ii, 477: Shrewsbury to Secretary [William] Blathwayt, Grafton, 9 June 1697.

26. H.M.C., *Bath MSS* I: 219: Shrewsbury to Oxford, Mon. [June 1712]. For Cardigan's sporting interests, see Eg. MSS 1695, f. 43 verso.

27. Add. MSS 61417, f. 186 verso.

28. Add. MSS 61423, f. 162 verso. This does not mean that continued employment in the bedchamber was contingent on a spouse's loyalty to the administration: see above, Chapter 3.

29. The five were Feilding, Holland, Townshend, Walpole, and Windham. All sat in parliament at the time of their appointments except Windham; his brother, Ashe, was knight of the shire for the county 1708–10 (see G. S. Holmes, *British Politics*, pp. 230–35, and sources noted Appendix B).

30. For the political leanings of these men, see the sources noted below, Appendix B. I am indebted to Drs. Eveline Cruickshanks and David Hayton for allowing me to examine material to be included in the forthcoming *History of Parliament, 1690–1715*.

31. Ladies Abingdon and Marlborough resigned their bedchamber places in 1705 and 1711, respectively. The removal of the two Churchill daughters in 1712, like the fall of their mother, involved personal as well as political considerations. It should also be pointed out that, apart from the bedchamber politicking of the Churchills, the Hill sisters, and the Duchess of Somerset, there was relatively little activity of this kind on behalf of parents, siblings, spouses, etc.: see below, Chapter 6, sub "Influence."

32. Add. MSS 61459, f. 52 recto and verso: Maynwaring to Sarah, "Tues. nine a clock" [?1708]. For Kent's reputation, see G. S. Holmes, *British Politics*, pp. 211, 227–28.

33. For Coke's Toryism, see Horwitz, *William III*, pp. 266, 300, 302; G. S. Holmes, *British Politics*, p. 50; but in the latter work cf. also pp. 138, 263 and n, 264, 270 n. For Offley's Whiggery, see *History of Parliament*, ed. Sedgwick, sub "Crewe Offley."

34. See sources noted below, Appendix B.

35. See H.M.C., *Buccleuch at Montagu House MSS* II ii, 637, for Stone; LS 13/115, ff. 58 verso, 60 verso; LS 13/176, p. 215, for the political significance of household purveyors.

36. H.M.C., *Eighth Report*, App. I (1881), p. 52; for Somerset's holdings, see R. Walcott, *English Politics in the Early Eighteenth Century* (Oxford, 1956), p. 50.

37. Burnet, *History* V: 141–42. In a similar vein, the French ambassador, d'Aumont, observed of Lord Steward Poulett that he was "tres riche, honneste homme, et d'un génie assez médiocre" (Salomon, *Geschichte*, p. 354).

38. See below, Chapter 6, sub "Household Officers in Parliament."

39. Officers are considered to have owned land if their discovered place of residence cannot be identified with a city or town. The wives or daughters of landowners are not considered in the above to have owned land. However, the landed estates possessed by the immediate male relatives of eleven ladies of the bedchamber, six maids of honor, and three dressers undoubtedly contributed to their appointments.

40. For example, while the great officers included nineteen lords lieutenant, below this level only nine sheriffs and eight justices of the peace have been identified.

41. Sir Charles Dalton of Hawkswell, Yorkshire, gentleman usher 1702–47, and his cousin Anne, daughter of Sir Marmaduke Wyvill of Constable Burton, Yorkshire, maid of honor 1707–14, were nephew and niece of Rosamunda, daughter of Sir Thomas Yarborough of Balne Hall and Snaith, Yorkshire. Rosamunda was a maid of honor 1702–4. The connections between these families dated from at least the Restoration, as did their record of court service: see sources cited, Appendix B. Sir Robert Dacres of Cheshunt, Hertfordshire, gentleman pensioner 1668–90, gentleman of the privy chamber 1691–1703, was the father of Thomas Dacres of the same, gentleman of the privy chamber 1705–27. Edmund Dummer of Swathling, Hampshire, clerk of the great wardrobe 1706–27, was the brother of Thomas Dummer of the same, portitior and tailor of the great wardrobe 1706–14, deputy master and underclerk of the great wardrobe 1707–?. Thomas's son, Thomas Lee Dummer, succeeded his uncle Edmund as clerk of the department in 1727. Solomon Eccles of Guildford, Surrey, musician in ordinary 1685–1710, was probably the brother of John Eccles of Kingston-upon-Thames, musician 1696–1700, master of the musick 1700–35. Both were probably related to Henry Eccles, musician in ordinary 1688–1711, who, however, settled in the parish of St. Martin's-in-the-Fields, Middlesex. Sir Charles Napier of Pucknall, Dorset, gentleman of the privy chamber 1697–1714, the son of Sir Robert Napier, gentleman of the privy chamber 1689–97, was a cousin of Sir Nathaniel Napier of Middlemarsh Hall and Mare Critchall, Dorset, gentleman of the privy chamber 1704–9.

42. They were William Bowen, comedian in ordinary 1689–1717; Nicholas Brady, chaplain in ordinary circa 1699–1714; Robert Bulkeley, purveyor and equerry 1696–1702; Joseph Burgeias, tailor to the great wardrobe ?–1707; Hugh, Earl of Cholmondeley, comptroller, then treasurer of the household 1708–13; Thomas Meredith, equerry 1704–10; Sir Hans Sloane, physician in extraordinary 1712–14, in ordinary 1727–53; Sir John Stanley, secretary to the lord

chamberlain 1697–1719; Nahum Tate, poet laureate 1692–1715; Agmondisham Vesey, gentleman of the privy chamber ?1704–14; John Walsh, instrument maker 1692–1731; Robert Wilks, comedian in ordinary 1699–1732. Meredith and Wilks had served in William's army as a captain and clerk of the camp, respectively (see sources noted Appendix B).

43. H.M.C., *Fourteenth Report*, App. III (1894), p. 207: Godolphin to Lord Seafield, 18 Aug. 1705.

44. Add. MSS 61456, f. 46. See ibid., f. 43 recto and verso, for the Countess's recommendation of her cousin Jeremiah Chaplaine to be a gentleman usher, stressing his family's poverty. She would later call the Queen's compliance "a great charity" (f. 46).

45. Burnet, *History* V: 141–42.

46. Add. MSS 22226, f. 52: Lady Strafford to the Earl of Strafford, 25 Dec. 1711.

47. Add. MSS 22229, ff. 144–45: William Wentworth, [gentleman usher to the Prince of Wales], to the Earl of Strafford, 13 Jan 1735/36.

48. At Huntercombe, Buckinghamshire; Dothill Park, Shropshire; and Sarsden, Oxfordshire, respectively.

49. See Harl. Soc. no. 8, *Le Neve's Pedigrees of the Knights*, for the possibility that Oldes may have started out as gentleman usher to the Duchess of Rutland.

50. Sources noted in Appendix B; L. Stone and J. C. Fawtier Stone, *An Open Elite? England 1540–1880* (Oxford, 1984), p. 199.

51. At Maplethorpe, Lincolnshire; Wormly, Hertfordshire; and East Combe, Kent, respectively. It is true that Chaplaine's estate was in financial difficulties (see above, n. 44), but so, apparently, were those of Griffith and Rowe: see Add. MSS 61422, f. 175; *C.T.B.* XIX: 63; XXI: 94; LS 13/175, f. 42 recto and verso.

52. Sources noted Appendix B.

53. To take three simple measurements of social status, out of a total of 71 gentlemen of the privy chamber, 34 can be shown to have owned land, 14 were M.P.s, and a further 15 can be shown to have been closely related to an M.P. or peer.

54. Gretton, clerk of the poultry and bakehouse, entered the household as an underclerk of the spicery, served for 42 years, and was probably related to Grace Gretton, whose husband had been a groom of Charles II's woodyard (*C.T.B.* VIII: 1644). Lowman, clerk of the kitchen, began as a clerk of the acatry, served 53 years, and was married to Mary Lowman, seamstress to William III and George I. Price, clerk of the acatry, began as an underclerk of the accompting house, served for 51 years, and was probably the son of William Price, chamber keeper to the grooms of the bedchamber (LS 13/231, f. 10); or was possibly related to William Price, yeoman of the salt stores to George I. Shaw, clerk of the poultry and bakehouse, began as a groom of the accompting house, and served for 42 years. Shaw married Mary Dryden, a relative of John Dryden, the poet laureate. For courtesy esquire status, see Appendix A.

55. Chatsworth House, Derbyshire, Whildon Collection, group B, v. 5; *Wentworth Papers*, p. 422; Add. MSS 31144, f. 413 verso; J. M. Beattie, *English Court*, p. 74.

56. See Aylmer, *King's Servants*, p. 111.

57. Sources noted Appendix B.

58. See below, Chapter 5, sub "Attendance and Work."

59. Add. MSS 61422, f. 197. In addition to Abigail and Alice Hill and Beata and Isabella Danvers, Isabella Arundell, woman of the bedchamber; Elizabeth Atkinson, laundress; and Anne Rhansford, seamstress, appear to fit the picture of decayed or impoverished gentility delineated above.

60. Burnet, *History* VI: 36–37 n. Dartmouth.

61. Sources noted Appendix B; Gregg, *Anne*, p. 290.

62. Sources noted Appendix B; Add. MSS 61424, f. 30 verso; 61425, f. 8.

63. Elizabeth Collier married the Earl of Dorset. Anne Duncombe married the Earl of Deloraine. Jane Warburton married the Duke of Argyll. In addition, Mary Stanhope married Charles, afterwards Viscount Fane.

64. Sir Charles Lodowick Cotterell, master of the ceremonies 1686–1710, had succeeded his father, Sir Charles Cotterell. Sir Charles Lodowick was in turn succeeded by his son, Sir Clement Cotterell, afterwards Cotterell-Dormer, who was succeeded, in turn, by *his* son, Sir Charles Cotterell-Dormer, in 1758. John Warner junior, master of the barges 1694–1713, had succeeded his father, John senior, who had previously succeeded *his* father, Noel Warner, circa 1663. Sir Philip Meadows, knight marshal 1700–1757, was succeeded at his death by his son, Sidney. Sir Philip had originally purchased the office from Edward Villiers, Earl of Jersey, who had succeeded his father, Sir Edward Villiers, in 1689. Anne's library keeper, Dr. Richard Bentley, surrendered that place to his son, Richard, in 1725. Her first sergeant trumpeter, William Shore, had succeeded his father, Matthias, in 1700.

65. See Gregg, *Anne*, pp. 141, 195–96, 325, 327–28.

66. Sources noted Appendix B; LS 13/174, pp. 149–51.

67. LS 13/175, f. 70.

68. Claud Arnaud senior, John Dissel, and Michael Hounsliffe procured places for their sons, Claud junior, Richard, and William, who rose to become a clerk and yeomen of the kitchen, respectively.

69. Altogether, "family"—whether at court or otherwise—can be identified for 624, or 40.9 percent, of the 1,525 individuals at the court of Queen Anne. This figure includes all 55 of those at the top and over half (319, or 58.6 percent) of the 544 officers at the middle rank of household service. Of this group, (i.e., the 624 household servants for whom family has been identified), 327, or 52.4 percent, can be demonstrated to have had relatives at court, 1660–1760 (Table 4.6, column 1). A comparison of this figure to the composite figures given in Table 4.6, columns 3–4, suggests that, if anything, the composite figures slightly underestimate the degree of interrelatedness among court servants.

70. The Tory families proscribed at the time of the Queen's death were one branch of the Duncombes, the Oglethorpes, Pinckneys, Progers, Somersets, Souths, Walters, and Yarboroughs.

71. Coke married Mary Hales in 1709; Fane married Mary Stanhope in 1707.

72. Sources noted Appendix B, esp. *Miscellanea Genealogica et Heraldica*, n.s., II: 270; and LC 5/157, pp. 289–92 (will of John Incledon).

73. Sidney, Earl of Godolphin, and Robert, Earl of Sunderland, had begun their careers as a page of honor and a gentleman of the bedchamber, respectively, in the bedchamber of Charles II.

74. Add. MSS 47027, p. 355, quoted in J. M. Beattie, *English Court*, pp. 158–59.

75. For evidence of the Marlboroughs' involvement in many of the above appointments, see Add. MSS 61415, f. 32 verso; 61416, f. 205 recto; 61443, f. 3; 61449, f. 1; 61450, ff. 224–25; 61454, ff. 133–36; Bodl. Lister MSS 4, ff. 5–6 verso, 10; Gregg, *Anne*, pp. 195–96; *Marlborough-Godolphin Correspondence*, pp. 162, 288, 310 and n. For their preferment of personal servants, see above, Chapter 3. It is probable that many of the 93 army officers preferred into Anne's household also owed their places to the captain general or his wife (Table 4.3, sub "Breakdown by Occupation"; sources noted Appendix B).

76. John, Lord Granville, underhousekeeper of St. James's 1703–7, was the son of John Granville, Earl of Bath, groom of the stole to Charles II. Bath's brother, Bernard Granville, was a groom of the bedchamber to the same monarch. His two sons were George Granville, Lord Lansdowne, comptroller 1712–13, treasurer of the household 1713–14; and Bernard junior, carver 1702–14. Their sister, Anne, married Sir John Stanley, baronet, secretary to the lord chamberlain 1697–1719. Lansdowne himself married Lady Mary Villiers, daughter of Edward, Earl of Jersey, thus allying the Granvilles with the other great Tory court family (see below, n. 77).

77. Sir Edward Villiers, knight marshal to Charles II and James II, master of the robes and groom of the bedchamber to the Duke of York, was related to the first and second Dukes of Buckingham, sometime masters of the horse and gentlemen of the bedchamber to James I, Charles I, and Charles II. Villiers's wife, Frances née Howard, was governess to Princesses Mary and Anne. Villiers's son, Edward, rose to be knight marshal 1689–1700, and, as Earl of Jersey, lord chamberlain 1700–1704. Jersey's sister, Barbara, was governess to the Duke of Gloucester and the wife of John, Lord Fitzharding, master of the horse to Princess Anne and treasurer of the chamber 1702–12. Another sister, Anne, married the Earl of Portland, groom of the stole and keeper of the privy purse to William III. A third sister, Elizabeth, married the Earl of Orkney, gentleman of the bedchamber to George I. Jersey himself married Barbara, daughter of William Chiffinch, closet keeper to Charles II. Their daughter, Mary, married George Granville, Lord Lansdowne, comptroller and treasurer of the household to Queen Anne.

78. William Cavendish, first Duke of Devonshire, was lord steward 1689–

1707. His son, the Marquess of Hartington and afterwards second Duke, was captain of the yeomen of the guard 1702–7, lord steward 1707–10 and 1714–16. The latter's wife, Rachel, was a lady of the bedchamber 1702–14. The first Duke's natural son, Philip Cavendish, was sergeant porter 1705–36. The third Duke was captain of the gentlemen pensioners 1726–31, lord steward 1733–37 and 1745–49. The fourth Duke was master of the horse 1751–55 and lord chamberlain 1757–62.

79. Among those with the surname Russell (whom I have largely been unable to link together), Lord Edward Russell was treasurer of the chamber 1693–1702. Francis Russell was an esquire of the body circa 1682–87 and a groom of the bedchamber 1685–86. Philip Russell was a groom of the great chamber in extraordinary from 1708. Robert Russell was a messenger of the chamber in 1695, a cupbearer 1701–18, and, if the same man, underhousekeeper at Newmarket from 1720. This suggests a connection with the William Russell who was sergeant of the hawks 1689–1703 and underhousekeeper at Newmarket 1707–20. The latter was, in turn, quite possibly related to George Russell, sergeant of the falconers to Charles II. Sir William Russell, baronet, a gentleman of the privy chamber 1690–1707, was, respectively, father and grandfather to two bedchamber women to Princess Amelia.

80. Charles Bland, who succeeded his brother, Edward, as page of the robes in 1700, was also clerk, storekeeper, and deputy master of the great wardrobe 1684–1707. A John Bland was tailor to the great wardrobe until 1705. For the Dummers, see above, n. 41. Francis, Thomas, and William Elrington were tailors to the great wardrobe 1709–26, 1689–21, and 1726–?, respectively. John Elrington was an arrasmaker 1703–7, clerk and storekeeper to the great wardrobe 1707–24. The first and second Dukes of Montagu between them held the mastership of the department 1671–86 and 1689–1749. The first Duke had succeeded a brother as master of the horse to Queen Catherine 1665–78. He purchased the mastership of the great wardrobe from his cousin, Edward Montagu, Earl of Sandwich, who had held it since the Restoration. The second Duke was also captain of the gentlemen pensioners 1734–40.

81. Joseph Centlivre, husband of the dramatist, was a yeoman and cook of the kitchen 1683–1725. He was probably related to Edward Centlivre, child of the kitchen 1708–14, and may have been the father of Joseph Centlivre, child of the chapel circa 1710–15. For Samuel and Robert Chambers, both of the scullery, see above. Thomas Chambers was a turnbroach of the kitchen to Charles II, and Hubert William Chambers was a child of the kitchen to George II. Alexander Murray was a breadbearer to James II. John Murray was first a page, then a groom of the buttery 1671–1707. A William Murray was a groom of the pastry 1689–95; another was a furner to the same department 1712–28. Charles Parsons was marshal of the hall 1689–1718. Edward Parsons was messenger of the avery 1689–1702 and, successively, tailcartaker, groom, and yeoman of the accompting house 1702–14 and clerk of the woodyard, scullery, and pastry 1714–52. He was succeeded in the last post by his son Philip. A Robert Parsons

served in Charles II's pantry; another was a yeoman harbinger 1717–30. A Charles Price was groom of the cellar 1702–12. John Price was an underclerk, then clerk of various offices 1693–1727. William Price was yeoman of the salt stores 1717–30. Charles Salter was a tallow chandler 1704–14. Edward Salter was an underclerk of the spicery circa 1708–28. Thomas Salter was, successively, child, groom, and yeoman of the pastry 1689–1729. The senior and junior John Webbs were both turnbroaches of the kitchen under James II and William III. Roger Webb was gentleman and yeoman of the buttery 1702–7. A Thomas Webb was clerk of, successively, the woodyard, the bakehouse, and the kitchen 1685–1702; another was, successively, a scourer, child, and groom of the kitchen 1702–21.

82. The Killigrew court connection dated at least to the reign of Queen Elizabeth, who employed Sir William Killigrew as a groom of the privy chamber. His son, Sir Robert Killigrew, was vice chamberlain to Henrietta Maria. *His* son Thomas Killigrew, the dramatist, was groom of the bedchamber and master of the revels to Charles II. His second wife, Charlotte, was keeper of the sweet coffers and lady of the privy chamber to Catherine of Braganza. Thomas's oldest son (by his first wife), Henry, was a groom of the bedchamber 1662–74 and gentleman of the privy chamber 1690–1705, and is listed in household records as a "jester" to William III (LC 5/43, f. 87 verso; LC 5/69, f. 79 verso). Henry's younger brother, Charles, was gentleman of the privy chamber 1670–1702, master of the revels 1680–1725. His son Guildford was page of honor 1714–27. Another son of Sir Robert Killigrew, Sir William, was a gentleman usher to Charles I and vice chamberlain to Catherine of Braganza. *His* son, William, was a gentleman of the privy chamber 1689–1708. Finally, a Sir Robert Killigrew was gentleman of the privy chamber circa 1670–1706, carver 1690–92. For the Russells, see above, n. 79.

83. Noel Warner, 1614–1663. John Warner senior, 1663–85 and 1687–94. Daniel Hill, 1685–87. John Warner junior, 1694–1713. Christopher Hill, 1713–19. John Hill, 1719–27. Robert Mason, 1727–36.

84. Add. MSS 61416, f. 106 recto and verso: Anne to Sarah, "Tues.," 29 June [1703].

Chapter V

1. For establishments and ordinances, see above, Chapter 2, n. 4; and *A Collection of Ordinances and Regulations for the Government of the Royal Household . . . from King Edward III to King William and Queen Mary* (Society of Antiquaries, 1790). The most useful guidebooks are E. (from 1704, J.) Chamberlayne, *Anglia Notitia; or, The Present State of England*, 22 edns. (1669–1707); J. Chamberlayne, *Magnae Britanniae Notitia*, 16 edns. (1708–55); G. Miege, *The New State of England*, 6 edns. (1691–1707); idem, *The Present State of Great Britain*, 11 edns. (1707–48); (anon.) *Present State of the British Court* (1720).

2. *Memoirs of the Life of Sir John Clerk of Penicuik, Baronet . . . 1676–1755*, ed.

J. M. Gray (Roxburgh Club, 1895), p. 72. The French envoy, Mesnager, found the court equally deserted during what was, admittedly, a secret audience with the Queen in September 1711: see P.R.O. 31/3/197, f. 98.

3. H.M.C., *Bath MSS* I: 201: Shrewsbury to [Robert Harley], 25 Apr. 1711. See also H.M.C., *Portland MSS* V: 463–64; Add. MSS 22225, f. 298; Burnet, *History* VI: 43–44 n. Dartmouth. Anne's court appears to have been equally deserted before her accession as Queen: see ibid. V: 8.

4. See Aylmer, "Officeholding to Civil Service," p. 106; idem, *King's Servants*, p. 132; G. S. Holmes, *Augustan England*, p. 255.

5. For household salaries and emoluments, see the establishments listed above, Chapter 2, n. 4. For biographical information, see sources noted Appendix B.

6. H.M.C., *Downshire MSS* I ii, 894: Poulett to Trumbull, 30 June 1711.

7. For great officers fulfilling each of these duties, see LS 13/21; LS 13/175, ff. 24 verso, 37 verso, 47, 81, 83 recto, 96, 98 verso, 103 verso, 104, 106 recto and verso; LC 5/3, pp. 3, 8; H.M.C., *Portland MSS* V: 19–20, 163; H.M.C., *Buccleuch at Montagu House MSS* II ii, 628–53. Lord steward's warrants of appointment are contained in LS 13/259; lord chamberlain's warrants are contained in LC 5/70–71; LC 5/116; LC 5/125–26; LC 5/153–55.

8. See, for example, LC 5/3, pp. 1, 3, 8–9; Luttrell, *Brief Relation* V: 463, 585; VI: 207; Boyer, *Annals* I: 139–41; III: 96–97; IV: 81–84; V: 151–53; VI: 224; VII: 247–49.

9. For Kent's delegating of authority, see Gloucester R.O., Lloyd-Baker-Sharp MSS, box 4, B-15: Kent to Archbishop Sharp, London, [18 Apr. 1706]. For the elder Montagu's absences from court, see Add. MSS 61450, f. 199 verso; for the younger Montagu's, see *Memoirs of the Duchess of Marlborough*, p. 304; J. M. Beattie, *English Court*, p. 51.

10. Boyer, *Annals* V: 4–5; LC 5/3, p. 8; H.M.C., *Twelfth Report*, App. III, p. 181.

11. Townshend was ambassador extraordinary and plenipotentiary to the States General from May 1709 to February 1711. Shrewsbury was ambassador extraordinary to France, November 1712 to September 1713; and lord lieutenant of Ireland, September 1713 to October 1714 (returned in June).

12. For Coke and Somerset, see above, Chapter 2, sub "Administration." For Sharp, see Sharp, *Life of John Sharp* I: 325–27, 330; Hart, *Life and Times of John Sharp*, pp. 220–22, 225–26.

13. For Ormonde's absences, see H.M.C., *Ormonde MSS*, n.s., VIII: xxxviii–xliv; Boyer, *Annals* II: 232. For the illnesses of other ladies, see H.M.C., *Buccleuch at Montagu House MSS* I, 352; *Hamilton Diary*, p. 57; *Wentworth Papers*, p. 395; Add. MSS 22226, f. 74; 61416, f. 205 verso; 61456, ff. 65, 70; Eg. MSS 1695, f. 5; Chatsworth House, Derbyshire, Devonshire MSS 117. For the ladies attending, see *Marlborough-Godolphin Correspondence*, p. 676; Swift, *Journal*, p. 451; Luttrell, *Brief Relation* V: 463, 492; H.M.C., *Hamilton MSS*, suppl. (1932),

p. 156; H.M.C., *Lindsey MSS*, suppl. (1942), p. 52; *Wentworth Papers*, p. 250; Add. MSS 17677 EEE, f. 119; HHH, f. 18; 22225, f. 298; 22226, ff. 66, 71 verso, 109, 258; 31144, f. 396; 61432, f. 82 recto and verso; 61442, ff. 5 verso, 40; 61456, f. 58; S.P. Dom. 34/32, f. 131; Chatsworth House, Derbyshire, Devonshire MSS 107.1, 117, 117.1; J. MacPherson, ed., *Original Papers Containing the Secret History of Great Britain, from the Restoration, to the Accession of the House of Hannover* (1775), II: 528, 533. For increased attendance during times of political crisis, see below, Chapter 6; and Add. MSS 61422, ff. 62–69 verso.

14. See note 13 above, and H.M.C., *Lindsey MSS*, suppl., p. 52; *Wentworth Papers*, p. 250; *Swift Correspondence* I: 214; Add. MSS 22225, f. 262; 22226, f. 244; 61422, ff. 62–63; S. S. Cohen, "The Diary of Jeremiah Dummer," *William and Mary Quarterly*, 3rd ser., XXIV (1967): 409; and below.

15. For gambling at Anne's court, see *Wentworth Papers*, p. 307; H.M.C., *Portland MSS* V: 463; Luttrell, *Brief Relation* V: 375; D. Green, *Queen Anne* (1970), pp. 281, 300; Add. MSS 17677 GGG, ff. 29 verso, 36, 67 verso; 61414, f. 119 verso; 61416, f. 3; 61422, ff. 62 verso, 175 verso.

16. *Memoirs of the Duchess of Marlborough*, p. 275; Add. MSS 61423, f. 1 verso: Sarah to [Sir David Hamilton], 16 Mar. 1710. For evidence of boredom among the other ladies, see Chatsworth House, Derbyshire, Devonshire MSS 117.1.

17. J. M. Beattie, *English Court*, pp. 73–83; and above, Chapter 2, sub "Administration."

18. See, for example, the career of Rachel Thomas, "yeowoman" of the robes: Add. MSS 61423, f. 163 verso; 61425, f. 3; and above, Chapter 3.

19. See above, Chapter 4, sub "A Good Family."

20. Small groups of gentlemen, ranging from 6 to 24, were required to attend coronations, funerals, thanksgivings, and ambassadorial entrances, upon which occasions they were allowed dinner: Boyer, *Annals* V: 4, 5, 152; LC 2/14; LC 5/3, pp. 4–5, 8–9; LC 5/70, p. 156; LC 5/153, p. 240; LC 5/156, p. 22; *Evening Post*, no. 610, 4–7 July 1713. The post had lost the remainder of its duties and payment under the later Stuarts: see N. Carlisle, *An Inquiry into the Place and Quality of the Gentlemen of His Majesty's Most Honourable Privy Chamber* (1829), pp. 154, 160, 163; J. M. Beattie, *English Court*, pp. 30–35.

21. While the yeomen of the guard, pages of the presence, and grooms of the great chamber were, technically, of inferior status at court (see Appendix A), their ceremonial role in the public rooms makes it advisable to include them in this discussion.

22. *A Collection of Ordinances and Regulations*, pp. 355, 369, 374. In 1729 the equerry Peter Wentworth described a similar schedule: Add. MSS 22227, f. 87 verso.

23. For the genesis of the public rooms, see H. M. Baillie, "Baroque Palaces," pp. 172–81; Starkey, "Intimacy and Innovation," passim; Cuddy, "Revival of Entourage," passim; J. M. Beattie, *English Court*, pp. 6–10.

24. *Household Ordinances*, pp. 353–57, 360–62, 368–79; J. M. Beattie, *English Court*, pp. 29–46. The gentleman usher assistant, who aided the daily waiter, appears to have attended year round: see J. M. Beattie, *English Court*, p. 39.

25. H.M.C., *Portland MSS* V: 222; H.M.C., *Lindsey MSS*, suppl., p. 52; *Hamilton Diary*, p. 64; *Wentworth Papers*, pp. 234–35; *Memoirs of the Duchess of Marlborough*, pp. 146–47, 170; Add. MSS 22225, f. 298; 22226, ff. 50, 66, 244, 258; 31143, f. 486 verso; 31144, ff. 357–58.

26. Add. MSS 31144, ff. 247, 257 verso, 274 verso; *Wentworth Papers*, pp. 184, 208.

27. Quoted in *Parl. Hist.* VI: 1370.

28. LC 5/154, p. 39.

29. Ibid., pp. 339, 366. The officer, Edward Harrison, was restored on 4 September and was dead by 10 December. It is probable that his earlier absence was due to illness.

30. Charles II's lords chamberlain issued fifteen orders for chamber servants to attend and suspended or dismissed four officers for not doing so in the course of his reign. (LC 5/14, p. 66; LC 5/16, pp. 35, 142; LC 5/141, pp. 32, 34, 298, 429, 464; LC 5/143, pp. 141, 175–76, 188–89, 255–56, 337; LC 5/144, p. 434; LC 5/145, p. 81). James II issued seven such orders and disciplined two men (LC 5/145, pp. 208–10, 212, 215; LC 5/147, p. 236; LC 5/148, pp. 87, 128, 196, 197, 251, 260). William III issued eight orders and disciplined three men (LC 5/149, p. 213; LC 5/150, pp. 130, 250; LC 5/151, p. 69; LC 5/152, pp. 40, 41, 228–29; LC 5/153, pp. 22, 60, 108; LC 5/201, p. 288). George I issued three orders and disciplined twelve officers (LC 5/157, pp. 59, 338; LC 5/158, pp. 59, 101–2, 224).

31. E 351/553–66 (Declared Accounts, Treasurer of the Chamber). For the attendance of servants below stairs away from London, see LS 13/175, f. 40 recto (List of Waiters Below Stairs at Kensington).

32. *Household Ordinances*, p. 355.

33. *Wentworth Papers*, pp. 205, 231–32, 248, 292, 345; Add. MSS 22225, f. 15; 22226, ff. 193 verso, 199; 31144, ff. 294, 318, 385, 405–6, 412 verso.

34. For Robert Chambers, who was too young, see above, Chapter 4, sub "Court Families." By contrast, James Clerke, who had begun his household career in 1673, was allowed in 1708, at age 74, to name James Eckersall, a doorkeeper to the kitchen, as his deputy. According to the warrant, Clerke "by reason of his great age is often indisposed, & thereby rend'red unable to attend Our Immediate Services as formerly" (LS 13/258, f. 65 verso). For other cases of permanent deputization, see LS 13/175, f. 102 recto; LC 5/154, p. 236.

35. Add. MSS 61417, f. 57 recto and verso: Anne to Sarah, "Friday night," n.d. [1707], copy by Sarah.

36. Add. MSS 22225, f. 15; 31143, f. 6 recto; 31144, ff. 247 recto and verso, 318, 405–6.

37. LC 5/145, p. 224.

38. Burrows, "Handel" II: 19–27. For another society with permission to decide its own waitings, see LC 5/145, p. 212.

39. *Marlborough-Godolphin Correspondence*, pp. 640 and n. 3, 928 and n. 3, 1395, 1439, 1458, 1607, 1649; Add. MSS 61422, f. 159 recto and verso; *Letters Illustrative of the Reign of William III . . . by James Vernon, Esq. Secretary of State*, ed. G. P. R. James (1841), III: 260–61; *D.N.B.*, sub "Horatio Walpole."

40. R. Masters, *History of the College of Corpus Christi* (1753), "A List of Members &c.," p. 14 and n. For Coleman's subsequent diplomatic career, which culminated in his appointment as Resident at Tuscany, see *British Diplomatic Representatives, 1689–1789*, ed. D. B. Horn (Camd. Soc., 1932), pp. 34–35, 77, 80. For the limits to the Queen's flexibility, see below.

41. *Letters to and from Henrietta, Countess of Suffolk*, ed. J. W. Croker (1824), I: 292–93: John Arbuthnot to Henrietta Howard, London, 39 [*sic*] May [1728].

42. For the attendance of Danvers and Fielding, see *Clarendon Correspondence* II: 207; Gregg, *Anne*, pp. 5, 65, 98, 235, 280. For their growing incapacity, see Add. MSS 61416, f. 205; 61417, ff. 181, 186.

43. Gregg, *Anne*, pp. 237, 332 and n.; Swift, *Journal*, pp. 351, 363, 560; H.M.C., *Fifteenth Report*, App. IV, pp. 454, 486, 495–96, 524, 525, 526, 536, 541; H.M.C., *Portland MSS* V: 222–23, 315, 369, 374.

44. Add. MSS 61417, f. 85: [Anne] to Sarah, "Saturday Night," n.d. [?Aug. 1707]. For Alice Hill's attendance, see *Swift Correspondence* I: 318 n. 2.

45. See, for example, *Hamilton Diary*, passim; E 351/553–66 (for payment of riding wages); Add. MSS 1968, f. 2; 4034, ff. 46–50; 4043, f. 157; 4076, ff. 106, 336; H.M.C., *Fifteenth Report*, App. VII, pp. 222–24; *Wentworth Papers*, p. 138; H. L. Snyder, "The Last Days of Queen Anne: The Account of Sir John Evelyn Examined," *H.L.Q.* XXXIV (1971): 264, 267. It is therefore understandable that Mary Stanhope worried that Malthus would be unable to treat her sick mother, "he being y[e] queen's apothecary" (Kent A.O., Stanhope of Chevening MSS U1590, C 7/16: Mary Stanhope to Alexander Stanhope, St. James's, 8 Feb. [1706]).

46. *Present State of the British Court*, p. 41. See also below, Chapter 7, sub "Art."

47. Burrows, "Handel" II: 23–24, 27; E 351/556–66 (for payment of riding wages).

48. This is the impression conveyed in Swift, *Journal*, pp. 350, 377–78 and the numerous sermons "preached before the Queen" that were published by individual chaplains.

49. H.M.C., *Portland MSS* V: 379: Bolingbroke to the Earl of Oxford, 6 Jan. 1713/14; see also *Bolingbroke Correspondence* II: 77–78; III: 51–52, 199; LC 3/53, p. 45. For the hectic schedule of Fortune Barton, one of Bolingbroke's favorite messengers, during the period 1713–14, see *Bolingbroke Correspondence* IV: 75–76, 78, 305, 450, 467–68, 569.

50. Duplication and rotation of attendance were of ancient standing at court. They were a holdover from a time when clientage was stronger: the servants of a great courtier had to be free to attend their noble master for extended periods of time. They also enabled the court to employ and, presumably, oblige

larger numbers of individuals. Unauthorized deputies appear to have been a problem below stairs. Three times the board of greencloth issued orders demanding "the personall & constant Attendance of all the Houshold Servants according to the Appointm[ts] and their severall waitings," on the last occasion (12 July 1714) expressly forbidding the exercise of office by deputy (LS 13/175, ff. 12 verso, 98 verso, 106 recto and verso). The practice appears to have been a problem at the early Stuart court as well: see Aylmer, *King's Servants*, pp. 127–28.

51. H.M.C., *Bathurst MSS*, p. 3: Bathurst to Lady Bathurst, Winchester, 13 Sept. 1683.

52. The established emoluments of household officers almost invariably came in the form of wages and boardwages, often from several paymasters. The latter figure tended to bulk much larger than the former, a vestigial reminder of the importance of the diet or "bouge" of court that every officer had once been entitled to. Thus, under Queen Anne, the lord chamberlain's established salary comprised £100 in wages, £1,100 in boardwages. Since this distinction had long since lost any practical meaning, wages and boardwages are added together when computing the "salaries" noted below.

53. LS 13/43 (Household Establishment, 1702); LC 3/5 (Chamber Establishment, 1702–13). These have been compared with LS 13/31–41 (Household Establishments, 1662–1701) and LC 3/2–4, 24–32 (Chamber Establishments, 1660–1702).

54. For the loss of tables, see above, Chapter 1, sub "Charles II." For the loss of fees and perquisites by the masters of the great wardrobe, robes, and jewel house; groom of the stole; and clerks of the greencloth, and for the compensatory increases in their established salaries, see *C.T.B.* II: 245; III: 131, 133; IV: 79; VIII: 485, 752; and above, Chapter 2, sub "Finance."

55. H.M.C., *Ormonde MSS*, n.s., V: 261–62: Sir William Boreman to Ormonde, Whitehall, 3 Jan. 1679–80. For evidence that other great household offices were thought to be declining in value, see Worcestershire R.O., Henning Papers, BA 2252/6 i, "An Account of the Lord Chamberlains Office by M[r.] Coling.," n.d. [1689]; Harl. MSS 1843, passim.

56. According to the Household Establishment of 1662 (LS 13/31), most tables for great officers were served between 14 and 28 dishes daily. Using the estimate quoted in Aylmer, *King's Servants*, p. 169, as a guide, these would have been worth between £1,700 and £3,400 per annum.

57. According to J. M. Beattie, *English Court*, p. 191, the master of the great wardrobe took his poundage at the rate of 12½ percent. At an average annual wardrobe expenditure of about £20,000 under Charles II, this would have yielded the master about £2,500, £500 more than the figure allotted him by the treasury (but cf. W. D. Montagu, Duke of Manchester, *Court and Society from Elizabeth to Anne* [1864], II: 303, for a different rate and yield).

58. The master of the robes, collecting his fees at the rate of 6*d*. in the pound, stood to make only £114 on his department's annual expenditure under

Charles II of £4,566. This figure is considerably less than the £500 per annum offered by the treasury.

59. H.M.C., *Ormonde MSS*, n.s., III: 452; V: 70, 79, 144–45, 147, 152.

60. LC 3/61, f. 77 recto; *C.T.B.* XV: 14–16, 206.

61. For the right to sell inferior places, see Worcestershire R.O., Henning Papers, BA 2252/6 i, "Account of the Lord Chamberlains Office," n.d. For its abolition, see above, Chapter 2, sub "Finance."

62. *C.T.B.* XXVII: 495, 503, 505, and XVII–XXVIII, passim, sub "Royal Bedchamber" and "Vice Chamberlain."

63. LS 13/175, f. 107. For the exemptions noted, see J. M. Beattie, *English Court*, p. 189 n. 1. Calculation based on average annual expenditure as calculated in Table 1.2.

64. Calculation based on figures quoted in J. M. Beattie, *English Court*, pp. 190–91; *C.T.B.* XXVIII: 251, 395–96; and above, Table 1.2.

65. See Tables 1.1, 1.2.

66. The largest were payments of £66 16*s.* per annum in livery money and an average of £48 per annum in fees of honor collected by the lord chamberlain: see E 351/3128–39 (Declared Accounts, Great Wardrobe); and below.

67. For the award and value of the plate itself, see LC 5/108, warrants of 6 July, 9 Nov. 1702; 27 Apr., 16 May 1704; 29 Apr. 1708; 11 May 1709; LC 5/109, pp. 13, 24, 30, 41, 65. For the cost of fashioning, see Hayward, *Huguenot Silver*, p. 78.

68. For attempts to recall old plate, see above, Chapter 2, sub "Finance." For examples of discharge, see LC 5/108, entries of 27 Apr. 1703; 23 Feb., 15 July, 30 Nov. 1708; 20 June 1709; LC 5/109, pp. 17–20, 23–24, 37–38, 53–54, 71–73, 77–78, 80–81. Lord Steward Devonshire's plate, with the arms of William III, was recently still in the Chatsworth Collection (Hayward, *Huguenot Silver*, p. 50). For the plate of Robert Harley as secretary of state, with the arms of Queen Anne, see A. G. Grimwade, *The Queen's Silver* (1953), p. 33.

69. *C.T.B.* XXIX: 237, 375; LC 5/156, p. 57; Add. MSS 61420, f. 107 verso.

70. LC 2/14; LC 5/153, pp. 361, 362, 367; LC 5/155, pp. 45–47, 53; LC 5/156, pp. 187–92.

71. *Marlborough-Godolphin Correspondence*, p. 1174 and n. 2; Luttrell, *Brief Relation* V: 154. For an appraisal of Prince George's horses, dated June 1709, in the private papers of his former master of the horse, the Earl of Bridgewater, see Huntington Library, San Marino, Calif., Ellesmere Calendar 10109.

72. For lists of lodgings and their inhabitants circa Anne's reign, see LC 5/201, pp. 171–73, and H.M.C., *Twelfth Report*, App. III, pp. 110–11 (St. James's, May 1695; Oct. 1714); LC 5/202, pp. 195–201 (Hampton Court, June 1710), 203–4 (Windsor, temp. Anne), 218–23 (Whitehall, May 1713); LC 5/201, pp. 434–36 (Kensington, July 1697); H.M.C., *Twelfth Report*, App. III, pp. 185–86 (Somerset House, circa 1714). See also lord chamberlain's warrants disposing lodgings in LC 3/153–55.

73. LC 5/201, p. 434; LC 5/202, p. 203. The accommodation at Whitehall had

been even more luxurious before the first fire there in 1691. As groom of the stole, the Earl of Portland had lodgings consisting of 23 rooms, closets, and garrets "with a Kitchen and shedds." Lord Steward Devonshire had 20 rooms, closets, and garrets, plus a kitchen and cellar (LC 5/196, ff. 1 verso–2 recto).

74. See, for example, *Wentworth Papers*, pp. 45–46; Add. MSS 61414, ff. 31, 51; 61416, ff. 73 recto and verso, 79, 108; 61417, f. 190; 61418, f. 2 verso; 61421, f. 120; 61422, ff. 23–26, 167–75.

75. Compare the treatment of Sir William Forrester—who, on his retirement and in recognition of 28 years' service, was allowed to keep his lodgings for the rest of his life "as a mark of Royal Favour" (LS 13/260, entry of 17 Apr. 1717)—with Anne's decision to turn Burnet out of his lodgings at her accession (Burnet, *History* V: 1 n. Macky).

76. Edward Griffith, a clerk of the greencloth, was reported to have spent nearly £1,200 on his lodgings (Add. MSS 61422, f. 175). The Duchess of Somerset was reimbursed £1,300 for furnishings and other "necessaries" upon vacating her apartments at St. James's as groom of the stole at the beginning of the next reign (*C.T.B.* XXXI: 699–700).

77. For grants of land or leases prior to 1702, see *C.T.B.* III: 1235; IX: 1602; X: 90; XV: 101, 392; XVI: 231. For grants made during the reign, see ibid. XXV: 375; *C.T.P. 1714–1719*, p. 184; and below. A few of Anne's servants received similar grants in subsequent reigns: see *C.T.B.* XXIX: 238–39; XXX: 420; *C.T.P. 1720–1728*, pp. 138–39.

78. *Memoirs of the Duchess of Marlborough*, p. 208.

79. 12–13 William III c. 2; 1 Anne c. 1.

80. 6 Anne c. 6. The Duchess of Marlborough was also granted a lease of choice land in St. James's Park: see *Memoirs of the Duchess of Marlborough*, p. 207.

81. Add. MSS 29267, ff. 33 recto and verso, 47 verso (Northumberland's figure calculated by adding his £3,000 per annum out of the excise to half of the £4,700 per annum out of the post office that he shared with his brother, the Duke of Grafton); *C.T.B.* V: 164–65, 1259–60; XVII: 690, 699, 736; XXV: 63; and information from Cruickshanks and Hayton.

82. *Memoirs of the Duchess of Marlborough*, pp. 207–10; Gregg, *Anne*, p. 329; *C.T.B.* XVIII: 211; XXII: 38, 372; Add. MSS 61420, ff. 74 verso–78, 79 verso–84; 61454, f. 133 verso.

83. Add. MSS 61420, ff. 74–78.

84. For the rates by which christening plate was awarded, see LC 5/108, p. 259. For the awards themselves, see LC 5/108, p. 289, and warrants of 22 July 1704, 20 Feb. 1706, 6 Jan. 1707, 4 May 1708; LC 5/109, pp. 12, 58; *C.T.B.* XXIV: 525; XXV: 447; XXIX: 718; XXX: 225.

85. *Memoirs of the Duchess of Marlborough*, p. 234.

86. For example, the Earl of Sunderland paid a total of £31 0s. 6*d*. to be sworn groom of the stole in 1719; £5 15*s*. upon receipt of his plate of office; and an average of roughly £500 per annum in fees (mostly at the exchequer) and taxes upon receipt of his total annual salary of £3,000 (Add. MSS 61597, ff. 128, 133,

135, 141, 144, 148, 151–54, 156, 158–61, 163, 165, 171). It is clear that many of the great (and some lesser) officers did entertain, particularly Master of the Horse Somerset and Lord Chamberlain Shrewsbury (H.M.C., *Downshire MSS* I ii, 867; *The Correspondence of Sir James Clavering*, ed. H. T. Dickinson [Surtees Soc., 1967], p. 103; Add. MSS 22226, ff. 37, 298 verso; 61422, f. 158 verso). For others, see *Wentworth Papers*, p. 208; Swift, *Journal*, pp. 29–30, 318, 320, 324, 327, 331, 335, 350, 356, 359, 362, 363, 374, 375, 377, 447, 461, 463, 470, 480, 522, 614, 617, 622, 643; Gregg, *Protestant Succession*, pp. 223, 251. However, it is difficult to know how much of this was done as part of one's official duties, and how much was simply a function of the aristocratic way of life.

87. See above, Chapter 2.

88. For Lord Fitzharding's salary and fees as treasurer of the chamber (which yielded between £1,400 and £1,800 per annum), see above. He also received £500 per annum as a teller of the exchequer (*C.T.B.* X: 479, 497). For his wife's pension of £600 per annum, later raised to £1,000 per annum, see above.

89. The Duke of St. Albans received £1,000 per annum as captain of the gentlemen pensioners; £1,000 per annum out of the logwood duty (*C.T.B.* XVIII: 76; XIX: 286); £800 on the Irish establishment (ibid. XXIII: 98); £500 out of the alienations office; and £500 out of the Welsh lands (ibid. XVII: 241). The Duke and Duchess of Somerset received £1,267 and £3,000 per annum as master of the horse and groom of the stole, respectively. There is evidence that the Duke may have had a pension of £4,000 per annum as well (J. M. Beattie, *English Court*, p. 214).

90. The Duchess of Marlborough received £3,000 per annum as groom of the stole; £2,000 per annum as keeper of the privy purse; and £600 per annum as mistress of the robes. Also included in the figure quoted above is the sum of £2,000 per annum that she collected retroactively out of the privy purse in 1711. See Gregg, *Anne*, p. 329, for evidence that she in fact collected far more in the years leading up to her fall.

91. Gregg, *Anne*, p. 153.

92. E. Chamberlayne, *Anglia Notitia* (1669), p. 454. Gregory King's figure of £2,800 per annum seems absurdly low. See G. S. Holmes, "Gregory King and the Social Structure of Pre-Industrial England," *T.R.H.S.*, 5th ser., XXVII (1977): 66.

93. Holmes, "Gregory King," p. 54 and n. For Newcastle, see above, Chapter 3. But cf. H.M.C., *Thirteenth Report*, App. II, p. 220.

94. The lord chamberlain, lord steward, treasurer, and comptroller of the household, along with the lord treasurer of England, all received long white staffs of office and, indeed, were known collectively as "the white-staves." The captains of the gentlemen pensioners and yeomen of the guard carried gold or gold-tipped staffs; their respective lieutenants and standard-bearers, black staffs with silver heads. In addition, the lord chamberlain, master of the ceremonies, and principal painter wore gold chains and medallions, while both the lord chamberlain and groom of the stole carried (and often wore) gold keys

with both a symbolic and practical significance. These various articles may often be seen prominently displayed in contemporary portraits of court officers. (*Shrewsbury Correspondence*, p. 510; H.M.C., *Sixth Report*, p. 370; H.M.C., *Eleventh Report*, App. V, p. 309; LC 5/153, pp. 249, 339; Add. MSS 61422, f. 119 recto and verso; Worcestershire R.O., Henning Papers, BA 2252/2, "Orders for the Government of Our Bedchamber . . . ," pp. 62–63; Sir R. Hennell, *The History of the King's Bodyguard of the Yeomen of the Guard* [1904], p. 186.)

95. For evidence that Seymour sat in the cabinet, see G. S. Holmes, *British Politics*, pp. 195–96 and n. For the others, see sources noted Appendix B.

96. Buckingham was promoted from lord steward to lord president of the council in 1711. Shrewsbury added the lord lieutenancy of Ireland and lord treasurer's staff to his lord chamberlainship in 1713 and 1714, respectively. Townshend added the position of plenipotentiary for the peace at Gertruyenberg to that of captain of the yeomen of the guard in 1709. Wyndham was promoted from master of the buckhounds to secretary at war in 1712.

97. See above, Chapter 4, sub "A Good Family."

98. *Hamilton Diary*, p. 56. For other evidence of long arrears at this level, see Gregg, *Anne*, pp. 371–72; *C.T.P. 1708–1714*, p. 394; *C.T.B.* XXVII: 495–514; Add. MSS 31144, ff. 405 verso, 410 recto and verso, 411; Curling, *Gentlemen at Arms*, pp. 179–80.

99. For fees in kind, see J. M. Beattie, *English Court*, pp. 194–96. For the abuse of this right, see below.

100. Among the exceptions, the clerk of the acatry made an average of £370 per annum in poundage on debentures for butcher's meat, bacon, fish, lard, brawn, and veal delivered into his office and for money paid out. The clerk of the spicery made about £90 in this way, that of the woodyard, scullery, and pastry about £45 per annum. These inequalities would not have been vicious if the "Ancient Order of Succession" had continued in operation. For the fees allowed to departmental clerks and subclerks below stairs, see LS 13/175, ff. 107–10. The above calculations are based upon the subtotals given for individual items taken in by the catering subdepartments in their quarterly accounts, contained in LS 4/13–20. These cover 109 of the 149 months of Anne's reign. I have divided the totals for each item by 109 and multiplied by 12 to give an annual average expenditure on each item, then calculated the poundage.

101. For a partial scale for this fee under Charles II, see LC 5/140, pp. 143–44. For an estimate of its yield, see J. M. Beattie, *English Court*, p. 193. In addition, the eldest gentleman usher, Black Rod, received a fee of £44 6*s*. 8*d*., a chain and medal worth about £60, a robe worth £29, and a wide range of other perquisites including knighthood, besides his salary of £150 per annum (LC 5/16, p. 133; LC 5/68, f. 31 recto; LC 5/71, f. 35 verso; LC 5/109, p. 6; J. Chamberlayne, *Magnae Britanniae Notitia* [1710], pp. 546–47).

102. For the rates at which fees of honor were collected, see LC 5/201, pp. 456–58, 464–65. I have followed Dr. Beattie in relying upon *The Handbook of*

British Chronology, ed. F. M. Powicke and E. B. Fryde, 2nd edn. (1961), pp. 202–66, for the appointment and translation of English bishops; pp. 273–80 for Welsh bishops; A. S. Turberville, *The House of Lords in the XVIIIth Century* (Oxford, 1927), App. A, for peerages; G. E. Cokayne, *Complete Baronetage*, 6 vols. (Exeter, 1900–1909), for baronets; *The Knights of England*, ed. W. A. Shaw, 2 vols. (1906), for K.G.'s and knighthoods. For evidence that fees of honor were becoming more difficult to collect, see LC 5/145, p. 44. However, Celia Fiennes maintained that they were still being collected in the early years of Anne's reign: *The Journeys of Celia Fiennes*, ed. C. Morris (1949), p. 329.

103. E 351/3128–39 (Declared Accounts, Great Wardrobe).

104. E 351/553–65 (Declared Accounts, Treasurer of the Chamber); E 2842–46 (Declared Accounts, Robes).

105. LS 13/43. This was the only form of material award allowed the chaplains and was "the worst provided table at court" according to Swift (*Journal*, p. 378). However, the position afforded other compensations: see above, Chapter 4, sub "Professional Standards and Reputation."

106. LS 13/43; LS 13/111.

107. Sources as for n. 72 above.

108. See LS 13/258, warrant of 31 Mar. 1707; LS 13/260, warrants of 17 Apr. and 20 Sept. 1717, for two such payments. Middling officers in the ordinance received reimbursement for lodgings ranging from £40 to £100 per annum (G. S. Holmes, *Augustan England*, p. 258).

109. LC 5/202, pp. 218–23; *Wentworth Papers*, pp. 45–46.

110. *Present State of the British Court*, p. 49. See also H.M.C., *Downshire MSS* I ii, 828. For the accuracy of these statements, see above, Chapter 4, sub "Professional Standards and Reputation."

111. This figure includes 28 holders of local offices that were, technically, without payment.

112. For example, Thomas Hutton, who made only £56 per annum as a gentleman usher, raised his income to over £200 per annum by holding simultaneous keeperships at Somerset House and St. James's. Philip Ryley received a little over £121 per annum as sergeant at arms to the lord treasurer, but made a substantial fortune out of his other posts, i.e., as an agent of the exchequer, surveyor of the woods south of the Trent, and commissioner on numerous revenue boards between 1685 and his death, in 1733. (In addition to the sources noted above, Chapter 2, n. 4, and below, Appendix B, see G. S. Holmes, *Augustan England*, pp. 249, 259–60.)

113. See Starkey, "Intimacy and Innovation," passim; Aylmer, *King's Servants*, p. 31; and above, Chapter 1, sub "Charles II."

114. See J. M. Beattie, *English Court*, pp. 6–16.

115. *C.T.B.* XXIII: 297–300.

116. Ibid. XXIV: 356. Later, she was awarded a pension of £200 per annum, "being a poor Old Sickly Creature that is quite starving" (Cambridge Univer-

sity Library, Cholmondeley [Houghton] Papers 53 item 37, quoted in *The London Diaries of William Nicolson, Bishop of Carlisle 1702–1718*, ed. G. S. Holmes and C. Jones [Oxford, 1985], p. 300 n. 114).

117. *C.T.B.* XX: 17.

118. G. A. Aitken, *The Life and Works of John Arbuthnot M.D., . . .* (Oxford, 1892), p. 159.

119. LC 5/70, pp. 295, 398; LC 5/71, ff. 21, 46, 71 recto and verso.

120. For example, William III spent at least £2,139 on the Earl of Albemarle's lodgings alone during the last three years of his reign (*C.T.B. Introduction 1695–1702*, pp. dxcvii–dxcviii; *C.T.B.* XVII: 1065). George I spent at least £4,400 on the lodgings of his principal female favorites during the first four years of his reign (LC 5/72, passim).

121. Gregg, *Anne*, p. 237.

122. *Parl. Hist.* VI: 1366.

123. *Evening Post*, no. 121, 20–23 May 1710; Gregg, *Anne*, pp. 235, 236; *C.T.B.* XXVII: 464–65, 483.

124. G. E. Cokayne, *The Complete Peerage of England, Scotland, Ireland, Great Britain and the United Kingdom*, ed. V. Gibbs et al., 14 vols. (1910–59), sub "Masham of Otes" n. "a" (no reference given for quotation).

125. For the Asiento contract, see B. W. Hill, *The Growth of Parliamentary Parties 1689–1742* (1976), pp. 140, 142, 145. For the accusation of peculation, see Green, *Anne*, p. 330; W. S. Churchill, *Marlborough, His Life and Times* (New York, 1938), VI: 614.

126. Gregg, *Anne*, 399; H.M.C., *Bath MSS* I: 225.

127. G. S. Holmes, *Augustan England*, pp. 15–16 and passim.

128. The groom porter received £550 per annum from the Queen in return for providing her lodgings "with Tables, Chairs, Firing etc. As also to provide Cards, Dice etc. when there is playing at Court: to decide Disputes which arise in Gaming." He also had the regulation of "common Billiards Tables, common Bowling Grounds, Dicing Houses, Gaming Houses and common Tennis Courts" in London and the vicinity, which service, according to Narcissus Luttrell, raised the value of his place to £1,000 per annum. (*Present State of the British Court*, p. 37; J. M. Beattie, *English Court*, p. 52 n. 1, quoting LC 5/156, p. 49; LC 5/147, p. 105; H.M.C., *Twelfth Report*, App. III, pp. 113–14; Luttrell, *Brief Relation* V: 515; *Daily Courant*, no. 2796, 9 Oct. 1710).

129. Sources as for n. 92 above.

130. For Lawrence, see Add. MSS 61425, f. 7 verso; 61475, ff. 74–75; information from Cruickshanks and Hayton; and the sources noted Appendix B.

131. Fees paid out at appointment could range from the £10 1*s.* 6*d.* paid by Casper Frederick Henning to be a carver (Worcestershire R.O., Henning Papers, BA 2252/2, no. 139) to the £49 19*s.* 6*d.* paid by Henry Lowman to be housekeeper at Kensington (Add. MSS 20101, f. 3), a far more lucrative office, held by patent for life. See also Add. MSS 4552, f. 206. According to Peter Went-

worth, "My Sallary is 300 a year but the taxes & cofferer's fees reduce it to 250" (Add. MSS 22227, f. 28; see also Worcestershire R.O., Henning Papers, BA 2252/2, no. 57).

132. Add. MSS 22227, ff. 62, 78 verso; 22229, ff. 144–45; 51324, f. 17 verso; *Wentworth Papers*, p. 250; Curling, *Gentlemen at Arms*, p. 180. In a similar vein, Mary Stanhope complained about the expenses incurred for clothes as a maid of honor: Kent A.O., Stanhope of Chevening MSS U 1590, C 7/16: 9 Feb. [1703].

133. For Wentworth, see *Wentworth Papers*, pp. 416, 468–69; Add. MSS 22226, f. 179; 22227, ff. 28 recto and verso, 101; 31143, ff. 239–40, 328; 31145, f. 13. For others, see Add. MSS 51324, f. 17 verso; H.M.C., *Tenth Report*, App. IV (1885), pp. 48–49; H.M.C., *Eleventh Report*, App. V, p. 59.

134. Add. MSS 22225, f. 262 recto and verso: Isabella Wentworth to the Earl of Strafford, 7 Apr. 1713; ibid., f. 298: same to same, 2 June 1713. For Mrs. Wentworth's earlier hopes, see ibid., ff. 88, 256 verso; 31143, ff. 72, 321 recto and verso, 369 verso.

135. *Wentworth Papers*, pp. 3–4, 533–34n; *D.N.B.*, sub "Thomas Wentworth, Earl of Strafford"; Add. MSS 22227, f. 87 verso.

136. *Wentworth Papers*, p. 198; Add. MSS 22229, ff. 144–45: William Wentworth to [the Earl of Strafford], 13 Jan. 1735/36.

137. *Swift Correspondence* II: 122: Arbuthnot to Swift, London, 12 Aug. 1714; II: 136: same to same, 19 Oct. 1714.

138. E. Chamberlayne, *Anglia Notitia* (1704), pp. 300–301.

139. See above, Chapter 2, sub "Finance."

140. *C.T.B.* XVII: 941–1078, passim.

141. See above, Chapter 2, sub "Finance."

142. LS 13/43.

143. With the loss of Whitehall, the groom of the vestry, the strewer of herbs, the fruiterer, and the yeoman of the woodyard lost their accommodation entirely, while other societies such as the laundresses and confectioners lost their most spacious accommodation of any in the royal palaces (LC 5/196, ff. 1–10). For those that remained, see sources quoted above, n. 72, esp. LC 5/201, pp. 434–36; LC 5/202, pp. 203–4.

144. E 351/553–65.

145. *C.T.B.* II: 225, 344; E 351/3128–39; LC 5/70–71, passim.

146. See above, n. 102.

147. New Year's gifts had been eliminated for great and middling officers as part of the retrenchment of the early 1680s. (H.M.C., *Ormonde MSS*, n.s. V: 541). Those remaining to menial servants were paid out of the privy purse: see the Privy Purse Accounts, Mar. 1702–July 1703, June 1708–June 1710 in Add. MSS 61420, ff. 74 verso–86 verso. There is evidence that the Queen's menial servants received additional New Year's gifts from other government officials: H.M.C., *Buccleuch at Montagu House MSS* II ii, 634; H.M.C., *Ormonde MSS*, n.s., VIII: 270–71; LC 5/201, pp. 460–61; S.P. Dom. 34/24, f. 118.

148. *Evelyn Diary* IV: 214–17 (2 Sept. 1680); Harl. MSS 1843, pp. 22–23.

149. *C.T.P. 1697–1702*, p. 29; *C.T.B.* XX: 82; XXIII: 297–300. Gostling was no longer an active member of the choir. His grant had originally been made by Charles II in order to allow him to maintain a curate at his living as rector of All Saints, Kent.

150. For wastage officially allowed, see J. M. Beattie, *English Court*, pp. 194–96.

151. LS 13/175, ff. 48 verso–50.

152. LS 13/173, p. 75.

153. See below, Chapter 7, sub "Art."

154. See above, Chapter 2, sub "Finance."

155. LS 13/43–45.

156. See above, n. 34.

157. See above, Chapter 4, sub "Court Families."

158. LS 13/43–50; LS 13/258–61, passim.

159. LS 13/262, warrants of 2 Dec. 1728, 12 Feb. 1728/9, and passim.

160. LC 9/6, pp. 24–25; Burrows, "Handel" I: 413–14; LC 9/343, entry of 30 Jan. 1733.

161. J. C. Sainty, "A Reform in the Tenure of Offices During the Reign of Charles II," *B.I.H.R.* XLI (1968): 151, 162; *C.T.B.* III: 381; VIII: 430, 457, 475. Under Queen Anne, the master of the revels, the knight marshal, and the housekeeper at Whitehall continued to hold their offices by patent for life. In addition, similar patents were granted, without intention of setting a precedent, to the first and second Dukes of Montagu as successive masters of the great wardrobe (H.M.C., *Twelfth Report*, App. VI (1889), p. 309; H.M.C., *Buccleuch at Montagu House MSS* I, 352) and to Ambrose Dickens as sergeant surgeon (LC 3/53, p. 87; LC 5/155, p. 312).

162. H.M.C., *Ormonde MSS*, n.s., IV: 139: Fox to Henry Gascoigne, Whitehall, 27 Apr. 1678.

163. Add. MSS 61414, f. 57: Anne to Sarah, "Thursday night," n.d. [?Sept. 1685].

164. His court career may have been even longer, if Tudway is correct that he received his training in the chapel royal as a boy: *D.N.B.*, sub "William Turner."

165. Sources noted Appendix B. According to Harl. Soc. no. 49, *Musgrave's Obituary*, p. 285, sub "Willis, Edw.," Wills was 101 years old at the time of his death in 1749.

166. Among the exceptions was Sir Thomas Felton, who began as a page of honor to Charles II and rose over a 43-year career to be comptroller of the household by the time of his death in 1709. Francis Newport, Earl of Bradford, served for 38 years as comptroller, then treasurer of the household and underhousekeeper at Ludlow Castle.

167. For removals of great officers during the reign, see above, Chapter 4, sub "Politics." Lord Chamberlain Shrewsbury, Lord Steward Poulett, Treasurer of the Household Lansdowne, Comptroller Stonehouse, Cofferer Masham,

Master of the Household Pole, Lord Almoner Smalridge, and Master of the Buckhounds Cardigan all resigned in opposition or were removed within a year of George I's accession. Below this level, political removals were rare. All occurred late in the reign. The Reverend Benjamin Palmer was removed in May 1710 for praying for Dr. Sacheverell (Boyer, *Annals* VIII: 355). Michael Messenger, a yeoman of the guard, and Daniel Damarie, one of the Queen's watermen, lost their places in the spring of 1710 for their prominent role in the Sacheverell riots (Luttrell, *Brief Relation* VI: 565; G. S. Holmes, *The Trial of Doctor Sacheverell* [1973], pp. 164–65). Damarie was restored to his place by the Tory ministry in August 1712, but lost it again in 1714. The equerry Thomas Meredith and several of the Churchill servants in the robes and bedchamber lost their places for their association with the Marlboroughs early in 1711 (Gregg, *Anne*, p. 327; Add. MSS 61422, f. 159 recto and verso). Finally, the gardener Richard Watts lost his place in 1712 for talking against the Queen and her ministry (see above, Chapter 2, sub "Finance").

168. Add. MSS 61456, f. 176 verso: Lady Portland to Sarah, 20 Feb. [1709].

169. For the stocks, see Dickson, *Financial Revolution*; and J. Carswell, *The South Sea Bubble* (1960). For the professions, see G. S. Holmes, *Augustan England*; Brewer, *Sinews of Power*, chap. 3; and *The Professions in Early Modern England*, ed. W. Prest (1987). For the political parties, see G. S. Holmes, *British Politics*. For the social and cultural opportunities to be found in London, see below, Chapter 7, sub "Art" and "Social Life."

170. For example, musicians, medical men, and master cooks were careful to advertise their court connections when dealing with the public. See Ashton, *Social Life*, p. 278; *The New Grove Dictionary of Music and Musicians*, ed. S. Sadie (1980), vol. X, sub "Jacob Kremberg"; *Daily Courant*, no. 210, 18 Dec. 1702; no. 644, 9 May 1704; *Evening Post*, no. 597, 4–6 June 1713; no. 606, 25–27 June 1713; P. Lamb, *Royal-Cookery: or, the Compleat Court-Cook . . . by Patrick Lamb, Esq; Near Fifty Years Master-Cook to their late Majesties King Charles II. King James II. King William and Queen Mary, and Queen Anne*, 2nd edn. (1716); R. Smith, *Court Cookery, or the Compleat English Cook* (1723), in which Smith, a former turnbroach, refers to himself as "Cook (under Mr. Lamb) to King William." For disputes and jealousies over the right to bear the royal warrant on tradesmen's goods, see LS 13/114, f. 10; LS 13/115, f. 128. This right remained highly prized through the eighteenth century: see N. McKendrick, J. Brewer, and J. H. Plumb, *The Birth of a Consumer Society: The Commercialization of Eighteenth-Century England* (Bloomington, Ind., 1982), pp. 71–72, 108–9.

171. For examples of court officers "running errands" for family members or friends in the localities, see *Wentworth Papers*, pp. 78, 139, 142–43, 192, 199, 200, 298–300; Add. MSS 22226, ff. 199, 219; 31143, f. 274; 31144, ff. 286–87 verso; H.M.C., *Twelfth Report*, App. II, pp. 427, 429, 430; App. III, p. 84; Kent A.O., Stanhope of Chevening MSS U1590 C 7/16: 8 Feb. [1706].

172. For the privilege itself, see LC 5/202, pp. 145–46. For its exercise, see ibid., pp. 146–47; Melbourne Hall, Derbyshire, Melbourne Hall MSS, old no.

67/new no. 108: Sir Edward Coke to Thomas Coke, 1 Oct. 1707. It may be this privilege that explains why Charles Napier, who had been in debtors' prison since 1696, was made a gentleman of the privy chamber in the following year (Cokayne, *Baronetage* IV: 127).

173. See J. M. Beattie, *English Court*, pp. 96–97; Pegge, *Curialia* I ii, 91–92.

Chapter VI

1. Larner, "Europe of the Courts," p. 669.
2. S.P. Dom. 34/32, f. 131; 36, f. 16
3. D. Allen, "Charles II's Chiffinch," p. 280; J. M. Beattie, *English Court*, pp. 15–16. See, for example, S.P. Dom. 34/12, f. 49. For an example of someone's being refused entrance to the guard chamber, see *Nicolson Diaries*, p. 176. Individuals could also be formally forbidden the court by written order of the secretary of state. This was the case with the Earl of Peterborough in 1708 (*Nicolson Diaries*, p. 442 n. 64) and Count Gallas in 1711 (LC 5/3, pp. 10–12; Gregg, *Anne*, p. 342).
4. For a good discussion of this process, see J. M. Beattie, *English Court*, pp. 6–16.
5. Worcestershire R.O., Henning Papers, BA 2252/2, pp. 67–69.
6. For her daily attendance at chapel, see Gregg, *Anne*, p. 137. For public drawing rooms, see below, sub "Information"; Chapter 7, sub "Social Life."
7. See below, Chapter 7, sub "Social Life."
8. Swift, *Journal*, p. 328. See also ibid., p. 451; *Wentworth Papers*, p. 312; Add. MSS 17677 CCC, f. 683 verso; HHH, ff. 9 verso, 89; 31144, f. 321.
9. H.M.C., *Fifteenth Report*, App. IV, pp. 322–23: B[ridget], Countess of Plymouth, to [Robert] Harley, [?25 Aug. 1706]. For other examples of presentation, see H.M.C., *Hamilton MSS*, suppl., p. 156; Add. MSS 61417, f. 181; 61456, f. 43 recto and verso; Snyder, "Last Days," pp. 262–63; *Nicolson Diaries*, pp. 126, 528; *Daily Courant*, no. 162, 23 Oct. 1702; *Evening Post*, no. 409, 22–25 Mar. 1712.
10. Worcestershire R.O., Henning Papers, BA 2252/2, pp. 67, 69. See also Add. MSS 17677 HHH, f. 18; 61425, f. 16 recto and verso; H.M.C., *Lindsey MSS*, suppl., p. 52; H.M.C., *Twelfth Report*, App. III, p. 1; *Hamilton Diary*, p. 64.
11. Worcestershire R.O., Henning Papers, BA 2252/2, p. 62. For the groom's unlimited access, see Add. MSS 61425, f. 16 recto and verso. For an interesting discussion of the key and its significance, see Starkey, "Representation Through Intimacy," p. 214.
12. Quoted in K. W. Campbell, *Sarah, Duchess of Marlborough* (Boston, 1932), p. 166.
13. J. Swift, "Memoirs Relating to That Change Which Happened in the Queen's Ministry in the Year 1710," in idem, *Historical and Political Tracts—English*, p. 374.
14. Gregg, *Anne*, pp. 169–70. For Sarah's absences and the remonstrations

of her friends, in particular Arthur Maynwaring, see Add. MSS 61423, f. 183 verso; 61442, f. 42 recto and verso; 61443, f. 44 verso; 61458, f. 22 verso; 61459, ff. 20 verso–21, 142, 180; 61461, ff. 27–32 verso; 61463, ff. 71–72; *Wentworth Papers*, p. 98; *Marlborough-Godolphin Correspondence*, pp. 285 and n. 1, 965–66, 1350; H.M.C., *Buccleuch at Montagu House MSS* I, 352. The portrait after Kneller is reproduced in black and white in Gregg, *Anne*, between pp. 244–45.

15. See Gregg, *Anne*, pp. 285, 298; B. L. Loan 29/38: Abigail Masham to Harley, "Thursday" 6th, n.d.; same to same, "Monday," n.d.; same to same, "Friday night past eleven," n.d. One indication of Abigail's effectiveness is the difficulty modern historians have encountered in attempting to date the beginning of Harley's secret access.

16. *Hamilton Diary*, pp. 63–64.

17. For Abigail's various pregnancies and illnesses, see Gregg, *Anne*, p. 332 and n; Swift, *Journal*, pp. 351, 363, 560; Add. MSS 22226, f. 219.

18. *Wentworth Papers*, p. 250: Peter Wentworth to the Earl of Strafford, London, 12 Jan. 1712.

19. Note, for example, the Whig charge that the Queen's Tory bedchamber attendants failed to deliver messages to the Duchess requesting her attendance, forcing Anne to resort to the post and a primitive form of registered mail: Burnet, *History* VI: 36 n. Onslow, quoting Oldmixon's *History*.

20. *Hamilton Diary*, p. 35.

21. "An Unpublished Political Paper by Daniel De Foe," *E.H.R.* XXII (1907): 132. As Thomas Hearne was well aware, it was no coincidence that this reign saw the publication of "Memoirs" of such previous favorites as Wolsey, Leicester, and the Duke of Buckingham: for Hearne's comment see *Remarks and Collections* I: 118.

22. *A Supplement to Burnet's History of My Own Time . . .*, ed. H. C. Foxcroft (Oxford, 1902), p. 292.

23. Burnet, *History* V: 230. For more evidence of Sarah's contemporary reputation, see H.M.C., *Fifteenth Report*, App. VII, p. 192; Add. MSS 61443, ff. 44 verso, 46 verso; 61459, f. 142; *Remarks and Collections* I: 61–62, 102, 123; G. S. Holmes, *British Politics*, p. 212; H. L. Snyder, "Queen Anne Versus the Junto: The Effort to Place Orford at the Head of the Admiralty in 1709," *H.L.Q.* XXXV (1972): 336.

24. G. S. Holmes, *British Politics*, p. 213; *Marlborough-Godolphin Correspondence*, p. 1588: Marlborough to Sarah, [Villers-Brûlin, 31 July /] "August the 11th 1710." For more evidence of Abigail's reputation with the Whigs, see *Marlborough-Godolphin Correspondence*, pp. 1055, 1073, 1149, 1157–58, 1356, 1584; Add. MSS 61459, f. 68 recto and verso; Manchester, *Court and Society* II: 281.

25. Add. MSS 61422, f. 107. For Abigail's reputation with the Tories, see Swift, *Journal*, p. 335; *Swift Correspondence* I: 69; II: 46; *Wentworth Papers*, p. 147; H.M.C., *Portland MSS* VII: 188; Add. MSS 22222, f. 74; B.L. Loan 29/38: Abigail Masham to Harley, Kensington, "Monday," n.d.

26. Swift, *Journal*, p. 435. For Swift's near obsession with the Duchess's sup-

posed power, see ibid., pp. 206, 364, 434, 437, 443, 451, 461, 471, 482. For other Tory viewpoints, see *Wentworth Papers*, pp. 270–71; *Swift Correspondence* II: 53, 100; G. S. Holmes, *British Politics*, p. 216; Add. MSS 22226, f. 171 recto and verso.

27. C. Hamilton, *Transactions During the Reign of Queen Anne; From the Union, to the Death of That Princess* (Edinburgh, 1790), Preface. For a more recent formulation of these sentiments, see E. Wingfield-Stratford, *The History of English Patriotism* (1913), I: 456.

28. Add. MSS 61422, f. 156 verso; *Memoirs of the Duchess of Marlborough*, pp. 234–35, 255–56.

29. Add. MSS 61434, f. 94: [Sarah to ?Godolphin], [27 Oct. 1709].

30. *The Private Diary of William, First Earl Cowper*, ed. E. C. Hawtrey (Roxburghe Club, Eton, 1833), p. 49.

31. For a contemporary reply to the *Conduct*, see J. Ralph, *The Other Side of the Question* (1742 and 1744). The Duke of Marlborough himself concluded of the Queen: "When she thinkes herself in the right, she needs no advice to help her to be very ferm and possative" (*Marlborough-Godolphin Correspondence*, p. 638).

32. For the Whig view of Queen Anne, see A. Cunningham, *The History of Great Britain from the Revolution in 1688, to the Accession of George I* (1787), I: 258; A. Strickland, *Lives of the Queens of England* (1842–48), XII: 378; F. W. Wyon, *The History of Great Britain During the Reign of Queen Anne* (1876), II: 531; W. E. H. Lecky, *The History of England in the Eighteenth Century* (1916–17), I: 38; G. M. Trevelyan, *England Under the Stuarts* (1949), p. 399.

33. The modern reappraisal of Anne's personality began with W. T. Morgan, *English Political Parties and Leaders in the Reign of Queen Anne 1702–10* (New Haven, Conn., 1920). It continued with G. M. Trevelyan, *England Under Queen Anne*, 3 vols. (1930–34), and G. S. Holmes, *British Politics*, esp. chap. 6.

34. Cf., however, G. S. Holmes, *British Politics*, pp. 210–16; and the revision implicit in Gregg, *Anne*.

35. *Memoirs of the Duchess of Marlborough*, pp. 86, 89–90.

36. Ibid., pp. 86–87.

37. See above, Chapter 3.

38. Sarah instructed Anne to burn her letters. Thus, only the copies taken by the former toward the end of their correspondence survive, along with the Queen's replies in Add. MSS 61416–18. Fortunately, the latter often give a good indication of what they were replying to. Many of these letters were printed in the *Conduct* and other collections of the Duchess's correspondence, with slight emendations.

39. See esp. Add. MSS 61416, ff. 24, 86–87 verso, 97, 197–203; *Memoirs of the Duchess of Marlborough*, pp. 90–91, 109–10, 111–12.

40. *Memoirs of the Duchess of Marlborough*, p. 112.

41. Ibid., pp. 112–13: Anne to Sarah, n.d. [15 Nov. 1705]. The Tories had,

among other things, opposed grants to the Duke of Marlborough in December 1702; promoted divisive Occasional Conformity Bills in 1702, 1703, and 1704, long after the Queen had ceased to support them, attempting, in the last case, to tack the measure onto the Land Tax Bill; and opposed the government's candidate for speaker in 1705. See ibid., p. 112, for the Duke of Buckingham's comment—made while the Queen was present, incognito, during the debate over the invitation in 1705—that she "might live till she did not know what she did and be like a child in the hands of others."

42. The Duke of Hamilton apparently thought her of some use in Scottish affairs early in the reign (see *C.S.P.D. 1702–03*, p. 142; *Letters Relating to Scotland in the Reign of Queen Anne by James Ogilvy, First Earl of Seafield, and Others*, ed. P. Hume Brown [Edinburgh, 1915], pp. 112, 115). In a fit of enthusiasm (or flattery) Lord Halifax credited her with having introduced the Queen to the Duke of Marlborough (Add. MSS 61458, f. 183 verso).

43. H.M.C., *Ninth Report*, App. II (1884), p. 474: Sarah to Mrs. Godolphin at "Eaton College," 3 Nov. 1718.

44. *Memoirs of the Duchess of Marlborough*, pp. 104, 258–59, 268; *Hamilton Diary*, p. 119.

45. Add. MSS 34518, f. 64, quoted in Morgan, *English Political Parties*, p. 209; *Memoirs of the Duchess of Marlborough*, pp. 181–82.

46. *Hamilton Diary*, p. 22. See also ibid., p. 120.

47. See *Marlborough-Godolphin Correspondence*, pp. 388 n. 1, 675; Morgan, *English Political Parties*, p. 209 n. 3.

48. *Private Correspondence of Sarah Duchess of Marlborough* . . . (1838), II: 103–4: Sarah to [Bishop Burnet], n.d. [after Jan. 1711].

49. *Memoirs of the Duchess of Marlborough*, p. 86.

50. See Add. MSS 61442, f. 176; 61450, f. 197 verso; 61455, ff. 92–93; 61456, ff. 172–73, 179; 61458, ff. 52–54 verso, 100 verso, 217 verso; 61474, ff. 69, 87 verso, 102, 161–63; Eg. MSS 1695, f. 6 verso; Kent A.O., Stanhope of Chevening MSS U1590 C 7/16, 9 Oct. 1704; 18 Jan. 1706; *Wentworth Papers*, p. 45.

51. Add. MSS 61450, f. 198 recto and verso: Sarah to the Duke of Montagu, [27 Aug. 1707].

52. *Wentworth Papers*, p. 45: Lady Wentworth to Lord Raby, Twickenham, 12 June 1705.

53. For other instances of Sarah's fielding, and in many cases discouraging, of petitions, see H.M.C., *Buccleuch at Montagu House MSS* I: 352; H.M.C., *Bathurst MSS*, pp. 4, 5, 8–9; Add. MSS 20778, f. 20 recto and verso; 61416, f. 205 verso; 61417, f. 173; 61423, ff. 183–84; 61455, ff. 94–95, 206; Eg. MSS 1695, ff. 6 verso, 10–13, 15; Huntington Library, Ellesmere Calendar, Bridgewater MSS 9990; Kent A.O., Stanhope of Chevening MSS U1590 C 7/26, 24 July 1702. For the Queen's appreciation of Sarah's services, see Add. MSS 61416, f. 205 verso; 61423, ff. 183–84.

54. Add MSS 61422, f. 6; 61458, ff. 100 recto and verso, 101; *Memoirs of the*

Duchess of Marlborough, pp. 90, 211–12. See also Add. MSS 31143, f. 6 verso. For Sarah's dominance of household patronage early in the reign, see above, Chapter 3.

55. Add. MSS 61418, ff. 60–61; 61442, ff. 171, 172 recto and verso, 176, 186 verso; 61456, f. 179; 61458, ff. 37–38, 136, 151; 61474, ff. 54, 61–64 verso, 79–80; D. Green, *Sarah, Duchess of Marlborough* (1967), p. 110.

56. H.M.C., *Downshire MSS* I ii, 828: Sarah to Sir William Trumbull, St. Alban's, 25 Apr. 1704.

57. Add. MSS 61416, f. 158 recto and verso: Anne to Sarah, "Wed. night," [17 May 1704]. See also ibid., f. 160 recto and verso.

58. Add. MSS 61444, f. 139 verso: Sarah to Humphrey Fyshe, 4 July 1727, quoted in F. Harris, "Accounts of the Conduct of Sarah, Duchess of Marlborough, 1704–42," *British Library Journal* VIII (1982): 30.

59. *Memoirs of the Duchess of Marlborough*, p. 130 and passim. For evidence of her earliest accusation to the Duke, see *Marlborough-Godolphin Correspondence*, p. 790. For subsequent accusations to friends and acquaintances, see H.M.C., *Downshire MSS* I ii, 855; Add. MSS 61441, f. 91 recto and verso; 61456, ff. 53, 174–75. It should be noted that Francis Atterbury noticed the Queen's favor for Abigail as early as June 1704: *Atterbury Correspondence* III: 208.

60. For Mrs. Masham's family relationship to both the Duchess of Marlborough and Robert Harley, see Gregg, *Anne*, p. 236.

61. Most of these letters are contained in B.L. Loan 29/38; many are printed in H.M.C., *Fifteenth Report*, App. IV; and H.M.C., *Portland MSS*, vol. V. The other face-to-face source is the *Hamilton Diary*: see below.

62. H.M.C., *Fifteenth Report*, App. IV, p. 525: [Abigail Masham to Robert Harley], 4 Sept. 1709. For other complaints by Mrs. Masham of the Queen's reserve toward her, see ibid., p. 524; B.L. Loan 29/38, "Tuesday night 12 a clock," n.d.

63. Swift, *Journal*, pp. 431, 433.

64. *Hamilton Diary*, p. 32; see also ibid., pp. 33–34.

65. Gregg, *Anne*, p. 347.

66. H.M.C., *Fifteenth Report*, App. IV, p. 499: Abigail to Harley, 27 July 1708. See also ibid., p. 524.

67. See Gregg, *Anne*, pp. 285, 298; B.L. Loan 29/38: "Thursday, 6th," n.d.; "Monday," n.d.; "Friday night past eleven," n.d.; "Sunday," n.d.; "Saturday night past eleven," n.d.

68. Gregg, *Anne*, p. 388; Royal College of Surgeons, Hunter-Baillie Collection, Arbuthnot Letterbook, f. 3: Earl of Mar to John Arbuthnot, 2 Aug. 1712.

69. Edward Gregg has found evidence of pregnancies, implying confinements and therefore absences from the Queen's side, in the late summer of 1708; sometime in 1709; the summer of 1711; the fall of 1712; and, possibly, the winter of 1713–14. In April 1713 Abigail was nursing a sick child (Gregg, *Anne*, p. 332 and n).

70. See H.M.C., *Portland MSS* V: 223, 315, 324, 360. For the earliest evidence of tension between Abigail and Oxford, see Gregg, *Anne*, p. 369.

71. Swift, *Journal*, p. 412 (entry of 14 Nov. 1711). For other visits, see pp. 333, 335, 351, 356, 433, 436, 447, 470, 480, 486, 489, 494, 504, 511, 514, 517, 521, 540, 614, 627.

72. For example, in April 1713, when the Queen was at St. James's and Mrs. Masham at Kensington nursing her eldest boy, who was seriously ill, Swift wrote: "She is so excessively fond it makes me mad; she should never leave the Qu, but leave every thing to stick to what is so much the Interest of the Publick as well as her own. This I tell her, but talk to the Winds." (Swift, *Journal*, p. 658.)

73. See H.M.C., *Fifteenth Report*, App. IV, pp. 657, 662; H.M.C., *Russell Astley MSS*, p. 198; Swift, *Journal*, p. 662; *Swift Correspondence* II: 79, 80; Add. MSS 22226, f. 239 recto and verso; B.L. Loan 29/38, "Monday, Kensington," n.d.

74. Burnet, *History* VI: 36 n. Dartmouth.

75. *Wentworth Papers*, p. 285: Lady Strafford to the Earl of Strafford, St. James's Square, 15 Apr. 1712.

76. H.M.C., *Bath MSS* I: 225; G. S. Holmes, *British Politics*, pp. 214–15 and n. 103; Burnet, *History* VI: 36 n. Dartmouth.

77. Burnet, *History* VI: 36 n. Dartmouth.

78. H.M.C., *Portland MSS* V: 49; G. S. Holmes, *British Politics*, pp. 201–2; E. Gregg, "Was Queen Anne a Jacobite?," *History* LVII (1972): 371.

79. Gregg, *Anne*, p. 353; Swift, *Journal*, pp. 660–63; for other examples of Abigail's soliciting through the ministry on behalf of others, see H.M.C., *Fifteenth Report*, App. IV, pp. 657, 662; B.L. Loan 29/38/1: Abigail to Harley, n.d.

80. B.L. Loan 29/38: Abigail to Oxford, "Monday, Kensington," n.d.

81. H.M.C., *Fifteenth Report*, App. IV, p. 536: [Abigail to Harley], 10 Mar. 1709/10.

82. *Journal inédit de Jean-Baptiste Colbert, Marquis de Torcy, ministre et secrétaire d'état des affaires étrangers pendant les années 1709, 1710 et 1711 . . .* , ed. F. Masson (Paris, 1884), p. 353.

83. G. S. Holmes, *British Politics*, p. 216, quoting B.L. Loan 29/10/8.

84. *Swift Correspondence* II: 81–82: Arbuthnot to Swift, [24 July 1714].

85. G. S. Holmes, *British Politics*, p. 216n, quoting B.L. Loan 29/10/8.

86. For Sarah's view, see Add. MSS 61422, f. 156 verso.

87. Burnet, *History* VI: 34 n. Dartmouth; Swift, *Journal*, pp. 206, 364, 434–35, 437, 443, 450, 461, 471, 482.

88. Add. MSS 22226, f. 171 recto and verso: Lady Strafford to the Earl of Strafford, 8 July 1712.

89. See Swift, *Journal*, p. 467; *Wentworth Papers*, pp. 208, 235; Burnet, *History* VI: 34 n. Dartmouth.

90. *Hamilton Diary*, p. 49. For Anne's agreement, see ibid., pp. 48, 57.

91. Gregg, *Anne*, p. 291; *Marlborough-Godolphin Correspondence*, pp. 1349, 1350; Add. MSS 61426, ff. 137–43; 61457, f. 4 verso.

92. See *Hamilton Diary*, pp. 37–40; *Wentworth Papers*, p. 258; Gregg, *Anne*, p. 352.

93. *Hamilton Diary*, p. 58.

94. Ibid.; for Hamilton's remonstrations, see ibid., pp. 46, 56, 58–59.

95. Ibid., p. 57; *Wentworth Papers*, p. 395; Chatsworth House, Derbyshire, Devonshire MSS 117.

96. *Wentworth Papers*, pp. 270–71: Lady Strafford to the Earl of Strafford, St. James's Square, 25 Feb. 1712; *Hamilton Diary*, p. 49.

97. *Hamilton Diary*, p. 124.

98. G. S. Holmes, *British Politics*, p. 215.

99. Gregg, *Anne*, p. 302, quoting Hertfordshire R.O., Panshanger MSS D/EP/F63, f. 31: Marlborough to Cowper, 18 Jan. [1710].

100. See above, Chapter 3.

101. This is an impression derived from a perusal of virtually all of the Duchess's pre-1730 correspondence as contained in Add. MSS 61414–76 and 62569. During this period she quarreled with nearly every major female relative or friend at one time or another, but never admitted any responsibility for these arguments.

102. Add. MSS 61416, f. 162. For the Queen's attitude to Jersey, see ibid.; G. S. Holmes, *British Politics*, p. 201. For Hedges's prudence, see G. S. Holmes, *British Politics*, pp. 255–56.

103. Gregg, *Anne*, p. 226, quoting Blenheim MSS G–17: Sarah to Anne, "Saturday morning ten a clock" [26 Sept. 1706].

104. *Memoirs of the Duchess of Marlborough*, p. 131. For Sarah's consistent attribution of royal behavior to Abigail's influence, see ibid., p. 162; H.M.C., *Downshire MSS* I ii, 855; *Marlborough-Godolphin Correspondence*, p. 1052; Add. MSS 61416, ff. 66, 96 verso, 159 verso, 185 verso, 211; 61417, ff. 74 verso, 75 verso–76, 102 verso–103, 137–40, 153–58 verso, 182, 183 verso, 190 verso; 61418, ff. 1 verso, 3 verso, 19; 61422, ff. 156 verso, 158 verso; 61434, f. 90.

105. *Hamilton Diary*, pp. 7, 11, 24–25, 34, 48. For Swift and the Tories, see above.

106. *The Letters and Diplomatic Instructions of Queen Anne*, ed. B. C. Brown (New York, 1968), p. 100: Anne to Sarah, St. James's, 21 Nov. [misdated 1702–4 by Brown; dated 1704 by Gregg, *Anne*, p. 193 n. 46].

107. *Hamilton Diary*, p. 44.

108. A full-scale discussion of contemporary attitudes toward gender, and female sovereignty in particular, is beyond the scope of this work. However, an interesting discussion of the problem in a Tudor context is to be found in P. L. Scalingi, "The Scepter or the Distaff: The Question of Female Sovereignty, 1516–1607," *The Historian* XLI (1978): 59–75.

109. Adams, "Faction, Clientage and Party," passim.

110. These factors, along with the happiness of her marriage and her prob-

able menopausal state at or soon after her accession, also ensured that marital, sexual, and obstetrical politics would play little part in Anne's reign. The only exception was the pair of parliamentary addresses urging her to remarry after Prince George's death. These were probably intended "to forestall any new proposal for an invitation to Hanover" (Gregg, *Anne*, p. 285). There is no evidence that Anne ever violated her marriage vows in either thought or deed. Sarah's charge of lesbianism is ludicrous even within the context of their bitter quarrel (ibid., pp. 272–78). Nevertheless, it still resurfaces upon occasion (see Somerset, *Ladies in Waiting*, pp. 182–84). Despite the Queen's high standards, a number of her courtiers and servants engaged in sexual and extramarital intrigues: notably Henrietta, Lady Godolphin, Jane, Lady Hyde, and the circle of rakes that included Thomas Coke, George Granville, and Henry St. John. However, such activity was far less common than at earlier courts, and it was of no discernable political significance.

111. *Hamilton Diary*, p. 15. See, for example, Add. MSS 61416, ff. 36 verso, 80 verso–81.

112. Gregg, *Anne*, p. 260; G. S. Holmes, *British Politics*, pp. 207, 212. There is no evidence that she had consulted the Prince previously.

113. Add. MSS 61416, f. 34: Anne to Sarah, [1702–3]. For the Duchess's opinion, see *Memoirs of the Duchess of Marlborough*, p. 88; Add. MSS 61426, ff. 41–46; for Nottingham, see Sharp, *Life of John Sharp* I: 312.

114. Sharp, *Life of John Sharp* I: 251, 318–19. For evidence of Sharp's frequent attendance on the Queen, see *Nicolson Diaries*, pp. 159, 167, 227, 387, 412, 451–52, 501.

115. Sharp, *Life of John Sharp* I: 319. For Sharp's deferring to a minister over patronage, see S.P. Dom. 34/19, f. 166.

116. Hart, *Life and Times of John Sharp*, pp. 115, 246, 255. For additional evidence of Sharp's influence on ecclesiastical affairs, see *Nicolson Diaries*, pp. 222, 451–52; S.P. Dom. 34/1, ff. 69–70; 12, f. 160; 15, ff. 84, 172; 16, ff. 68–69, 79; 18, f. 80; 19, f. 133 verso; 34, f. 38.

117. Sharp, *Life of John Sharp* I: 306; Gregg, *Anne*, pp. 178–79.

118. Sharp, *Life of John Sharp* I: 383–400; *Swift Correspondence* I: 176.

119. Sharp, *Life of John Sharp* I: 315.

120. For Sharp's appointment of preachers, see Sharp, *Life of John Sharp* I: 326–28; Hart, *Life and Times of John Sharp*, pp. 225–27. For his influence on Nicolson's appointment at Carlisle in 1702, see Hart, *Life and Times of John Sharp*, p. 238; on Hooper at St. Asaph in 1703, see ibid., p. 239; on Beveridge at St. Asaph in 1704, see Sharp, *Life of John Sharp* I: 337; on Bull at St. David's in 1705, see ibid., I: 337, and Hart, *Life and Times of John Sharp*, p. 240; on Moore at Ely, Dawes at Chester, and Blackall at Exeter, all in 1707, see ibid., p. 241; on Dawes at York, see ibid., p. 245; and, possibly, on Bisse at St. David's and Robinson at Bristol in 1710, and Ottley at St. David's in 1712, see ibid. For his influence on the disposal of other livings, see ibid., pp. 15, 186, 239, 245; Sharp, *Life of John Sharp* I: 336–37 and n; H.M.C., *Fifteenth Report*, App. IV, p. 141; Add. MSS

61416, f. 160; S.P. Dom. 34/1, f. 69 verso; 2, ff. 129–30; 12, f. 160; 16, f. 69; 18, f. 80; 34, f. 38. See also G. V. Bennett, "Robert Harley, the Godolphin Ministry, and the Bishoprics Crisis of 1707," *E.H.R.* LXXXII (1967): 726–46.

121. For Drake, see Hart, *Life and Times of John Sharp*, p. 245; H.M.C., *Bath MSS* I: 222. For the bishoprics, see above, n. 120.

122. Hart, *Life and Times of John Sharp*, p. 103; Swift, *Journal*, pp. 665 n. 38, 667.

123. For example, in 1707 Sharp failed to procure the see of Lincoln for Dawes, the regius professorship of divinity at Oxford for Smalridge, and a prebend's stall at St. Paul's for a Finch (Hart, *Life and Times of John Sharp*, pp. 240, 243; H.M.C., *Fifteenth Report*, App. IV, p. 388). In 1711 he failed to procure the deanery of Christ Church for Smalridge (*Nicolson Diaries*, pp. 510, 523).

124. See H.M.C., *First Report* (1870), App., p. 22; H.M.C., *Portland MSS* V: 58; S.P. Dom. 34/2, f. 130; 19, f. 133; Hart, *Life and Times of John Sharp*, pp. 223–25.

125. Add. MSS 61422, f. 156 verso. See also f. 158 verso. For a good sketch of Somerset's character, see G. S. Holmes, *British Politics*, p. 226.

126. *Memoirs of the Duchess of Marlborough*, pp. 42, 241; *Shrewsbury Correspondence*, pp. 634–35.

127. G. S. Holmes, *British Politics*, pp. 205, 226; Add. MSS 61422, ff. 158 recto and verso; *Wentworth Papers*, pp. 143–44, 149–50, 152, 232–33, 235; Swift, *Journal*, pp. 332, 437, 461; *Swift Correspondence* I: 248, 283–84.

128. See G. S. Holmes, *British Politics*, p. 195.

129. Gregg, *Anne*, p. 351; G. S. Holmes, *British Politics*, p. 390.

130. In July 1706 he is reported to have "been extreamly pressing with the Queen" to allow Lord Walden to sell his regiment (*Marlborough-Godolphin Correspondence*, p. 619; Add. MSS 61134, ff. 57 verso–58). In August 1707 he petitioned Anne and the ministry for his son to be made governor of Teignmouth (Add. MSS 61134, f. 59 recto and verso; *Hamilton Diary*, p. 21). In 1708–9 he pushed for regiments or lesser commands to be given to Lords Brooke, Lumley, and Winchester; Messrs. Berkeley, Dormer, and MacCartney, and his son Hertford (*Marlborough-Godolphin Correspondence*, pp. 1154, 1294, 1346, 1371–72, 1397–98; Add. MSS 61134, ff. 65, 68–69, 70, 72 recto and verso, 74 recto and verso, 76–77). Arthur Maynwaring thought that the preferment of John Hill to be a colonel "was certainly 13's [Somerset's] advice, who fancies he made Honiwood a Col." (Add. MSS 61461, f. 36). Outside of military appointments, he was "zealous for Mr. Stanhope" to be appointed envoy to the Archduke in 1703; "stickled hard" for Nicholas Rowe to be appointed to Secretary Queensberry's office in 1709; and designed "to get 10 [Rivers] a pension" in 1709 (*Marlborough-Godolphin Correspondence*, pp. 218 and nn. 1–2, 227 n. 6, 1402 n. 1; Kent A.O., Stanhope of Chevening MSS U1590 C 9/28: 2 July 1702, 8 June 1703; O/48: 30 July 1703, 23 Aug. 1703; Add. MSS 61134, f. 61 recto and verso; *Wentworth Papers*, pp. 140–41). Of these solicitations, only those on behalf of Hertford, Rowe, and—if Maynwaring was correct—Hill and Honiwood can be shown to

have been successful (*Hamilton Diary*, p. 21; Charles Dalton, *George the First's Army, 1714–27* [1910–12], I: 96; Luttrell, *Brief Relation* VI: 404).

131. *Marlborough-Godolphin Correspondence*, pp. 1497: Godolphin to the Duke of Marlborough, 16 May 1710; 1501: Godolphin to Sarah, "Fryday evening at 8," [19 May 1710]. See also ibid., pp. 1350, 1512; Add. MSS 61418, ff. 91, 107; 61422, ff. 72–79 verso; 61425, ff. 137–43.

132. Add. MSS 61426, f. 182 verso; *Marlborough-Godolphin Correspondence*, pp. 1464–65.

133. *Wentworth Papers*, p. 128: Peter Wentworth to Lord Raby, 4 Aug. 1710.

134. Add. MSS 61460, f. 209: [Sarah to Arthur Maynwaring, circa 18 Apr. 1710].

135. H.M.C., *Fifteenth Report*, App. IV, p. 553: Somerset to [Robert Harley], "Sunday night, six o'clock," 30 July 1710. For additional examples of Somerset's role as an intermediary between Harley and the Queen, see ibid., pp. 545, 548, 552, 557.

136. *Marlborough-Godolphin Correspondence*, pp. 1613, 1634; Burnet, *History* VI: 14; Add. MSS 61461, f. 85 verso.

137. See *Marlborough-Godolphin Correspondence*, pp. 1539, 1613, 1632; Add. MSS 61460, f. 217.

138. Burnet, *History* V: 453 n. Dartmouth. For Dartmouth's criticisms, see the rest of the passage. For the Duchess's views, see *Memoirs of the Duchess of Marlborough*, pp. 176, 241–46; Add. MSS 61422, ff. 127 verso, 156 verso; 61423, ff. 175, 176 verso–177.

139. *Memoirs of the Duchess of Marlborough*, p. 241; *Shrewsbury Correspondence*, pp. 634–35. For his relationship to Anne and the Churchills, see Gregg, *Anne*, pp. 82, 97, 100.

140. *Marlborough-Godolphin Correspondence*, p. 1478: Godolphin to Sarah, "29 Aprill at noon" [1710]. Late in William's reign, when Shrewsbury was first prevailed upon to take up the lord chamberlainship, Lord Somers pointed out to him: "[The office will] most naturally bring you near the king . . . without the toil and danger of a secretary's place, and without the ruin of your health." (*Shrewsbury Correspondence*, p. 522: Somers to Shrewsbury, 29 Dec.–8 Jan. 1697–98.)

141. Add. MSS 61422, f. 156 verso. See also H.M.C., *Thirteenth Report*, App. II, p. 210; H.M.C., *Bath MSS* I: 199, 221, 360; *Wentworth Papers*, pp. 128–29.

142. Staffordshire R.O., Dartmouth MSS D 1778 I ii, nos. 163, 336; V, no. 777: Shrewsbury to Dartmouth, n.d.; H.M.C., *Portland MSS* V: 12; H.M.C., *Bath MSS* I: 199, 220, 221, 360; H.M.C., *Downshire MSS* I ii, 888–89; Swift, *Journal*, p. 21; S.P. Dom. 34/19, f. 25.

143. See H.M.C., *Fifteenth Report*, App. IV, p. 658, 660; H.M.C., *Bath MSS* I: 219, 231.

144. Eg. MSS 1695, f. 51: Shrewsbury to Lady Longueville, Windsor, 11 Oct. 1713; see also f. 49 for a similar diffidence. However, cf. *Nicolson Diaries*, p. 566.

145. H.M.C., *Bath MSS* I: 210: Anne to Oxford, 19 Sept. [1711].

146. Gregg, *Anne*, pp. 386–87.

147. H.M.C., *Bath MSS* I: 216: Anne to Oxford, 15 Nov. [1711]; see also Gregg, *Protestant Succession*, p. 58.

148. Gregg, *Anne*, pp. 344–45.

149. D. Szechi, "The Duke of Shrewsbury's Contacts with the Jacobites in 1713," *B.I.H.R.* LVI (1983): 230–31; MacPherson, *Original Papers* II: 479–80.

150. Gregg, *Anne*, pp. 388–89; E. Cruickshanks, "The Tories and the Succession to the Crown in the 1714 Parliament," *B.I.H.R.* XLVI (1973): 183–84.

151. For the period prior to Coke's appointment as vice chamberlain, see H.M.C., *Twelfth Report*, App. III, p. 17; Melbourne Hall, Derbyshire, Melbourne Hall MSS, old no. 67 / new no. 107: Francis Mundy to Coke, 19 Feb. 1703[/04]; old no. 67 / new no. 110: Richard Wilmot to same, 17 Nov. 1705; old no. 94: John Coke to same, 22 Oct.; old no. 99: Edward Coke to same, 23 Oct. 1703; same to same, 10 Nov. 1703; old no. 104: Godfrey Clarke to same, 15 Nov. 1706; old no. 105: Ralph Burton to same, 16 Feb. 1703/04. For the period following his appointment, see H.M.C., *Twelfth Report*, App. III, pp. 75–76, 84, 97, 103, 104, 107, 183; Melbourne Hall, Derbyshire, Melbourne Hall MSS, old no. 67 / new no. 108: Sir Edward Coke to Thomas Coke, Richmond Green, 1 Oct. 1707; Martin Gonzalez de Belslaza to same, 11 Apr. 1708; old no. 67 / new no. 109: Henry Gilbert to same, 14 June 1712 (also 30 June; 19, 28 July); old no. 97: Elizabeth Coke to same, 11 Jan. [1710].

152. Bishop Compton is supposed to have persuaded the Queen to drop the ecclesiastical commission in 1702, but in other matters he tended to solicit through the ministry (Morgan, *English Political Parties*, p. 160; B.L. Loan 29/37, letters dated 5 Nov. and 8 Dec. 1712; 25 Apr. and 19 June 1713; S.P. Dom. 34/2, f. 92; 13, f. 168; 14, f. 92; 16, f. 171; 20, ff. 9, 74, 123; 21, f. 64; 33, f. 49. However, cf. also S.P. Dom. 34/14, f. 66; 16, f. 235; 19, ff. 1, 32; 34, f. 32; 35, f. 107; H.M.C., *Bath MSS* I: 97, 152, for direct applications). The first Duke of Devonshire's chaplain was made a prebend of Westminster in May 1702, and he was one of three peers who successfully recommended Parker to be chief justice in 1705 (Luttrell, *Brief Relation* V: 177, 560). The second Duke influenced White Kennett's appointment as dean of Peterborough in 1707, but failed in his solicitations for Somers in 1708. He petitioned the Marlboroughs, not the Queen, for a garter for Orford in 1709. (G. V. Bennett, *White Kennett, 1660–1728, Bishop of Peterborough* [1957], pp. 99 and n. 3, 134; *Marlborough-Godolphin Correspondence*, pp. 958–59; H.M.C., *Thirteenth Report*, App. II, pp. 203, 210–11; Add. MSS 61459, f. 62 verso; 61474, ff. 201–2.) The Duke of Montagu frequently petitioned his in-laws, the Marlboroughs, for places and pensions; Lords Paget and Poulett tended to go through their longtime political chief, Oxford, rather than petition the Queen directly (Add. MSS 61303, f. 16; 61450, ff. 195–99 verso; H.M.C., *Portland MSS* V: 195, 283, 423, 437, 446–47, 449–50).

153. H.M.C., *Russell Astley MSS*, p. 91: A[nne, Lady] Frescheville to Lady Russell, 30 July [1702–?]. For another, similar example, see S.P. Dom. 34/18, f. 63.

154. Add. MSS 61459, f. 102 verso: Arthur Maynwaring to Sarah, Duchess of Marlborough, "Sat. morn.," [11 Sept. 1708].

155. See, for example, Peter Wentworth's attributions of influence to Henry Lowman, clerk of the kitchen, and Charles Scarborough, clerk of the green-cloth (Add. MSS 31144, f. 413 verso; *Wentworth Papers*, p. 139).

156. Kent A.O., Stanhope of Chevening MSS U1590 C 8/4: Mary Stanhope to Philip Stanhope, endorsed 11 July 1707, written after the Duchess of Marlborough informed Mary that her request for prize money had been denied. For Mary's reliance upon the Duchess for favors, see ibid., C 7/16, letters dated 7 Oct. 1704, 18 Jan. 1706.

157. For Arbuthnot's supposed influence, see *Wentworth Papers*, p. 138; *Swift Correspondence* II: 75; Swift, *Journal*, pp. 329, 370–72. For evidence of his influence on minor appointments, see Swift, *Journal*, pp. 329, 370–72; Aitken, *Arbuthnot*, pp. 40–41; *Swift Correspondence* II: 33. On a higher plane, Arbuthnot exerted himself in conjunction with Lord Treasurer Oxford for Arthur Charlett to be made a bishop, and failed (Aitken, *Arbuthnot*, p. 50).

158. *Hamilton Diary*, p. 20.

159. Ibid., pp. 22, 23–24, 25–27, 29, 30, 31, 37, 38, 48, 49, 50, 57. See also Add. MSS 61423, f. 14 verso.

160. *Hamilton Diary*, pp. 20, 34.

161. Ibid., pp. 13, 16–17.

162. Burnet, *History* V: 455. For the others, see H.M.C., *Eighth Report*, App. I, p. 38; Swift, *Journal*, p. 206; *Memoirs of the Duchess of Marlborough*, pp. 260–61; Add. MSS 61460, f. 26 verso; *Hamilton Diary*, pp. 47, 50.

163. See above, sub "Access."

164. Add. MSS 31144, f. 410 verso: Wentworth to the Earl of Strafford, Windsor, 2 Sept. 1713; see also MacPherson, *Original Papers* II: 505.

165. Gregg, *Anne*, p. 347.

166. *Hamilton Diary*, pp. 62–63. During the politically sensitive summer of 1710, Hamilton was also sometimes asked about public opinion: see ibid., p. 11.

167. Add. MSS 31143, f. 580; G. S. Holmes, *British Politics*, p. 210.

168. For the Whig attempt in January 1710 to purge Masham by parliamentary address, see Gregg, *Anne*, pp. 302–3; G. S. Holmes, *British Politics*, p. 209. For the Tory attempt to have Hamilton removed, see *Hamilton Diary*, p. xxxii.

169. Burnet, *History* V: 457.

170. Sharp, *Life of John Sharp* I: 299–311; *Nicolson Diaries*, pp. 392–93 n. 22. The Queen also canvassed Archbishop Tenison, unsuccessfully, in 1703 over legislation concerning Prince George (*Nicolson Diaries*, pp. 159–67).

171. Gregg, *Anne*, p. 303.

172. G. S. Holmes, *British Politics*, p. 209, quoting Finch MSS G. S., bundle 23, anon. letter, 28 Jan. 1709[/10].

173. For example, in the winter of 1711–12 Anne closeted, largely unsuccessfully, with Whig peers over the peace and the Hamilton peerage (Gregg,

Anne, pp. 344, 351; *Parl. Hist.* VI: 1034; Burnet, *History* VI: 76n; Add. MSS 22226, f. 41). She did so with success in January 1714 to oppose another proposed invitation to the Electress (Gregg, *Anne*, pp. 377–78). For additional examples of closeting, see MacPherson, *Original Papers* II: 574, 612; Szechi, *Jacobitism*, pp. 86, 89, 128, 145.

174. For Coke, see *Wentworth Papers*, p. 103. For Shrewsbury, see *Hamilton Diary*, p. 29. For Somerset, see below.

175. Gregg, *Anne*, p. 254; *Marlborough-Godolphin Correspondence*, p. 1416.

176. *Marlborough-Godolphin Correspondence*, p. 1437: Godolphin to the Duke of Marlborough, 17 Mar. 1709/10; see also ibid., p. 1440.

177. For the Queen's rather complicated position on Sacheverell—which coincided roughly with her ministry's position on the idea of trying the clergyman, but not with their position on his punishment—see G. S. Holmes, *British Politics*, p. 187.

178. *Swift Correspondence* I: 284: Swift to Archbishop William King, London, 8 Jan. 1711/12.

179. Sharp, *Life of John Sharp* I: 391; *Nicolson Diaries*, p. 528; S.P. Dom. 34/35, f. 17; H.M.C., *Portland MSS* VIII: 260; H.M.C., *Bath MSS* I: 218; *Hamilton Diary*, p. 10; Swift, *Journal*, p. 21; Add. MSS 61414, ff. 29, 111; 61442, f. 40; Aitken, *Arbuthnot*, p. 33.

180. *Hamilton Diary*, pp. 65–67. Earlier, Hamilton had also been used as a go-between with the Churchills, Godolphin, and Lord Cowper (ibid., pp. 7–8, 10, 12, 13, 15, 20–21, 25, 26, 30, 36–37, 38–39, 45).

181. R. M. Hatton, "New Light on George I of Great Britain," in *England's Rise to Greatness*, ed. Baxter, p. 252 n. 112.

182. Burnet, *History* VI: 37 n. Dartmouth.

183. Gregg, *Anne*, pp. 85, 98; Add. MSS 61414, f. 150 recto and verso; 61421, ff. 130–31 verso; 61474, f. 15.

184. Add. MSS 61418, f. 91; 61422, f. 24; 61425, f. 15 verso; *Memoirs of the Duchess of Marlborough*, p. 172; Gregg, *Anne*, p. 244; H.M.C., *Eighth Report*, App. I, p. 38.

185. Add. MSS 61418, ff. 11, 91. See also *Memoirs of the Duchess of Marlborough*, p. 172.

186. See above, Chapter 3.

187. See, for example, *Memoirs of the Duchess of Marlborough*, pp. 147, 261; H.M.C., *Tenth Report*, App. IV, p. 51; Add. MSS 22225, f. 342 verso; 61416, f. 131; 61417, f. 185; 61422, f. 24 verso.

188. Add. MSS 31144, f. 412 verso: Wentworth to Strafford, Windsor, 13 Sept. 1713.

189. *Wentworth Papers*, pp. 68–69, 82, 92, 124, 154, 193, 218, 247, 312, 325, 347, 354, 358, 359, 387, 407–9; Add. MSS 22225, ff. 331 verso–332; 31143, ff. 263 verso, 401, 486 verso, 580; 31144, ff. 257 verso, 274, 321 recto and verso, 359 verso; 416 verso–417.

190. *Wentworth Papers*, pp. 128–29, 147–48, 149, 152, 208, 213, 250; Add. MSS 31144, ff. 410 verso–411.

191. *Wentworth Papers*, pp. 103, 232–33, 235, 371.

192. The political, social, and cultural significance of the London ambassadorial community during the later Stuart period is a subject deserving of study in its own right. Because of this, and because the limits of the present study had to be drawn somewhere, the great caches of diplomatic correspondence housed in continental archives have not been consulted for this work. However, the Netherlands Transcripts (Add. MSS 17677 XX–EEE; GGG–HHH) and Stowe MSS (nos. 222–27) in the British Library; the Baschet Transcripts (P.R.O. 31/3/199–203) in the Public Record Office; the ambassadorial correspondence printed by Kemble, Klopp, Legrelle, MacPherson, Morandi, and Salomon; and the various printed reminiscences left by the Marquis de Torcy have been examined. The overall impression left by this admittedly partial survey is that several of the foreign ambassadors (L'Hermitage, Hoffmann, Kreyenberg) were keen and observant reporters of the day-to-day activities of the English court, government, and parliament, often surpassing the newspapers and newsletters of the day in the completeness of their reportage. However, their "inside" political information (regarding the Queen and her courtiers, at least) tended to be superficial and stereotypical, deriving as it did from sources within whichever political party the respective ambassador's government happened to favor. The resulting information tended to be based upon rumor: numerous sentences begin "On dit . . ." In short, because of the Queen's physical isolation and native prudence, her court lacked a Barillon (French ambassador at the courts of Charles II and James II), i.e., a foreign observer of keen intelligence who was admitted into the monarch's confidence.

193. For the importance attached to the Queen's well-being by contemporaries, see H.M.C., *Bath MSS* I: 233; *Hamilton Diary*, p. 54; *Bolingbroke Correspondence* III: 76.

194. Add. MSS 17677 HHH, ff. 87 verso–88.

195. P.R.O. 31/3/202, f. 8: Charles d'Iberville to Louis XIV, 8 Jan. 1714 (n.s.). See also ibid., ff. 19 verso, 29, 37.

196. See below, Chapter 7, sub "Social Life."

197. *Wentworth Papers*, p. 302n (passage noted, but not copied, by Cartwright); *Swift Correspondence* II: 35, 93–95; Swift, *Journal*, pp. 515, 561; *Hamilton Diary*, pp. 4–5, 50; *Parl. Hist.* VI: 1240n; Snyder, "Last Days," p. 263; Add. MSS 4043, f. 157; Aitken, *Arbuthnot*, pp. 55–56.

198. *Wentworth Papers*, p. 188: Wentworth to Lord Raby, 20 Mar. 1711.

199. Add. MSS 31144, f. 442: Wentworth to the Earl of Strafford, London, 30 Mar. 1714. For examples of Arbuthnot's deception, see H.M.C., *Downshire MSS* I ii, 854; Add. MSS 22226, f. 225 verso. For a virtual admission that this was a conscious policy, see below, n. 204.

200. H.M.C., *Portland MSS* V: 305: [Defoe to Oxford], 18 July 1713. For evi-

dence of Defoe's charge, see Add. MSS 22226, f. 85 recto and verso; Gregg, *Anne*, pp. 374, 378; MacPherson, *Original Papers* II: 405, 440.

201. *Hamilton Diary*, p. 60; H.M.C., *Downshire MSS* I ii, 854.

202. For Arbuthnot's lodgings, see LC 5/154, pp. 84, 423; LC 5/155, pp. 163, 203.

203. *Hamilton Diary*, p. xxxi.

204. H.M.C., *Eighth Report*, App. I, p. 50. Regarding this reasoning, Arbuthnot wrote to Swift: "Shadwell says he will have my place at Chelsea. Garth told me his merit was giving intelligence about his mistress's health. I desired he would do me the favour to say, that I valued myself upon quite the contrary; and I hoped to live to see the day when his Majesty would value me the more for it too" (Aitken, *Arbuthnot*, p. 82: Arbuthnot to Swift, 19 Oct. 1714; see also ibid., p. 52).

205. Add. MSS 22226, f. 258: Lady Strafford to the Earl of Strafford, 30 Dec. 1712. For other examples of this practice, see Add. MSS 17677 CCC, f. 616 verso; HHH, f. 18; 22226, ff. 50, 66, 71 verso, 241 verso, 244; *Wentworth Papers*, pp. 234–35; *Swift Correspondence* I: 214.

206. Add. MSS 22226, f. 66: Lady Strafford to the Earl of Strafford, 8 Jan. 1711[/12]; see also f. 244.

207. Swift, *Journal*, p. 139.

208. Ibid., p. 440. Similarly, after James II's flight in 1688, the Earl of Clarendon resolved to go to court "to see how the world went": *Clarendon Correspondence* II: 231, 239.

209. Add. MSS 31144, ff. 286–87; 61460, ff. 43 verso–44 verso; *Wentworth Papers*, pp. 72, 74, 87, 142–43, 215; Burnet, *History* VI: 34 n. Dartmouth; H.M.C., *Portland MSS* V: 171; Klopp, *Stuart* XIII: 4; Swift, *Journal*, pp. 135, 285, 320, 327, 499, 633.

210. Swift, *Journal*, p. 603. In the first two cases he was quite correct, but overly optimistic in the last: see below, Chapter 7, sub "Social Life."

211. Add. MSS 31144, f. 329 verso: Peter Wentworth to the Earl of Strafford, 23 Jan. 1712/13; see also Add. MSS 17677 GGG, f. 40 verso; P.R.O. 31/3/201, ff. 9 verso–10; Swift, *Journal*, p. 633; *Atterbury Correspondence* III: 226.

212. Add. MSS 31144, f. 288 recto and verso: Peter Wentworth to the Earl of Strafford, Windsor, 24 Aug. 1712; see also ibid., ff. 274 verso–275, 296–97; *Wentworth Papers*, p. 184.

213. See, for example, *Wentworth Papers*, p. 184; H.M.C., *Portland MSS* V: 436; Add. MSS 31144, ff. 274 verso–275, 296–97; 61443, f. 44 verso.

214. In this section, "government" refers to the ministry and its adherents; "court" with a lowercase "c" continues to stand for the royal household. For contemporaries, as seen above, "Court" with a capital "C" conflated "ministry" and "royal household."

215. This is in marked contrast to the situation under Charles II, when "great pains were taken to have some of the king's menial servants chosen; so that there was a very great number of men in all stations in the court, as well

below stairs as above, who were members of the house of commons": Edward, Earl of Clarendon, *The Life of Edward, Earl of Clarendon* (Oxford, 1857), I: 608. See also *Savile Correspondence*, p. 45.

216. G. S. Holmes, *British Politics*, pp. 121, 130; Plumb, *Political Stability*, chap. 4.

217. [S. Clement], *Faults on both Sides; or an Essay upon the original Cause, Progress, and mischievous Consequences of the Factions in this Nation . . .*, printed in *A Collection of Scarce and Valuable Tracts . . . Selected From . . . Public, as Well as Private, Libraries . . .*, ed. Sir W. Scott (1809–15; repr., 1965), XII: 691.

218. James Lowther to William Gilpin, 2 Sept. 1710, quoted in W. A. Speck, *Tory & Whig: The Struggle in the Constituencies, 1701–1715* (1970), p. 79; see also ibid., pp. 84–85.

219. See G. S. Holmes, "The Attack on 'The Influence of the Crown' 1702–16," *B.I.H.R.* XXXIX (1966): 47–68, esp. pp. 67–68.

220. G. S. Holmes, *British Politics*, pp. 121, 366, 436–39; C. Jones, "'The Scheme Lords, the Neccessitous Lords, and the Scots Lords': The Earl of Oxford's Management and the 'Party of the Crown' in the House of Lords, 1711–14," in *Party and Management in Parliament, 1660–1784*, ed. C. Jones (Leicester, 1984), p. 126 and passim.

221. Speck, *Tory & Whig*, pp. 72–73, 80, 84–85; W. A. Speck, "The House of Commons, 1702–14: A Study in Political Organization" (D. Phil. thesis, Oxford University, 1965), pp. 311–12. However, cf. L. Colley, *In Defiance of Oligarchy: The Tory Party 1714–60* (Cambridge, Eng., 1982), pp. 19–20, 120–25, for an alternate view.

222. Roberts, "Party and Patronage," passim.

223. Specifically, the lists of members in attendance, committee members, managers with the Commons, and reporters to the House contained in the *Lords Journals* have been made to yield averages per session for each peer (1) over the whole of his parliamentary career and (2) over the period of his household employment (a subset of [1]). These averages have themselves been averaged for the entire population of household peers in Table 6.2. The same procedure was applied to the lists of committee members, chairs of committees, reporters, and tellers contained in the *Commons Journals*, to yield the composite averages for household M.P.s in Table 6.3. The alternate procedure of dividing members' careers into discrete periods in household office and out of it raises the complicating factor of a period in an office outside of the household, which proved far too cumbersome to include in the tables.

224. A comparison with the averages for all members of both Houses, though useful, proved to be beyond the scope of this work.

225. Delawarr's interest in this aspect of parliamentary business seems to have run in the family: his son was the earliest documented lord chairman of committees (S. Lambert, *Bills & Acts* [Cambridge, Eng., 1971], p. 91).

226. Add. MSS 22221, f. 289: Delawarr to the Earl of Strafford, 3 Sept. 1713; see also G. S. Holmes, *British Politics*, pp. 385–86.

227. For the political affiliations of these men, see the sources noted Appendix B; and information provided by Cruickshanks and Hayton.

228. *Parl. Hist.* VI: 492–93, 860; Gregg, *Anne*, p. 166; *Nicolson Diaries*, pp. 122, 173, 286, 321–22; G. S. Holmes, *British Politics*, p. 73; H.M.C., *Fifteenth Report*, App. IV, pp. 50, 75; *Marlborough-Godolphin Correspondence*, p. 159; Sharp, *Life of John Sharp* I: 268–69; Hart, *Life and Times of John Sharp*, p. 211; *Wentworth Papers*, p. 223; Swift, *Journal*, p. 433; MacPherson, *Original Papers* II: 401.

229. Gregg, *Anne*, p. 348; Szechi, *Jacobitism*, p. 104.

230. For the lists upon which this study is based, see Appendix D.

231. The one significant exception for this analysis is the list for the Commons' division on whether to agree with the Lords' amendments to the bill for extending the time for taking the Abjuration Oath on 13 February 1703 (Hayton and Jones no. 79). The government's position on the first two Occasional Conformity Bills was not unequivocal, so these divisions have not been counted in calculating government/opposition votes (see H. L. Snyder, "The Defeat of the Occasional Conformity Bill and the Tack: A Study in the Techniques of Parliamentary Management in the Reign of Queen Anne," *B.I.H.R.* XLI [1968]: 172–86).

232. This is demonstrated clearly in the ministry's equivocal position on the Schism Act (see Gregg, *Anne*, p. 386). The various lists associated with this issue have therefore not been counted in calculating government/opposition votes.

233. See Speck, "House of Commons," p. 157. My reference to these dichotomies is not meant to suggest that there was ever an organized opposition independent of the two parties under Queen Anne. Thus, "opposition" remains lowercase.

234. Even the Lords' division on the Hamilton peerage (20 Dec. 1711, Hayton and Jones no. 74) which Wentworth, for one, thought devoid of party significance (*Wentworth Papers*, p. 229) did more or less divide along party lines. This is understandable: it is hardly likely that the Whigs would not feel strongly about giving Lord Treasurer Oxford another potential supporter and the Tories another hereditary seat in the Lords.

235. Hayton and Jones, no. 60. See C. Jones, "Godolphin, the Whig Junto and the Scots: A New Lords' Division List from 1709," *Scottish Historical Review* LVIII (1979): 158–74.

236. Specifically, the recorded votes of each household peer and M.P. were individually classified as either Whig or Tory, then added up and expressed as a percentage of whichever side the member in question voted with most frequently. Thus, a member who voted seven times Whig and three times Tory is classified as 70 percent Whig, and would appear in the Whig side of column 1 (Tables 6.4 and 6.5) in the 51–75 percent rank. The same members' votes on the same issues (where the categories apply) were then classified along government/opposition lines, expressed as a percentage, and so on.

237. Court loyalties also prevailed for Cholmondeley, Kent, Sharp, and

Somerset in the vote on the rights of Scots peers in 1709, but this was not an issue with a clear-cut party component (Hayton and Jones, no. 60).

238. See the lists noted in Appendix D and *Nicolson Diaries*, pp. 392–95, 415, 518, 541–42, 612. Nottingham forecast that Cholmondeley would join his fellow Whigs in opposing the Schism Bill in the spring of 1714 (Hayton and Jones, no. 82).

239. See above, Chapter 4, sub "Politics."

240. See the lists noted in Appendix D.

241. See esp. G. S. Holmes, *British Politics*, chap. 2. However, cf. Colley, *Defiance of Oligarchy*, pp. 12–17, for the suggestion that Augustan politics was far more stylized and consensual than has previously been thought.

242. The following discussion is confined to the household officers in parliament. However, there is considerable evidence to suggest that the argument set forth is applicable to placemen in general. See G. S. Holmes, *British Politics*, chaps. 11–12; Speck, "House of Commons," chap. 3; idem, "The Choice of a Speaker in 1705," *B.I.H.R.* XXXVII (1964): 29–30; Snyder, "Occasional Conformity," p. 186; C. Jones, "Scheme Lords," passim.

243. Snyder, "Occasional Conformity," p. 186 n. 3; Speck, *Tory & Whig*, p. 100.

244. Information provided by Cruickshanks and Hayton.

245. G. S. Holmes, *British Politics*, p. 255, and the lists noted in Appendix D.

246. *Wentworth Papers*, p. 226: Peter Wentworth to the Earl of Strafford, London, 18 Dec. 1711.

247. G. S. Holmes, *British Politics*, p. 227.

248. See above, sub "Influence."

249. Lists noted in Appendix D; *Parl. Hist.* VI: 1343; *Nicolson Diaries*, p. 612; C. Jones, "Scheme Lords," p. 146 n. 43.

250. C. Jones, "Scheme Lords," p. 130; Szechi, *Jacobitism*, p. 157.

251. For the court's financial difficulties under Oxford, see above, Chapter 2, sub "Finance."

252. C. Jones, "Scheme Lords," passim.

253. For Buckingham's parliamentary expertise, see *Parl. Hist.* VI: 881, 955–56, 962–67, 1037. For Shrewsbury's reputation, see above, sub "Influence." For their sometimes equivocal parliamentary behavior, see above; *Wentworth Papers*, p. 179; *Parl. Hist.* VI: 1037; Szechi, *Jacobitism*, pp. 127, 174.

254. For Beaufort, see Speck, "House of Commons," pp. 289–90; idem, *Tory & Whig*, p. 11; G. S. Holmes, *British Politics*, p. 270; Szechi, *Jacobitism*, pp. 61–62, 146. For Somerset, see Walcott, *English Politics*, pp. 10n, 50, 207, 226; Speck, "House of Commons," p. 289; idem, *Tory & Whig*, p. 11. For the Granville interest, see Walcott, *English Politics*, pp. 62–63, 112 n. 4; Speck, "House of Commons," p. 290; H.M.C., *Portland MSS* V: 312, 315, 322, 330–31. For Seymour, see Walcott, *English Politics*, pp. 63–66; Speck, *Tory & Whig*, p. 11.

255. Walcott, *English Politics*, pp. 22 n. 1, 48–49, 67–68; Speck, "House of

Commons," p. 188 n. 1; G. S. Holmes, *British Politics*, pp. 230–31, 261–62; H.M.C., *Fifteenth Report*, App. IV, p. 330; *Prideaux Letters*, p. 200.

256. G. S. Holmes, *British Politics*, p. 324 and n. Sir John Holland's similarly equivocal behavior eventually left him bereft of his interest, his seat, and his household place: ibid., pp. 229–34, 327; Swift, *Journal*, pp. 44, 226; information provided by Cruickshanks and Hayton.

257. Speck, *Tory & Whig*, p. 107.

Chapter VII

1. Quoted in Philip, Earl Stanhope, *History of England Comprising the Reign of Queen Anne Until the Peace of Utrecht, 1701–1713* (1872), II: 310.

2. W. H. Craig, *The Life of Lord Chesterfield* (1907), pp. 46, 52.

3. For the Duc d'Aumont's comments, see P.R.O. 31/3/201, ff. 3–4, 9 verso–10, 17 verso; for the Duchess of Marlborough, see *Memoirs of the Duchess of Marlborough*, pp. 230–31; for the Countess of Orkney, see H.M.C., *Portland MSS* V: 463–64; for Bishop Burnet, see Burnet, *History* VI: 230; for Sir John Clerk, see *Memoirs of Sir John Clerk*, p. 72; for Uffenbach, see Z. C. von Uffenbach, *London in 1710: From the Travels of Zacharias Conrad von Uffenbach*, trans. and ed. W. H. Quarrell and M. Mare (1934), p. 133; for Swift, see Swift, *Journal*, pp. 328, 580.

4. See *Memoirs of the Duchess of Marlborough*, pp. 230–31; Add. MSS 61422, f. 199; LC 5/3, pp. 9–10.

5. J. Swift, "Memoirs Relating," p. 367; see also *Parl. Hist.* VI: 1370.

6. See H.M.C., *Buccleuch at Montagu House MSS* I: 353; *Bolingbroke Correspondence* III: 373–74; IV: 290; Add. MSS 61417, f. 178; LC 5/3, pp. 3, 8, 9–10; *Wentworth Papers*, p. 82; E. J. Sheppard, *Memorials of St. James's Palace* (1894), I: 81–82; F. W. Fairholt, *Costumes in England* (1846), I: 351–52; Wray, *Ancient Royal Palaces*, p. 95; Gregg, *Anne*, pp. 71–72; Green, *Anne*, pp. 40, 107.

7. Add. MSS 61422, f. 199; *Memoirs of the Duchess of Marlborough*, p. 232.

8. *Memoirs of the Duchess of Marlborough*, p. 275; see also Add. MSS 61414, f. 25; *Memoirs of Sir John Clerk*, p. 72; Gregg, *Anne*, p. 81; Sheppard, *St. James's* I: 81.

9. Millar, *Tudor, Stuart . . . Pictures* I: 25, 144.

10. *Memoirs of the Duchess of Marlborough*, p. 230.

11. Note, for example, the frequent disputes among court officials and others over rights of precedence: LC 5/2, pp. 173–74; LC 5/201, pp. 355–67; H.M.C., *Seventh Report*, App., p. 469; H.M.C., *Twelfth Report*, App. III, p. 183; H.M.C., *Fifteenth Report*, App. VI, pp. 11–12; H.M.C., *Hastings MSS* II: 349.

12. Gregg, *Anne*, pp. 88–89, 94–96; *Memoirs of the Duchess of Marlborough*, pp. 62–70, 72–73, 79–82; Add. MSS 61414, f. 166 recto and verso; 61415, f. 13; 61421, f. 87; *Marlborough-Godolphin Correspondence*, pp. 34–35.

13. *Evelyn Diary* IV: 433, 491; LC 3/56, warrant of 20 Feb. 1684[/85]; LC 5/201, pp. 53–54; Dearnley, *Church Music*, p. 55; *Seafield Correspondence*, p. 30. See also

Gregg, *Anne*, p. 51, for her behavior at the reception of the papal nuncio in 1687.

14. Green, *Anne*, p. 60.

15. See above, Chapter 3; Chapter 6, sub "Influence." For another example, also involving Somerset, see *Nicolson Diaries*, p. 238.

16. Burnet, *History* V: 2; see also H.M.C., *Twelfth Report*, App. III, p. 1, for Anne's gracious reception of the old Earl of Chesterfield, and his comparison of her to Queen Elizabeth.

17. H.M.C., *Second Report* (1871), App., p. 242: Sir Robert Southwell to Bishop William King, Spring Garden, 14 Mar. 1701/2.

18. Burnet, *History* V: 2 n. Dartmouth. See also *Nicolson Diaries*, p. 98.

19. H.M.C., *Seventh Report*, App., p. 246: John Percival to Thomas Knatchbull, 21 Mar. 1701/2; Burnet, *History* V: 2 n. Onslow; H.M.C., *Second Report*, App., p. 242; *Flying Post*, no. 1068, 10–12 Mar. 1702.

20. E. Hamilton, *The Backstairs Dragon: A Life of Robert Harley, Earl of Oxford* (1969), p. 43. For Anne's ability to rise to a great occasion, see below; and Bodl. Lister MSS 37, f. 80.

21. H.M.C., *Fifteenth Report*, App. IV, p. 34: [Godolphin to Harley], 8 Mar. 1701/2.

22. Gregg, *Anne*, p. 152.

23. For the association with William III, see Burnet *History* V: 3. The phrase was suggested for inclusion in the speech by the Tory Earl of Rochester (Gregg, *Anne*, p. 152).

24. J. E. Neale, "November 17th," in idem, *Essays in Elizabethan History* (1958), p. 17; *The Past Speaks*, ed. L. B. Smith and J. R. Smith (Lexington, Mass., 1981), p. 225.

25. Gregg, *Anne*, p. 130. It should be noted that William had referred to himself at the opening of his last parliament as "the common Father of all My People" (*Commons Journals* XIII: 647).

26. G. R. Elton, *England Under the Tudors* (1955; repr., 1971), p. 399.

27. Boyer, *Annals* I: 162. For evidence that Anne had long identified personally with Elizabeth, see Gregg, *Anne*, p. 96.

28. Boyer, *Annals* I: 75–76; Add. MSS 17677 YY, f. 190. For this itinerary, see below, Table 7.2.

29. Boyer, *Annals* I: 139–41; Luttrell, *Brief Relation* V: 232, 235; Gregg, *Anne*, p. 165. See also the commentary in *Observator* I, no. 59, 11–14 Nov. 1702.

30. For an eyewitness account of Anne's coronation, see *Journeys of Celia Fiennes*, pp. 300–305; see also C. A. Edie, "The Public Face of Royal Ritual: Sermons, Medals and Civic Ceremony in Later Stuart Coronations," *H.L.Q.* LIII (1990): 324–28; E. C. Ratcliffe, *The English Coronation Service* (1936), pp. 136–37; Luttrell, *Brief Relation* V: 155, 158, 166; Harl. MSS 6118. For a description of a garter ceremony, see Boyer, *Annals* III: 187. For the Queen's reviewing troops in Hyde Park, see *English Post*, no. 238, 17–20 Apr. 1702; no. 377, 8–10 Mar.

1702[/3]; *Evening Post*, no. 621, 30 July–1 Aug. 1713; Add. MSS 17677 GGG, f. 298 verso. For the Queen's reviewing parades of the standards taken at Blenheim and Ramillies, see *Daily Courant*, no. 849, 4 Jan. 1705; no. 1459, 17 Dec. 1706; no. 1462, 20 Dec. 1706.

31. Luttrell, *Brief Relation* V: 462–63; Boyer, *Annals* I: 140–41. For detailed accounts of the day's events and order of procession at a public thanksgiving, see esp. *The Monthly Register*, Aug. 1705, pp. 258–59; and *Daily Courant*, no. 1312, 28 June 1706.

32. Boyer, *Annals* I: 75–78, 99–100; IV: 178; Luttrell, *Brief Relation* V: 223; *London Gazette*, no. 3852, 8–12 Oct. 1702.

33. Luttrell, *Brief Relation* V: 210; *English Post*, no. 309, 30 Sept.–2 Oct. 1702; *Post Man*, no. 1006, 22–25 Aug. 1702; Add. MSS 17677 YY, f. 175.

34. L. Melville, *Bath Under Beau Nash* (1907), pp. 34–35; W. Connely, *Beau Nash* (1955), pp. 21, 23; D. Gadd, *Georgian Summer: Bath in the Eighteenth Century* (Bath, 1971), pp. 20, 78. For the nobility and gentry following the court to Bath, see Kent A.O., Stanhope of Chevening MSS U1590 C 8/4, 9 Sept. [1703]; H.M.C., *First Report*, App., p. 19; H.M.C., *Ninth Report*, App. II, p. 467; P. Borsay, *The English Urban Renaissance: Culture and Society in the Provincial Town 1660–1770* (Oxford, 1989), p. 241.

35. Smuts, *Court Culture*, p. 18.

36. See, for example, Boyer, *Annals* I: 78; III: 97; IV: 82–83.

37. Ibid., I: 78. For a similar reception on the Winchester progress of 1705, see *London Gazette*, no. 4154, 30 Aug.–3 Sept. 1705; *The Monthly Register*, Aug. 1705, p. 260.

38. Smuts, "Public Ceremony," p. 78.

39. Boyer, *Annals* I: 18.

40. Boyer, *Annals* I: 99–100.

41. Ibid., IV: 10–13; H.M.C., *Fifteenth Report*, App. IV, p. 178.

42. For local celebrations of such national events and anniversaries (excepting the obligatory, government-sponsored celebrations in Edinburgh and Dublin) see, for Accession Day, *Post Man*, no. 1251, 11–14 Mar. 1704; *Post Boy*, no. 2470, 10–13 Mar. 1710/11; for Coronation Day, see *English Post*, no. 243, 29 Apr.–1 May 1702; *London Gazette*, no. 3805, 27–30 Apr. 1702; no. 3810, 14–18 May 1702; *Post Man*, nos. 961–62, 25–30 Apr. 1702; no. 965, 5–7 May 1702; nos. 970–71, 16–27 May 1702; for the royal birthday, see *Post Man*, no. 1089, 13–16 Feb. 1703; no. 1735, 8–11 Feb. 1707; *London Gazette*, no. 4409, 9–12 Feb. 1707[/8]; *Post Boy*, no. 2617, 16–19 Feb. 1711/12; no. 2771, 10–12 Feb. 1712/13; *Daily Courant*, no. 3852, 27 Feb. 1714; for the proclamations of war and peace, see *Post Man*, no. 971, 19–21 May 1702; *Post Boy*, no. 2810, 12–14 May 1713; nos. 2812–13, 16–21 May 1713; no. 2815, 23–26 May 1713; for the news of victories and thanksgivings, see *Post Man*, no. 1048, 10–12 Nov. 1702; no. 1051, 19–21 Nov. 1702; no. 1058, 5–8 Dec. 1702; no. 1061, 12–15 Dec. 1702; no. 1072, 7–9 Jan. 1703; nos. 1315–16, 7–12 Sept. 1704; no. 1618, 25–28 May 1706; no. 1634, 4–6 July 1706; *Flying Post*, nos. 1183–85, 3–10 Dec. 1702; *London Gazette*, nos.

3868–69, 3–10 Dec. 1702; no. 4053, 11–14 Sept. 1704; *Daily Courant*, no. 2035, 26 Aug. 1708; *Post Boy*, no. 2679, 10–12 July 1712; no. 2682, 17–22 July 1712; nos. 2835–40, 9–23 July 1713; for examples of extraordinary charity or the initiation of corporate projects on such days, see *Evening Post*, no. 83, 21–23 Feb. 1710; *Post Boy*, no. 2463, 22–24 Feb. 1710/11; no. 2838, 16–18 July 1713; C. Rose, "London's Charity Schools, 1690–1730," *History Today* XL (Mar. 1990): 21.

43. References to Anne as the second Elizabeth were particularly common in the addresses that flowed in after the victory at Blenheim: see *London Gazette*, no. 4052, 7–11 Sept. 1704; nos. 4054–56, 14–25 Sept. 1704; nos. 4064–67, 19 Oct.–2 Nov. 1704; nos. 4070–71, 9–16 Nov. 1704; no. 4073, 20–23 Nov. 1704. The image of Anne as the "nursing mother of her people" persisted to the end of the reign: see *Flying Post*, no.1164, 20–22 Oct. 1702; *London Gazette*, no. 4020, 18–22 May 1704; no. 4048, 24–28 Aug. 1704; no. 4058, 28 Sept.–2 Oct. 1704; no. 4076, 30 Nov.–4 Dec. 1704; no. 4116, 19–23 Apr. 1705; no. 4643, 21–24 Jan. 1709[/10]; *Post Man*, no. 1632, 29 June–2 July 1706; no. 1649, 16–18 July 1706; no. 1653, 25–27 July 1706; no. 1662, 17–20 Aug. 1706; *Rehearsal* I, no. 199, 12 Apr. 1707; *British Apollo* I, no. 32, 28 May–2 June 1708; *Post Boy*, no. 2612, 5–7 Feb. 1711/12; *Britain* XXVIII, 8–11 Apr. 1713. Anne was also frequently identified with Deborah: see *Daily Courant*, no. 215, 24 Dec. 1702; no. 773, 6 Oct. 1704; no. 828, 9 Dec. 1704; no. 857, 13 Jan. 1705; no. 1321, 9 July 1706; *London Gazette*, no. 4058, 28 Sept.–2 Oct. 1704. Finally, references to her "English heart" were not uncommon: see *Observator* I, no. 1, 1 Apr. 1702; *Post Boy*, no. 2678, 8–10 July 1712.

44. See, for example, Boyer, *Annals* III: 97; Luttrell, *Brief Relation* V: 462; VI: 122, 167. Indeed, beginning with the 1707 thanksgiving, publicans and innkeepers frequently advertised balconies or rooms overlooking the parade route, which could be rented for the day, a classic early example of the marriage of royal ceremony and commercial ingenuity: *Daily Courant*, no. 1624, 29 Apr. 1707; nos. 3658–59, 4–6 July 1713; *Evening Post*, no. 609, 2–4 July 1713.

45. Boyer, *Annals* I: 78; Green, *Anne*, p. 118. See also the testimony of L'Hermitage in Add. MSS 17677 YY, f. 201.

46. Boyer, *Annals* I: 126. See also Add. MSS 17677 YY, f. 260; *English Post*, no. 321, 28–30 Oct. 1702.

47. Turner describes structure as "all that which holds people apart, defines their differences and constrains their actions"; communitas as "the desire for a total, unmediated relationship between person and person, a relationship which nevertheless does not submerge one in the other but safeguards their uniqueness in the very act of realizing their commonness." See V. Turner, *Dramas, Fields and Metaphors* (Ithaca, N.Y., 1974), p. 274.

48. Smuts, "Public Ceremony," pp. 78–82.

49. Boyer, *Annals* I: 121–22.

50. Ibid., III: 98 (describing the Blenheim thanksgiving, 1704).

51. See G. S. Holmes, *British Politics*, p. 187; H.M.C., *Bath MSS* I: 199. But cf. also J. P. Kenyon, *Revolution Principles: The Politics of Party 1689–1720* (Cambridge, Eng., 1977), p. 120.

52. For contemporary belief in the priestly character of the British monarch, see J. C. D. Clark, *English Society 1688–1832: Ideology, Social Structure and Political Practice During the Ancien Régime* (Cambridge, Eng., 1985), p. 135; Starkey, "Representation Through Intimacy," pp. 192–94; G. Straka, "The Final Phase of Divine Right Theory in England, 1688–1702," *E.H.R.* LXXVII (1962): 639.

53. Add. MSS 61416, f. 150 recto and verso: Anne to Sarah, Kensington, 29 Apr. [1704].

54. Sharp to William Lloyd, Bishop of Worcester, 31 Mar. 1703, printed in *E.H.R.* V (1890): 122. For evidence of belief in the royal healing power among the elite, see P. Ziegler, *Crown and People* (New York, 1978), pp. 15–16; among the general populace, see Clark, *English Society*, p. 162.

55. Luttrell, *Brief Relation* V: 223, 249, 285, 288, 414, 548; *Wentworth Papers*, pp. 325, 375; Gregg, *Anne*, p. 148; *Nicolson Diaries*, p. 300; *English Post*, no. 382, 19–22 Mar. 1702[/3]; *Flying Post*, no. 1180, 26–28 Nov. 1702; no. 1189, 17–19 Dec. 1702; *London Gazette*, no. 3901, 29 Mar.–1 Apr. 1703; no. 4019, 15–18 May 1704; no. 4126, 24–28 May 1705; no. 4172, 1–5 Nov. 1705; no. 4185, 17–20 Dec. 1705; no. 4276, 31 Oct.–4 Nov. 1706; no. 4289, 16–19 Dec. 1706; no. 4552, 23–25 June 1709; no. 4657, 23–25 Feb. 1709[/10]; no. 4684, 25–27 Apr. 1710; no. 4971, 26–28 Feb. 1711[/12]; no. 4993, 17–19 Apr. 1712; *Evening Post*, no. 558, 5–7 Mar. 1713.

56. J. Boswell, *The Life of Samuel Johnson LL.D.*, ed. M. Morris (1914), p. 8; Clark, *English Society*, pp. 161–65; M. Bloch, *The Royal Touch: Sacred Monarchy and Scrofula in England and France*, trans. J. E. Anderson (1973), pp. 182–83, 222–23; Starkey, "Representation Through Intimacy," p. 220 n. 16. The author has in his possession courtesy of Dr. Peter Jackson of Wilmslow, Cheshire, a Queen Anne shilling, minted in 1711, with a small hole drilled through the top of the coin above the effigy, presumably so that it might be worn as a talisman or memorial.

57. Uffenbach, *London in 1710*, p. 115; see also E. Chamberlayne, *Anglia Notitia* (1669), p. 237.

58. For this political calendar and its increasing politicization, see D. Cressy, *Bonfires and Bells: National Memory and the Protestant Calendar in Elizabethan and Stuart England* (1989); de Krey, *Fractured Society*, pp. 59–60, 253; Kenyon, *Revolution Principles*, pp. 69–82; B. S. Stewart, "The Cult of the Royal Martyr," *Church History* XXX (1970): 181–85; *Rehearsal* I, no. 29, 10–17 Feb. 1705.

59. For the day's schedule, see W. B. Ewald, *The Newsmen of Queen Anne* (Oxford, 1956), p. 43, quoting the *Post Boy* of 5–7 Feb. 1706. See also R. McGuinness, "The Origins and Disappearance of the English Court Ode," *Proceedings of the Royal Musicological Society* LXXXVII (1960–61): 69–82; and idem, "A Fine Song on Occasion of the Day Was Sung," *Music and Literature* L (1969): 290–95.

60. Boyer, *Annals* I: 215. See also the maid of honor Mary Stanhope's account in Kent A.O., Stanhope of Chevening MSS U1590 C 7/16.

61. Ewald, *Newsmen*, p. 43.

62. Luttrell, *Brief Relation* V: 281.

63. Manchester, *Court and Society* II: 275; Gregg, *Anne*, p. 258.

64. *Journeys of Celia Fiennes*, p. 300.

65. See Gregg, *Anne*, pp. 182, 231–32, 234, 258; Add. MSS 17677 BBB, f. 40 verso; *Marlborough-Godolphin Correspondence*, pp. 931, 933, 934–35; E. von Spanheim, "Spanheim's Account of the English Court," ed. R. Doehner, *E.H.R.* II (1887): 764.

66. *Memoirs of Sir John Clerk*, p. 62.

67. Luttrell, *Brief Relation* VI: 29, 154, 357, 359. For the Prince's chronic health problems, see Add. MSS 17677 YY, ff. 84 verso, 190, 259–60, 267 verso; BBB, ff. 104, 107, 116 verso; CCC, f. 510; Kent A.O., Stanhope of Chevening MSS U1590 C 7/16, 8 Feb. [1706].

68. Luttrell, *Brief Relation* VI: 368; A. Boyer, *The Political State of Great Britain* (1711–40), I: 53.

69. Luttrell, *Brief Relation* VI: 382, 390; Add. MSS 17677 CCC, ff. 683 verso, 686; *Clavering Correspondence*, p. 21.

70. Luttrell, *Brief Relation* VI: 403; *Wentworth Papers*, p. 108: Peter Wentworth to Lord Raby, 14 Feb. 1710.

71. See Speck, *Tory & Whig*, pp. 100–101. While the Winchester progress occurred in late summer, long after final returns were in, the Queen's dining with the Duke of Bolton, a prominent local Whig, could only have been regarded as a portent of royal favor in the coming session.

72. *Daily Courant*, no. 2588, 8 Feb. 1710.

73. Add. MSS 61460, f. 118: Arthur Maynwaring to Sarah, Duchess of Marlborough, "Tuesday afternoon" [15 Nov. 1709].

74. Add. MSS 31143, f. 613; *The Complete Letters of Lady Mary Wortley Montagu*, ed. R. Halsband (Oxford, 1965), I: 70–71.

75. Boyer, *Annals* IX: 335; Luttrell, *Brief Relation* VI: 688; see also H.M.C., *Fifteenth Report*, App. IV, p. 657.

76. Curtis, *Queen Anne*, p. 180.

77. Boyer, *Annals* IX: 335; Burrows, "Handel" I: 141; *The London Stage 1660–1800*, ed. E. L. Avery (Carbondale, Ill., 1960), II: 255.

78. H.M.C., *Fifteenth Report*, App. IV, p. 657: [Edward Harley] to Abigail Harley at Eywood, 6 Feb. 1710/11.

79. *Swift Correspondence* I: 214; *Nicolson Diaries*, pp. 556–57.

80. Torcy, *Journal inédit*, p. 354; Swift, *Journal*, pp. 158–59, 267, 328, 331, 350, 366; H.M.C., *Portland MSS* V: 4; *Letters of Lady Mary Wortley Montagu* I: 81, 100.

81. Swift, *Journal*, p. 363; H.M.C., *Portland MSS* V: 15; Add. MSS 17677 EEE, ff. 234, 243 verso.

82. *Wentworth Papers*, pp. 247–48; Boyer, *Political State* V: 89; *Swift Correspondence* II: 11.

83. *Hamilton Diary*, p. 56; Add. MSS 17677 GGG, f. 29 verso; 31144, ff. 321 recto and verso, 324 verso.

84. Add. MSS 17677 EEE, f. 119 verso; 22226, ff. 37, 298 verso; *British Mer-*

cury, no. 390, 24 Dec. 1712; no. 446, 13–20 Jan. 1713/14; *Post Boy*, no. 2772, 12–14 Feb. 1712/13.

85. *British Mercury*, no. 391, 31 Dec. 1712; nos. 412–13, 27 May–3 June 1713; no. 424, 19 Aug. 1713; *Evening Post*, no. 591, 21–23 May 1713; *Post Boy*, no. 2814, 21–23 May 1713; Add. MSS 17677 GGG, ff. 101 verso–102, 125 verso, 145 verso, 183, 276 verso–277.

86. See above, Chapter 6, sub "Information."

87. For the period before the Queen's illness, see *British Mercury*, no. 422, 5 Aug. 1713; *Evening Post*, no. 494, 7–9 Oct. 1712; *Bolingbroke Correspondence* III: 440, 477–78; *The Correspondence of Sir Thomas Hanmer, Bart. Speaker of the House of Commons with a Memoir of His Life . . .* , ed. H. E. Bunbury (1838), pp. 147, 150. For the period immediately after, see *Wentworth Papers*, pp. 358, 359, 375, 387, 395; H.M.C., *Downshire MSS* I ii, 901; Green, *Anne*, p. 308.

88. *Verney Letters of the Eighteenth Century from the MSS at Claydon House*, ed. Margaret, Lady Verney (1930), I: 356: Mary Lovett to Lord Fermanagh, 15 May 1714.

89. H.M.C., *Portland MSS* V: 433: Newsletter, 1 May 1714. For additional evidence that Anne made an effort to appear in public more often during the last few months of her life, see *Wentworth Papers*, p. 358; Add. MSS 17677 HHH, ff. 9 recto and verso, 71 verso, 79, 87 verso–88, 89 recto and verso, 94, 195, 200 verso, 206; P.R.O. 31/3/202, ff. 37, 43 verso, 68 verso, 77.

90. The question of why Queen Anne (or, for that matter, any other early modern ruler) was popular (or unpopular) requires more detailed consideration than it can receive here. A preliminary analysis suggests that her well-known Anglocentrism and xenophobia, her staunch Protestantism and anti-Catholicism, her good husbandry and charitable nature appealed to some of the most long-standing, pervasive, and deeply held attitudes among her English subjects (see esp. T. Harris, *London Crowds in the Reign of Charles II: Propaganda and Politics from the Restoration until the Exclusion Crisis* [Cambridge, Eng., 1987], chaps. 2, 4). No previous Stuart sovereign had shared them so completely. Anne's gender, a handicap in dealing with her administration and ruling class, may also have been an asset with her people. It clearly reminded them of Gloriana, a parallel that Anne was careful to underline. Some may have sympathized with her tragic obstetrical history, or the loss of her only surviving son in 1700, or the loss of her husband in 1708. On a more subtle level, what has been said about Elizabeth may have been true of Anne as well: that in a Protestant country such as England, a female sovereign may have fulfilled the role performed by the Virgin Mary in Catholic countries. That is, Queen Anne may have represented a more maternal, and therefore softer and more comfortable, embodiment of political and religious authority than her male predecessors. (For the idea of the Virgin Queen's replacing the Virgin Mary, see Strong, *Cult of Elizabeth*, pp. 15–16; idem, *Portraits of Queen Elizabeth I*, p. 36; Loades, *Tudor Court*, p. 36.) Nor should it be forgotten that in the eyes of many of her Protestant subjects, Anne had entered the nation's political and

religious hagiography by her resistance to and daring escape from her father before and during the Revolution. Finally, as the reign wore on, her subjects may have come to the sort of collective verdict that professional historians are conditioned to avoid: that, when all is said and done, she was a rather good queen. She prosecuted a successful war, won a favorable (if controversial) peace, defended the Church, continued (albeit unenthusiastically) the Toleration, respected constitutional proprieties, and avoided the fiscal extravagance and institutional cruelty sometimes associated with the early modern English monarchy. What Stuart—nay, what Tudor—could boast so much?

91. *Journeys of Celia Fiennes*, pp. 300, 302. See also the account in the *Flying Post*, no. 1087, 23–25 Apr. 1702, in which spectators are reported to have experienced "great Satisfaction to see her Majesty look so well, and with an Air of so much Royalty and good Nature."

92. *Memoirs of the Duchess of Marlborough*, p. 273.

93. Anon., *The Life of her late Majesty Queen Anne, As well before her Accession to the Throne as after* (1721), I: 415. For the Queen's accessibility out of doors, see above, Chapter 6, sub "Access."

94. See Green, *Anne*, p. 271; LS 13/175, f. 99 recto and verso; *Daily Courant*, no. 2635, 4 Apr. 1710; *Evening Post*, no. 365, 11–13 Dec. 1711; nos. 515–16, 25–29 Nov. 1712; no. 556, 28 Feb.–3 Mar. 1713; *Post Boy*, no. 2766, 29–31 Jan. 1712/13; *British Mercury*, no. 420, 22 July 1713; no. 423, 12 Aug. 1713; no. 433, 21 Oct. 1713; no. 459, 14–21 Apr. 1714; but cf. *Britain* XIX, 7–11 Mar. 1713.

95. Boyer, *Annals* XI: 306–7; P.R.O. 31/3/201, ff. 16 verso–17; *Memoirs of the Marquis of Torcy, Secretary of State to Lewis XIV* . . . (1757), II: 277–78; H.M.C., *Bath MSS* I: 201; H.M.C., *Twelfth Report*, App. III, pp. 99–100, 107–8; *Wentworth Papers*, p. 248; *British Apollo* III, no. 156, 21–23 Mar. 1711; *Evening Post*, no. 515, 25–27 Nov. 1712. According to Edward Gregg, the Oxford ministry was not above manufacturing plots to discredit the Whigs: see *Protestant Succession*, p. 145.

96. See Gregg, *Anne*, p. 150.

97. The reason given for Anne's absence from St. Paul's for the thanksgiving of 7 Nov. 1710 was "to avoid giving the Mob an Opportunity to assemble, and commit Riots" (Boyer, *Annals* IX: 253). While there were good political reasons for Anne not to be present at a celebration of the "successes" of the 1710 campaign when she was about to pursue a peace policy, the experience of nearly causing a riot among a Tory-Royalist crowd during the Sacheverell trial earlier that year would not have encouraged her to make further public appearances. It should be noted that the Duke of Marlborough likewise avoided "the Mobility" on his return from the continent in November 1711 (Boyer, *Annals* X: 54). In 1711 and 1712 Tory crowds used the Queen's birthday as an excuse for anti-Whig rioting (de Krey, *Fractured Society*, pp. 254, 256). In short, the political situation during the Queen's last four years was so explosive that any public appearance by a political celebrity, whether popular or unpopular, might provoke a riot. The Queen's reluctance to appear in public during these last years

should therefore not necessarily be interpreted as an indication that she herself feared for her life.

98. George Beaumont to Dr. Radcliffe, 2 Aug. 1714, quoted in C. R. Hone, *The Life of Dr. John Radcliffe, 1652–1714* (1950), pp. 102–4; but cf. *Wentworth Papers*, p. 410.

99. As we have seen, Anne's behavior was not always scrupulously nonpartisan. In particular, much of her early rhetoric, such as her assertion of Englishness or her promise at the dismissal of parliament on 25 March 1702 to "countenance those who have the truest zeal" to support the Church of England (*Parl. Hist.* VI: 25), was legitimately subject to partisan interpretation: see Defoe's trenchant analysis of Dissenting reaction to the Queen's equivocal behavior early in the reign in *The Letters of Daniel Defoe*, ed. J. H. Healey (Oxford, 1955), pp. 50–56. For High Church dissatisfaction, see *Hearne Remarks and Collections* I: 61; II: 88, 90, 93, 360–61; G. V. Bennett, *The Tory Crisis in Church and State 1688–1730: The Career of Francis Atterbury, Bishop of Rochester* (Oxford, 1975), chaps. 4–9. I am grateful to Professor Gary de Krey for calling this point to my attention.

100. See, for example, Campbell, *Duchess of Marlborough*, p. 166.

101. Burrows, "Handel" I: 104–5; Boulton, *Amusements of Old London* II: 149; Add. MSS 22226, ff. 113 verso–114; 31144, f. 334; *Wentworth Papers*, pp. 108, 247, 318; Swift, *Journal*, p. 481; Klopp, *Stuart* XIV: 4.

102. H.M.C., *Twelfth Report*, App. V, p. 177: John Charlton to Lady Granby, Totteridge, 11 Nov. 1703. For similar activities in 1704, though without mention of Kit-Cat Club sponsorship, see Add. MSS 17677 ZZ, f. 483 verso.

103. *British Apollo* II, no. 70, 23–25 Nov. 1709. It should be noted that the Dutch and imperial ambassadors had been supplementing the court's activities in this way since the 1706 thanksgiving: see Add. MSS 17677 BBB, ff. 343 verso–344; CCC, ff. 557–58; DDD, f. 81; *Post Boy*, no. 2148, 17–19 Feb. 1708/9; *Post Man*, no. 1708, 17–19 Feb. 1709.

104. Speck, *Tory & Whig*, p. 93; Boyer, *Annals* X: 278–80; H.M.C., *Eleventh Report*, App. V, p. 307; *Evening Post*, no. 354, 15–17 Nov. 1711, postscript.

105. *Flying Post*, no. 3280, 4–7 Oct. 1712; no. 3293, 4–6 Nov. 1712; no. 3299, 18–20 Nov. 1712; no. 3304, 29 Nov.–2 Dec. 1712; no. 3334, 7–10 Feb. 1712/[13]; no. 3377, 19–21 May 1713; de Krey, *Fractured Society*, pp. 256–58; MacPherson, *Original Papers* II: 446; Add. MSS 17677 HHH, ff. 70 verso–71.

106. *Flying Post*, no. 3308, 9–11 Dec. 1711; no. 3335, 10–13 Feb. 1712/[13]; no. 3353, 24–26 Mar. 1713.

107. De Krey, *Fractured Society*, pp. 256–58.

108. *Wentworth Papers*, pp. 208, 210, 215.

109. Ibid., p. 248; see also MacPherson, *Original Papers* II: 270–71.

110. *British Mercury*, no. 283, 11–14 Jan. 1712; no. 293, 4–6 Feb. 1712; *Protestant Post-Boy*, no. 58, 12–15 Jan. 1711/12; no. 62, 22–24 Jan. 1711/12; MacPherson, *Original Papers* II: 270–71, 273, 280.

111. Cowles, *The Great Marlborough*, p. 373.

112. Green, *Anne*, p. 13.

113. Foss, *Age of Patronage*, p. 111. For similar verdicts, see Millar, *Queen's Pictures*, p. 87; F. A. Parsons, *The Psychology of Dress* (1923), p. 240; N. Armstrong, *Jewellery: An Historical Survey of British Styles and Jewels* (Guildford, Eng., 1973), p. 129; Mitchell, "Command Performances . . . Anne," p. 117.

114. I have been unable to discover evidence that Pope spent any time at Anne's court prior to writing his great mock-epic. Nor is there any proof that the incident so immortalized took place there: see *The Poems of Alexander Pope* II, ed. G. Tillotson (1940), p. 83. It may be significant that the action of the poem is set at Hampton Court, Anne's least favorite residence.

115. For some idea of the size and breadth of the collection, see Millar, *Queen's Pictures*, pp. 66–70, 82–83.

116. E. Boswell, *Restoration Court Stage*, p. 180; Burnet, *History* V: 2 n. Dartmouth.

117. A. Boyer, *The Life and Reign of Queen Anne* (1735), pp. 715–16; E. Chamberlayne, *Anglia Notitia* (1679, 1682); Add. MSS 38863; Westrup, "Foreign Musicians," p. 81.

118. Dearnley, *Church Music*, pp. 214, 222, 231; *London Stage* I: 495; Burrows, "Handel," I: 22–23, 32.

119. Burrows, "Handel," I: 32–33; II: 29; *Post Boy*, no. 2158, 12–15 Mar. 1708/9; LS 13/258, warrants of 10 Apr. 1706, 17 Apr. 1708, 31 Aug. 1708, 29 June 1709, 12 Jan. 1712, 7 Feb. 1714, 8 Mar. 1714; *C.T.B.* XXII: cdxcix (for Elford).

120. Dearnley, *Church Music*, p. 58; Fellows, *Cathedral Music*, p. 29; Burrows, "Handel," I: 33–34. Tudway's opinion is supported by the publication in 1712 of *Divine Harmony; or A New Collection of Select Anthems Used at Her Majesty's Chappel-Royal, Westminster-Abbey, St. Paul's, Windsor, Both Universities, Eaton, and Most Cathedrals in Her Majesty's Dominions. . . .*

121. E. Boswell, *Restoration Court Stage*, p. 174; La Fontaine, *King's Musick*, p. 434; H.M.C., *Twelfth Report*, App. II, p. 365; *London Stage* I: 409.

122. Add. MSS 61414, f. 141: Anne to Sarah, "Tuesday," n.d. [c. 1691].

123. E. 351/554–57 (Declared Accounts, Treasurer of the Chamber, sub "riding wages").

124. Luttrell, *Brief Relation* V: 429.

125. J. Hawkins, *A General History of the Science and Practise of Music* (1853), p. 718n.

126. Manchester, *Court and Society* II: 337: Sarah to Charles, Duke of Manchester, St. James's, 13 Apr. 1708.

127. For Anne's schedule, see Gregg, *Anne*, chap. 5.

128. Sharp, *Life of John Sharp* I: 317.

129. *Memoirs of the Duchess of Marlborough*, p. 274.

130. Luttrell, *Brief Relation* V: 222, 448, 450, 578; *Daily Courant*, no. 87, 29 July 1702.

131. *Wren Society VII*, pp. 209–12.

132. Ibid., p. 215.

133. Ibid., p. 139 and plate XXI.

134. Wray, *Ancient Royal Palaces*, p. 151; Nash, *Hampton Court*, pp. 144–45; Minney, *Hampton Court*, pp. 194–98; Hedley, *Windsor Castle*, p. 134.

135. See Uffenbach, *London in 1710*, p. 104; J. M. Beattie, *English Court*, p. 9.

136. Curtis, *Anne*, p. 128.

137. *C.T.B.* XX: 18.

138. Ibid. XVII: 58.

139. Ibid. XVIII: 214–15; XX: 82; XXI: ccxxx–ccxxxi; Burrows, "Handel" I: 153; *D.N.B.*, sub "Thomas Betterton."

140. See above, Chapter 4, sub "Professional Standards and Reputation."

141. Add. MSS 61416, f. 4 verso: Anne to Sarah, 19 May [1702]. See also Add. MSS 17677 DDD, f. 203 verso.

142. D. Green, *Gardener to Queen Anne*, p. 74.

143. Ibid., pp. 68, 80–81, 89, 93–94. For Anne's relationship to Wise, see ibid., pp. 82, 89.

144. *D.N.B.*, sub "Charles Boit"; Stewart, *Kneller*, p. 57.

145. *C.T.B.* XIX: 60, 286; XX: 347; XXI: 181, 500; XXII: 299, 441; XXIII: 133, 376; XXIV: 298, 456; XXVI: 128, 427–28; M. Reynolds, *The Learned Lady in England, 1650–1760* (Gloucester, Mass., 1964), p. 180; Aitken, *Arbuthnot*, p. 36; G. N. Davis, *German Thought and Culture in England 1700–1770* (Chapel Hill, N.C., 1969), p. 47.

146. Burnet, *History* V: 252–53; *C.T.B.* XXI: 11–13, 26, 102, 504.

147. Gregg, *Anne*, pp. 6–7, 182; D. Green, *Anne*, p. 335. See also Add. MSS 61422, f. 111 verso.

148. See, for example, Add. MSS 22226, f. 290; 61414, f. 55; 61415, f. 135 recto and verso; *Memoirs of the Duchess of Marlborough*, p. 230.

149. Blenheim MSS E-17: Anne to Sarah, n.d. [1708], quoted in D. Green, *Duchess of Marlborough*, p. 80.

150. Add. MSS 61424, f. 15.

151. See above, Chapter 2, sub "Finance."

152. Boyer, *Annals* IX: 363. For evidence that these rules were enforced, see *Clavering Correspondence*, p. 58. Some indication of the seriousness with which court mourning was viewed by the upper classes may be found in the profusion of advertisements in London's daily newspaper for mourning coaches and chariots following the death of Prince George: *Daily Courant*, no. 2092, 3 Nov. 1708; no. 2094, 5 Nov. 1708; nos. 2097–99, 9–11 Nov. 1708; no. 2202, 15 Nov. 1708; no. 2226, 13 Dec. 1708.

153. Talbot Williamson, gentleman usher to Princess Amelia, quoted in Fritz, "Trade in Death," p. 308. For commentary from Anne's reign, see *The Correspondence of Alexander Pope*, ed. G. Sherburn (Oxford, 1956), I: 53; *Observator* VIII, nos. 86–88, 23 Nov.–2 Dec. 1709; *Clavering Correspondence*, pp. 18–19.

154. H.M.C., *Fifteenth Report*, App. IV, p. 161: [Anon. Newsletter], London, 6 Feb. 1704/5. For the petitions of tradesmen, see Ewald, *Newsmen*, pp. 59–60; H.M.C., *Twelfth Report*, App. III, pp. 183–84; S.P. Dom. 34/35, ff. 114–16; 36, f.

97. In 1709 parliament received nine separate petitions, which barrage led in February of that year to a parliamentary inquiry and proposal of a bill to limit court mournings. The bill failed, but the court did bow somewhat to this pressure in the spring by relaxing the requirements for Prince George's mourning: Fritz, "Trade in Death," p. 313; *London Gazette*, no. 4526, 24–28 Mar. 1709; *Post Boy*, no. 2179, 30 Apr.–3 May 1709.

155. The one possible exception was the hoop skirt, introduced around 1710: I. Brooke, *A History of English Costume* (1937), p. 133.

156. C. W. Cunnington and P. Cunnington, *Handbook of English Costume in the Eighteenth Century* (Boston, 1972), pp. 72, 113, 114; M. Sichel, *Costume Reference 4: The Eighteenth Century* (1977), pp. 21, 34; Kelly and Schwabe, *Costume and Armour* II: 44.

157. Mitchell, "Command Performances . . . Anne," pp. 112–14; Uffenbach, *London in 1710*, p. 66.

158. See Killanin, *Kneller*, pp. 79–82; Gaunt, *Court Painting*, p. 168; Foss, *Age of Patronage*, pp. 147–51; J. Loftis, *The Politics of Drama in Augustan England* (Oxford, 1963), pp. 40–41; R. J. Allen, "The Kit-Cat Club and the Theatre," *Review of English Studies* VII (1931): 56–61; idem, *The Clubs of Augustan London* (Cambridge, Mass., 1933), pp. 232–35.

159. For the shift in subject matter at the turn of the eighteenth century, see Nicoll, *History of English Drama* II: 161; J. Loftis, "The Court and the Stage" in *Revel's History* V: 15; idem, *Politics of Drama*, pp. 29–35.

160. For the rise of public patronage of the arts in general, see Foss, *Age of Patronage*, esp. chap. 8; G. S. Holmes, *Augustan England*, esp. chap. 2; and J. H. Plumb, *The Commercialisation of Leisure in Eighteenth-Century England* (Reading, 1973).

161. Burrows, "Handel" II: 152–55.

162. Stewart, *Kneller*, pp. 57, 59.

163. G. S. Holmes, *Augustan England*, p. 29.

164. M. Quennell and C. H. B. Quennell, *A History of Everyday Things in England . . . 1500–1799* (1950), p. 201.

165. See J. M. Beattie, "The Court of George I and English Politics, 1717–1720," *E.H.R.* LXXXI (1966): 26–37; and idem, *English Court*, pp. 264–75.

166. See Add. MSS 61414, passim; Cowles, *The Great Marlborough*, pp. 93, 96; Curtis, *Anne*, pp. 42–43.

167. For Anne's hunting, see Luttrell, *Brief Relation* V: 205, 586; Add. MSS 17677 AAA, f. 457; BBB, ff. 388, 479 verso; CCC, f. 165; 22225, ff. 331–32; 31143, f. 6 recto; 31144, f. 417; *Marlborough-Godolphin Correspondence*, p. 1110; Swift, *Journal*, p. 324; H.M.C., *Bath MSS* I: 182; Ashton, *Social Life*, p. 232.

168. Swift, *Journal*, p. 324. For Anne's obesity, see Green, *Anne*, p. 336; *Wentworth Papers*, p. 301; B.L. Stowe MSS 226, f. 176 verso.

169. Swift, *Journal*, p. 328.

170. Luttrell, *Brief Relation* V: 536, 542, 544; VI: 82, 91, 96, 218, 224; *Marlborough-Godolphin Correspondence*, pp. 922, 934–35.

171. B. Bevan, "Queen Anne's Sporting Interests," *Country Life*, 30 July 1964, pp. 288–89; Luttrell, *Brief Relation* V: 587; Swift, *Journal*, p. 330.

172. E. Wenham, *Old Silver for Modern Settings* (1964), p. 64; Borsay, *English Urban Renaissance*, p. 182; LC 5/108, warrants of 30 June 1703, 22 July 1704, 21 June 1705, 10 June 1707, 14 May 1709, 5 June 1710; LC 5/109, pp. 31, 32, 42, 66, 79, 84, 110; Ashton, *Social Life*, pp. 229–30.

173. *C.T.B.* XXVII: 136, 148; LS 13/43; LS 13/199, pp. 121–23, 124; LS 13/258, p. 77.

174. Bevan, "Anne's Sporting Interests," p. 289; *D.N.B.*, sub "Tregonwell Frampton."

175. Add. MSS 17677 YY, f. 142; BBB, f. 107; CCC, f. 505; EEE, ff. 172 verso, 243 verso; GGG, ff. 38, 96; HHH, f. 9 verso; 22226, ff. 177, 270; 31143, f. 263 verso; 31144, f. 274; 61416, f. 7; 61432, f. 72 verso; D. Green, *Anne*, pp. 280, 300; Swift, *Journal*, pp. 366, 588, 603, 604, 606; H.M.C., *Thirteenth Report*, App. II, p. 224; H.M.C., *Portland MSS* V: 4; *Letters of Lady Mary Wortley Montagu* I: 81, 100, 117. Drawing rooms could also be held in the morning: see Add. MSS 17677 GGG, f. 40 verso; 31144, f. 329 verso.

176. Add. MSS 17677 HHH, f. 9 recto and verso; 22226, f. 32; *Wentworth Papers*, p. 213; Swift, *Journal*, p. 356.

177. H.M.C., *Twelfth Report*, App. V, p. 176 [following the commission's dating]; Gregg, *Anne*, p. 232; Add. MSS 17677 BBB, ff. 40 verso, 104; 31144, ff. 321 verso, 324 verso; Uffenbach, *London in 1710*, pp. 132–33.

178. See, for example, *Wentworth Papers*, p. 312.

179. *Memoirs of Sir John Clerk*, p. 72.

180. Swift, *Journal*, p. 328.

181. Jusserand, *French Ambassador*, p. 91.

182. See above, Chapter 5, sub "Attendance and Work."

183. Foss, *Age of Patronage*, p. 24; J. M. Beattie, *English Court*, p. 14.

184. See P. Tillemans's "Queen Anne in the House of Lords," reproduced in Somerset, *Ladies in Waiting*, facing p. 214; or J. Gerhard Huck's drawing "Presentation of the Treaty of Union," reproduced in C. H. Dand, *The Mighty Affair* (Edinburgh, 1972), facing p. iii.

185. Add. MSS 61422, f. 62 verso.

186. *Journeys of Celia Fiennes*, p. 359. For evidence from the previous reign that this screen was indeed designed "to keep off companyes coming near [the Queen]," see ibid., p. 279. For the Queen's receiving in her bedchamber, see Add. MSS 17677 CCC, f. 686 recto and verso; HHH, ff. 9 verso, 89 recto and verso; 31143, f. 263 verso; 31144, f. 321 recto and verso; *Wentworth Papers*, p. 312; Swift, *Journal*, p. 361; D. Green, *Anne*, pp. 149, 247, 280.

187. See above, Chapter 6, sub "Access."

188. *Memoirs of the Duchess of Marlborough*, pp. 230–31; see also Burnet, *History* VI: 230.

189. B.L. Loan 57/71, f. 15 verso: [Anne to Frances, Lady Bathurst], Windsor, "Fri.," n.d. The *Nicolson Diaries* for 9 Nov. 1705 record the following ac-

count of the bishop's reception by Anne upon his return to London for the season: "She was pleased to enquire what weather and Roads I met with in comeing to Town, &c" (p. 300). For her conversations with Masham, see above, Chapter 6, sub "Influence"; for those with Hamilton, see *Hamilton Diary*, passim. However, cf. the Duc d'Aumont's claim of a "plus facile" conversation in January 1713 in P.R.O. 31/3/201, f. 4.

190. Swift, *Journal*, p. 328.

191. Anne's reputed prudery has often been used to explain the dullness of her court (see, for example, Lord Chesterfield's comment, above). It is certainly true that her private conduct was above reproach, especially in the years following the Revolution. As Queen, she issued a general proclamation against vice at her accession (Tudor and Stuart Proclamations, no. 4314), suppressed the wearing of masks at the public theater in 1704 (Nicoll, *History of English Drama* I: 14 n. 3), and closed down Mayfair in 1708 (C. De La Roche Francis, *London Historic and Social* [Philadelphia, 1902], II: 101). In general, her reign was notable for an increased regulation of the moral standards of the public stage by the lord chamberlain's office, but it can be argued that this owed at least as much to a change in public opinion as it did to the Queen's own inclinations. It is significant that though Anne supported reform, she nevertheless appointed Vanbrugh and Congreve to head one of the theater companies in 1705, despite their having figured prominently in the attacks of Jeremy Collier (see R. D. Hume, ed., *The London Theatre World 1660–1800* [Carbondale, Ill., 1980], pp. 291–94; *Revels History* V: 29, 124). Anne's virtuousness does not appear to have prevented her from enjoying the theater and opera when it came to court, or the pleasures of the ballroom or the turf when she was able to pursue them, as noted above. Nor did it stop her from receiving the old Duchess of Cleveland in 1705 (Add. MSS 17677 BBB, ff. 6–7; Petherick, *Restoration Rogues*, p. 392) or impel her to dismiss Ladies Godolphin or Hyde from the royal bedchamber, despite their dubious reputations (see *D.N.B.*, sub "Francis, Earl of Godolphin"; Gregg, *Anne*, p. 327; *Letters of Lady Mary Wortley Montagu* I: 60 n. 2). The effect of Anne's moral standards upon the aesthetic and social life of the court is impossible to assess, and must therefore remain a moot point.

192. Chatsworth House, Derbyshire, Devonshire MSS 117.1: Duchess of Somerset to [Duchess of Devonshire], Windsor, 30 Sept. [1707].

193. Uffenbach, *London in 1710*, p. 133.

194. H.M.C., *Portland MSS* V: 463: Lady Orkney to [?Lady Henrietta Holles, June–Oct. 1711]—my identification of recipient and dating. The Commission's dating of this letter as "1714, June ?" cannot be correct, since Anne's last visit there ended in February. A reference elsewhere in the letter to "Lord Harley" must refer to Edward, Lord Harley, indicating that it must have been written after his father's creation as Earl of Oxford on 23 May 1711. The Commission's identification of the recipient as "Lady Harriet Harley" would suggest a dating after her marriage in September 1713, but there is no internal evidence to suggest that she had yet married. The presence of the Dukes of Saint Albans and

Somerset suggests, rather, that the Countess of Orkney's visit took place before the loss of their court places in January 1712. Thus, the most likely date for the letter is sometime from late June to mid-September 1711, during the court's extended stay at Windsor (see *Post Boy*, nos. 2514, 21–23 June 1711; 2548, 8–11 Sept. 1711).

195. *D.N.B.*, sub "Elizabeth Villiers, Countess of Orkney."

196. Swift, *Journal*, pp. 84–85, 200–201, 214, 228, 316, 318, 320, 322, 323, 324, 328, 329–30, 363, 373, 374, 421, 424, 451, 463, 490, 522, 595–96, 614, 617, 622, 623, 624, 629, 633, 643, 645, 650–51, 659.

197. Ibid., p. 522.

198. Ibid., pp. 421, 490, 585.

199. *Lady Mary Wortley Montagu Letters* I: 81, 100, 117

200. See above, Chapter 6, sub "Information."

201. For full drawing rooms, see D. Green, *Anne*, p. 300; H.M.C., *Portland MSS* V: 4; *Wentworth Papers*, p. 308; B.L. Stowe MSS 226, f. 216; P.R.O. 31/3/201, f. 67 verso; 202, f. 66; Add. MSS 17677 BBB, f. 287 verso; EEE, f. 243 verso; GGG, f. 310; 31144, f. 274; Swift, *Journal*, pp. 158–59, 267, 350, 361, 366, 467, 490, 595, 603, 604. For sparsely attended drawing rooms, see Swift, *Journal*, pp. 130, 137, 328, 364; *Wentworth Papers*, p. 312.

202. For Oxford, see Swift, *Journal*, pp. 283, 323; but cf. also p. 268; for Bolingbroke, see ibid., pp. 214, 623; for Burlington, see p. 451; for Arbuthnot, p. 356; for Winchilsea and Bacon, p. 138.

203. For Buckingham, see ibid., p. 467; for Berkeley, see p. 659.

204. Even the Hanoverian envoy, Schütz, complained, "Sa Cour est nombreuse alors, mais il y a tres peu de belle femmes" (B.L. Stowe MSS 226, f. 216: [Schütz to Robethon], 26 Feb./9 Mar. 1714). For similar sentiments expressed by an Englishman, Edward Stanhope, see Kent A.O., Stanhope of Chevening MSS U1590 C 7/16, 11 Dec. [1705].

205. This is the picture that emerges from the admittedly hostile assessments of White Kennett, Bishop of Peterborough, and Charles, Earl of Orrery: see *The Works of Jonathan Swift D.D.*, ed. W. Scott (1824), I: 137–41.

Conclusion

1. L. Colley, "The Apotheosis of George III: Loyalty, Royalty and the British Nation 1760–1820," *Past and Present*, no. 102 (1984): 94–129, esp. pp. 95–96.

2. Starkey, "Representation Through Intimacy," p. 188.

Select Bibliography

The sources listed in this bibliography fall under three headings: Manuscripts, Newspapers, and Printed Primary and Secondary Sources. For sources not listed below, see the Abbreviations and Appendix B.

Manuscripts

Bodleian Library, Oxford

MSS Lister 2–4, 35, 37	Dr. Martin Lister
MSS Rawlinson A. 286	Bishop Robinson Correspondence, 1710–14

British Library

ADDITIONAL MSS:

Add. MSS 1783, 1786, 1823, 1968, 3198, 3984, 4034, 4038, 4039, 4041, 4043, 4049, 4060, 4061, 4075, 4076, 4078, 4199	Correspondence of Sir Hans Sloane with Dr. John Arbuthnot, Charles Bernard, John Chamberlayne, etc.
Add. MSS 4552, f. 206; 4572, f. 101	Papers of Thomas Madox
Add. MSS 5750–51, 5756, 5763, 5841	Warrants, Royal Household
Add. MSS 6283, 6286, 6305, 6307–9, 6339	Collections Relating to Coronations, Royal Funerals, and Other Court Ceremonies
Add. MSS 15624	An Account of Arrears Owed the Servants of William III as of 31 Mar. 1702
Add. MSS 15897	Hyde Papers (household accounts of the Duke of York and family, 1685)
Add. MSS 17677 XX–EEE; GGG–HHH (FFF unavailable)	Netherlands Transcripts (dispatches of L'Hermitage and other Dutch envoys to the States General, 1702–14)
Add. MSS 20101	Kensington Palace
Add. MSS 20778, f. 20	Sarah, Duchess of Marlborough, to the Duchess of Ormonde

Add. MSS 22209, 22221–22, 22225–29, 31141, 31143–45	Strafford Papers (the Wentworth family)
Add. MSS 24927–28, 38863	Revenue Papers, Duke of York, 1682–85
Add. MSS 28080, 29267	Revenue Papers, Household
Add. MSS 29589	Nottingham Papers
Add. MSS 34195, ff. 100–101	Account of Queen Mary's Activities, Summer of 1690
Add. MSS 40791	Vernon Papers (lord steward's papers, 1688–93)
Add. MSS 40794	Vernon Papers (memoirs of James Vernon, Jr.)
Add. MSS 51324	Correspondence and Papers of Sir Stephen Fox
Add. MSS 61101, 61118, 61131, 61134, 61148–49, 61163–64, 61303, 61346, 61407, 61414–51, 61453–76, 61479–80, 61597, 61602, 61615–16, 61655, 62569	Blenheim Papers (Sarah, Duchess of Marlborough; Charles, Earl of Sunderland)
Add. MSS 61830	Paget Papers
Add. MSS 63079	Townshend Papers
EGERTON MSS:	
Eg. 1695	Yelverton Papers (Sarah, Duchess of Marlborough, and Charles, Duke of Shrewsbury, to Viscountess Longueville)
Eg. 2678, ff. 6–11	Marlborough Papers (privy purse account, 1706–7)
Eg. 3350	Leeds Papers (bedchamber ordinances, papers)
HARLEIAN MSS:	
Harl. 124	Revenue Papers
Harl. 1843	Jewel House
Harl. 6118	Coronation of Queen Anne
LANSDOWNE MSS:	
Lansdowne MSS 805	Satirical List of Court M.P.'s Temp. Charles II
Lansdowne MSS 1215	Chamber Establishment, 1690
LOANS:	
Loan 29/31–32, 34, 36–38, 64, 311	Portland (Harley papers)
Loan 57/71, 83–84, 102	Bathurst Papers

STOWE MSS:

Stowe MSS 222–27	Hanover Papers, 1702–14
Stowe MSS 322, f. 106	Revenue Papers (account of the civil list debt, 25 June 1713)
Stowe MSS 751	Sarah, Duchess of Marlborough

Chatsworth House, Derbyshire

Devonshire MSS 18, 51, 69, 107, 117	Devonshire Papers
Whildon Collection, groups B, C, E	Devonshire Estate Papers

Gloucestershire R.O.

Lloyd-Baker-Sharp MSS: Sharp Correspondence D3549 (77a–b)	John Sharp, Archbishop of York

Greater London R.O.

Jersey Archives (accs. no. 510)	Edward Villiers, Earl of Jersey

Huntington Library, San Marino, California

Ellesmere Calendar 9986–10259	Bridgewater Papers (Prince George's stables)
Hastings MSS X–3	Band of Gentlemen Pensioners

Kent A.O.

Stanhope of Chevening MSS U1590; C 7–9; O 30, 48	Stanhope Papers

Melbourne Hall, Derbyshire

Melbourne Hall MSS: Parliamentary Papers; bundles 3, 64, 67–71, 93–111, 122, 149 (old numbering)	Hon. Thomas Coke

Public Record Office, Chancery Lane

EXCHEQUER PAPERS:

E351/553–66	Declared Accounts, Treasurer of the Chamber, 1701–14
E 351/1764–68	Declared Accounts, Master of the Horse, 1702–15
E 351/1867–73	Declared Accounts, Cofferer of the Household, 1702–13
E 351/2842–46	Declared Accounts, Robes, 1702–14
E 351/3128–39	Declared Accounts, Master of the Great Wardrobe, 1702–14

E 403/2203–14	Issues on Debentures, 1690–1716
E 407/2, nos. 67–120	Gentlemen Pensioners Rolls, 1682–1727

LORD CHAMBERLAIN'S PAPERS:

LC 2/14–20	Royal Coronations, Funerals, Etc., 1700–1714
LC 3/2–13, 24–32, 73	Chamber Establishments, 1660–1734
LC 3/37–41	Salary, Livery, and Pension Books, 1667–1720
LC 3/33, 56–57, 61–63	Appointment Books, 1660–1733
LC 3/53	Sign Manual Warrants for Appointments, 1689–1720
LC 5/2–3	Notebooks of the Cotterell Family, 1660–1758
LC 5/11–18	Treasurer of the Chamber, Pay Office Warrant Books, 1660–1732
LC 5/39–47, 52–53, 60–73, 79–90, 101	Great Wardrobe Warrants and Papers, 1660–1752
LC 5/107–9, 112–14	Jewel Office Warrant Books, 1618–1793
LC 5/115–16, 118–29, 131, 137–60, 165–66	Lord Chamberlain's Warrants, 1660–1737
LC 5/195–96, 201–2, 205	Lord Chamberlain's Orders; Precedent Books, 1660–1820
LC 7/1–3	Theater Papers, 1660–1797
LC 9/6	Chamber Assignments (of pay), 1702–18

LORD STEWARD'S PAPERS:

LS 4/13–20	Pedes Parcellarum (quarterly accounts), 1702–13
LS 13/11	Cheque Roll, 1702–14
LS 13/21	Contract Book, 1702–14
LS 13/31–50	Establishments, Household Below Stairs, 1662–1727
LS 13/71–81	Expeditions to Holland, Germany (expenses), 1693–1727
LS 13/104–6	Letterbooks, 1661–1710
LS 13/111	Liveries, 1703–11, 1727–38
LS 13/114–16	Minutes, Board of Greencloth, 1685–1760
LS 13/170–77	Entry Book of Records, 1660–1746
LS 13/197–201	Admissions Books, 1672–1749

LS 13/231–34, 342–44 — Assessment of Taxes (for household servants), 1689, 1695–1753

LS 13/252–63 — Warrants of Appointment, Entry Books, 1660–1760

P.R.O. TRANSCRIPTS:

31/3/199–203 — Baschet Transcripts (French diplomatic correspondence, 1710–14)

STATE PAPERS, DOMESTIC:

SP 34/1–38 — State Papers, Domestic, 1702–14

Royal College of Surgeons

Hunter-Baillie Collection — Arbuthnot Correspondence

Staffordshire R.O.

Dartmouth MSS D 742/Q, nos. 130–31; D 1778/V, nos. 132–34, 147, 177, 194, 563, 777; I ii 163, 336 — Dartmouth Papers (stables papers, 1660–88; civil list accounts, 1710–14; Shrewsbury correspondence)

W. Sussex R.O.

Petworth House Archives: Somerset Papers, P.HA. 14–16, 243–52, 255–56, 300, 322, 6304, 6306–7, 6323–25, 6330–31 — Duke of Somerset (correspondence; stables papers)

Worcestershire R.O.

Casper Frederic Henning Papers: BA 2252; Ref: 705: 366; Parcels 1–6 — Royal Bedchamber, Privy Purse, and Gardens

Newspapers

(The following have been examined on microfilm from the Burney Collection in the British Library.)

Athenian News; or Dunton's Oracle, 1710
Britain, 1713
British Apollo; or, Curious Amusements, 1708–11
The British Mercury, 1711–14
Daily Courant, 1702–14
Dublin Gazette, 1708–9
English Post. with News Foreign and Domestick, 1702–3
Evening Post, 1710–13
Flying Post; or, The Post-Master, 1702, 1712–13

London Gazette, 1702–12
Medley, 1710–12
Observator, 1702–12
Post-Angel, 1702
Post Boy, 1711–14
The Post Man; and The Historical Account, 1702–10
Protestant Post-Boy, 1712

Printed Primary and Secondary Sources

Place of publication is London unless otherwise indicated.

Aitken, G. A., *The Life and Works of John Arbuthnot M.D., Fellow of the Royal College of Physicians* (Oxford, 1892).
Allen, D., "The Political Function of Charles II's Chiffinch," *Huntington Library Quarterly* XXXIX (1976).
Allen, R. J., *The Clubs of Augustan London* (Cambridge, Mass., 1933).
———, "The Kit-Cat Club and the Theatre," *Review of English Studies* VII (1931).
Armstrong, N., *Jewellery: An Historical Survey of British Styles and Jewels* (Guildford, Eng., 1973).
Ashton, J., *Social Life in the Reign of Queen Anne, Taken from Original Sources* (1883; repr., Detroit, 1968).
Atterbury, F., *The Epistolary Correspondence, Visitation Charges, Speeches, and Miscellanies, of the Right Reverend Francis Atterbury, D.D. Lord Bishop of Rochester*, 5 vols. (1783).
Avery, E. L., and Van Lennep, W., eds., *The London Stage 1660–1800*, vols. I–II (Carbondale, Ill., 1960).
Aylmer, G. E., "Attempts at Administrative Reform, 1625–40," *English Historical Review* LXXII (1957).
———, *The King's Servants: The Civil Service of Charles I, 1625–1642*, 2nd edn. (1974).
———, "The Last Years of Purveyance 1610–1660," *Economic History Review*, 2nd ser., X (1957).
———, "Officeholding as a Factor in English History, 1625–42," *History* XLIV (1959).
———, "Officeholding, Wealth and Social Structure in England . . . c.1580–c. 1720," paper presented at the Istituto Internazionale di Storia Economica, Prato, April 1974.
———, *The State's Servants: The Civil Service of the English Republic, 1649–1660* (1973).
Baillie, George, *The Correspondence of George Baillie of Jerviswood 1702–1707* (Edinburgh, 1842).
Baxter, S. B., *The Development of the Treasury, 1660–1702* (London and Cambridge, Mass., 1957).

———, *William III and the Defense of European Liberty 1650–1702* (New York, 1966).

Beattie, J. M., "The Court of George I and English Politics, 1717–1720," *English Historical Review* LXXXI (1966).

———, *The English Court in the Reign of George I* (Cambridge, Eng., 1967).

Beattie, L. M., *John Arbuthnot: Mathematician and Satirist* (New York, 1967).

Bennett, G. V., "Robert Harley, the Godolphin Ministry, and the Bishoprics Crisis of 1707," *English Historical Review* LXXXII (1967).

———, *The Tory Crisis in Church and State 1688–1730: The Career of Francis Atterbury, Bishop of Rochester* (Oxford, 1975).

Berkeley, George, *The Correspondence of George Berkeley Afterwards Bishop of Cloyne and Sir John Percival Afterwards Earl of Egmont*, ed. B. Rand (Cambridge, Eng., 1914).

Bolingbroke, Henry St. John, Viscount, *Letters and Correspondence, Public and Private, of the Right Honourable Henry St. John, Lord Visc. Bolingbroke; During the Time He Was Secretary of State to Queen Anne*, ed. G. Parke, 4 vols. (1798).

———, *Letters of Bolingbroke to James Grahme*, ed. H. T. Dickinson (Transactions of the Cumberland and Westmoreland Archaeological Society LXVIII, 1968).

Bond, R. P., *Queen Anne's American Kings* (Oxford, 1952).

Boswell (Murrie), E., *The Restoration Court Stage* (Cambridge, Mass., 1932).

Boulton, W. B., *The Amusements of Old London . . . from the 17th to the Beginning of the 19th Century*, 2 vols. (New York, 1901; repr., 1969).

Boyer, A., *History of the Reign of Queen Anne, Digested into Annals*, 11 vols. (1703–13).

Brooke, I., *English Costume of the Seventeenth Century* (1950).

———, *A History of English Costume* (1937).

Buck, A., *Dress in Eighteenth-Century England* (1979).

Burnet, G., *History of His Own Time*, 6 vols. (Oxford, 1833).

Burrows, D. J., "Handel and the English Chapel Royal During the Reigns of Queen Anne and King George I," 2 vols. (Ph.D. diss., Open University, 1981).

Caritt, E. F., *A Calendar of British Taste from 1600 to 1800* (?1948).

Carpenter, E., *The Protestant Bishop Being the Life of Henry Compton 1632–1713 Bishop of London* (London, New York, and Toronto, 1956).

Chandaman, C. D., *The English Public Revenue 1660–1688* (Oxford, 1975).

Clarendon, Henry Hyde, Earl of, *The Correspondence of Henry Hyde, Earl of Clarendon and of His Brother Laurence Hyde, Earl of Rochester; with the Diary of Lord Clarendon from 1687 to 1690*, ed. J. W. Singer, 2 vols. (1828).

Clark, J. C. D., *English Society 1688–1832: Ideology, Social Structure and Political Practice During the Ancien Régime* (Cambridge, Eng., 1985).

Clavering, Sir James, *The Correspondence of Sir James Clavering*, ed. H. T. Dickinson (Surtees Society, 1967).

Cobbett, W., ed., *The Parliamentary History of England*, vol. VI, 1702–14 (1810).

Cohen, S. S., "The Diary of Jeremiah Dummer," *William and Mary Quarterly*, 3rd ser., XXIV (1967).

Coke, T., *Vice Chamberlain Coke's Theatrical Papers, 1706–1715*, ed. J. Milhous and R. Hume (Carbondale, Ill., 1982).

Collection of Ordinances and Regulations for the Government of the Royal Household . . . from King Edward III to King William and Queen Mary (Society of Antiquaries, 1790).

Colley, L., "The Apotheosis of George III: Loyalty, Royalty, and the British Nation 1760–1820," *Past and Present*, no. 102 (1984).

Cowles, V., *The Great Marlborough and His Duchess* (1983).

Cruickshanks, E., "The Tories and the Succession to the Crown in the 1714 Parliament," *Bulletin of the Institute of Historical Research* XLVI (1973).

Cunnington, C. W., and Cunnington, P., *Handbook of English Costume in the Eighteenth Century* (Boston, 1972).

Curtis, G., *The Life and Times of Queen Anne* (1973).

Davis, G. N., *German Thought and Culture in England 1700–1770* (Chapel Hill, N.C., 1969).

Dearnley, C., *English Church Music 1650–1750* (New York, 1970).

de Beer, E. S., "King Charles II's Own Fashion: An Episode in Anglo-French Relations 1666–1670," *Journal of the Warburg Courtauld Institute* II (1938).

de Krey, G. S., *A Fractured Society: The Politics of London in the First Age of Party, 1688–1715* (Oxford, 1985).

Dickens, A. G., ed., *The Courts of Europe: Politics, Patronage and Royalty 1400–1800* (New York, 1977).

Dickinson, H. T., *Bolingbroke* (1970).

———, "The October Club," *Huntington Library Quarterly* XXXIII (1970).

———, "The Poor Palatines and the Parties," *English Historical Review* LXXXII (1967).

Dickson, P. G. M., *The Financial Revolution in England: A Study in the Development of Public Credit* (1967).

Douglass, J., *Sir Godfrey Kneller* (1971).

Dugdale, G. S., *Whitehall Through the Centuries* (1950).

Dutton, R., *English Court Life from Henry VII to George II* (1963).

Ede, M., *Arts and Society in England Under William and Mary* (1979).

Elias, N., *The Court Society*, trans. E. Jephcott (New York, 1983).

Evans, M., *Costume Throughout the Ages* (Philadelphia, 1950).

Evelyn, J., *The Diary of John Evelyn, Now First Printed in Full from the Manuscripts Belonging to Mr. John Evelyn and Edited by E. S. de Beer*, 6 vols. (Oxford, 1955).

Ewald, W. B., *The Newsmen of Queen Anne* (Oxford, 1956).

Fastnedge, R., *English Furniture Styles from 1500 to 1830* (1962).

Fiennes, C., *The Journeys of Celia Fiennes*, ed. C. Morris (1949).

Ford, W. K., "The Chapel Royal at the Restoration," *Monthly Musical Record* XC (1960).

Foss, M., *The Age of Patronage: The Arts in England 1660–1750* (Ithaca, N.Y., 1972).

Gaunt, W., *Court Painting in England from Tudor to Victorian Times* (1980).

Giffard, Lady M., *Martha, Lady Giffard: Her Life and Correspondence (1664–1722)*, ed. J. G. Longe (1911).
Green, D., *Gardener to Queen Anne: Henry Wise (1653–1738) and the Formal Garden* (Oxford, 1956).
———, *Grinling Gibbons: His Work as Carver and Statuary 1648–1721* (1964).
———, *Queen Anne* (1970).
———, *Sarah, Duchess of Marlborough* (1967).
Gregg, E., *The Protestant Succession in International Politics, 1710–1716* (New York, 1986).
———, *Queen Anne* (1980).
———, "Was Queen Anne a Jacobite?," *History* LVII (1972).
Halsband, R., *The Life of Lady Mary Wortley Montagu* (Oxford, 1956).
Hamilton, Sir David, *The Diary of Sir David Hamilton 1709–1714*, ed. P. Roberts (Oxford, 1975).
Hanmer, Sir Thomas, *The Correspondence of Sir Thomas Hanmer, Bart. Speaker of the House of Commons with a Memoir of His Life to Which Are Added Other Relicks of a Gentleman's Family*, ed. H. E. Bunbury (1838).
Harbage, A., *Thomas Killigrew: Cavalier Dramatist 1612–83* (Philadelphia, 1930).
The Harcourt Papers, ed. E. W. Harcourt (Oxford, n.d.).
Harley, J., *Music in Purcell's London: The Social Background* (1968).
Hart, A. T., *The Life and Times of John Sharp, Archbishop of York* (1949).
Hatton, R. M., *George I Elector and King* (Cambridge, Mass., 1978).
Hayton, D., "The 'Country' Interest and the Party System, 1689–1720," in *Party and Management in Parliament, 1660–1784*, ed. C. Jones (Leicester, 1984).
Hearne, Thomas, *Remarks and Collections of Thomas Hearne*, ed. C. E. Doble, vols. I–IV (Oxford, 1885–1921).
Hedley, O., *Windsor Castle* (1967).
Heyward, J. F., *Huguenot Silver in England 1688–1727* (1959).
Hibbard, C., *Charles I and the Popish Plot* (Chapel Hill, N.C., 1983).
Hill, B. W., *Robert Harley: Speaker, Secretary of State and Premier Minister* (New Haven, Conn., and London, 1988).
Hill, R., *The Diplomatic Correspondence of the Right Hon. Richard Hill Envoy Extraordinary from the Court of St. James to the Duke of Savoy in the Reign of Queen Anne*, ed. W. Blackley (1845).
Historical Manuscripts Commission, *First Report* (1870), Hatton MSS.
———, *Third Report* (1872), Northumberland MSS, Bath MSS.
———, *Fifth Report* (1876), Sutherland MSS.
———, *Sixth Report* (1877), Graham MSS, Ingilby MSS, Ormonde MSS.
———, *Seventh Report* (1879), Graham MSS, Verney MSS, Ormonde MSS.
———, *Eighth Report*, Appendix I (1881), Marlborough MSS.
———, *Eighth Report*, Appendix II (1881), Manchester MSS.
———, *Ninth Report*, Appendix II (1884), Morrison MSS.
———, *Tenth Report*, Appendix IV (1885), Westmoreland MSS, Stewart MSS, Bagot MSS.

———, *Eleventh Report*, Appendix IV (1887), Townshend MSS.
———, *Eleventh Report*, Appendix V (1887), Dartmouth MSS.
———, *Twelfth Report*, Appendices II–III (1888–89), Cowper MSS.
———, *Twelfth Report*, Appendix V (1889), Rutland MSS.
———, *Twelfth Report*, Appendix VII (1890), Le Fleming MSS.
———, *Twelfth Report*, Appendix IX (1891), Beaufort MSS.
———, *Thirteenth Report*, Appendix II (1893), Portland MSS.
———, *Fourteenth Report*, Appendix II (1894), Portland MSS.
———, *Fourteenth Report*, Appendix IV (1894), Kenyon MSS.
———, *Fourteenth Report*, Appendix VII (1895), Ormonde MSS.
———, *Fourteenth Report*, Appendix IX (1895), Lindsey MSS.
———, *Fifteenth Report*, Appendix I (1896), Dartmouth MSS.
———, *Fifteenth Report*, Appendix II (1897), Hodgkin MSS.
———, *Fifteenth Report*, Appendix IV (1897), Portland MSS.
———, *Fifteenth Report*, Appendix VII (1898), Ailesbury MSS.
———, *Bath MSS*, vols. I–III (1904–8).
———, *Bathurst MSS* (1924).
———, *Buccleuch at Montague House MSS*, vols. I–II (1899–1903).
———, *Buccleuch at Drumlanrig Castle MSS* (1903).
———, *Downshire MSS*, vol. I, pts. i–ii (1924).
———, *Hamilton MSS*, suppl. (1932).
———, *Hastings MSS*, vol. II (1930).
———, *House of Lords MSS*, n.s., vols. II–VIII (1903–12).
———, *Lindsey MSS*, suppl. (1942).
———, *Ormonde MSS*, n.s., vols. III–VIII (1902–20).
———, *Portland MSS*, vols. V–X (1899–1931).
———, *Russell Astley MSS* (1900).
———, *Stuart MSS*, vols. I–IV (1902–10).
Holmes, G. S., "The Attack on 'The Influence of the Crown' 1702–16," *Bulletin of the Institute of Historical Research* XXXIX (1966).
———, *Augustan England: Professions, State and Society, 1680–1730* (1982).
———, *British Politics in the Age of Anne* (1967).
———, "The Commons' Division on 'No Peace Without Spain,' 7 December 1711," *Bulletin of the Institute of Historical Research* XXXIII (1960).
———, "Gregory King and the Social Structure of Pre-Industrial England," *Transactions of the Royal Historical Society*, 5th ser., XXVII (1977).
———, "Harley, St. John and the Death of the Tory Party," in *Britain After the Glorious Revolution*, ed. G. S. Holmes (1969).
Holmes, G. S., and Speck, W. A., "The Fall of Harley in 1708 Reconsidered," *English Historical Review* LXXX (1965).
Holmes, R. R., *Windsor* (1908).
Horn, D. B., "Rank and Emolument in the British Diplomatic Service 1689–1789," *Transactions of the Royal Historical Society*, 5th ser., IX (1959).

Horwitz, H., *Parliament, Policy and Politics in the Reign of William III* (Manchester, 1977).
———, *Revolution Politicks: The Career of Daniel Finch Second Earl of Nottingham, 1647–1730* (Cambridge, Eng., 1968).
———, "The Structure of Parliamentary Politics," in *Britain After the Glorious Revolution*, ed. G. S. Holmes (1969).
Hughes, B. R. T., *Three Centuries of English Domestic Silver 1500–1820* (New York, 1968).
Hughes, T., *Old English Furniture* (New York, 1969).
Hume, R. D., ed., *The London Theatre World 1660–1800* (Carbondale, Ill., 1980).
Hutton, R., *The Restoration: A Political and Religious History of England and Wales 1658–1667* (Oxford, 1985).
Jones, C., "The Division That Never Was: New Evidence on the Aborted Vote in the Lords on 8 December 1711 on 'No Peace Without Spain,'" *Parliamentary History* II (1983).
———, "Godolphin, the Whig Junto and the Scots: A New Lords' Division List from 1709," *Scottish Historical Review* LVIII (1979).
———, "'The Scheme Lords, the Neccessitous Lords, and the Scots Lords': The Earl of Oxford's Management and the 'Party of the Crown' in the House of Lords, 1711–14," in *Party and Management in Parliament, 1660–1784*, ed. C. Jones (Leicester, 1984).
———, "Seating Problems in the House of Lords in the Early Eighteenth Century: The Evidence of the Manuscript Minutes," *Bulletin of the Institute of Historical Research* LI (1978).
Kendrick, A. F., *English Needlework* (1967).
Kenyon, J. P., *Robert Spencer, Earl of Sunderland, 1641–1702* (1958).
Killanin, M. Morris, Lord, *Sir Godfrey Kneller and His Times, 1646–1723, Being a Review of English Portraiture of the Period* (1948).
Klopp, O., *Der Fall des Hauses Stuart und die Succession des Hauses Hannover in Gross-Britannien und Irland im Zusammenhange der Europäischen Angelegenheiten von 1660–1714*, vols. X–XIV (Vienna, 1881–88).
Lambert, S., *Bills & Acts* (Cambridge, Eng., 1971).
Larner, J., "Europe of the Courts," *Journal of Modern History* LV (1983).
Latham, J., *The Pleasure of Your Company: A History of Manners and Meals* (1972).
Lawrence, W. J., "Foreign Singers at the Court of Charles II," *Musical Quarterly* IX (1923).
Legrelle, A., *La diplomatie française et la succession d'Espagne*, 4 vols. (Gand, 1888–92).
Lister, R., *Decorative Wrought Ironwork in Great Britain* (Rutland, Vt., 1970).
Lloyd, H. A., *Old Clocks* (1970).
Loades, D., *The Tudor Court* (Totowa, N.J., 1987).
Loftis, J., "The London Theatre in Early Eighteenth Century Politics," *Huntington Library Quarterly* XVIII (1954–55).

———, *The Politics of Drama in Augustan England* (Oxford, 1963).

Luttrell, N., *A Brief Historical Relation of State Affairs from September 1678 to April 1714*, 6 vols. (Oxford, 1857).

MacPherson, J., ed., *Original Papers Containing the Secret History of Great Britain, from the Restoration, to the Accession of the House of Hannover*, 2 vols. (1775).

Manchester, W. D. Montagu, Duke of, *Court and Society from Elizabeth to Anne*, vol. II (1864).

Marchmont, P., Earl of, *A Selection from the Papers of the Earl of Marchmont in the Possession of the Right Hon[ble] Sir. George Henry Rose Illustrative of Events from 1685 to 1750* (1831).

Marillier, H. C., *English Tapestries of the Eighteenth Century: A Handbook to the Post-Mortlake Productions of English Weavers* (1930).

Marlborough, J., Duke of, et al., *The Correspondence 1701–1711 of John Churchill First Duke of Marlborough and Anthonie Heinsius Grand Pensionary of Holland*, ed. B. van 'T Hoff (The Hague, 1951).

Marlborough, J., Duke of; Marlborough, S., Duchess of; and Godolphin, S., Earl of, *The Marlborough-Godolphin Correspondence*, ed. H. L. Snyder, 3 vols. (Oxford, 1975).

Marlborough, S., Duchess of, *Memoirs of the Duchess of Marlborough*, ed. W. King (1930).

Marshall, D., *The English Domestic Servant in History* (1949; repr., 1968).

Mason, J. E., *Gentlefolk in the Making: Studies in the History of English Courtesy Literature and Related Topics from 1531 to 1744* (Philadelphia, 1935).

McGuinness, R., "A Fine Song on Occasion of the Day was Sung," *Music and Literature* L (1969).

———, "The Origins and Disappearance of the English Court Ode," *Proceedings of the Royal Musicological Society* LXXXVII (1960–61).

McInnes, A., "The Appointment of Harley in 1704," *Historical Journal* XI (1968).

———, *Robert Harley, Puritan Politician* (1970).

McKendrick, N.; Brewer, J.; and Plumb, J. H., *The Birth of a Consumer Society: The Commercialization of Eighteenth-Century England* (Bloomington, Ind., 1982).

Melville, L., *Bath Under Beau Nash* (1907).

Metzger, E. C., *Ralph, First Duke of Montagu 1638–1709* (Lewiston, N.Y., and Queenston, Ont., 1987).

Millar, O., *The Queen's Pictures* (New York, 1977).

———, *The Tudor, Stuart and Early Georgian Pictures in the Collection of Her Majesty the Queen*, 2 vols. (1963).

Miller, J., "Faction in Later Stuart England, 1660–1714," *History Today* XXXIII (1983).

———, *James II: A Study in Kingship* (1978).

Minney, R. J., *Hampton Court* (1972).

Mitchell, L. D., "Command Performances During the Reign of George I," *Eighteenth Century Studies* VII (1974).

———, "Command Performances During the Reign of Queen Anne," *Theatre Notebook* XXIV (1970).
Montagu, Lady M. W., *The Complete Letters of Lady Mary Wortley Montagu*, ed. R. Halsband, 2 vols. (Oxford, 1965).
Moore, T. K., and Horwitz, H., "Who Runs the House? Aspects of Parliamentary Organization in the Later Seventeenth Century," *Journal of Modern History* XLIII (1971).
Morandi, C., ed., *Relazioni di Ambasciatori Sabaudi, Genovesi e Veneti durante il periodo della grande alleanza e della successione di Spagna (1693–1713)*, I (Bologna, 1935).
Morgan, W. T., *English Political Parties and Leaders in the Reign of Queen Anne 1702–10* (New Haven, Conn., 1920).
Nash, R., *Hampton Court* (1983).
Nicoll, A., *A History of English Drama 1660–1900*, vols. I–II (1962–67).
Nicolson, W., *Letters on Various Subjects Literary, Political, and Ecclesiastical to and from William Nicolson D.D. Successively Bishop of Carlisle and of Derry; and Archbishop of Cashell; Including the Correspondence of Several Eminent Prelates from 1683 to 1726–27 Inclusive*, ed. J. Nichols (1809).
———, *The London Diaries of William Nicolson, Bishop of Carlisle 1702–1718*, ed. G. S. Holmes and C. Jones (Oxford, 1985).
The Norris Papers, ed. Thomas Heywood (Chetham Society, 1846).
Oman, C., *English Silversmiths' Work, Civil and Domestic: An Introduction* (1965).
Patrick, S., *Autobiography of Symon Patrick: A Brief Account of My Life, with a Thankful Remembrance of God's Mercies to Me* (Oxford, 1839).
Peck, L. L., *Northampton: Patronage and Policy at the Court of James I* (1982).
Pegge, S., *Curialia: or An Historical Account of Some Branches of the Royal Household, &c.* (1791).
Pepys, S., *The Diary of Samuel Pepys*, ed. R. Latham and W. Matthews, 11 vols. (1970–83).
Petherick, M., *Restoration Rogues* (1951).
Plumb, J. H., *The Commercialisation of Leisure in Eighteenth-Century England* (Reading, 1973).
———, *Georgian Delights* (Boston, 1980).
———, *The Growth of Political Stability in England, 1675–1725* (1967).
Present State of the British Court (1720).
Price, C. M., *Music in the Restoration Theatre* (Ann Arbor, Mich., 1979).
Quennell, M., and Quennell, C. H. B., *A History of Everyday Things in England, Done in Two Parts of Which This Is the Second, 1500–1799* (1950).
Ranke, L. von, *A History of England Principally in the Seventeenth Century*, vol. V (Oxford, 1875; repr., New York, 1966).
Ratcliffe, E. C., *The English Coronation Service* (1936).
Redington, J., ed., *Calendar of Treasury Papers*, 6 vols. [1557–1738] (1868–89).
Reitan, E. A., "From Revenue to Civil List, 1689–1702: The Revolution Settle-

ment and the 'Mixed and Balanced' Constitution," *Historical Journal* XIII (1970).
The Revels History of Drama in English V 1660–1750 (1976).
Rimbault, E. F., ed., *The Old Cheque-Book, or Book of Remembrance, of the Chapel Royal, from 1561–1744* (Camden Society, 1872).
Roberts, C., "The Constitutional Significance of the Financial Settlement of 1690," *Historical Journal* XX (1977).
———, "'Party and Patronage in Later Stuart England," in *England's Rise to Greatness, 1663–1763*, ed. S. B. Baxter (Berkeley, Calif., 1983).
Rosenheim, J. M., *The Townshends of Raynham: Nobility in Transition in Restoration and Early Hanoverian England* (Middletown, Conn., 1989).
Roseveare, H., *The Treasury: The Evolution of a British Institution* (1969).
Sainty, J. C., "The Origin of the Leadership of the House of Lords," *Bulletin of the Institute of Historical Research* XLVII (1974).
———, "A Reform in the Tenure of Offices During the Reign of Charles II," *Bulletin of the Institute of Historical Research* XLI (1968).
———, "The Tenure of Offices in the Exchequer," *English Historical Review* LXXX (1965).
Salomon, F., *Geschichte des Letzten Ministeriums Königin Annas von England (1710–1714) und der Englischen Thronfolgefrage* (Gotha, 1894).
Scott, H. A., "London Concerts from 1700 to 1750," *Musical Quarterly* XXIV (1938).
———, "London's Earliest Public Concerts," *Musical Quarterly* XXII (1932).
Seafield, James Ogilvie, Earl of, *Letters Relating to Scotland in the Reign of Queen Anne by James Ogilvie, First Earl of Seafield, and Others*, ed. P. Hume Brown (Edinburgh, 1915).
———, *Seafield Correspondence from 1685 to 1708*, ed. J. Grant (Edinburgh, 1912).
Sharp, T., *The Life of John Sharp, D.D., Lord Archbishop of York: Collected from His Diary, Letters and Other Authentic Testimonies*, 2 vols. (1825).
Shaw, W. A., ed., *Calendar of Treasury Books*, 31 vols. [1660–1718] (1904–62).
———, ed., *Calendar of Treasury Books and Papers*, 5 vols. [1727–45] (1897–1903).
Sheppard, E. J., *Memorials of St. James's Palace*, 2 vols. (1894).
———, *The Old Royal Palace of Whitehall* (1902).
Shrewsbury, C., Duke of, *The Private and Original Correspondence of Charles Talbot, Duke of Shrewsbury*, ed. W. Coxe (1821).
Smith, E., *Foreign Visitors in England and What They Have Thought of Us ...* (1889).
Smuts, R. M., *Court Culture and the Origins of a Royalist Tradition in Early Stuart England* (Philadelphia, 1987).
———, "The Political Failure of Stuart Cultural Patronage," in *Patronage in the Renaissance*, ed. G. F. Lytle and S. Orgel (Princeton, N.J., 1981).
———, "Public Ceremony and Royal Charisma: The English Royal Entry in London, 1485–1642," in *The First Modern Society*, ed. A. L. Beier, D. Cannadine, and J. M. Rosenheim (Cambridge, Eng., 1989).

Snyder, H. L., "The Defeat of the Occasional Conformity Bill and the Tack: A Study in the Techniques of Parliamentary Management in the Reign of Queen Anne," *Bulletin of the Institute of Historical Research* XLI (1968).

———, "Godolphin and Harley: A Study of Their Partnership in Politics," *Huntington Library Quarterly* XXX (1967).

———, "The Last Days of Queen Anne: The Account of Sir John Evelyn Examined," *Huntington Library Quarterly* XXXIV (1971).

———, "A New Parliament List for 1711," *Bulletin of the Institute of Historical Research* L (1977).

———, "Party Configurations in the Early Eighteenth-Century House of Commons," *Bulletin of the Institute of Historical Research* XLV (1972).

———, "Queen Anne Versus the Junto: The Effort to Place Orford at the Head of the Admiralty in 1709," *Huntington Library Quarterly* XXXV (1972).

Somerville, D. H., *The King of Hearts: Charles Talbot, Duke of Shrewsbury* (1962).

Speck, W. A., "The Choice of a Speaker in 1705," *Bulletin of the Institute of Historical Research* XXXVII (1964).

———, "The House of Commons, 1702–14: A Study in Political Organization," (D.Phil. thesis, Oxford University, 1965).

———, *Tory & Whig: The Struggle in the Constituencies, 1701–1715* (1970).

———, ed., "An Anonymous Parliamentary Diary, 1705," *Camden Miscellany* XXIII, 4th ser., VII (1969).

Sperling, J. G., "The Division of 25 May 1711 on an Amendment to the South Sea Bill: A Note on the Reality of Parties in the Age of Anne," *Historical Journal* IV (1961).

Starkey, D., "Representation Through Intimacy: A Study in the Symbolism of Monarchy and Court Office in Early-Modern England," in *Symbols and Sentiments: Cross-Cultural Studies in Symbolism*, ed. I. Lewis (London, New York, and San Francisco, 1977).

———, ed., *The English Court: From the Wars of the Roses to the Civil War* (1987).

State Papers and Correspondence Illustrative of the Social and Political State of Europe from the Revolution to the Accession of the House of Hanover, ed. J. M. Kemble (1857).

Stewart, J. D., *Sir Godfrey Kneller and the English Baroque Portrait* (Oxford, 1983).

Sutherland, J., "The Impact of Charles II on Restoration Literature," in *Restoration and Eighteenth-Century Literature*, ed. C. Camden (Chicago, 1963).

Swift, J., *The Correspondence of Jonathan Swift*, ed. H. Williams, vols. I–II (Oxford, 1963).

———, *Historical and Political Tracts—English*, vol. 5 of *The Prose Works of Jonathan Swift D.D.*, ed. T. Scott (1911).

———, *Journal to Stella*, ed. H. Williams, 2 vols. (Oxford, 1948).

Symonds, R. W., "Charles II Couches, Chairs and Stools 1660–1670," *Connoisseur* XCIII (1934).

———, *Thomas Tompion, His Life & Work* (1951).

Szechi, D., "The Duke of Shrewsbury's Contacts with the Jacobites in 1713," *Bulletin of the Institute of Historical Research* LVI (1983).

———, *Jacobitism and Tory Politics 1710–14* (Edinburgh, 1984).
Taylor, L., *Mourning Dress: A Costume and Social History* (1983).
Thomson, F. P., *Tapestry: Mirror of History* (New York, 1980).
Timbs, J., *Clubs and Club Life in London; with Anecdotes of Its Famous Coffee-Houses, Hostelries and Taverns, from the Seventeenth Century to the Present Time*, 2 vols. (1879; repr., Detroit, 1967).
Tomlinson, H., "Financial and Administrative Developments," in *The Restored Monarchy, 1660–1688*, ed. J. R. Jones (Totowa, N.J., 1979).
Torcy, Jean-Baptiste Colbert, Marquis de, *Journal inédit de Jean-Baptiste Colbert, Marquis de Torcy, ministre et secrétaire d'état des affaires étrangères pendant les années 1709, 1710 et 1711 . . .*, ed. F. Masson (Paris, 1884).
———, *Memoirs of the Marquis of Torcy, Secretary of State to Lewis XIV. Containing the History of the Negotiations from the Treaty of Ryswic to the Peace of Utrecht*, 2 vols. (1757).
Turberville, A. S., *The House of Lords in the XVIIIth Century* (Oxford, 1927).
———, *The House of Lords in the Reign of William III* (Oxford, 1913).
Uffenbach, Z. C. von, *London in 1710: From the Travels of Zacharias Conrad von Uffenbach*, trans. and ed. W. H. Quarrell and M. Mare (1934).
Vernon, J., *Letters Illustrative of the Reign of William III from 1696 to 1708 . . . by James Vernon, Esq. Secretary of State*, ed. G. P. R. James, 3 vols. (1841).
Walcott, R., *English Politics in the Early Eighteenth Century* (Oxford, 1956).
Warner, R., *The History of Bath* (Bath, 1801).
Wentworth, P., et al., *The Wentworth Papers, 1705–1739*, ed. J. J. Cartwright (1883).
Western, J. R., *Monarchy and Revolution: The English State in the 1680s* (1972).
Westrup, J. A., "The Chapel Royal Under James II," *Monthly Musical Record* LXX (1940).
———, "Domestic Music Under the Stuarts," *Proceedings of the Royal Musicological Association* LXVIII (1941–42).
———, "Foreign Musicians in Stuart England," *Musical Quarterly* XXVII (1941).
Wheatley, H. B., *London Past and Present: Its History, Associations and Traditions*, 3 vols. (1891).
Wildeblood, J., *The Polite World: A Guide to the Deportment of the English in Former Times* (1973).
Williams, A. S., "Panegyric Decorum in the Reigns of William III and Anne," *Journal of British Studies* XXI (1981).
Wilson, J. H., *The Court Wits of the Restoration* (Princeton, N.J., 1948).
Wray, R. T., *Ancient Royal Palaces in and near London* (1902).
Wren Society IV: Hampton Court Palace 1689–1702 (Oxford, 1927).
Wren Society VII: The Royal Palaces of Winchester, Whitehall, Kensington, and St. James's 1660–1715 (Oxford, 1930).
Wright, A. R., *British Calendar Customs* (1968).

Index

This Index gives the following identifying information for persons mentioned in the text: titles, parliamentary memberships, household offices, and, for married women, maiden names. Where a person came to hold more than one title of nobility, only the highest is listed unless the person is mentioned under a previous title in the text. Dates are given only for total service in the main household contiguous with Anne's reign. Household offices held in succession are separated with semicolons; offices held simultaneously are separated with a comma or an unpunctuated "and." No attempt is made to list non-household offices held. Thus Robert Harley, Earl of Oxford, is identified as housekeeper of St. James's Palace rather than by his most famous post, lord treasurer of England.

In this Index an "f" after a page number indicates a separate reference on the next page, and an "ff" indicates separate references on the next two pages. A continuous discussion over two or more pages is indicated by a span of page numbers, e.g, "pp. 57–58." *Passim* is used for a cluster of references in close but not consecutive sequence.

Library of Congress Cataloging-in-Publication Data
Bucholz, R. O., 1958–
The Augustan court : Queen Anne and the decline of court culture / R. O. Bucholz.
p. cm.
Includes bibliographical references and index.
ISBN 0-8047-2080-0 (cloth : acid-free paper)
1. Great Britain—History—Anne, 1702–1714. 2. Great Britain—Court and courtiers—History—18th century. I. Title.
DA495.B83 1993
941.06′9′092—dc20
[B] 92-440
CIP